ECONOMIC TRANSFORMATIONS IN EAST AND CENTRAL EUROPE

ECONOMIC TRANSFORMATIONS IN EAST AND CENTRAL EUROPE

Legacies from the Past and Policies for the Future

Edited by David F. Good

London and New York

First published 1994
by Routledge
11 New Fetter Lane, London EC4P 4EE

Simultaneously published in the USA and Canada
by Routledge
29 West 35th Street, New York, NY 10001

Typeset in Garamond by
Florencetype Ltd, Kewstoke, Avon

Printed and bound in Great Britain by
T.J. Press (Padstow) Ltd, Padstow, Cornwall

British Library Cataloguing in Publications Data
A catalogue record for this book is available from the British Library

Library of Congress Cataloging in Publication Data
Economic transformations in Eastern Europe: legacies from the past and policies for the future / edited by David F. Good.
p. cm.
Includes bibliographical references and index.
1. Europe, Eastern – Economic conditions – 1989– 2. Europe, Eastern – Economic policy – 1989– I. Good, David F.
HC244.E24475 1994 94–5476
338.947 – dc20

ISBN 0–415–11266–4

CONTENTS

FIGURES

TABLES

CONTRIBUTORS

Lee J. Alston, Professor of Economics, University of Illinois – Champaign/Urbana

Ivan T. Berend, Professor of History, Director of the Center of European and Russian Studies at the University of California, Los Angeles

Ivo Bićanić, Professor, Faculty of Economics, University of Zagreb

Felix Butschek, Univ.-Doz and Deputy Director of the Austrian Institute of Economic Research

Scott M. Eddie, Professor, Department of Economics, University of Toronto

David F. Good, Professor of History and Director, Center for Austrian Studies, University of Minnesota

Janusz Kaliński, Professor, Department of Economic History, Warsaw School of Economics

Daniel E. Miller, Assistant Professor, Department of History, University of West Florida

Jürgen Nautz, Assistant Professor, Department of Modern History, Gesamthochschule Universität, Kassel

Michael Palairet, Senior Lecturer in Economic History, University of Edinburgh

Anton Pelinka, Professor of Political Science, University of Innsbruck, and Director of the Institute of Conflict Research, Vienna

Roumyana Preshlenova, Research Associate, Institute for Balkan Studies, Sofia

Marko Škreb, National Bank of Croatia, Research and Analysis Department, and University of Zagreb, Faculty of Economics

Jan Stankovsky, Austrian Institute of Economic Research

Alice Teichova, Emeritus Professor of Economic History, Girton College, Cambridge, and The London School of Economics and Political Science

Richard Tilly, Professor and Director, Institut für Wirtschafts-und Sozialgeschichte, Westfälische Wilhelms-Universität, Münster

PREFACE

This volume has its origins in two conferences organized by the Center for Austrian Studies and held at the University of Minnesota. The earlier conference compared the former Habsburg empire and the then still existing Soviet Union as imperial structures. The idea blossomed in spring 1989 just before the revolutions of 1989 began to unfold in Eastern Europe. The conference was held one year later as the Soviet empire was crumbling and by the time the papers were published as Richard L. Rudolph and David F. Good (eds.) *Nationalism and Empire: The Habsburg Empire and the Soviet Union* (St. Martin's Press) in 1992, the Soviet Union itself was in the final stages of disintegration.

The second conference took the story a step further by dealing with the implications of imperial collapse in Central and Eastern Europe for the economic future of the region. In spring 1992 two dozen historians, economists, and political scientists gathered at Minnesota for a conference to explore how the current economic transition in the former East bloc states fits into the region's economic history. The essays here are revised versions of the papers delivered at the 1992 conference and together represent a companion volume to *Nationalism and Empire*.

Since 1977, the Center for Austrian Studies has served as the focal point in North America for the interdisciplinary study of Austria thanks to a generous gift of 1 million dollars from the Austrian people to the University of Minnesota. Both the 1992 conference and this volume symbolize Austria's historic and geographic position in the heart of Central Europe, which gives the Center for Austrian Studies a unique and significant role in discussions on the shape of the new Europe.

I wish to thank several participants in the conference who contributed indirectly to the success of the volume by serving as commentators or panelists at the conference: from Minnesota – Zbigniew Bochniarz, Robert Kudrle, Richard Rudolph, and Vernon Ruttan; and from outside Minnesota – Kurt Bayer, Karen Brooks, Daniel Chirot, John Lampe, Marvin Jackson, Larry Neal, and Erich Streissler. Carol Duling did superb work as the conference coordinator. Major funding for the conference was supplied by the Austrian Ministry of Science and Research and by the Austrian Cultural Institute in New York. Two units of the University of Minnesota also supplied generous funding – the Center for European Studies and the Freeman Center for International Economic Policy. I am grateful to Ellen Comisso for her valuable comments on revised versions of the individual contributions.

Louise Guenther prepared the manuscript with exceptional care and thoroughness as Assistant Editor. Eve Dvorak also provided valuable editorial assistance.

Both the Austrian Cultural Institute and the Center for Austrian Studies have generously subsidized the publication of this volume.

David F. Good
Minneapolis, Minnesota

Part I
INTRODUCTION

1

THE ECONOMIC TRANSFORMATION OF CENTRAL AND EASTERN EUROPE IN HISTORICAL PERSPECTIVE

Main themes and issues

David F. Good

The collapse of Communism in Central and Eastern Europe marks a watershed in the region's economic history. Most observers on both sides of the cold war divide initially greeted the events of 1989 with considerable euphoria. They conjured up visions of a brighter future in which the region's economies would throw off the shackles of their central planning systems, integrate fully with the rest of Europe, and begin catching up with their wealthier neighbors in the West. Euphoria has given way to more sober reflections in face of post-1989 realities. In Western Europe the push for further unity within the European Community (EC) ran out of steam in 1992 and is now in danger of collapsing under the weight of popular fears about its consequences. In Eastern Europe social conflict, economic stagnation, and challenges to democratic values threaten to derail the transition from Communism. The vision of European-wide integration is giving way to neo-cold war images of a "fortress EC" sealing itself off from its poorer, more unstable neighbors in the East.

What lies ahead? Will the states of Central and Eastern Europe successfully negotiate the transition to market economies and begin catching up with Western Europe? Or will they lapse into a lengthy period of social and political conflict and fall further behind? In the early stages of the transition, most policy-makers and specialists quite understandably did not address these questions but focused instead on the more immediate technical issues (see Blanchard *et al.* 1991; Campbell 1991). Growing concerns about the region's economic future, however, make the questions increasingly compelling. The contributions below demonstrate that useful answers to them require knowledge of the region's economic past.[1]

HISTORICAL APPROACH

History "matters" in the obvious sense that it can provide useful lessons. The current watershed in Central and Eastern Europe is only the most recent in a series of dramatic turning points in the region's long-term economic development. Examining the current transformation in light of earlier ones offers insights that cannot be gained without such historical perspective. But history "matters" in a more fundamental sense because it passes on legacies from generation to generation. Reflecting choices made in the past, these inherited legacies limit the range of choices available to successive generations and give history its path-dependent character (Arthur 1988; David 1985; North 1990). While the collapse of the Soviet empire will mark a major discontinuity in the economic history of Central and Eastern Europe, it has not left behind a blank slate. The events of 1989 destroyed the old regime, but left intact ideas and institutions that will continue to shape behavior well into the future.

Despite the variety of experience within Central and Eastern Europe, the economies of the region have two things in common that differentiate them from the economies of Western Europe. One is their long-standing relative economic backwardness. Even a rudimentary knowledge of European history suggests that the current lag of the region is not simply a legacy of the Communist era, but in large measure reflects the long-standing West to East economic gradient in Europe. In addition, the same history tells us that great watersheds in the European past have had especially far-reaching consequences for Central and Eastern Europe. The end of the cold war actually marks the fourth major shock in the past century or so. The first came in the late nineteenth century as the uneven spread of modern economic growth through Central and Eastern Europe uprooted traditional agrarian societies. World War I delivered the second shock; in its wake successor states were created from the fallen Russian and Habsburg empires in much the same way that war led to the fragmentation and ultimate collapse of the decaying Ottoman empire during the nineteenth century. World War II delivered the third shock as the region became incorporated into the Soviet empire during the cold war. Each of these shocks was followed by significant changes in the region's underlying economic institutions and/or its international economic relations. The transition periods were painful and marked by economic difficulties, social conflict, and political instability.

A look at the region's economic history over this period will uncover the legacies that will shape its economic future. Tracing out the long-term pattern of relative backwardness will give clues about the region's potential for catching up. Analyzing long-term patterns of continuity and change in institutions and international economic relations will provide a perspective on their likely path in the post-cold war era. Here I show how the individual contributions illuminate these themes within a chronology dictated by the previous system shocks: the late nineteenth century up to World War I, the era including the two world wars, and the cold war era.

RELATIVE ECONOMIC BACKWARDNESS IN HISTORICAL PERSPECTIVE

Comparing international income levels is tricky, especially when the comparisons involve countries with sharply different economic systems and different levels of development. However, even if the available data have a substantial margin of error, they demonstrate the substantial lag of the former East bloc economies within Europe.[2]

In his essay Felix Butscheck (Ch. 2) argues that much of this current lag reflects the late appearance of modern economic growth in the region. Abundant evidence shows that the origins of economic backwardness in Central and Eastern Europe lie deep in the past, at least as far back as the early modern period when proto-industrialization sprouted in some rural areas of Western Europe and the "second serfdom" took hold throughout much of Eastern Europe (Kriedte *et al.* 1981; Chirot 1989).

Containing a large chunk of today's Central and Eastern Europe, the Habsburg empire stood in the middle of the European economic gradient; relatively backward compared with France and relatively advanced compared with Russia. In addition, the sprawling Habsburg realm itself displayed a pronounced West to East economic gradient (Good 1984: Chs 2, 5). We do not know how rapidly the lands of Central and Eastern Europe grew under Habsburg rule before 1870, but Table 1.1 shows that they failed to keep pace with the economies of Western Europe and the USA. By that year, gross domestic product (GDP) per capita in the Habsburg empire as a whole stood at a level just over one-third that of the USA and just under one-third that of the UK, a gap that was surely not so large a century before. Furthermore, regional disparities within the empire mirrored the larger economic gradient in Europe; income levels were two to three times higher in the empire's western lands than in its eastern lands (Good 1993b: Tables 2, 3).

Table 1.1 also shows that the rise of the USA to economic leadership between 1870 and World War I coincided with a deterioration in the relative standing of almost all European countries, including the lands of Central and Eastern Europe.[3] Yet a closer look confirms previous work that challenges overly pessimistic views of economic performance in the region during the final decades of Habsburg rule (Gerschenkron 1977; Jaszi 1929). The Habsburg empire grew more rapidly in the late nineteenth century than most European economies, including even Germany. In addition, regional income disparities within the Empire began to close in the four pre-World War I decades.[4] As a result, between 1870 and 1910, much of Central and

Table 1.1 Catching up and falling behind in Europe. Indices of gross domestic product per capita 1870–1987 (present-day, pre-1989 boundaries) (USA=100)

Country	*1870*	*1910*	*1950*	*1987*
USA	100.0	100.0	100.0	100.0
Northwest				
UK	113.4	80.6	62.0	69.3
Belgium	87.5	65.7	46.4	64.8
Netherlands	88.9	62.9	52.9	67.5
France	65.4	49.2	45.2	70.6
Germany	54.1	49.3	37.3	73.4
Switzerland	73.6	58.7	68.3	76.4
Northern				
Denmark	65.4	63.0	58.0	74.1
Finland	39.8	32.9	38.9	70.2
Norway	51.2	39.9	51.1	87.3
Sweden	54.5	48.4	57.7	77.6
Mediterranean				
Italy	52.1	40.3	31.3	66.7
Portugal	40.0	22.2	20.2	42.6
Spain	48.5	41.4	25.0	47.3
Central and Eastern				
Habsburg empire	36.5	34.2	–	–
[a]Austria	59.4	51.0	31.6	64.4
[a]Czechoslovakia	45.7	41.9	38.6	46.0
[a]Hungary	30.2	35.2	33.7	44.3
[a]Poland	23.9	21.4	27.2	30.1
[a]Yugoslavia	24.6	24.9	14.4	30.2
[a]Romania	21.7	23.2	13.3	28.8
Bulgaria	–	20.5	16.3	32.9
Russia (Soviet Union)	38.6	26.2	33.7	44.0

Notes and Sources:

[a] Indicates the successor states and territories of the Habsburg empire.

1870 and 1910: For the successor states, the indexes are computed from Good (1993c, Table 3). For Romania and Poland in 1870 and 1910 and for Yugoslavia in 1870 the data are for the Habsburg portions only of the present-day states. For the remaining states, the indices are computed from Maddison (1990, Table 1a: 83). See Good (1993c, Section I, Table A-1) for details.

1950 and 1987: For all states (and for Yugoslavia in 1910), the indexes are calculated from Maddison (1990, Table 1a: 83). See Good (1993c, Section I, Table A-1) for details.

Eastern Europe began to catch up with the more developed states of Western Europe even as it lost ground to the USA.

Within the overall pattern of instability and stagnation in the period 1910–1950, most European economies, including the successor states to the Habsburg empire and their neighboring states in Central and Eastern Europe, continued to fall further behind the USA.[5] On average, however, the states of Central and Eastern Europe seemed to have performed no better and no worse than other European states. Taken as a whole, the data for 1870, 1910, and 1950 show clearly that the Communist regimes in post-1945 Central and Eastern Europe inherited a sizable legacy of relative economic backwardness. On the eve of the Communist takeover, income levels throughout most of the region were still below the European average and were from one-quarter to one-third the level of GDP per capita in the USA.

At first glance, Table 1.1 suggests that the former East bloc economies performed rather well in the cold-war era. In response to vigorous programs of economic modernization, incomes grew faster in Central and Eastern Europe than in the USA, especially in the 1950s and 1960s, so the relative position of the region improved in the cold war era. Yet most European economies grew faster than the American economy after World War II. Although the East bloc economies also experienced an "economic miracle," the growth rates were not unusually fast considering the low starting point in 1950 and, compared with Western Europe, they were significantly lower in the 1970s and 1980s.

THE STATE AND ECONOMIC INSTITUTIONS

The issues

Despite deepening concern over the future of Central and Eastern Europe, the drive to introduce markets and to privatize state-owned property will push ahead. The current economic restructuring in the region occurs during a major sea change in international discourse on political economy. Beginning in the late 1970s, the state came under steady fire as the major source of economic ills in the developed, capitalist economies. Deregulation and tax cuts aimed at reducing the size of government became the buzz-words of economic policy.

In this climate the standard criticisms of the central planning regimes, described at length in the essays of Michael Palairet (Ch. 6), Scott Eddie (Ch. 7), and Jan Stankovsky (Ch. 15), took on even greater weight. Of course, long before 1989 debate within the socialist world led to economic reforms that decentralized decision-making even within the most rigid planning systems (Campbell 1991; Johnson 1989). As Eddie points out, the collapse of Communism has now brought the complete discrediting of central planning and deep skepticism about state controls and intervention in economic affairs. Both inside and outside the region, the double vision of "market economies" and "privatization" guides policy discussions.

While the overall vision of the future seems clear, its precise content and timing are not. How quickly will these economies transform? What will they look like in the end? These are critical questions because, as Lee Alston argues in his essay (Ch. 3), markets do not "just happen." They arise from conscious decisions to set up institutions that permit a society to capture the gains from exchange by reducing uncertainty. Whether they are formal (rules and laws backed by the coercive power of the government) or informal (codes of behavior enforced by small groups or associations), Alston's review of economic history shows that institutions "matter." They foster economic growth if they encourage "positive-sum" productivity-raising behavior; they retard economic growth if they promote "negative-sum" behavior aimed at redistributing income.

Both the Alston essay (Ch. 3) and the essay by Richard Tilly (Ch. 12) point to another lesson of economic history – that the state has played a critical role in defining and enforcing the rules of the game that encourage growth-promoting institutions. In this respect, the state's lack of credibility in post-Communist Central and Eastern Europe is particularly worrisome. Under the present conditions it is hard to imagine effective policies of promoting economic growth in Central and Eastern Europe that fail to include a substantial role for the state. Developing infrastructure, creating new institutions of production and exchange, and brokering the social tensions of transition cannot be accomplished through private contracting alone. They require an active public sector that is far smaller and less oppressive than in the typical centrally planned economy, but far larger and more interventionist than is implicit in more naive Western blueprints of the region's future.

Just as specialists and policy advisors debate the future shape of the new market economies so, too, do they disagree about the speed at which change should be implemented. There are certainly strong arguments in favor of the "shock treatment" implemented, for example, in Poland. In theory, as Alston argues, a rapid transition to new institutional arrangements offers potential losers less chance to resist. In addition, as both Alston (Ch. 3) and Eddie (Ch. 7) note, by reducing uncertainty a rapid transition may stimulate investment and increase the willingness of society to play by the new rules of the game.

In the current situation, however, change appears to be unfolding slowly and where "shock treatment" has been applied it has generated considerable grumbling and open conflict.

Institutional arrangements have a certain inertia. When they do change, they do so gradually because in reality those who stand to lose do form coalitions and resist change. Slow change may actually bring benefits if, as

Alston notes, it allows time for the underlying population to adjust and perceive the changes as fair and equitable. In the current transition, elites are not managing popular perceptions very well. Some people argue that little has changed because much of the old elite still seems to be in power. Others believe that a lot has changed because new policies have hit some groups harder than others. Still others see a link between the two – that it is precisely the old elites who did well under Communism that are now being enriched in the transition to capitalism.

Historical legacies

The economic history of the region, too, should make us wary of visions of Central and Eastern Europe based on rapid, friction-less transitions to full-blown market economies. It is a history marked by ongoing efforts at both state-building and economy-building and by both change and continuity in the wake of system shocks. With respect to economic development, decision making came as much from above as from below. Adam Smith's invisible hand becomes increasingly visible as we move eastward in Europe. Although Alexander Gerschenkron's approach to European industrialization has been picked apart in its details, his vision of Central and Eastern Europe as the home of hierarchical modes of resource allocation and income distribution has much value.[6]

In Central and Eastern Europe, state-building began in earnest in the eighteenth-century Habsburg empire. Maria Theresa and Joseph II promoted fundamental economic reforms, especially in agriculture, as the levels of spending needed to maintain the monarchy's great power status began to outstrip government revenue (Matis 1981; Komlos 1990). In the nineteenth century modern economic growth in Britain and Northwestern Europe further destabilized great power politics in Europe. Having survived the revolutions of 1848, the Habsburg crown once again instituted major economic reforms in agriculture, finance, trade, and transportation as a way of shoring up its great power status (März, 1968; Matis, 1972). The tradition of state intervention in economic activity carried on after the Dual Settlement of 1867 even as control over some important areas of economic policy shifted to separate governments in Vienna and Budapest. Scholars are correct in emphasizing the role of market forces in promoting economic development in the Habsburg empire, but they are remiss in denying the key role of the state in determining the rules of the game underlying economic decision-making and in behaving as an autonomous economic actor in its own right.[7]

In the last half of the nineteenth century, the large universal banks, Gerschenkron's other "special institutional factor" under conditions of economic backwardness, emerged in Central Europe to substitute for its missing capital market and pool of entrepreneurs. As Alice Teichova argues in her essay (Ch. 4), Austria–Hungary and not Germany should be considered the quintessential universal bank economy before 1914. The ties of the Viennese great banks to industry were pervasive and close. Although much like their German counterparts the Viennese banks were not especially entrepreneurial and instead provided "development assistance for the strong" (Tilly 1986), few would deny their strategic role in mobilizing and allocating capital by virtue of their sheer weight in the economy.

In the late nineteenth century, top-down decision-making in economic affairs tended to be the order of the day in the Balkans, too. As the independent states of Bulgaria, Greece, Romania, and Serbia were formed out of the decaying Ottoman empire, state-building and economy-building went hand in hand, which meant that relative to their level of economic development, the Balkan states had large, modern-looking state structures (see, for example, Lampe 1989; Berend and Ránki 1982).

The creation of small states in Central and Eastern Europe out of pre-1914 empires marks a watershed in the region, but it did not end the pattern of hierarchical modes of resource allocation. The tradition persisted and took on new forms. The tasks of state building, post-war reconstruction, and national integration meant that the actual involvement of the state in economic life far transcended the restricted role reserved for it by the prevailing liberal orthodoxy (Ránki and Tomaszewski 1986). Public officials in the new successor states had to deal with the problems of post-war demobilization and with the devastating consequences of hyperinflation. In addition, much public sector energy went into building new institutional arrangements and mechanisms of policy formation, as is seen in the essays of Ivo Bićanić and Marko Škreb (Ch. 9) on Yugoslavia, Janusz Kaliński on Poland, and Daniel Miller (Ch. 11) on Czechoslovakia. The state intervened even further in the great depression with bail-outs of failing enterprises, controls on foreign exchange, supports for commodity prices, and bilateral trade agreements. The Bićanić and Škreb essay (Ch. 9) confirms Alston's point (Ch. 3) about the special role of the state in creating the institutions of the market economy. In addition, the Yugoslav case clearly demonstrates that institution-building does not happen overnight. Uniform rail tariffs were put in place in 1925 and a uniform tax system only in 1928. The Serbian dinar became the national currency in 1925, but was stabilized only in 1931, and it took twenty years to set up fully the national bank.

The interwar history of the Central European universal banks shows how institutional inertia persists in the face of changed circumstances. Teichova (Ch. 4) argues that World War I and the peace treaties dramatically changed the environment in which the universal banks operated, but not their strategies. With the dissolution of the Habsburg empire, the Viennese banks became multinational enterprises instead of domestic enterprises operating in a large internal market. They tried to shore up their close ties with industry throughout Central and Eastern Europe by borrowing short-term in Western Europe. The resulting bank failures led to several key mergers and a further concentration in Austrian banking. The crisis came to a head in 1931 with the crash of the Creditanstalt; the state bailed out the bank and became the major shareholder guarantor of a one-bank system.

In contrast, pursuing pre-1914 strategies in the new interwar circumstances did not lead to such disastrous results in the case of the Czech banks. Although they, too, cultivated the imperial capital market before World War I, Alice Teichova (Ch. 4) and Daniel Miller (Ch. 11) point out that the Czech banks had a more national than imperial focus. Their strong pre-war ties with the central organizations of the Czech credit cooperatives and savings banks carried over into the interwar period and, according to Teichova (Ch. 4), made the Czech financial system relatively resilient in the 1930s crisis.

The economic history of the cold war era provides further support for my two central points – that unbridled market forces are unlikely to carry the day in Central and Eastern Europe and that the new institutional arrangements will develop slowly. The experience of post-1945 Western Europe provides some evidence on both issues. In the recent disillusionment with state intervention and hierarchical coordination of market forces, it is easy to forget the major role these played in resurrecting Western Europe from the ashes of the great depression and World War II. French indicative planning and the neo-corporatist arrangements of the small neutral countries typify the range of mixed capitalist institutions that underpinned economic growth in the period (Freeman 1989; Katzenstein 1984; Shonfield 1965; Van der Wee 1986: Chs. 7, 8).

It is especially useful to look at post-1945 Austria, which was the only small state of Central and Eastern Europe to land on the Western side of the iron curtain and the most socialist of Western market economies (Kramer and Butschek 1985; Abele *et al.* 1989). Austria developed an extensive welfare state and its unique brand of "Austro–Keynesian" macroeconomic stabilization policy, nationalized the bulk of German-controlled industry at the end of the war, and, as discussed in the essay of Anton Pelinka (Ch. 8), gradually put into place its "social partnership" to control wages and prices. It is worth noting, too, that even with the pressure of the cold war and the umbrella of the USA, these institutions of mixed capitalism in Austria and elsewhere in Western Europe evolved over time and only became firmly entrenched by the end of the 1950s.

A more fundamental issue raised by the Austrian case is whether its social partnership, the centerpiece of its neo-corporatist system, is exportable to the east. Pelinka argues from the initial experience of post-1989 Czechoslovakia that it is not, despite striking parallels with Austria after 1945. In contrast to Austria during the cold war, labor and capital have no centralized organizations and the political party system is highly fragmented in post-1989 Czechoslovakia (and currently in the Czech Republic). Reflecting this, the neo-corporatist look-alike institution, the Council of

Economic and Social Associations, actually bears only a faint and superficial resemblance to the social partnership of Austria or the neo-corporatist arrangements of Scandinavia. While Pelinka's assessment certainly holds for the near-term, it is still possible that over time a network of extra-parliamentary institutions may arise in the former East bloc states to prop up the weak democracies and weak economies.

Of more direct relevance, of course, is the experience of the East bloc economies during the cold war. By the late 1940s, the small states of Central and Eastern Europe were rapidly and systematically transforming their economies along Soviet lines by introducing central planning, nationalizing property, and collectivizing agriculture. The lessons to be drawn from the Communist experience, however, are by no means obvious, especially if it is viewed in light of the region's past. To what extent was the Soviet model artificially implanted on viable market economies? To what extent was it an unusually coercive version of previous state-building and economy-building experiments designed to promote catching up? Both views receive support from this volume depending on the country under discussion.

Eddie for Hungary (Ch. 7) and Miller for Czechoslovakia (Ch. 11) argue that the changes were revolutionary, both in substance and in the pace of introduction. Miller shows that forming the new Czechoslovak state out of the Habsburg empire after World War I did not alter the fundamental character of the Czech agrarian political movement. The newly organized Republican Party of Agriculturalists and Small Farmers used existing institutional structures to advance its interests in the Land Reform of 1919 and the tariff legislation of the 1920s. The real discontinuity began with the Nazi invasion of 1938, which led to a rapid dismantling of agrarian political structures. The economic foundations were subsequently demolished after the Communist take-over in 1948. The new regime took over all agrarian financial institutions, including the credit cooperatives, and it nationalized or collectivized most land in private hands – 83 per cent by 1960. In Miller's view the Communist era marks such a sea change in Czech agrarian politics that the pre-Communist interwar years leave almost no legacy for the post-Communist Czech Republic. Today's agrarian parties lay claim to the pre-1939 Republican past in their rhetoric, but parties extolling the virtues of small independent farms have not done well in the polls. As a result of their experiences in collective farms under Communism, Czech farmers are skeptical about running small and medium size farms and tend to prefer employment in large agricultural enterprises.

Eddie (Ch. 7), too, argues for the inherently revolutionary character of the Hungarian experience under Communism. He argues that the current transition in Hungary, as elsewhere in the former East bloc, resembles an era of reconstruction after a destructive war. But, he argues, the current situation is actually far worse because of the devastating legacies left behind by Communism – a client–patron legal system with no culture of abiding by the law and a labor force with no work ethic; in the old regime motivation and effort counted for less than who one knew.

Other authors recognize the revolutionary nature of the Communist experiment, yet stress its continuities with the pre-Communist past. Kaliński, for example, stresses the persistence of relatively small peasant farms despite the large scale institutional changes in the Polish economy after World War I and World War II. In his essay Ivan Berend analyses the collapse of the post-1945 Communist regimes in light of the ongoing attempts by modernizing elites in the region to overcome the region's relative economic backwardness. He also outlines a possible pessimistic scenario in which sluggish, conflict-ridden transitions give way to a new round of authoritarian regimes without, of course, the ideology or institutions of Communism. Bićanić and Škreb read the entire economic history of the Yugoslav state from its creation in 1919 to its disintegration in 1991 as a series of experiments in centralized decision-making that ultimately failed to weld together the Yugoslav economy and enable it to catch up with Western Europe. These views remind us that the Communist regimes ushered in a new chapter in the ongoing and rather tumultuous story of political modernization and economic development in Central and Eastern Europe.

REORDERING INTERNATIONAL ECONOMIC RELATIONS

The issues

The collapse of the Soviet Union's external empire not only set in motion institutional changes in Central and Eastern Europe; it also put an end to the artificial division of Europe into two distinct, largely independent economic blocs. Inflexible bilateral trade agreements, low levels of foreign investment, and severe restrictions on emigration weakened economic integration within the East bloc and isolated it from the West. High levels of multilateral trade, large scale foreign investment, and relatively open borders integrated the economies of the West and tied them into the world economy. With the exception of Austria, the economies of Central and Eastern Europe functioned in a socialist division of labor with the Soviet Union based on favorable terms of trade; they imported raw materials and energy at less than world prices and exported manufactured goods at more than world prices (Holzman 1987; Marer 1989). By contrast, Austria became closely tied to the market economies of Western Europe, especially the Federal Republic of Germany.

Now that the cold war is over, the stage is set for the reintegration of Europe from the Atlantic to the Urals. But what form will this take and what will be its timetable? Initially some observers offered impressive visions of an expanded EC that would include former East bloc states as they successfully made the transition to market economies and democratic institutions. Indeed Czechoslovakia, Poland, and Hungary quickly applied for and received associate status in the EC. More recently, debate within the EC over the Maastricht Treaty and pessimism about the transition in the former East bloc have dashed expectations that reintegration would take the form of a European-wide EC in the foreseeable future.

Reintegration will occur, of course, but in a much less formal and visible form. It will take shape as economies gradually adjust to the disequilibrium implicit in the economics of the cold war divide. Taking the West to East income gradient as a starting point, economic theory would predict an adjustment involving some combination of migration westward, capital flows eastward, and trade flows in both directions based on comparative advantage. The rise of anti-foreigner sentiment and restrictions on immigration in Western Europe insure that migration out of Eastern Europe will play only a limited role in the adjustment, which means that the burden will fall more heavily on some combination of capital and trade flows (Holzmann *et al.* 1993).

Historical legacies

The dismemberment of the Habsburg empire after World War I and the creation of the Soviet empire after World War II greatly altered the political framework of international economic relations in Central and Eastern Europe. The economic history of the past century, however, shows strong continuities despite the watersheds associated with the two world wars.

Taking a long view means seeing the post-cold war reintegration of Europe as part of the long-standing evolution of a European-wide division of labor. The trend accelerated sharply in the nineteenth century as economic forces (the railroad) and political forces (the free trade movement and the formation of customs unions among the German states, within the Habsburg empire, and within unified Italy) sharply reduced both natural and legal barriers to the free flow of goods, capital, and people across Europe (Pollard 1981; Berend and Ránki 1982). Resource and trade flowed predictably along the West to East economic gradient; capital moved eastward from the more developed areas of Northwestern Europe – France, England, the Low Countries, and Rhineland–Westphalia. People migrated westward (many eventually to the New World) from the agrarian regions of Central and Eastern Europe. Manufactured goods from Western Europe exchanged for agricultural goods from Eastern Europe. At the same time, resource endowment and the uneven spread of modern technology prevented a complete regional specialization along these lines. Higher-income economies in the West exported some agricultural goods and lower-income economies in the East exported some manufactured goods on the basis of lower wages or specialized technological niches.

Much of today's Central and Eastern Europe participated in this growing international division of labor either as regions inside the Habsburg empire or as independent states strongly tied to it. Just as the empire's regional economic disparities mirrored the overall pattern of spatial inequality within Europe, so too did its interregional linkages mirror Europe's overall pattern of international economic relations (Good 1984: Ch. 4). After the revolutions of 1848, railroad expansion reduced transportation costs and the empire formally became a customs union. Along the West to East gradient within the empire, Vienna acted as a filter for the flow of capital eastward and the flow of people westward (März 1968; Rudolph 1976). Manufactured goods from the Western regions exchanged for agricultural goods from the Eastern regions. But here, too, exports of processed foodstuffs, semi-manufactures and manufactures became an increasing portion of total exports from some lands in the East; Hungary, for example, found its own industrial niche in flour milling.

The Habsburg economy was quite self-sufficient as is shown by the low level of its foreign trade compared with its internal trade. However, the empire became increasingly tied to Western Europe by virtue of its strong ties to Germany.[8]

Tilly's essay (Ch. 12) shows that Central and Eastern Europe accounted for an increasing share of capital exports from Germany, which by the end of the nineteenth century had become the third largest capital exporter behind England and France. German interests in the region centered on the Habsburg empire more than Russia or the independent Balkan states with Vienna providing the main channel for the flow of funds into the peripheral areas of the empire.

Moving further east, Roumyana Preshlenova shows in her essay (Ch. 13) the extent to which the independent Balkan states were tied into the Habsburg empire. The empire was the single most important trading partner of the Balkan states and might have been even more important had there been more complementarity between the two trading areas. As it turned out, however, competition between the heavily agricultural areas of Hungary and the largely agrarian Balkan economies led to tariff wars between Austro–Hungary and the Balkan states. The competition heightened political tension and led to the redirection of some trade toward Germany and Western Europe, but the share of the Habsburg lands in Balkan trade still remained high.

Tilly's essay (Ch. 12) provides valuable perspective on a key question: Will sizable amounts of private capital flow into post-cold war Central and Eastern Europe? Tilly argues that in the late nineteenth century German capital flows to Austria–Hungary and the Balkans reflected the profit expectations of private investors, not the political will of the German government. According to his calculations, German investment in the region paid, that is, the risk-adjusted rate of return on foreign debt and equity issues approximated the return on domestic issues. Although the flows were private, they did not reflect "market forces" *per se* but the institutional strategies of the big universal banks, which preferred lending to strong and stable governments. The increased importance of the Habsburg empire as an outlet for German capital is consistent with the narrowing of the gap between the return on Austro–Hungarian securities and domestic issues in response to the greater stability of Habsburg finances and the introduction of the gold standard. Tilly argues the same point for the Balkan states; they attracted Western capital by using restrictive fiscal policies to build up credibility as borrowers. From this experience he concludes that private capital will play a major role in Central and Eastern Europe only after the region attains some political stability, which he argues depends on financial and technical support from Western governments.

The pre-1914 and interwar experiences also demonstrate the historical legacy of Central and Eastern Europe as an economic area. Tilly's essay provides support for the prediction of most present-day observers that Germany will assume a major role in the region despite the difficulties brought on by its reunification. In turn Preshlenova's work (Ch. 13) suggests the potential for significant economic interaction among the Central and Eastern European small states apart from Germany. We are already seeing more intense economic relations between Austria and its successor state neighbors of the former East bloc – the Czech and Slovak Republics, Hungary, Slovenia, and Croatia – and between this former Habsburg core and Poland, Romania, and Bulgaria. Taken together both essays belie the widely held notion that trade potential within the former East bloc states is limited.

These pre-1914 trends persisted into the interwar war period despite the destabilizing shocks delivered by World War I and the territorial settlements of the Paris peace treaties. The dismemberment of the Habsburg empire into the successor states in 1919 marks a sharp break in the *political* relations among the peoples of Central and Eastern Europe, but it did not automatically lead to new economic relations. Previously domestic (interregional) flows of goods and resources now became external (international) flows. The persistence of these links despite conscious efforts on the part of successor state governments to undo them, show how powerful they were (März 1984; Stiefl 1988: Ch. 4; Ránki and Tomaszewski 1986). It is true that German financial and trade penetration declined in the region after World War I despite Nazi attempts to revive it in the late 1930s. Also, successor state governments followed protectionist trade policy to build up domestic industry and sought to nationalize firms previously controlled by Vienna (nostrification). Jürgen Nautz's essay (Ch. 14) shows, however, that protectionist policies had the effect of sharply reducing the overall volume of trade, but did not lead to a sudden change in its geographic patterns. Austria's efforts in cultivating ties with the other successor states apparently paid off.

The share of the successor states in Austria's trade declined somewhat in the interwar period, but still accounted for almost 50 per cent on the eve of World War II. Also, Teichova (Ch. 4) makes the point that Vienna's financial control over the former Habsburg lands changed more in legal form than in reality (see also Matis 1983).

As Stankovsky (Ch. 15) notes (echoed also by Butschek (Ch. 2) and Nautz (Ch. 14)), the real break in the nineteenth-century pattern of international economic relations in Central and Eastern Europe occurred after World War II. As part of the Council of Mutual Economic Assistance (CMEA), the former East bloc states were not closed economies, but the direction and character of their external relations did change significantly. The small states of Central and Eastern Europe continued to trade extensively with one another, but their ties to the rest of Europe shifted dramatically from Western Europe to the Soviet Union. Producers in the CMEA bloc found its markets appealing because they were relatively easy to exploit and because the Soviet Union offered favorable terms of trade.

The 1970s brought a challenge to the socialist economies as a relatively self-contained economic bloc. As described in Ivan Berend's essay (Ch. 5), the initial post-1945 policy of extensive growth via import substitution had reached its limits. In response to the growth slow-down, the socialist regimes turned to the world market. The crisis in the region deepened, however, in part because the world economy itself was undergoing its own structural transformation. But, according to Berend (Ch. 5), state socialism faced an additional obstacle – its "quasi-religious, post-Stalinist ideology" that called for continuing the policy of forced industrialization. In the context of the world-wide crisis, this policy led to widening trade deficits and rising external debt whose service soaked up a large and increasing proportion of hard currency income.

Michael Palairet's case study (Ch. 6) of Zastava, Yugoslavia's large automobile producer, offers clear-cut microeconomic support for the macroeconomic perspective outlined by Berend. Zastava, supported with Fiat capital, had prospered in the 1960s by supplying finished cars to its own home market and by supplying components to the Polish and Soviet auto industries. In the 1970s it successfully exported finished cars to CMEA markets. Under pressure from the government to become a hard currency earner despite its status as a high-cost import substituter, Zastava staked out a strategy for penetrating the American market with its Yugo model. Despite huge subsidies the strategy failed in the face of growing supply bottlenecks and problems of internal coordination that made quality control impossible. According to Palairet, the Zastava experience was not unique; over 75 per cent of Yugoslavian exports into hard currency markets were sold at a price less than the home price. In the end, the turn to world markets not only spelled the downfall of Zastava, but ultimately, Palairet argues, deepened the crisis of state socialism in Yugoslavia. The Zastava story also serves as a foreshadowing to policymakers in the former East bloc economies of the pressures they will face as their economies become truly open economies.

Of course, the shape of international economic relations in the future is uncertain, but the contributions offer important clues. Jan Stankovsky argues in his essay (Ch. 15) that the former East bloc economies have a comparative advantage in sectors that use skilled labor and human capital, a positive legacy from the Communist era that suggests a strategy of export-led growth around high-tech manufacturing. Of course, this strategy also requires a sizable inflow of capital and technological know-how from abroad, which may not be forthcoming in the near future. In the short-run, he argues, these economies may have to follow a low-wage strategy of export promotion in the steel, textiles, and agricultural sectors.

We can also speculate about the changing geographical character of Central and East European international relations based on the pre-1989 patterns. Cut loose from the limitations of CMEA, the small states of Central and Eastern Europe will seek out new relationships in a more complex European-wide specialization and division of labor. The end of CMEA marks a major break, but new patterns will emerge gradually. History suggests that the relative importance of former CMEA partners, especially Russia, will fall, while the relative importance of Western Europe, especially Germany and Austria, will rise. At the same time, it suggests that economic relations *within* the region may remain strong even as its states cultivate new economic ties.

IMPLICATIONS

The main message of these contributions is that the relative economic backwardness of Central and Eastern Europe has deep roots in the past and will not be overcome simply because the Communist regimes have fallen from power. From the late nineteenth century until the end of World War II most of Europe fell behind the USA as it took over economic leadership from Britain. Within Europe the long-standing West to East economic gradient became less steep in the decades before World War I as much of Central and Eastern Europe began to catch up, but then stayed much the same in the interwar period. After World War II, both Western Europe and Eastern Europe began to close the gap with the USA in the context of their economic miracles. But the world-wide slow down in growth from the early 1970s was especially pronounced in the states of the East bloc and over the next two decades the region's relative backwardness with respect to Western Europe once again deepened. Taken as a whole the cold war era represents a missed opportunity for the socialist states of Central and Eastern Europe, especially considering the potential for high rates of growth inherent in the low level of income per capita in 1950.

The contributions here provide strong evidence that the sources of the missed opportunity were both internal and external. In part they lay in the institutional mechanisms of state socialism even in its reformed versions – the system's striking inability to provide incentives for "positive-sum" productivity-raising behavior and its rigidity in face of changing external circumstances. In part the causes lay in the region's fundamental isolation from the more dynamic Western economies, which persisted despite some opening up in the 1980s. With only limited access to Western markets and capital, the region could not tap the sources of economic growth that continued to fuel the closing of the gap between Western Europe and the USA. Obviously the internal and external factors are related. In the early years the closed nature of the economic system and the self-sufficiency of CMEA were mutually reinforcing. The internationalization of the socialist economies in the 1970s sought to restart their sputtering growth engines; ultimately it may have undermined the system itself.

At one level the economic history of Central and Eastern Europe justifies the initial optimism that greeted the fall of the Communist regimes. The region possesses clear potential for overcoming its relative economic backwardness with respect to the rest of Europe. Its states now have a considerable history of sustained economic growth in the sense developed by Kuznets (1966). In the Czech lands, Slovakia, Hungary, and Slovenia, modern economic growth began before World War I. In the rest of the region, it began under Communist rule on foundations that had been laid down in the late nineteenth century and the interwar period. As a result, the region's level of development today (as measured by per capita income) is high compared with most Third World countries. In absolute terms it is equal to that of Western Europe in the early 1960s. In relative terms, the current gap in relation to the USA is equal to the lag of Western Europe behind the USA on the eve of World War II. The low value of its antiquated and polluting capital stock must be weighed against the large endowment of human capital that was fueled by social spending on education and health in the Communist era.

A deeper reading of the region's economic history, however, offers substantial grounds for more pessimistic assessments of its economic prospects. Although the economic potential of the region is high, catch-up will be neither rapid nor automatic. The timing and pace of catch-up will depend heavily on the future path of institutional change and on the international environment. To engineer sustained catch-up, the drive toward market economies based on private property must continue, but it will most probably proceed slowly and reach its limits well short of textbook versions of the "market economy." The character, sheer magnitude, and social consequences of the transition suggest prominent and ongoing roles for the state and for non-market hierarchies in post-1989 Central and Eastern Europe. In this regard the mixed capitalist systems of the post-1945 Western European economic miracle provide a useful historical analogy. Of course, states and hierarchies are nothing new to the region as the pre-Communist history of state-building and economy-building clearly demonstrates. These legacies will prevent full-blown market systems from forming.

Of course, the former East bloc states may have to use free-market rhetoric to cover over these tendencies toward institutional inertia in much the same way that states in the region had to cultivate fiscal orthodoxy in order to gain credibility in pre-1914 and interwar international financial markets. But ultimately the key to attracting foreign capital is the state's ability to foster and preserve political stability. The economic history of the region suggests that foreign investors are less interested in the ideological nature of political regimes than in the expected profits generated by their economies; even at the height of the cold war some Westerners did not hesitate to take advantage of profitable trade and investment opportunities in East Europe.

The region's economic history also suggests that the pace and timing of catch-up hinges on how successfully the region reintegrates into the world economy and on the future health of the world economy itself. Before World War I, German capital played an important role in the emergence of modern economic growth in the lands of Central and Eastern Europe under Habsburg rule. Trade with the West, especially with the Habsburg empire, apparently did not have the same impact on the independent Balkan states, but may have laid the important foundations for future economic growth.[9] In the interwar period, the instability and shrinkage of international trade contributed to poor economic performance in both Western and Eastern Europe. In the cold war era, the economic isolation of the East bloc states from Western capitalism, which persisted even after the opening up in the late 1970s and 1980s, explains much of the relatively poor economic performance.

The geographical reorientation may be neither dramatic nor come quickly. Although its bilateral framework no doubt hindered intraregional trade within CMEA before 1989, the experience of the Habsburg successor states after World War I suggests there may be some inertia in the region's trading patterns. The same experience suggests a gradual reorientation of trade away from Russia toward Western Europe, especially Germany and Austria, as trading partners and as sources or conduits of foreign capital.

In closing it may be useful to look at the economic future of the formerly socialist Central and Eastern European states in light of post-1919 Austria, with whom they shared a common history up to 1945. The cold war era offers, perhaps, the best case scenario: Austria, the only small state in the region to escape Soviet domination, experienced an economic miracle and political stability as an integral part of Western Europe. The interwar period offers perhaps the worst case scenario: Austria, like most of the Habsburg successor states, experienced sluggish economic growth and political conflict that ushered in an authoritarian regime and foreign domination.

Surely the post-1945 scenario is too rosy. In the cold war, the Austrians rebuilt institutions on a modest scale (compared with the task now facing its neighbors to the east) within the hothouse of what may turn out to have been a uniquely favorable international environment. We can only hope that the interwar scenario is not on the horizon. Under the pall of its alleged non-viability as a small state, post-1919 Austria, like all the Habsburg successor states, began state-building in the hostile environment of a disintegrating world economy, which few observers think is around the corner.

The future no doubt lies somewhere in between these two scenarios. The world economy will likely function neither as well as in the 1950s and 1960s nor as poorly as in the 1920s and 1930s. Whatever happens to the world economy, the economic history of the last century shows that the twin tasks of state-building and economy-building are particularly difficult in the lands between Germany and Russia. The region seems fated to reinvent itself every half century; the late nineteenth century and World War I ushered in a new era in state-building while World War II brought new strategies of economic development. These dramatic twists and turns alone may explain much of the region's persisting relative backwardness.[10] This suggests the value of an important research agenda that focuses on the relationship between the region's relative economic backwardness and its crisis-prone history. Has its relative economic backwardness made it more prone to crisis in the wake of European-wide system shocks? Have the system shocks in turn promoted the region's relative backwardness? Getting answers to these questions may hold the key to developing a more stable pattern of political modernization and economic development in post-1989 Central and Eastern Europe.

NOTES

I wish to thank Diana Mishkova for her valuable comments on earlier versions of this essay.

1 Even policymakers now recognize this. Douglass C. North, one of two economic historians who shared the 1993 Nobel Prize in economics, is much sought after as a consultant in the former East bloc because of his work on the role of institutional change in economic history.

2 Data for 1989 show that they fall in the lower half of 23 European countries. Czechoslovakia with the highest income in the former East bloc ranked only 13 and Romania with the lowest income ranked 20. *The Economist*, 7 July 1990: 15. Based on UN, OECD, IMF, and CIA data.

3 On the general issue of changing economic leadership see Maddison (1991: Ch. 2) and Baumol *et al.* (1989).

4 These results confirm my earlier conclusions in Good (1984: 148–56) about the path of regional disparities in the empire, which were based on far less systematic evidence. But they run counter to Lampe (1989: 193).

5 There were exceptions; the Soviet Union in the East and Finland, Norway, Sweden, and Switzerland in the West, grew faster. See Table 1.1

6 Gerschenkron (1962) offers the clearest statement of his approach. Harley (1991) argues that Gerschenkron's approach is consistent with theories of economic development in which institutions are endogenous. Gerschenkron applies his approach to nineteenth-century Austria in Gerschenkron (1977). Rudolph (1972) tests his view on the role of banking for the Austrian half of the Habsburg empire. For a more general evaluation of Gerschenkron's views in the context of the empire see Good (1991a).

7 For views that downplay the role of the state see Eddie (1989), Huertas (1977), Komlos (1983), and Rudolph (1980).

8 This was more true for the Alpine lands and the Bohemian lands in the West than for the eastern lands of Hungary and Galicia, which relied more heavily on imperial markets, based on data in Eddie (1977) and Eddie (1980). On balance, the flows of goods, financial capital, and people narrowed regional differences in commodity prices, interest rates and wages, which demonstrates that economic union in the Empire was becoming a reality. See details in Good (1984: Ch. 4) and Mesch (1984).

9 However, as with the East bloc states in the cold war, the problem may have been their low level of trade with the outside world. See Hanson (1986).

10 This idea was suggested to me by Ellen Comisso after she had read the individual contributions.

REFERENCES

Abele, H., Nowotny, E., Schleicher, S., and Winckler, G. (eds.) (1989) *Handbuch der österreichischen Wirtschaftspolitik*, Vienna.

Arthur, W. B. (1988) "Self-reinforcing mechanisms in economics," in P. W. Anderson, K. J. Arrow and D. Pines (eds.) *The Economy as an Evolving Complex System*, Reading, MA.

Baumol, W. J., Blackman, S. A. B. and Wolff, E. N. (1989) *Productivity and American Leadership: The Long View*, Cambridge, MA.

Berend, I. and Ránki, G. (1974) *Economic Development in East–Central Europe in the 19th and 20th Centuries*, New York.

Berend, I. and Ránki, G. (1982) *The European Periphery & Industrialization 1780–1914*, London, New York.

Blanchard, O. *et al.* (1991) *Reform in Eastern Europe*, Cambridge, MA.

Butschek, F. (1985) *Die österreichische Wirtschaft im 20. Jahrhundert*, Stuttgart.

Butschek, F. (1990) "'Austrifizierung' der Oststaaten auch in der Wirtschaftspolitik?," *Europäische Rundschau* 18: 11–24.

Campbell, R. W. (1991) *The Socialist Economies in Transition*, Bloomington, IN.

Chirot, D. (ed.) (1989) *The Origins of Backwardness in Eastern Europe. Economics and Politics from the Middle Ages until the Early Twentieth Century*, Berkeley.

David, P. (1985) "Clio and the economics of QWERTY," *American Economic Review* 75: 332–7.

Drabek, Z. (1985) "Foreign trade performance and policy," in M. C. Kaser and E. A. Radice (eds.) *The Economic History of Eastern Europe 1919–1975*, vol. I, Oxford.

Eddie, S. (1977) "The terms and patterns of Hungarian foreign trade, 1882–1913," *Journal of Economic History* 37: 329–58.

Eddie, S. (1980) "Austria in the Dual Monarchy: Her trade within and without the Customs Union," *East Central Europe* 7 (2): 225–47.

Eddie, S. (1989) "Economic policy and economic development in Austria–Hungary, 1867–1913," in *The Cambridge Economic History of Europe*, vol. 8, Cambridge.

Freeman, J. R. (1989) *Democracy and Markets: The Politics of Mixed Economies*, Ithaca, NY.

Gerschenkron, A. (1962) *Economic Backwardness in Historical Perspective*, Cambridge, MA.

Gerschenkron, A. (1977) *An Economic Spurt that Failed*, Princeton, NJ.

Good, D. (1984) *The Economic Rise of the Habsburg Empire 1750–1914*, Berkeley.

Good, D. (1991a) "Austria–Hungary," in R. Sylla and G. Toniolo (eds.) *Patterns of European Industrialization: The Nineteenth Century*, London, New York.

Good, D. (1993a) "Ökonomische Ungleichheit in der Vielvölkerstaat," in J. Nautz and R. Vahrenkampf (eds.) *Die Wiener Jahrhundertwende*, Vienna.

Good, D. (1993b) "The economic lag of Central and Eastern Europe: Evidence from the late nineteenth-century Habsburg empire". Center for Austrian Studies Working Paper Series, 93–8.

Good, D. (1993c) "Estimating pre-1914 incomes in the post-1919 successor states of the Habsburg empire: Supplementary notes and tables." Unpublished manuscript.

Hanson, J. R. II (1986) "Export shares in the European periphery and the Third World before World War II: Questionable data, facile analogies," *Explorations in Economic History* 23: 85–99.

Harley, C. K. (1991) "Substitution for prerequisites: endogenous institutions and comparative economic history," in R. Sylla and G. Toniolo (eds.) *Patterns of European Industrialization: The Nineteenth Century*, London, New York.

Holzman, F. D. (1987) *The Economics of Soviet Bloc Trade and Finance*, Boulder, CO.

Holzmann, R., Thimann, Ch. and Petz, A. (1993) "Eastern European economic reform and Western European economic adjustment: Some macroeconomic considerations," Paper prepared for Empirica Economic Policy Forum, Vienna, 18 October 1993.

Huertas, T. (1977) *Economic Growth and Economic Policy in a Multinational Setting*, New York.

Janos, A. C. (1982) *The Politics of Backwardness in Hungary 1825–1945*, Princeton, NJ.

Jaszi, O. (1929) *The Dissolution of the Habsburg Monarchy*, Chicago, IL.

Johnson, P. M. (1989) *Redesigning the Communist Economy: The Politics of Economic Reform in Eastern Europe*, Boulder, CO.

Katzenstein, P. (1984) *Corporatism and Change: Austria, Switzerland, and the Politics of Industry*, Ithaca, NY.

Komlos, J. (1983) *The Habsburg Monarchy as a Customs Union: Economic Development in Austria–Hungary in the Nineteenth-Century*. Princeton, NJ.

Komlos, J. (1990) *Stature, Nutrition, and Economic Development in the Eighteenth-Century Habsburg Monarchy: The "Austrian" Model of the Industrial Revolution*, Princeton, NJ.

Kramer, H. and Butschek, F. (1985) *Vom Nachzügler zum Vorbild(?). Österreichische Wirtschaft 1945 bis 1985*, Stuttgart.

Kriedte, P., Medick, H. and Schlumbohm, J. (1981) *Industrialization before Industrialization*, Cambridge, New York.

Kuznets, S. (1966) *Modern Economic Growth: Rate, Structure and Spread*, New Haven, CT.

Lampe, J. (1989) "Imperial borderlands or capitalist periphery? Redefining Balkan backwardness, 1520–1914," in D. Chirot (ed.) *The Origins of Backwardness in Eastern Europe*, Berkeley, London.

Lampe, J. and Jackson, M. (1982) *Balkan Economic History 1550–1950: From Imperial Borderlands to Developing Nations*, Bloomington, IN.

Maddison, A. (1990). "Measuring European growth: The core and the periphery," in E. Aerts and N. Valério (eds.) *Growth and Stagnation in the Mediterranean World*

in the 19th and 20th Centuries, Leuven: Leuven University Press.
Maddison, A. (1991) *Dynamic Forces in Capitalist Development*, New York.
März E. (1968) *Österreichische Industrie -und Bankpolitik in der Zeit Franz Josephs I*, Vienna.
März, E. (1984) *Austrian Banking and Financial Policy: Creditanstalt at a Turning Point, 1913–1923*, New York.
Marer, P. (1989) "The economies and trade of Eastern Europe," in W. E. Griffith (ed.) *Central and Eastern Europe: The Opening Curtain?*, Boulder, CO.
Matis, H. (1972) *Österreichs Wirtschaft. Konjunkturelle Dynamik und gesellschaftlicher Wandel im Zeitalter Franz Josephs I*, Berlin.
Matis, H. (ed.) (1981) *Von der Glückseligkeit des Staates. Staat, Wirtschaft und Gesellschaft in Österreich im Zeitalter des aufgeklärten Absolutismus*, Berlin.
Matis, H. (1983) "Disintegration and multi-national enterprises in Central Europe during the post-war years (1918–1923)," in A. Teichova and P. L. Cottrell (eds.) *International Business and Central Europe, 1918–1939*, New York.
Matis, H. (1991). "Österreichs Wirtschaftsgeschichte – ein Modell für Osteuropa?" *Österreich in Geschichte und Literatur* 35: 119–31.
Mesch, M. (1984) *Arbeiterexistenz in der Spätgründerzeit – Gewerkschaften und Lohnentwicklung in Österreich 1890–1914*, Vienna.
North, D. C. (1990) *Institutions, Institutional Change and Economic Performance*, Cambridge.
Pollard, S. (1981) *Peaceful Conquest: The Industrialization of Europe 1760–1970*, Oxford, New York.
Ránki, Gy. and Tomaszewski, J. (1986) "The role of the state in industry, banking, and trade," in M. C. Kaser and E. A. Radice (eds.) *The Economic History of Eastern Europe 1919–1975*, Vol. II, Oxford.
Rudolph, R. (1972) "Austria, 1800–1914," in R. Cameron (ed.) *Banking and Economic Development*, New York.
Rudolph, R. (1976) *Banking and Industrialization in Austria-Hungary*, Cambridge.
Rudolph, R. (1980) "Social structure and the beginning of Austrian economic growth," *East Central Europe* 7 (2): 207–24.
Shonfield, A. (1965) *Modern Capitalism*, London, New York.
Stiefl, D. (1988) *Die Grosse Krise in einem kleinen Land. Österreichische Finanz-und Wirtschaftspolitik 1929–1938*, Vienna.
Tilly, R. (1986) "German banking 1850–1914: Development assistance for the strong," *Journal of European Economic History* 15: 113–52.
Van der Wee, H. (1986) *Prosperity and Upheaval: The World Economy 1945–1980*, Berkeley, Los Angeles.

Part II

THE LONG VIEW

2

EXTERNAL SHOCKS AND LONG-TERM PATTERNS OF ECONOMIC GROWTH IN CENTRAL AND EASTERN EUROPE

Felix Butschek

Many argue that socialism in Eastern Europe broke down in part because of its economic inefficiency, the evidence for which lies in the comparatively low per capita income in the former CMEA (Council of Mutual Economic Assistance) countries. Their democratic successors and their Western counterparts hope that economic conditions will improve and that after a successful transformation into a market economy, these economies will begin to approach Western standards. The implication is that the main source of economic backwardness in these countries has been their "wrong" economic system. The assumption needs closer examination if only because of the considerable differences in average income levels within Western Europe and even within the European Community.

As the former East bloc economies were managed according to socialist principles during the last four decades, it is difficult to assess their economic potential and level of development had they remained capitalistic. One useful approach is to rely on historical analysis; to assess past levels of development in these countries in comparison with Western economies of similar size, starting points and environmental conditions. Analyzing the former successor states of the Austro–Hungarian Monarchy seems especially illuminating. All of them, with the exception of Austria, belonged to the former East bloc. During the period of industrialization and proto-industrialization they belonged to the same political unit and after the dissolution of the Habsburg Monarchy they faced similar political and economic problems. So comparing these states before the break between East and West after World War II with a capitalist state like Switzerland might provide some useful insights into their potential economic capacity. (This approach was also chosen because comparable time series data for the whole period are not available.) For the whole period, of course, comparing the socialist successor states of the Habsburg Monarchy with Austria, the only capitalistic one after 1945, makes the most sense. Italy seems useful as an additional yardstick. Although only its northern regions were once part of the Habsburg Monarchy and they were severed from the Monarchy before its total dissolution, Italy belongs to the more-or-less peripheral areas of Europe that developed under similar institutional conditions.

THE TIMING OF INDUSTRIALIZATION

Differences among states in levels of national income today are still determined to a considerable degree by the timing of initial industrialization. Despite the great length of time, countless endogenous and exogenous influences on economic development, and the general tendency of convergence in the Organization of Economic Cooperation and Development (OECD)-area (Dowrick and Nguyen 1989), the hierarchy of countries according to per capita income is still dominated by early industrializers such as the USA and Switzerland. To be sure, the "first" industrializer UK has fallen back to an average level, while the latecomer Japan is nearing the top. In general, however, latecomers in Europe, such as Spain, Portugal and Greece, are still way behind.

So the beginning of industrialization might provide the first important information about the economic potential of Central and Eastern European countries. Industrialization proceeded in Europe and in North America in a regional–sequential pattern that was dependent on institutional prerequisites (Hoffmann 1931; Rostow 1960). It started in Great Britain in the late eighteenth century and was followed quickly by Switzerland and the USA. The second phase of industrialization comprised most of the Western and Central European states between 1820 and 1850 and the third phase included Scandinavia and the Netherlands between 1860 and 1890. The Eastern and Southeastern European countries followed around 1900 (Hoffmann 1931: 70).

The task of dating the onset of industrialization has turned out to be a rather complicated procedure for the Austro–Hungarian Monarchy, which in 1918 numbered 52 million inhabitants and consisted of regions that varied greatly in ethnic background and in economic and educational achievement. In the territory of present-day Austria and in the Bohemian crownlands, conditions for industrialization were similar to those in much of Western and Central Europe. Hungary industrialized in the third phase while Galicia, Bukowina, Dalmatia, and the coastal areas along the Adriatic are to be counted among those regions that industrialized only around 1900. Therefore, the sequential pattern that was typical for Europe as a whole also held for the Monarchy, which like a microcosm reflected European conditions on its own soil (Good 1984: 243). This time-sequence meant, of course, that economic growth in the Monarchy, as an average of its regions, was rather slow up to the end of the nineteenth century and gained momentum only around 1900.

My analysis relies on historical statistics of per capita Gross National

Table 2.1 Per capita income in OECD 1990

	US-$	Switzerland = 100
USA	21,449	102.2
Switzerland	20,997	100.0
Luxembourg	19,340	92.1
Canada	19,120	91.1
Germany	18,291	87.1
Japan	17,634	84.0
France	17,431	83.0
Sweden	16,867	80.3
Denmark	16,765	79.8
Austria	16,620	79.2
Finland	16,453	78.4
Belgium	16,405	78.1
Italy	16,021	76.3
Australia	15,951	76.0
Norway	15,921	75.8
Iceland	15,851	75.5
Netherlands	15,766	75.1
UK	15,720	74.9
New Zealand	13,258	63.1
Spain	11,792	56.2
Ireland	10,659	50.8
Portugal	8,389	40.0
Greece	7,349	35.0
Turkey	3,316	15.8
OECD–Total	7,000	81.0
OECD–Europe	14,070	67.0

OECD: Organization of Economic Cooperation and Development

Source: OECD (1992)

Product (GNP) (see Statistical Appendix). To provide a common denominator, the GNP data are expressed as percentages of the Swiss GNP. I chose Switzerland because it is one of the first countries to industrialize and shows a comparatively undisturbed development until after World War II.

Of course, statistics for this period are not too reliable, but they allow at least an approximate picture of relative income levels on the eve of World War I. These figures correspond to the pattern described above. In 1913, today's Austria had the highest income level within the Monarchy; 70 per cent of the Swiss income level, 90 per cent of the German level and more than 150 per cent of the Italian level. It was followed by Czechoslovakia, which reached only three-quarters of the Austrian level, the average being lowered by the relatively underdeveloped Slovakia. Hungary's level was

Table 2.2 Per capita gross national product 1913–90 (in real terms)
Switzerland = 100

	1913	*1925*	*1929*	*1933*	*1938*	*1948*	*1990*
Austria	70.7	64.2	56.9	45.2	58.8	35.6	79.2
Czechoslovakia	54.4	49.4	46.3	41.0	45.5	44.2	38.5
Germany/FGR	78.6	69.8	60.9	58.5	93.5	36.3	87.1
Hungary	38.6	35.8	33.5	32.4	37.5	22.2	28.9
Italy	45.8	47.1	40.9	40.2	45.8	23.8	76.3
Poland	–	20.0	27.7	27.2	30.9	32.0	21.1
Romania	–	31.0	26.2	24.2	28.5	–	15.1
Yugoslavia	29.5	29.6	27.0	23.9	28.2	–	25.3
Switzerland	100.0	100.0	100.0	100.0	100.0	100.0	100.0

Sources: Bairoch (1976), UN (1949), ERECO (1992). Austrian figures were corrected. All figures use boundaries for the 1919–39 period.

barely half of Austria's, while Yugoslavia's income was roughly 40 per cent of the Austrian level. Data for Poland and Romania are not available for 1913.

WORLD WAR I AND THE DISSOLUTION OF THE HABSBURG MONARCHY

World War I caused the first major exogenous shock for Central and Eastern Europe. It was the first war to utilize huge parts of the demographic and economic capacities of the countries involved. The Monarchy especially was strained to complete exhaustion, as one of the weaker participants in the war. Some believe the war would have ended even without military defeat in the winter of 1918 because of economic reasons alone (Gratz and Schüller 1930: 200; März 1981: 171–93).

The economies of the new successor states suffered severe setbacks. The war had depleted stocks, worn out machinery, weakened workers through hunger, and devalued the currency. In many countries, especially Poland, Yugoslavia, and Romania, there was heavy war damage (Berend and Ránki 1974: 176; Teichova 1988: 15). Political and military turmoil accompanied the birth of the new states. So it is not surprising that in many countries the economy broke down. In 1919 industrial production in Poland fell to roughly one-fifth the level of 1913 and in Romania the level in 1918 stood at one-third the 1913 level (Teichova 1988: 16). The catastrophic economic collapse found its expression in hyperinflations in Austria, Hungary and Poland; only Czechoslovakia was able to regain very early its internal financial equilibrium (Berend and Ránki 1974: 180).

But even when these immediate post-war difficulties, which also affected other European countries, were overcome, the new states faced special economic problems that arose from the dissolution of the Habsburg Monarchy. Up to 1914 the lands of East–Central Europe were to some extent members of a huge sheltered market. After 1919, they were small economies that were forced to compete on international markets. What had been internal flows of goods became foreign trade. But since these countries were concerned mainly with emphasizing their independence in economic as well as political matters, they built up national industry, put up tariff-walls, and issued trade restrictions (Kofman 1990: 191). These measures did not much change the direction of foreign trade because the trade relations among the successor states remained very close (Nautz 1992). They did, however, reduce its volume significantly (Hertz 1947: 79). This caused detrimental effects especially for Austria, which had the highest foreign trade share of all the successor states (Hertz 1947: 57).

So even when the economic situation improved and the boom of the 1920s spread to the countries of Central and Eastern Europe, growth in Austria could not compensate for the losses suffered due to the war and political changes. The same seems to be true for Hungary, whereas the comparatively poor performance of Czechoslovakia might be partly the result of the radical stabilization policy after the war. No comparable figures exist for Poland and Romania, but data on industrial production indicate that Poland resembled Austria and Hungary, while Romania reached at least its pre-war level (Teichova 1988: 176). Compared with 1913, the position of all countries in East–Central Europe, with the exception of Yugoslavia, deteriorated with respect to Switzerland.

When the post-war boom reached its peak in 1929, an ambivalent picture is presented. Austrian GDP had improved marginally by 6 per cent compared with 1913. The gap with respect to Western and Northern European countries increased. But the other countries of Central and Eastern Europe fared better, so their income gap *vis-à-vis* Austria narrowed: to above 80 per cent in Czechoslovakia to almost 60 per cent in Hungary, and to nearly 50 per cent in Poland and Romania. While the performance of Germany and Italy remained comparatively weak, the Swiss economy grew extraordinarily well, so that the relative distance of the states in Central and Eastern Europe to Switzerland increased again. But this was not typical for Europe. It seems, therefore, that in the second half of the 1920s, the successor states, with the exception of Austria, performed relatively well.

The Great Depression hit world wide. Most strongly affected were countries that had suffered heavily during World War I, such as Germany and Austria, but also those, like the USA, that were less involved. Among the successor states, Czechoslovakia and Yugoslavia were seriously affected by the slump.

The setback in Hungary, Poland, and Romania seems to have been less severe in spite of the agrarian crisis, perhaps because real production did not decline as much as agricultural prices fell (Berend and Ránki 1974: 244).

The subsequent recovery was rather weak with the notable exception of Germany. There the combination of expansionist employment policy and rearmament led to a steep upswing that pushed GDP upwards by nearly 60 per cent (Temin 1989). For the countries of Central and Eastern Europe the recovery remained modest, although some of them, especially Hungary and Yugoslavia, seem to have profited from being included in the German *Großraumwirtschaft* (Berend and Ránki 1974: 266). The data for Austria are misleading; until 1937 GDP grew by only 11 per cent, the slowest for all of Europe. But after the German occupation in March 1938, German employment policy and rearmament increased GDP by 15 per cent in that year alone, such that total growth in GDP since 1933 reached 26 per cent and exceeded the European average. But as the Swiss economy stagnated in this period, all countries improved their relative position.

To sum up, the income level of the states in Central and Eastern Europe was determined to a great extent by the time they began to industrialize. With the exception of Austria and Czechoslovakia they ranked distinctly below the European average prior to World War I, but above the states of southern Europe like Spain, Portugal, and Greece. World War I and the dissolution of the Habsburg Monarchy strained these economies to such an extent that their income level decreased more than the rest of Europe after 1919. This setback was partly overcome in the second half of the 1920s. The great depression was no worse in the region than elsewhere and the recovery from it was weak, as it was for most other countries. On balance, it appears that before World War II these countries had not yet regained fully their relative position of 1913.

WORLD WAR II AND THE COLD WAR DIVISION OF EUROPE

World War II strained the economies of the region even more than World War I. It was not only that a great part of GDP was destined for military use, but also that the German occupation meant an additional burden for the resources of the various countries (Ambrosius and Hubbard 1986: 261). Air raids enlarged the damages of fighting and the war lasted considerably longer than the previous one. Nevertheless, the situation in the European countries differed considerably from that after World War I. According to the available figures, no country had an income level seven years after the war that was lower than in 1938. Indeed, in most states it was actually much higher, so it seems that the far more severe consequences of World War II had been overcome remarkably faster than those of World War I.

Of course, data are scarce and not very reliable, but they seem to show that some countries of East–Central Europe fared well in these years. According to the calculations for 1948, Czechoslovakia, for example, was able to increase its per capita income by nearly 11 per cent compared with

1938 (UN 1949: 235; see Statistical Appendix). The reason for this especially good performance was that war damages were limited and Nazi Germany had invested much in the economy, because it did not expect air raids there. The Polish gain of 35 per cent seems highly improbable, considering the extensive war damage and the consequences of the German occupation, although it may be explained by the territorial changes. Other countries did not fare so well; income levels in 1948 were lower than in 1938 in Hungary (−12.5 per cent) and especially in Austria (−24 per cent). At that point, per capita income in Czechoslovakia clearly exceeded that of Austria.

On balance, it seems that the income-position of Central and Eastern Europe relative to the rest of Europe in 1948 remained more or less unchanged. The decisive shock for this region was the partition of Europe. A sign of the deteriorating political and economic relations between East and West was the pressure of the Soviet Union upon the Czechoslovak government not to participate in preparing the Marshall Plan and Czechoslovakia became one of the last to adapt to the Communist pattern.

Over time, the two blocs intensified their internal relations through economic integration. This tendency is apparent in the development of foreign trade, especially between Austria and the other successor states. Although the dissolution of the Habsburg Monarchy had far-reaching consequences for the Austrian economy, e.g., the sheltered markets were lost and tariff-walls were erected by the other successor states, the trade links among these countries remained far stronger than would have been expected for purely economic reasons as suggested by gravitation models (Linnemann 1966: 34). In 1924 46.3 per cent of Austrian exports went to this group of countries, compared with only 13.1 per cent to Germany, Austria's largest neighbor. Import figures were similarly impressive (48.7 per cent compared with 14.9 per cent). And although the economic forces tended to equilibrate those politically determined trade flows, in 1937 the successor states still accounted for 31.5 per cent of Austria's exports and 38.5 per cent of its imports while Germany still accounted only for 14.8 per cent of Austria's exports and 16.1 per cent of its imports (Karner *et al.* 1987).

The occupation of Austria by the German Reich in 1938 caused a considerable redirection of trade flows. There are no statistics for this period either, but according to my estimates, trade with Germany tripled in 1938, while exports to other countries decreased by 24 per cent (Butschek 1978: 47). Undoubtedly, the linkage between the Austrian economy and the German economy intensified during the following war years.

After the end of World War II, trade flows reverted somewhat to the pre-1938 pattern; in 1948 the successor states received 18.5 per cent of Austrian exports and delivered 29.7 per cent of Austria's imports. Subsequently, however, the foreign trade shares of these countries diminished continuously. For historical reasons and because parts of the Austrian industry under Soviet occupation regime (USIA) had been integrated into the East

Table 2.3 Regional structure of Austrian foreign trade

	1924	*1937*	*1948*	*1985*
Exports		*Shares of total exports*		
Germany	13.1	14.8	5.8	30.1
Italy	10.1	14.0	17.0	9.0
Switzerland	6.6	5.1	13.3	6.7
Czechoslovakia	11.0	7.1	7.5	1.1
Poland	9.7	4.3	1.5	1.2
Romania	6.5	5.6	0.9	0.3
Yugoslavia	10.3	5.4	4.9	2.3
Hungary	8.8	9.1	3.7	2.6
World	100.0	100.0	100.0	100.0
Imports		*Shares of total imports*		
Germany	14.9	16.1	17.9	40.9
Italy	7.2	5.5	11.0	8.2
Switzerland	5.6	3.2	8.5	4.5
Czechoslovakia	22.6	11.0	10.8	1.9
Poland	7.5	4.6	8.6	1.1
Romania	2.5	6.0	0.9	0.4
Yugoslavia	4.4	7.9	4.8	1.1
Hungary	11.7	9.0	4.6	2.0
World	100.0	100.0	100.0	100.0

Source: Bundesamt für Statistik, Österreichisches Statistisches Zentralamt

bloc markets, Austria's trade with the region reached the highest level of all OECD-countries, but the relative importance of these flows permanently decreased. In 1985 the post-1919 successor states received only 5.2 per cent of Austrian exports and shipped 5.4 per cent of total imports.

The example of Austria shows clearly the increasing economic separation of the two trading blocks. In the 1950s political intentions might have been behind this development. However, with "coexistence" at the beginning of the 1970s, it was clearly the different economic mechanisms in the two systems that reduced the importance of economic ties. Foreign trade in a planned economy does not contribute fundamentally to the optimal allocation of resources; its only role is to fill gaps in the planned home production (Levcik and Stankovsky 1988: 155).

SETBACK AND TRANSITION

These different economic mechanisms also changed decisively the position of the successor states in Europe's income hierarchy. Austria was the only one to become part of the community of Western industrialized nations and it joined the OECD. The Western countries realized the great Anglo–Saxon post-war design of Bretton Woods, which was based politically on parliamentary democracy and economically on the free flow of goods, services, and payments. The Western system was intensified at the end of the 1950s with several steps toward closer economic integration. It achieved enormous success, not only by increasing the real income of the population, but by building up the safety net of social security and education that became its characteristic features. And even when difficulties arose in the 1970s as a consequence of external shocks, the oil crisis, and of internal flaws, e.g., overstrained budgets, the system stabilized. In the 1980s a new upswing set in.

The system in the East bloc was based politically on totalitarianism and economically on central planning and public ownership of the means of production. Although the system was early criticized by Austrian economists like Ludwig von Mises and Friedrich Hayek, its economic flaws did not become immediately obvious. On the one hand economic growth in the West was in its first phases in the 1950s and not yet evident. On the other hand, the inefficiencies of the socialist economic systems became more visible over time; only from the 1960s onward did its flaws become evident.

Although there was also economic growth in the East, supply was never able to adapt to demand, which resulted in both stocks of unwanted goods and queues of consumers. Production technology become more and more obsolete and hardly able to participate in new technical developments, like electronics.

While supporters of socialism frequently claimed that planned economies were immune to cyclical influences, they, too, were affected by the oil crisis. Yet, as the Western countries succeeded in stabilizing budgets and current accounts in the 1980s, the debt burden grew in many countries in the East bloc, which led them to the brink of a payments crisis. This must be borne in mind in explaining the sudden breakdown of Communism in the East.

As all of the successor states but Austria were part of the East bloc, they experienced the same type of inefficiencies. But the statistical evidence is not easy to interpret as national income accounting in the East differed from that in the West. In the past, most estimates were grossly misleading, which might explain in part why no one anticipated the breakdown of the Communist system. Estimates using the Western system of national accounts have been made by the United Nations only for Hungary and Poland. For Czechoslovakia, Romania, and Yugoslavia, I rely on other estimates that provide at least correct orders of magnitude (see Statistical Appendix).

According to these figures, after more than 40 years of separation, the immediate post-war standing of the two blocs has changed completely. In 1990 per capita GDP in Austria was five times the level of 1950 in real terms.

It reached 79.2 per cent the level of Switzerland, the richest European country, and remained about 10 per cent below the former Federal Republic of Germany. Italy shows a similar performance, which is an expression of the convergence-tendency in post-1945 Western Europe. In contrast, the Eastern countries lagged drastically behind. Czechoslovakia, which had a considerably higher income per capita than Austria in 1948, lost ground and in 1990 its level was only half of Austria's. Of course, the situation in 1948 might have been unfavorable for Austria because its reconstruction was in full force and would have probably altered the relative position *vis-à-vis* Czechoslovakia within a few years and the GDP of the successor states is now shrinking as a consequence of the transition since 1989. But what matters is the dramatic change in the magnitudes in the post-World War II era, and the fact that the other successor states fell further behind: in 1990 income per capita in Hungary stood at 36.4 per cent of the Austrian level and in Poland at 25 per cent. So it seems beyond doubt that the most severe relative setback for the economies of East–Central Europe came in the Communist period.

But the story is not yet finished. The enormous problems of transition remain to be solved. I cannot adequately discuss here the ways and means to change the economic system in these countries. The "shock program" of American economists and the International Monetary Fund stands in the foreground. Approaches that rely on converting to the market system by a series of small steps, as was done in Austria after 1945 (Butschek 1990), have not been widely discussed. Agreements between the government and the major social groups in the Austrian model have appeared only in Czechoslovakia (Begg 1991: 270). In the impasse over policy, Gross Domestic Product continues to decrease in both relative and absolute terms.

It is difficult at the present time to predict the duration of this transition period. It may be that the more advanced reforming countries like Czechoslovakia, Hungary, and Poland will soon reach a turning point in

Table 2.4 Gross domestic product development in East–Central Europe 1990, 1991 (as % of previous year)

	1990	*1991*	*1992*
		Estimate	
Czechoslovakia	0	−16	−7
Hungary	−3	−10	−2
Poland	−12	−9	−1
Romania	−7	−13	−10

Source: Gabrisch (1993: 13)

their development (Gabrisch 1993). But whatever the future path, it is clear that the countries of Central Europe formed a group, whose per capita income after World War II was lower than most other European states, the states of southern Europe being an exception for similar historical reasons. According to the experience of Western Europe, one might have expected that the economies of East–Central Europe should have grown at least at the average rate of OECD Europe. Perhaps in the course of capitalist convergence, their growth rate would have been a little above average, so there is a double loss caused by their socialist economic systems. But still, all things being equal, the East bloc, except for Czechoslovakia, would have been expected to remain in the lower range of the European income hierarchy.

Austria, as a point of reference, was the sole successor state that remained within Western Europe yet it still needed nearly half a century to catch up to the Western European average. Its GDP per capita in purchasing power parity terms was only one-third the Swiss level in 1950, but reached a level equal to 50 per cent in 1960, 75 per cent in 1980, and 80 per cent in 1990. The idea that the East–Central European countries might approach the level of OECD-Europe (excluding the southern states) within the next decade is pure illusion. If it is possible within a couple of years to provide the economies of these countries with workable market systems, some "economic miracle" might occur. History shows, however, that reaching the Western European income level will certainly take time.

STATISTICAL APPENDIX

Bairoch (1976) is one of the rare studies that contains comparable data for Western and Eastern industrialized countries. Other studies do not include the Eastern European countries (Maddison 1984; Flora 1987). Still others include some, but not all, Eastern European countries or use data that are not directly comparable (Mitchell 1975; Lethbridge 1985).

Bairoch's data were calculated in 1960 US dollars and therefore offer income estimates in real terms on the basis of exchange rates. I use them here only for the period 1913–38. For Austrian GNP in 1938, I rely on my estimates in Butschek (1978: 127). According to data published by Lethbridge, Bairoch underestimates the growth of Hungary and especially of Czechoslovakia, which should have exceeded Austrian per capita income by the late 1920s, and overestimates the growth of Yugoslavia. This suggests that Bairoch's figures must be used with caution, but they do provide orders of magnitude.

I did not use Bairoch's figures for the post-1945 period for two reasons. First, they begin only in 1950 and therefore do not provide comparable data for the countries of Central and Eastern Europe for the years just prior to the final establishment of the Communist system. Second, the estimates of GNP for East–Central Europe in the 1960s and 1970s seem to be inaccurate.

According to these calculations, in 1973 the GDP of both the German Democratic Republic and Czechoslovakia exceeded that of Austria by nearly 13 per cent! Certainly comparing Gross National Product according to the System of National Accounts (SNA) calculation and the Net Material Product estimates of the former centrally planned economies is extremely difficult (see as an overview Havlik 1991). Bairoch's estimates used Economic Commission for Europe (ECE) calculations on the basis of the indirect indicators method (Bairoch 1976: 339). But his figures are not only in sharp contrast to any visible evidence towards the end of the 1960s, when traffic between these countries intensified; they also imply a falling back of the per capita income of the German Democratic Republic and Czechoslovakia to one-half of the Austrian level within one decade. Although a general bias toward overvaluing per capita income in Eastern Europe certainly existed, other sources seem to have obtained more realistic

Table 2.5 Volume of per capita gross national product at market prices: Constant 1970 geographical boundaries (in 1960 US dollars and prices)

	1913	*1929*	*1950*	*1960*	*1970*	*1973*
Austria	681	720	721	1,232	1,855	2,168
Belgium	894	1,099	1,167	1,484	2,295	2,654
Bulgaria	(263)	(306)	(423)	(750)	(1,461)	(1,755)
Czechoslovakia	(524)	(586)	(785)	(1,488)	(2,163)	(2,438)
Denmark	862	945	1,277	1,650	2,475	2,716
Finland	(520)	590	1,027	1,503	2,428	2,797
France	695	983	1,137	1,669	2,645	3,029
Germany (West)	731	795	931	1,781	2,627	2,873
Germany (East)	–	–	(571)	(1,368)	(2,116)	(2,445)
Greece	(322)	(390)	445	718	1,440	1,769
Hungary	372	424	(560)	(958)	(1,576)	(1,851)
Ireland	(611)	662	744	919	1,334	1,474
Italy	441	517	590	978	1,557	1,694
Netherlands	754	1,008	1,019	1,418	2,127	2,334
Norway	749	1,032	1,652	2,078	3,125	3,495
Poland	–	–	(556)	(891)	(1,454)	(1,842)
Portugal	(292)	(320)	383	514	954	1,247
Romania	–	–	(319)	(579)	(1,047)	(1,360)
Spain	367	455	367	529	986	1,179
Sweden	680	897	1,712	2,263	3,226	3,411
Switzerland	963	1,265	1,368	1,841	2,468	2,661
UK	996	1,038	1,352	1,686	2,079	2,284
USSR	326	(293)	(585)	(939)	(1,651)	(1,887)
Yugoslavia	(284)	(341)	(339)	599	1,019	(1,182)
Europe	534	571	749	1,157	1,828	2,077

Source: Bairoch (1976: 307)

Table 2.6 Per capita gross domestic product in US dollars at official exchange rates and in international (Int) dollars, 1975

	Per capita GDP			
	In US dollars converted at exchange rate		In international dollars	
	US-$	US=100	Int-$	US=100
Austria	5,010	69.8	4,995	69.6
Belgium	6,298	87.8	5,574	77.7
Denmark	7,498	104.5	5,911	82.4
France	6,428	89.6	5,877	81.9
Germany	6,797	94.7	5,953	83.0
Hungary	2,125	29.6	3,559	49.6
Ireland	2,673	37.2	3,049	42.5
Italy	3,440	47.9	3,861	53.8
Luxembourg	6,472	90.2	5,883	82.0
Netherlands	6,061	84.5	5,397	75.2
Poland	2,586	36.0	3,598	50.1
Romania	1,742	24.3	2,387	33.3
Spain	2,946	41.0	4,010	55.9
UK	4,134	57.6	4,588	63.9
Yugoslavia	1,664	23.2	2,591	36.1

GDP: Gross domestic product

Source: Kravis (1982: 12)

results (Kravis 1982). According to these, Hungary reached 71.3 per cent of the Austrian level in 1975 in contrast to the 85.3 per cent of the level in Bairoch's calculations. If one applies Bairoch's income relatives, this implies that Czechoslovakia was 93.9 per cent of the Austrian level instead of 124.5 per cent. The former estimates still seem too high, but they come nearer to the actual situation than do Bairoch's figures.

Considering that up to now no reliable national income figures exist for the former centrally planned economies, I avoided any comparison for the last 40 years. Only the most recent estimates provide plausible data for the present study.

For 1948, I used the calculations in the *Economic Survey of Europe* in 1948 (UN, 1949). They provide National Income figures for 1938, 1947, and 1948 in US dollars at 1938 prices. These figures are also in real terms, but at purchasing power parities, which of course reduced the comparability with the older figures. Here again, this does not preclude arriving at rough orders of magnitude because the 1929 exchange rates were used as the basis for purchasing power parities (p.229). The data for Austria were corrected according to the most recent income calculations, which show a more

Table 2.7 National income per capita 1938, 1947, 1948

Country	*Income per capita (dollars in 1938 prices)*		
	1938	*1947*	*1948*
Northwestern Europe			
Denmark	316	276	307
Ireland	252	247	287
Norway	255	248	253
Sweden	367	413	413
UK	378	363	401
Total Northwestern Europe:	362	352	384
Western Europe			
Belgium–Luxembourg	275	255	278
France	236	207	228
Netherlands	323	219	250
Switzerland	367	451	441
Total Western Europe:	262	233	254
Central and Northeastern Europe			
Austria	179	114	157
Czechoslovakia	176	165	195
Finland	178	151	173
Hungary	112	82	98
Poland	104	114	141
Total Central and Northeastern Europe:	132	120	147
South and Southeastern Europe			
Bulgaria	68	51	66
Greece	80	58	62
Italy	127	100	105
Other European countries	72	72	73
Total South and Southeastern Europe:	89	77	82

Source: UN (1949: 235). The pre-war data refer to 1937 in the case of Austria, Czechoslovakia, and the USA, but are expressed in 1938 prices.

favorable development in 1948 compared with 1937 (1937 rather than 1938 data were used for Austria and Czechoslovakia in the UN-calculations). The correct figure was 157 dollars instead of 130 dollars.

The data for 1990 are based on OECD-figures for Western European countries. For the Eastern European countries, both UN-data and Central Intelligence Agency estimates were used. They are compared using purchasing power parities, because at the present time comparisons on the basis of exchange rates would be highly misleading.

REFERENCES

Ambrosius, G. and Hubbard, W.H. (1986) *Sozial- und Wirtschaftsgeschichte Europas im 20.Jahrhundert*, Munich.

Bairoch, P. (1976) "Europe's gross national product 1800–1975," *The Journal of European Economic History*, 5: 273–340.

Begg, D. (1991) "Economic reform in Czechoslovakia: Should we believe in Santa Klaus?," *Economic Policy*, October: 243–86.

Berend, I.T. and Ránki, G. (1974) *Economic Development in East–Central Europe in the 19th and 20th Centuries*, New York, London.

Butschek F. (1978) *Die österreichische Wirtschaft 1938 bis 1945*, Vienna, Stuttgart.

Butschek, F. (1990) "'Austrifizierung' der Oststaaten auch in der Wirtschaftspolitik?," *Europäische Rundschau*, 1: 11–24.

Dowrick St. and Nguyen D.-T. (1989) "OECD comparative economic growth 1950-1985: Catch up and convergence", *American Economic Review*, 5.

ERECO. (1992) *Europe in 1996*, Paris.

Flora, P. (1987) *State Economy and Society in Western Europe 1815–1975*, Frankfurt, London, Chicago.

Gabrisch, H. (1993) "Under the impact of Western recession", *WIIW-Forschungs berichte*, No. 184: 197b, Vienna.

Good, D.F. (1984) *The Economic Rise of the Habsburg Empire 1750-1914*, Berkeley.

Gratz, G. and Schüller, R. (1930) *Der wirtschaftliche Zusammenbruch Österreich-Ungarns. Die Tragödie der Erschöpfung*, Vienna, New Haven.

Havlik, P. (1991) "East–West GDP Comparisons: Problems, Methods and Results." *WIIW Forschungsberichte*, no.174, Vienna.

Hertz, F. (1947) *The Economic Problems of the Danubian States*, London.

Hoffmann W.G. (1931) *Stadien und Typen der Industrialisierung*, Jena.

Karner, St., Kubin, J. and Steiner, M. (1987) "Wie real war "Mitteleuropa'?," *Vierteljahreshefte für Sozial – und Wirtschaftsgeschichte*, 2.

Kofman J. (1990) "Economic nationalism in East–Central Europe in the interwar period," in H. Szlajfer (ed.), *Economic Nationalism in East–Central Europe and South America 1918–1939*, Geneva.

Kravis, I.B. (1982) *World Product and Income*. Baltimore, London.

Lethbridge, E. (1985) "National income and product," in M.C. Kaser and E.A. Radice (eds.) *The Economic History of Eastern Europe 1919–1975*, Oxford.

Levcik F. and Stankovsky J. (1988) "Eastern Europe's trade problems: between the USSR and the West," in J.P. Hardt and C.H. McMillan (eds.) *Planned Economics: Confronting the Challenges of the 1980s*, Cambridge.

Linnemann, H. (1966) *An Econometric Study of International Trade Flows*, Amsterdam.

Maddison, A. (1984) *Phases of Capitalist Development*, Oxford, New York.

März, E. (1981) *Österreichische Bankpolitik in der Zeit der grossen Wende 1913–1923*, Vienna.
Mitchell, B.R. (1975) *European Historical Statistics*, London, Basingstoke.
Nautz, J. (1992) "Die Entwicklung der Handelsbeziehungen Österreichs zu den anderen Nachfolgestaaten nach dem Ersten Weltkrieg", *Wirtschaft und Gesellschaft*, 4: 539–59.
OECD. (1992) *National Accounts*, vol. 1: *1960–1990*, Paris.
Rostow, W.W. (1960) *The Stages of Economic Growth*, Cambridge.
Teichova, A. (1988) *Kleinstaaten im Spannungsfeld der Großmächte*, Vienna.
Temin, P. (1989) *Lessons from the Great Depression*, Cambridge, London.
UN. (1949) *Economic Survey of Europe in 1948*, Geneva.

3

INSTITUTIONS AND MARKETS IN HISTORY

Lessons for Central and Eastern Europe

Lee J. Alston

INTRODUCTION

Former Communist countries have embarked on a mission to transform their planned economies into market economies. The task is immense for contrary to what some economists may believe, markets do not just happen.[1] In order for anything but primitive non-simultaneous exchange to take place, in particular for international exchange and exchange in intermediate product markets, the traders must have some assurance that each side of the transaction will uphold its side of the contract. The assurance is given by the formal and informal institutions in an economy. Institutions are constraints on behavior that influence the costs of exchange and production.

Among economists, economic historians look at the long-run and thereby are accustomed to looking at the role of institutions in economic growth.[2] For the most part, the history of the world has been a history of economic stagnation. Only for the past one hundred and fifty years have we had modern economic growth and then only for a small percentage of the world's population. I suggest that the reason for a lack of economic growth has not been a problem of technology but rather a failure of most governments to establish the appropriate institutions that support markets, which in turn produce economic growth. The intent of my chapter is not to specify which institutions the former Communist countries should adopt, but rather to see what lessons we might learn from the work of economic historians who have studied the role of institutions in economic growth. The first lesson relates to the functioning of institutions. Did they increase or decrease the gains from trade? Also, what determines why people adopted or failed to adopt an institution? At times the historical record shows that societies and individuals sometimes opted for the long-run cooperative solution, and at other times they opted for short-run gains associated with redistributive behavior.

The second lesson from history is that institutions do not change rapidly, so when countries like those in Central Europe today are at historical junctures they must choose their institutions with care. Institutions, once adopted and operating credibly, are not easily reversed. People build up special interests around the new rules and develop informal institutions to solidify their gains.[3] Thus, if a society develops institutions that reward negative-sum redistributive activity as opposed to cooperative growth-enhancing activity, it finds it difficult to reverse the path.

Choosing with care does not imply that countries should delay moving towards markets. Indeed, the longer the delay in assigning secure property rights, the greater the uncertainty to potential investors and hence the slower the pace of economic activity.[4] Furthermore, delays may allow the potential losers from the transformation to have the time and political ammunition (resulting from the low level of economic activity) to resist the transformation altogether.

Across Central and Eastern Europe and the former Soviet Union there is considerable variation in the speed at which countries are privatizing state-owned assets. For example, Poland and more recently the Czech Republic have moved aggressively towards privatization while Hungary and Russia are further behind. What seems to plague countries is not the issue of whether to privatize but the issue of who will gain from privatization. There are a myriad of ways to privatize assets that may well end up with similar results in the long-run. As a consequence, the delays associated with a concern over distribution may strike some as excessive yet it is important for the ultimate success of institutional change that the changes are perceived as equitable. If not, the changes may not be stable. For example, the issue of restitution is important particularly in Central Europe, because many of the citizens who owned assets before the Communist take-overs are still alive.

The historical examples to be discussed also shed some light on a third issue: whether the institutions that support markets need to be created exogenously by the government or allowed to develop endogenously by the market participants themselves. The evidence that I present on private institutions developed endogenously by market participants suggests that the initial role of the government is *crucial*, but that it should be limited to allow for competition among private institutions.

THE BENEFITS AND THE COSTS OF TRADE

Voluntary trade produces wealth among both nations and individuals.[5] The wealth creation comes because the participants have different endowments, costs of production, or tastes. For trade to produce gains for all market participants, the parties to the transaction must live up to their contractual obligations. Parties must be constrained to choose cooperative growth-enhancing activity rather than activity designed to produce short-run gains.

Local trade is more likely to result in contractual compliance than long-distance trade. Local exchanges are personal. Trust and the likelihood of repeat dealings either in commercial or social affairs, increase the likelihood of contractual compliance. Most traders know one another and may have kinship ties. However, the benefits from trading locally are limited: 1) endowments do not differ much; and 2) economies of scale in production may not be realized because the extent of the market is small, i.e., demand may be too low.

Long-distance trade allows traders to reap the benefits from different endowments and potential scale economies in production. But long-distance trade entails higher transaction costs of exchange. The volume and extent of trade will depend on the transaction costs of trade and the benefits of trade. Institutions can augment economic growth by reducing the per unit costs of exchange leading to more trading over time and space.

The costs of exchange involve issues of measurement, opportunism, contractual enforcement, and ideology. I will illustrate with a description of land markets in the Brazilian Amazon.[6] Because of past titling practices and overlapping state and federal jurisdiction over the disposal of public land, there exists considerable uncertainty over land security. To secure title to land in the early part of the twentieth century, a survey was not necessary; people simply described the land to which they laid claim according to various physical characteristics. The individual landowners had the responsibility of demarcating their plot and registering it. The imprecision in measuring the boundaries led to overlapping claims. In a counterfactual world where all claims were surveyed, demarcated and registered by a government agency, the degree of conflict would be minimal and people could transfer and use land according to its highest valued use. The imprecision in measuring land claims was not a serious problem until the land rose in value with government road building in the 1970s and an influx of colonists.

Adding to the uncertainty over titles in the 1970s was a conflict in jurisdiction over the disposal of public lands. With the exception of land deemed essential for national security (usually land bordering other countries), state governments had the sole authority to dispose of public lands within their boundaries until 1971. In that year the federal government claimed 100 kilometers on either side of all federal roads constructed, under construction, or projected in Legal Amazonia. With this move the federal government ostensibly had authority over 80 per cent of the remaining public land in Pará. Naturally, the state of Pará challenged this decree and aggressively began titling land, often without proper surveys.

As if the dual authority over land did not lead to enough confusion, individuals can claim land through squatters' rights. One can even squat on private land and, if not evicted in ten years, acquire title.

The uncertainty in land titles may result in a dissipation of potential rents from the land.[7] Because users of land are not always certain that they will be on the land in the future, the incentive to make land-specific investments by using fertilizers, fences, and drainage is diminished.[8]

The climate of uncertainty also allows for more opportunistic behavior.[9] With titles unclear the costs of forgery fall, resulting in fake titles that are difficult to discriminate from real titles, particularly in a society where judges are known to accept bribes.

In addition to high information costs, frontier societies are typified by an absence or at least lack of third-party government enforcement of contracts. The result is "might makes right:" over 1,000 Brazilians have died in land conflicts since 1980 (Schneider 1992; Human Rights Watch 1991).[10]

Compounding the chaotic conditions of exchange on frontiers is the lack of a commonly accepted set of beliefs or ideology, an informal constraint on behavior. The settlers on the Brazilian frontier are from different regions of Brazil with different attitudes and endowments. Consequently, there is no common practice on how to do business nor is there trust among the traders. Beliefs matter because they can reduce or increase the resources devoted to measuring the attributes of goods, constraining opportunism, or enforcing contracts.[11]

When behavior is not readily constrained as in the market for land in Brazil, the transaction costs of exchange are high with the result that wealth is lower than would be the case if constraints existed. I will present historical examples of institutions that arose to reduce the costs of exchange, but first discuss briefly the ways in which formal and informal institutions promote cooperative behavior.

FORMAL AND INFORMAL CONSTRAINTS

Institutions are the formal and informal constraints that allow us to capture the gains from complex exchange. For the most part formal constraints are the laws enforced by governments. Informal institutions are perhaps more important.[12] Informal institutions consist of the culture, customs, religions, ideologies, and voluntary arrangements that discourage individuals from cheating and other forms of opportunistic behavior. In a game theoretic framework, people should opt for the cooperative solution. For example, if all labor held the view of "an honest day's work for an honest day's pay," then employers could dispense with costly monitoring and workers and employers could be better off. Clearly, if all people firmly believed in honest dealings, the costs of exchange would be less. Ideologies matter in part because it is not always evident what type of allocative procedures best promote economic growth. Precise cause and effect relationships are not available and the competing models can not be definitively tested. Moreover, what "works" in one country, county, or city may not "work" in another because people have different models of reality. Even if people have the same view of how the world works, they may have different preferences over redistribution. This is why different ideologies can exist and compete with one another. For example, in the post-World War II era many of the Western economies posted similar rates of economic growth with varying degrees of redistribution and government intervention.

The cause of ideological change can be either incremental or continuous, but the recognition of an ideological change is usually abrupt. That is, ideologies almost by definition are shorthand views of how the world works that can be used to interpret a set of facts. If the model is always changing, such interpretations are impossible. For this reason people often report having had a *gestalt* experience even though in actuality they may have been continuously accumulating evidence that conflicts with their stated ideology. This, of course, does not refute the possibility of discrete ideological change. An event may be so compelling as to prompt an immediate rejection of one's world view.[13]

Ideologies or other informal mechanisms must be enforced if they are to affect behavior. Informal constraints may be self-enforcing when there is no third-party enforcer, e.g., in the practice of walking on the right side of the hallway. Ideologies, too, can be self-enforcing; for example, I may refrain from stealing because I simply view it as wrong. Or a prevailing ideology can be imposed on a minority. Other informal constraints such as norms of behavior observed in families or business are generally enforced through second parties. Retaliation or some sort of societal sanction such as ostracism can enforce compliance. Third-party, non-governmental enforcement of informal constraints is also a possibility and is more likely when exchange is complex or in situations where the participants do not share a common set of beliefs.

Institutions add stability to our lives and ease the cost of contracting. This is not to say that all institutions aid contracting or promote economic growth. Ideally, institutions both constrain behavior but also adapt to changes in relative prices. If institutions do not change in response to relative prices, growth may be choked off. This result is not inevitable, but it is all too common. Economic growth is a process of what Schumpeter termed "creative destruction" by which he meant that it generates winners and losers. Depending on political power, the potential losers from institutional change may be able to block institutional responses to relative prices. For example, it is feared by many in the West that entrenched bureaucrats may be able to slow down and even prevent some countries in Central and Eastern Europe from moving fully to a market system.

HISTORICAL EXAMPLES OF INFORMAL INSTITUTIONS

Codes of behavior among nomadic tribes in Africa

Robert Bates (1983, 1989) describes tribes in Africa, where despite the high potential for cattle stealing, tribe members tended to live in relative harmony, without formal mechanisms for upholding order such as police or courts.[14] Bates argues that tribes adopted codes of behavior against intra-tribe raiding to avoid the threat of feud. Family members monitored each other because they would bear part of the costs should raiding occur.

The codes of behavior worked in part because the trading groups were relatively homogeneous. If one of them raided, there was a credible threat of retaliation. Under such conditions the long-run gains from cooperation exceed the short-run benefits from raiding.

Cultural constraints or norms of behavior are more likely to be successful in situations where the trading group is small and geographically restricted. Where trade exists across culturally different groups of people or vast territories other institutions are needed to constrain opportunistic behavior.[15]

The Maghribi traders coalition

Avner Greif (1989) has examined the relationships among a group of traders in the Middle East in the twelfth century.[16] Trade was carried out over a vast territory and in order to reap the benefits from trade a merchant had to entrust his goods to an agent. Furthermore, it was difficult to monitor whether the agent was acting in the interest of the merchant because of asymmetrical information. Asymmetries arose because of the uncertainties associated with trade at that time. When goods were shipped, the prices they would fetch upon arrival or the costs of shipping were never known. To limit opportunism, merchants formed a coalition under which they would act both as principals (merchants) and agents (traders). If a trader were reported cheating, others were absolved of their debts to the cheater. For this reason, parties had an incentive to trade in the presence of other traders who could attest to the principal on the honesty of their dealings. Here the institution was successful in achieving the cooperative solution by making the parties post a bond of sorts: the debts that others owed them.

Gold mining camp rules in the "Wild" West

Gold was discovered in the USA in 1848 in what is now California and sparked a rush of people to an otherwise deserted area.[17] No laws governed mineral extraction and even if there were, there was no one to enforce them. One might have expected either chaos to have ensued or that the gains would have been monopolized by some powerful Mafia-type organization. Neither happened. Instead, miners established rules that gave individuals exclusive rights to an area of land called a claim. Collectively, miners banded together to prevent outsiders from claim-jumping, i.e., stealing a miner's exclusive right to a piece of land. The property rights established encouraged the efficient use of resources. For example, as population grew, the size of claims that miners could establish fell. In addition, because protection was a public good, there were laws on how many days a year a claim had to be worked. Most importantly, general acceptance of the laws meant that miners spent their time working rather than dissipating the rents from gold-mining by having to protect their claims.

Here, even though most of the miners had relatively short-term horizons, the reasons the rules worked were that: 1) the gains from cooperating were large; and 2) the miners were relatively equal in their potential for violence. Most miners carried guns as a visible indication of their willingness to defend their rights. It might be argued that culture determined the rules because most of the miners were from the USA where private property was the norm; the miners simply transferred what "worked" in their towns to the mines. Although there may be some merit to the argument, miners from very different cultures, e.g., China and South America, established rules similar to those of the American miners.

US Land policy and cattlemen's associations

The disposal of land in the USA was established early in the country's history with a series of ordinances in 1784, 1785, and 1787.[18] Essentially, it was decided to sell land and to enforce transferable property rights. The government set prices and people then bought according to their demands. The government did not auction off land to the highest bidder. This system worked reasonably well for settling agricultural land until the late nineteenth century. One exception to this generalization was the Homestead Act, which stipulated the amount of land that a settler could claim by residing on and improving the land. The problem with the law was that in many areas of the country the size that could be claimed was economically insufficient. However, the damage by this form of transfer was limited because eventually settlers could sell land so that landholdings were ultimately restructured to appropriate sizes. Nevertheless, there may have been some irreversabilities associated with environmental degradation.

Around 1870 migration had reached land whose prices as set by the US government were too high relative to the land's potential use value. As a consequence, most of the land in the American West went unsold. This did not mean that the land had no use; it was particularly well suited to cattle ranching. No one owned the land because everyone had a right to use it. This is the typical problem of common ownership: 1) individuals are reluctant to invest capital in the land because they are not guaranteed they will reap the return; 2) the land tends to be overused because each rancher only considers the marginal benefit from additions to herd size and not the marginal cost, which is spread across all ranchers; and 3) individuals expend resources defending their assets. The federal government allowed the commons problem to persist because both the Departments of Agriculture and Interior desired bureaucratic control over the range and timber resources. Furthermore, politicians believed that most citizens would perceive transfers of large tracts of land as subsidizing the rich, even though it was not very valuable. Here was a case where ideology appears to have mattered.

To limit the losses from common ownership, cattlemen banded together to limit stocking and reduce entry. Grazing rights were tied to prior legal claims to water. The group limited entry by denying rights to new entrants and by observing cheaters in the annual roundup of cattle. Being excluded from the vast economies of scale inherent in the roundup made it unprofitable to remain in the cattle business.

Like the gold-mining case, a cooperative solution was reached among cattlemen in part because they were a relatively homogeneous group. But here, one might have anticipated more cheating because the gains from cooperation lay far further in the future in the form of capital appreciation in range rights. What apparently prompted the cattlemen to adopt the long-run horizon on the range, i.e., to avoid overstocking, was that being precluded from the roundup had a large cost relative to the gain from overstocking.

HISTORICAL EXAMPLES OF FORMAL CONSTRAINTS

Formal constraints are the rules or laws of society that are backed by the coercive power of the government. Because there is a third party enforcer, the rules established are not necessarily in the interests of all parties to the contract. Nor are the rules that are established necessarily conducive to economic growth. Below I will outline some historical cases of formal constraints and trace out their impact on the economy. It is not simply the formal constraints such as laws and constitutions that create the incentives for economic growth but also and perhaps more importantly the informal beliefs or constraints that gave rise to the formal constraints. Beliefs or ideologies matter because they affect people's willingness to play by the rules, which affects the enforcement costs necessary to induce compliance.

The Glorious Revolution and the rise of Parliament[19]

North and Weingast (1989) argue that the long-run economic growth of England was set in motion by the Glorious Revolution, which led to the financial supremacy of Parliament. In the early part of the seventeenth century the crown often acted arbitrarily to raise revenue. The Stuarts at times forced constituents to give them loans, confiscated their wealth, and in general rendered property rights less secure. This led to an ongoing struggle with the courts and parliament, and finally to a civil war. The end result was a weakening of the monarchy. Parliament gained control over financial matters and the judiciary became more independent. In short, the property rights of citizens became more secure. The security from arbitrary confiscation had a profound impact on the government's ability to raise capital. Government borrowing from its citizens increased dramatically yet the rates of interest did not increase, which suggests that lenders believed the government would honor its commitments.

The Bank of England was established in 1694 to intermediate the growing public debt, but it soon began to undertake private operations. The development of capital markets surely was instrumental in England's rapid economic development and political hegemony. For over the next century the ability of England to raise capital contributed to its military supremacy over France. Bordo and White (1990) argue that during the Napoleonic era England was able to borrow to finance the war because the Parliament assured creditors that England would repay, while France had to rely on taxes because it lacked credibility in the capital markets.

Here is a case where reputation based on past performance encouraged Britain to continue taking a long run perspective and not confiscate wealth. To maintain its reputation as a worthy creditor, the government occasionally had to take steps to assure creditors of its commitment to pay off its debt. For example, in the course of the Napoleonic Wars England raised taxes which signaled to lenders their willingness and ability to repay in full once the war was over.

Not only is the design of governmental institutions important but so too is the government's need to make credible its promise not to confiscate wealth. For example, in the past several years the Mexican government has privatized several industries. Over time, private parties have paid higher prices for public assets because the Mexican government has demonstrated its commitment to privatization by neither renationalizing the industries nor over-regulating them such that the assets are less valuable to the private sector.

Restriction on the rights of creditors

In 1934 in the midst of the Great Depression in the USA, the Supreme Court upheld a moratorium ruling in Minnesota that prevented private creditors from foreclosing on farms held by delinquent debtors.[20] As a result of the decision, twenty-four other states patterned laws after the one in Minnesota. What impact did these laws have on willingness of creditors to make future loans? One would expect that faced with higher costs from default creditors would either raise interest rates or ration credit. The evidence indicates that they relied most on rationing credit. The short-run impact of the ruling was perhaps not all that harmful, but to the extent that it established a precedent the long-run impact of the ruling on the sanctity of contracts was serious indeed.

Clearly, the Supreme Court ruling involved a case where expropriation occurred and to this extent increased the uncertainty of future contracting, which in turn reduced the gains from trade. The important point to highlight is that the law was not purely re-distributional because some incompetent farmers remained in farming while more capable farmers were rationed out of the market. Consequently, output was lower than it otherwise would have been. Furthermore, because of the higher risk associated with farm loans, creditors invested less than optimally in the farm sector.

A more sanguine view of the Supreme Court decision was that it prevented the restrictions on private contracting from being even more severe. By 1934 many people believed that capitalism and private property had outlived their usefulness. People had taken to demonstrating and many farm foreclosure auctions had been disrupted by angry farmers. Indeed the Supreme Court justified its ruling on the basis of emergency. The moratoria could only be temporary; once normal times returned the rights of contractors would again reign absolute. The Supreme Court ruling may have taken some of the wind out of the sails of those who had lost faith in markets and the sanctity of private contracting.

The unitization of US oilfields

Unitization means that an oil field is drained as if there were one owner and the proceeds are divided according to some agreed-upon rights, the simplest being surface rights.[21] The losses from failing to unitize are staggering. Total recovery rates fall because sub-surface pressure is dissipated too quickly. Oil is exploited too rapidly because the rights to oil go to whoever extracts it first, and too much capital is used in order to speed the extraction process. Excess oil wells in the USA are testimony to the waste. Libecap (1989) reports that in 1980 the USA had 88 per cent of the world's oil wells and only 14 per cent of the world's production.

Despite the recognized losses, the parties to oil contracts could not reach a consensus to unitize, because small oil companies would lose by unitization and they had the political clout to maintain the status quo. The value of the losses are bounded by the costs of horizontal integration but these may not be small because of differences of opinion over the value of claims. These same differences blocked private unitization efforts. Here is a case where the transactions costs of determining the proper side-payments were too large to allow private contractors to establish the proper institutions to prevent rent dissipation. Also, the government failed to initiate unitization because of the political bargaining strength of the special interest groups who won by preventing unitization.[22]

Social control and paternalism in agriculture in the American South

Joseph Ferrie and I (1989) chronicled the co-evolution of paternalism, a contract of sorts, and social control, a formal and informal institution that was imposed on blacks and lower class whites in the South by the rural plantation elite.[23] Under paternalism, workers exchanged dependable labor services for a variety of goods and services such as credit, housing, medical and old-age assistance and, most importantly, protection from acts of violence. The protective aspect of paternalism became more valuable to workers as social control became more oppressive. By the turn of the century and until changes in federal law and its enforcement in the 1960s, the rural South was typified as an "armed camp for intimidating black folk." Social control, comprised of disfranchisement and a variety of laws and practices, was the means by which Southern elites fostered and condoned intimidation, especially of blacks. In short, Southern state governments did not provide blacks and many poor whites with civil rights. Furthermore, markets where blacks could purchase protection or legal assistance did not exist. A black accused of wrongdoing could not readily hire either a white or a black lawyer to represent him. In the absence of civil rights and governmentally supplied welfare in the rural South, paternalism arose to fill the need.

Landlords willingly supplied paternalism because it was cheaper than cash in inducing work effort. Pre-mechanized agriculture had a severe monitoring problem. Production took place over a wide geographic space and labor effort could not be assessed ex-post by judging output, which varied from natural conditions that were not readily assignable either to nature or to the worker.

There were no formal rules but it was in the interest of both sides of the arrangement to fulfill obligations. Blacks had an incentive to work because, if caught shirking, they would lose their protector and with the low cost of information that existed in rural areas they could not readily find another protector. Landlords had an incentive to deliver protection and other services like medical care because if they did not they would have a more difficult time securing reliable labor in the future.

To maintain paternalism, landlords had to prevent state and federal governments from providing substitutes for their services. By the early twentieth century the rural elite controlled legislation at the state level disfranchising blacks and poor whites. After Reconstruction the federal government did not attempt to intervene in Southern race or labor relations until the 1930s. From that time, the federal government tried to introduce welfare and other programs, which would have raised the costs of agricultural labor in two ways: directly by raising reservation wages and indirectly by reducing the benefits to workers from welfare arrangements provided by the landlord. Because of their disproportionate political power, Southern landlords successfully used their political agents to prevent federal intervention in race or labor relations. For example, agricultural workers were exempted from the social security bill, which provided old-age assistance, and from the Fair Labor Standards Act, which established minimum wages. Although several Civil Rights bills were introduced into Congress, none passed until 1964.

Paternalism began to disappear around 1960, the same time that Southern agriculture became fully mechanized. Mechanization, along with complementary technology, standardized production by reducing the discretionary input of labor. As a result, the benefits from paternalism as a monitoring device for landlords fell. Moreover, labor displacement, brought about by mechanization, further eroded the benefits of paternalism for monitoring. Fear of unemployment was now sufficient to induce work effort.

Because we do not have a direct measure of paternalism, it is difficult to establish the impact of mechanization. We do, however, have indirect measures. First, Southern Congressmen who maintained their disproportionate political power allowed the passage of bills that encouraged rural out-migration. They surely would not have done so had paternalism not been burdensome. Secondly, mechanization prompted a change in the mix of contracting. Sharecropping, which went hand in glove with paternalism, virtually disappeared.

Within the institution of social control, paternalism was an implicit contractual arrangement that reduced the high transaction costs associated with pre-mechanized, labor intensive agriculture. Because paternalism was costly, it disappeared and the welfare state allowed to expand once the economic incentive for its maintenance disappeared. Until mechanization, both sides had an incentive to maintain paternalism and abide by its rules: workers because there were few substitutes for landlord paternalism and landlords because paternalism was a low-cost way of inducing work effort.

IMPLICATIONS

Institutions, formal and informal, are necessary for all but the most rudimentary forms of exchange. My chapter illustrates how institutions function and discusses some of the factors that give rise to institutional change. It is critical for economic growth that politicians promote those institutions that give incentives for people to engage in productive as opposed to negative-sum redistributive activities. Most importantly, institutions must be designed with care, not only because they determine incentives in a society, but also because once established, they are not easily changed; groups hurt by change will invest in behavior that supports the existing institutions.

Taking care does not imply delay in establishing the minimal institutions, such as private property rights, that undergird markets. The former East bloc countries should move boldly, yet not blindly, towards markets. There are several reasons for moving to markets as quickly as is politically feasible.[24] The ideological change that accompanied the downfall of Communism discredited central planning and brought with it a sense that markets are the solution to all woes. Yet, the people in these countries have only a rudimentary understanding of how markets actually work. They observe that the West has markets and is rich and believe, therefore, that markets are all that they need to become rich. They do not understand that markets work through a process of creative destruction, which brings about winners and losers. Behind the belief that markets will save Central Europe is the idea of an initial honeymoon period during which people will be more willing to sacrifice than they would be later once the rules of the game are established.

Another reason for moving quickly on some fronts, especially in establishing private property rights, is that market institutions tend to develop endogenously once property rights are in place. Moreover, allowing private institutions to develop right away may lead to results that are superior to those produced by planning institutions, which do not allow for competition among institutions. The variety of institutions that developed historically to generate the cooperative solution suggests that it would have been impossible to plan the same institutions.

Politicians can change (and I have argued *should* change) formal institutions (the laws of society) quickly, but they have little direct influence on informal institutions such as norms of behavior or culture, which have an equal if not more important impact on market behavior. Nevertheless, the formal rules may have an indirect impact on norms of behavior. For example, we know that people's willingness to sacrifice the present for the future, a norm of sorts, varies across countries. Part of the reason may be that the laws in some societies make consumption in the future uncertain. Under conditions of future uncertainty, people will rationally consume more today, but this in turn may affect other forms of behavior like the willingness to work. The argument can be stated succinctly: the laws of society determine the link between effort and reward and, if rewards are believed to be arbitrary, effort will decrease as will other forms of growth-enhancing behavior. Furthermore, to the extent that elected officials are respected they help shape the norms of society through their words and actions. In short, politicians can be opinion-makers, especially in times of uncertainty such as those facing the former Communist countries today.

The final rationale for prescribing rapid change has to do with the role of the state. The state is essential for economic growth. It defines and enforces the rules of the game and the consequent payoffs to cooperative growth-enhancing activity rather than redistributive activity. The dilemma facing former Communist countries is that the state lacks credibility. The only way to establish credibility, once it is lost, is to begin acting credibly. The longer the delay in establishing private property rights, the more citizens will believe that it is "politics as usual." What trust existed between citizens and their new leaders will wither away over time and make the move to markets nearly impossible.

Societies are seldom at historical junctures where the basic societal institutions are revamped. For this reason leaders should strike while the iron is hot and there is ideological support for change. Delay could mean that societies might never hit their target of private markets because either the potential losers may organize sufficiently to block change or the ideological support for change may fall. Delaying change could lead to enormous losses in terms of economic growth and welfare.

NOTES

Unlike the other authors in this volume, I am not a specialist in Central or Eastern Europe. My area of expertise is in the interplay between markets and institutions in general. A preliminary version of my chapter was presented at a conference in Moscow in the fall of 1990. The conference was entitled "Moving to Markets" and included Soviet academics and policy-makers. Over the course of the conference I benefitted greatly from comments received from George Akerlof, Gary Becker, Victor Goldberg and the other participants. I thank Jeremy Atack, David Good, Larry Neal and Douglass North for comments on subsequent drafts.

1 Individuals only have a natural propensity "to truck, barter and exchange" if they are given the appropriate incentives. Adam Smith's oft quoted observation was relevant for only a small part of the world. It is perhaps accurate to say that most economists believe that institutions are important but treat them as exogenous and focus on optimizing behavior, *given the institutional constraints*.
2 Douglass C. North more than any other economic historian has stressed the importance of institutions on economic growth. In particular I refer you to North (1981) and (1990).
3 Redistributive activities are seldom zero-sum, but rather negative-sum because people expend resources to effect the transfer.
4 Currently in Brazil property rights to land in the Amazon are not clearly defined and as a result people expend resources to define property rights and dissipate some of the inherent rent from land through a lack of investment, environmental degradation, and violence. In a recent report authored jointly by the International Monetary Fund, The World Bank, the Organization for Economic Cooperation and Development and the European Bank for Reconstruction and Development a clear message emerges: ". . . security of private property must be assured at the outset in order to encourage private initiative" (International Monetary Fund 1991: 17).
5 For the analytical structure in this section I have relied heavily on North (1990).
6 The following observations come from my ongoing research on property rights and resource use in the state of Pará in the Brazilian Amazon. The description of land markets that follows is specific to Pará, although other states in the Amazon have similar problems.
7 I use the cautionary word "may" because the work is still in progress and I lack documented evidence on this point. Furthermore, because land is still relatively abundant, part of the observed lack of investment is no doubt due to relative prices.

8 Uncertain security over agricultural land in Eastern and Central Europe is no doubt in part responsible for the decline in production. See *The Economist*, 7–14 August 1993: 57–8.

9 By opportunistic behavior I mean the incentive that people have to lie, cheat, swindle, and shirk. Oliver Williamson (1985) pioneered the term "opportunistic" behavior and explores the safeguards contractors erect to limit it.

10 Most violence does not occur on the frontier where land is abundant and consequently cheap, but rather in the areas where government has not yet asserted a monopoly on enforcing contracts and where land values are relatively high. It is the potential for capturing rents from high valued land that leads to violence, although violence itself may result in the ultimate form of rent dissipation – death.

11 For example, when government enforcement is absent such as in drug dealing or other illegal activities trust amongst traders becomes more important. The result is frequently trade among blood relatives.

12 More important because unless a society is closed and willing to use considerable coercion (e.g., the former communist countries of Eastern and Central Europe) citizens must believe in the laws or the laws will be impossible to enforce. This of course begs the question as to whether laws alone can be binding. A discussion of this issue is beyond the scope of this essay but I refer those interested to Alston *et al.* (1993).

13 It is beyond the scope of my chapter to speculate on the factors that give rise to ideological change. Some scholars like Robert Higgs (1987) argue that ideologies are most subject to change during periods of crisis and that certain elites are ideological makers during these crises. I do not dispute this view but suggest that ideologies can also "creep up on one." Certain arguments or statements made in economic self-interest can, if repeated frequently enough, become internalized and take on a life of their own without changing rapidly in response to relative prices. For example, racial animosity in the USA in the nineteenth century can be explained by economic self-interest on the part of those with political power. Attitudes about the racial inferiority of blacks was buttressed through the mid-twentieth century by the continued economic self-interest of Southern politicians and their principals. For those with political power, the pure economic stake in keeping blacks in an inferior status diminished with the mechanization of Southern agriculture. Yet, the ideology of racial animosity only changed with a lag. For an elaboration of the linkage between the mechanization of Southern agriculture and political behavior, see Alston and Ferrie (1993).

14 This section draws heavily on Bates (1983, 1989).

15 Part of the reason for the fighting and redistributive activities among ethnic groups in the former Communist countries is the result of the lack of formal institutions that would constrain fighting among people with differing beliefs.

16 This section draws heavily on Greif (1989).

17 This section draws heavily on Umbeck (1977).

18 This section draws on Dennen (1976), Libecap (1989) and North (1990).

19 This section draws on North and Weingast (1989) and Bordo and White (1990).

20 This section draws on Alston (1984).

21 This section draws on Libecap (1989).

22 This does not necessarily imply that government ownership of the asset would have been preferable. The losses from a failure to unitize would presumably have been lower than what existed but this would come at the expense of inefficiencies associated with the incentives under government ownership. Higgs (1982) de-

scribes another case where political interests led to legislation fostering technical regress rather than economic growth.

23 This section draws on Alston and Ferrie (1989, 1993).

24 What follows is prescriptive rather than predictive. I am actually relatively pessimistic about the prospects for rapid institutional change. Change necessarily brings about winners and losers and many of the politicians and bureaucrats who are in charge of change would be sowing the seeds of their own destruction. For this reason many of the less than very senior ranking officials have an incentive to block change. They argue that the reason for moving slowly towards markets is a concern over the redistributional consequences of change, e.g., the future of the elderly. My guess is that much of the rhetoric masks self-interested concern over future livelihood.

REFERENCES

Alston, L.J. (1984) "Farm foreclosure moratorium legislation: A lesson from the past," *American Economic Review*, 74 (3) (June): 445–57.

Alston, L.J. and Ferrie, J.P. (1989) "Social control and labor relations in the American South before the mechanization of the cotton harvest in the 1950s," *Journal of Institutional and Theoretical Economics*, 145 (1) (March): 133–57.

Alston, L.J. and Ferrie, J.P. (1993) "Paternalism in agricultural labor contracts in the U.S. South: Implications for the growth of the welfare state," *American Economic Review*, 83 (4): 852–76.

Alston, L.J. and Gillespie, W. (1989) "Resource coordination and transaction costs: a framework for analyzing the firm/market boundary," *Journal of Economic Behavior and Organization* ,11: 191–212.

Alston, L.J. and Schapiro, M.O. (1984) "Inheritance laws across colonies: Causes and consequences," *Journal of Economic History*, 44(2) (June): 277–87.

Alston, L.J., Eggertsson, T. and North, D.C. (eds.) (1993) *Empirical Studies in Institutional Economics*, draft manuscript under review.

Bates, R. (1983) *Essays on the Political Economy of Rural Africa*, Cambridge.

Bates, R. (1989) *Beyond the Miracle of the Market: The Political Economy of Agrarian Development in Rural Kenya*, Cambridge.

Bordo, M. and White, E. (1990) "A tale of two currencies: British and French finance during the Napoleonic Wars," Working Paper.

Dennen, T. (1976) "Cattlemen's associations and property rights in land in the American West," *Explorations in Economic History*, 13: 423–36.

The Economist (1993) "Trouble on the farm," (August 7–14): 57–8.

Greif, A. (1989) "Reputation and coalitions in the medieval trade: Evidence on the Maghribi traders," *Journal of Economic History*, 49 (4) (December): 857–82.

Higgs, R. (1982) "Legally induced technical regress in the Washington salmon fishery," *Research In Economic History*, 7: 55–86.

Higgs, R. (1987) *Crisis and Leviathan: Critical Episodes in the Growth of American Government*, New York.

Human Rights Watch (1991) *Rural Violence in Brazil*, New York.

International Monetary Fund, The World Bank, Organisation for Economic Co-operation and Development and the European Bank for Reconstruction and Development. (1990) *The Economy of the USSR*, Washington DC.

Libecap, G.D. (1989) *Contracting for Property Rights*, Cambridge.

North, D.C. (1981) *Structure and Chance in Economic History*, New York.

North, D.C. (1990) *Institutions, Institutional Change and Economic Performance*, Cambridge.

North, D.C. and Weingast, B.R. (1989) "Constitutions and commitment: The evolution of institutions governing public choice in seventeenth-century England," *Journal of Economic History*, 49 (4) (December): 803–32.
Schneider, R. (1992) "Brazil: An analysis of environmental problems in the Amazon," World Bank Report.
Umbeck, J. (1977) "The California Gold Rush: A study of emerging property rights," *Explorations in Economic History*, 14: 197–226.
Williamson, O. (1985) *The Economic Institutions of Capitalism*, New York.

Part III

THE STATE, INSTITUTIONS, AND ECONOMIC GROWTH

4

CONTINUITY AND DISCONTINUITY

Banking and industry in twentieth-century Central Europe

Alice Teichova

For almost a century, the interaction between banks and industry has been the subject of speculation and debate. Scholars have analyzed the role of banks in industrialization, the nature and causes of concentration in industry, and the general impact of banks on business cycles and on long-term economic growth.

This discussion gained further momentum among economic historians in the mid-1960s with Alexander Gerschenkron's views on the role of banks under conditions of relative economic backwardness (Gerschenkron, 1965) and the rediscovery of Rudolf Hilferding's *Finanzkapital* (published in English for the first time in 1981), which looked at the nature of the interaction between banking and industrial capital. The issue now confronts Central and Eastern Europe where financial markets and commercial banks were completely absent under Communism. Policymakers must consider the role of banks in turning the former planned economic systems into functioning capitalist, market economies. Therefore, looking critically into the past is not only an academic exercise. Analyzing the history of bank–industry relations in Central Europe will show that the region's current lack of investment capital is a long-standing, chronic problem.

I will focus here on "universal" or "mixed" banks – those institutions that combined the short-term business of deposit banking with the long-term activity of investment banking, and in addition, performed stockbrokering functions, managed clients' portfolios, acquired shares and voting rights in joint-stock companies on their own account. With the exception of the UK, and, possibly, also France, universal banks spread throughout Europe during the phase of buoyant expansion in capitalism from the 1880s to 1914. Close relationships between industrial companies and banks developed everywhere, although the pace at which this happened differed somewhat from country to country.

I limit my analysis to Central Europe, where the union of banking and industry was especially marked. Germany is often seen as a "model" of this trend. There is less agreement among scholars about the rest of Central Europe – Austria–Hungary until 1918; Austria and the successor states to the Dual Monarchy thereafter – where the intertwining of bank–industry relations has been interpreted negatively.[1] I draw on a current international research project under my direction that investigates the financing of industry by banks in Austria, Czechoslovakia, Hungary, and Sweden.[2]

I

The geographical diffusion of universal banking across Europe accompanied the rapid, parallel rise of large-scale enterprise, of formal cartels, and of other monopolistic and oligopolistic formations. These trends led to concern about the excessive concentration of economic power in banks and their apparent dominance of industry. Awareness of this issue by contemporaries is shown by the early appearance of the first book on cartels, by Kleinwächter and published in Innsbruck in 1883. It may seem strange that this first systematic description of modern concentration in industry, trade, and finance should have been produced within the Habsburg Monarchy, which is often viewed by economic historians as a laggard in industrialization. But the backwardness of the Austro–Hungarian economy has often been overstated in macroeconomic assessments. This view of "sluggishness" has continued largely because of the Monarchy's uneven economic development (Good 1984; Komlos 1983; Rudolph 1976). Too much attention is often focused on the Monarchy's southeastern regions – among the most economically backward of Europe – and too little on its western regions (Bohemia, Moravia, Silesia, and the Alpine lands), which experienced an industrial revolution comparable with Western Europe. This spatially differentiated capitalist development in Austria–Hungary cannot exclusively be explained by Gerschenkron's approach to relative economic backwardness.[3]

Contrary to the widespread assumption among scholars that Germany became the home of universal banking *par excellence* after the failure of the *Crédit mobilier* in France, its purest form actually can be found in Austria–Hungary, certainly from at least the last quarter of the nineteenth century. Contemporaries, even senior officials within the Austrian Ministry of Finance, regarded the relationship between industrial and banking capital as one of power and they assumed that the power in its most expressive form lay with the banks (März 1968: 14). As with cartels, the first attempt to analyze the bank–industry relations emanated from this part of Europe. Hilferding's *Finance Capital*, completed in 1909 and first published in Vienna in 1910, was influenced by conditions in the author's homeland:

> Austria . . . provides the clearest example of the direct and deliberate influence of bank capital upon cartelization. (Hilferding 1981: 213)

Of course, Hilferding examined the interlocking of bank and industrial capital not only in Austria, but also in Germany. There the financing of large industrial concerns by and through banks intensified to such a degree before 1914 that he drew the hasty political conclusion from his assumption of the supremacy of banks over industry that capitalism could be replaced by socialism in one stroke:

> Even today, taking possession of six large Berlin banks would mean taking possession of the most important spheres of large-scale industry, and would greatly facilitate the initial phases of socialist policy. (Hilferding 1981: 368)

The power of banks over industry was, and largely *is still*, assumed. A few years ago the prestigious German newspaper the *Frankfurter Allgemeine Zeitung* published a voluminous survey of the world's bankers and banking systems by Kruk (1977), which stressed the historical context of European banks and the role of their universality as a foundation for their power. Although perhaps an oversimplification, a hypothesis about the *potential* hierarchical relationship between banks and industrial enterprises can be a useful tool in empirical research.

Gerschenkron, who like Hilferding also had an Austro–Hungarian background (see Rosovsky 1979), reproduced essentially Hilferding's chain of thought, when he assessed the role of banks in both financing industrial companies and furthering concentration. Moreover, his ideas are not unlike those of Hilferding with respect to how banks assume control over their clients' industrial enterprises, especially through financial operations and by serving on the boards of their subsidiary companies. However, Gerschenkron drew a fundamentally different conclusion about the implications of this relationship. He did not regard the dependence of industrial enterprises on banks as a necessary result of capitalist development, but as a feature of "latecomer" industrial economies that marked only a limited phase in their overall development and persisted only until the initial scarcity of capital was overcome (Gerschenkron 1977: 14).

Consequently, Gerschenkron assigned a "missionary" task to the credit banks (*Kreditbanken*) in relatively backward European countries before 1914. Yet, in the view of some authors, the banks continued with this "missionary" activity without any break into the interwar period. In my opinion, after 1918 the banks were not so much promoting industrial enterprise as rescuing their own industrial subsidiary enterprises from collapse (März and Weber 1983: 342).

Gerschenkron's plausible generalizations greatly stimulated empirical work by his own students and by other scholars, especially in Austria, Germany, and Sweden, on the role of banks in "latecomer" economies, a term that has become universally accepted for every European country with the exception of Britain and, perhaps, also France. However, the evidence arising from these studies has called into question Gerschenkron's approach on almost every count. With respect to the pre-1914 period, the assumptions about the scarcity of capital and the decisive role of banks in overcoming it were tested and found wanting. Similarly the widely held idea about the banks' supremacy over industry, first postulated by Hilferding, has recently been scrutinized by Wellhöner (1989) and Wixforth (1989). In examining the extent of bank supremacy in the German economy during both the Wilhelmine and Weimar periods, they utilized the surviving records of the largest combines within German heavy industry, and demonstrated the need for a more differentiated approach to the issue. Tilly (1986), also qualifies the role of the mixed banks in Germany between 1870 and 1913 by calling their support for industry "development assistance for the strong," and my own research shows this to be true for the large Viennese banks as well.

Although studies of bank–industry relations in Europe during the pre-1914 period are now available, very few exist for the interwar period. Lack of access to company and bank archives has been a major stumbling block, and has led to fragmentary, uncoordinated and almost random research efforts. Yet, the principal findings on the nature of pre-1914 European universal banking provide signposts for the interwar period, especially as World War I was not a discontinuity for concentration of either industrial or financial capital. Rather, the War accelerated such concentration. Similarly the need for the financing of industry by banks was not diminished – indeed, the turmoil of post-war inflations and financial crises intensified such demand. Therefore, I focus on bank–industry relations within the context of universal banking from the turn of the century until the end of the 1930s.

II

Before 1914 the level of joint-stock banking assets in the Austrian financial sector compared very favorably with that of other developed European economies. As in Germany, the universal banks of the Habsburg empire preferred to extend credits to enterprises that were profitable or had a long-standing customer relation (Rudolph 1976: 104). From its very foundation in the 1850s, the leading Austrian commercial bank, the Credit-Anstalt für Handel und Gewerbe, placed no special emphasis on encouraging the entrepreneurial spirit when it undertook the promotion of industrial companies (März 1981: 55). As in Germany, the archival evidence for Austria does not support the idea that the banks performed a "missionary" task in furthering industrialization.

Legal and fiscal regulations determined the specific nature of the relationship between banks and industry within Austria–Hungary. Industrial joint-stock companies avoided long-term credit and instead chose financing by floating new shares through the banks because tax laws unfavorably affected the growth of joint-stock enterprise. Until its amendment in 1899, company law hindered the development of an adequate capital market (Matis and

Bachinger 1973: 216; Mosser 1980: 184); the large credit banks stepped in to fill the void.

According to Alois Mosser's analyses of Austrian company balance sheets for the period 1880 to 1914, the majority of joint-stock companies obtained capital in two main ways: first, through the plough-back of their own financial resources; and, second, by taking up short-term credit from the banks, with the latter being eventually amortized by the issue of shares. In aggregate, credit to joint-stock companies rose four-fold over the period 1880–1913, while long-term credit decreased relative to short-term credit (Mosser 1980: 113, 134). The Austrian banking system performed the usual functions of accumulating and mobilizing capital as in other developed countries, but it played a much greater active role in the allocation of capital (Rudolph 1976: 159). As there were no legal constraints to the ownership of shares by banks, bank credits were secured by shares, preferably those of the largest and soundest industrial enterprises. The banks strengthened their supervision of client companies through interlocking directorships, while they encouraged cartelization and initiated or mediated mergers. The banks frequently performed marketing operations for enterprises within their spheres of interests or, in the case of cartels, acted as the cartel bureau for whole industrial sectors, especially in sugar, coal, and wood.

By 1914 the eight great Viennese banks accounted for about two-thirds of the total capital of all the financial institutions of the empire (Weber 1985: 232). These institutions had secured strategic positions in almost all branches of industry and their influence radiated out from Vienna to encompass all the territories of the Dual Monarchy. In the Hungarian portion of the Monarchy, only one bank was on a par with the leading Viennese institutions – the Hungarian General Credit Bank – which itself was linked to the Austrian Credit-Anstalt. Ránki has estimated that in 1913 this bank controlled 63 industrial enterprises, which, in aggregate, accounted for 16 per cent of the total capital of Hungarian joint-stock companies (Ránki 1983: 356).

The League of Nations' examination of the shattered post-war Austrian financial system yielded the famous Layton–Rist Report, which assessed the pre-1918 functions of the Viennese banks:

> They served every relatively important operation in all areas: shares issues, formation of syndicates, placing of loans or any larger industrial credit. Relations with international finance are concentrated in Vienna – here foreign credits were taken up and administered for the entire Empire. Viennese banks led the penetration of Eastern and Southeast Europe with Austrian capital. (Layton and Rist 1925)

With the break-up of the Monarchy in 1918, the large Viennese universal banks found themselves suddenly standing at the center of what were now multinational diversified concerns.[4] During the short period from 1919 to

1923, the leading Viennese banks were penetrated by international capital. Despite these sudden transformations, the evolution of bank–industry relations within the successor states during the inter-war period was strongly marked by characteristics carried over from the pre-war system. Accordingly, a parallel development of the bank–industry structure in Austria, Czechoslovakia, Hungary, Italy, Poland, and Yugoslavia occurred after the dissolution of the Empire.

The banking system inherited by the successor states had several common features. The tradition of the "universal" banks serving as the source of finance for industrial enterprises continued unbroken. The banks' assets consisted largely of industrial equities, whose prices fell under crisis conditions and rendered them illiquid. Domestic deposits were mostly insufficient and, towards the end of the 1920s, decreased. Liquidity problems arose perennially, the banks defaulted on their enormous debts in the crisis of the 1930s, and concentration within banking, through mergers, intensified. By 1937, 75 per cent of the equity of commercial banks in Romania and Yugoslavia, and at least 30 per cent in Poland and Bulgaria were in foreign, mainly Western hands. While the share of foreign ownership was relatively high (no precise figures are known as yet) in the case of Austrian universal banks, no more than 15 per cent of the total capital of all joint stock banks in Czechoslovakia were foreign-owned (Teichova 1974: 342, 1989: 924).

In many respects the development of the Czech banking system both in the Habsburg Monarchy and during the existence of the independent Czechoslovak state between 1918 and 1938 differed from that of the other successor states. As early as the upswing in the business cycle between 1907 and 1912 the Czech banks had achieved a dominating position in the local (Bohemian, Moravian, and Silesian) money market. They had succeeded in ousting the Bohemian–German banks by a tighter concentration of banking capital, and by building up both stronger industrial concerns and centrally controlled networks of branches and affiliates throughout the Austro–Hungarian Empire, and, to a lesser extent, beyond its eastern and south-eastern borders (Nečas 1987). The Czech universal banks, especially the strongest among them – the Živnostenská banka – constituted a threat to the Viennese financial institutions. In their competitive expansion into the Slavic areas of the Austro-Hungarian Empire, they employed the nationalist slogans of "mutual Slavonic interests" and "Slav brotherhood" against the established Viennese and Budapest banks. Although by the outbreak of World War I the capital of the 22 largest Viennese banks still amounted to 71.4 per cent of the total banking capital of the Austrian half of the Dual Monarchy, the number of Czech banks rose from four banks to thirteen, and their share in total banking capital from 1900 to 1913 rose from 7.9 per cent to 13.3 per cent (Riesser 1912; Jindra 1957).

From the turn of the century, the Czech national movement in Bohemia and Moravia built up a financial presence in the credit cooperatives movement and the small savings banks. Through their central organizations, these institutions provided capital for the large Czech banks and their powerful industrial clients in Prague and Brno, where the actual reins of financial and economic power were concentrated in the independent Czechoslovak Republic after 1918 (Teichova 1988a: 29, 47).

In post-1918 Austria, the savings banks still provided hardly any domestic resources for the commercial banks and created a centralized organization, the *Girovereinigung der Sparkassen*, only in December 1937. In contrast, the Czech savings institutes founded the *Ústřední banka českých spořitelen (Sporobanka)* (Central Bank of the Czech Savings Institutes) already in June 1903, which became a constant source of funds for the large Czech banks where the concentrated savings were deposited. While the Czech banking system was not immune to the vagaries of crises in the interwar period, it avoided the crashes that characterize the Austrian system. The policies of the Živnostenská banka were, in the historical context, more cautious than the Viennese banks in granting credit to industrial enterprises and in paying out dividends, and were more farsighted in building up reserves (Lacina 1983: 1990).

In the case of Vienna, the former financial center of the Danube basin, bank–industry relations were dramatically affected by the disintegration of the empire. The large Viennese commercial banks attempted to carry on "business as usual," but in very much changed circumstances. Expecting to resume their role as the financial leaders, the Viennese banks retained a hand in financing at least a part of the business in the former imperial lands (März 1981: 352–3). This policy was pursued despite their having lost most of their branches; of the 143 branches possessed by the ten largest Viennese banks outside Austria in 1918, only nine had remained by 1924 (*Compass* 1919, 1925). They lost great chunks of their subsidiary industrial enterprises through "nostrification," which involved transferring head offices of companies from Vienna to the new successor states. Above all, the Viennese banks lost control of their most profitable industrial enterprises, which were now located beyond its border with Czechoslovakia (Teichova 1974: 339–40, 1979: 372, 1988b: 57–63).

Unlike German banks and industry, which after 1918 opposed foreign penetration (Feldman 1989), the Viennese banks were anxious to attract capital from the countries of the Entente. The bankers and Austrian politicians assumed that the shrunken Austrian economy would not be viable without external support (Teichova 1988b: 87–9). During the inflation of the early 1920s industrial demand for credit rose steeply and was met by the banks, but at the price of plunging the Austrian financial sector further and further into foreign debt. This eventually dire situation arose because a prerequisite for the expansion of bank advances to industry was lending to the Viennese banks from Western Europe and the USA. With respect to only the short-term foreign indebtedness of the largest Viennese banks, this lending increased approximately three-fold from 1924 to 1930, rising from 370 million to 980 million schilling (Kernbauer and Weber 1986: 193).

Compared with the pre-1913 period, industry became dependent to a much higher degree on bank loans while, in turn, the banks increased their share ownership of dependent client companies. Bank financing became increasingly marked by financial institutions borrowing short and then re-lending the funds on a longer-term basis. This was in no way altruistic; to sustain their own creditworthiness, the banks had to keep their industrial debtors afloat. An illusion of prosperity was created to cover industrial losses and sustain industrial dividends. Although such desperate procedures were not unknown in other countries, the extent of such camouflaging in persistent crisis conditions was, in my opinion, specific to Austria. The banks were encouraged by expectations of an economic revival, but this proved to be illusory and, moreover, Vienna never regained its regional leadership in finance and trade.

As in other economies, bank mergers in Austria took place from the mid-1920s, but to a much greater degree. Fusions of the Viennese banks occurred after rampant speculation that marked the period until 1924 and had been unchecked in the absence of effective banking legislation. In the chaos of hyperinflation, the Austrian government established a Banking Commission in 1922 and charged it with preparing legislation both to control banking practices and restrict fraudulent dealing on the stock exchange. However, its work was stymied and, eventually, the Commission was disbanded in 1926 without result.[5] Crashes and financial crises continued and led to more amalgamations. In 1929 only four of the eight great Viennese banks remained. As a result of merger and consolidation, each surviving bank had a greater number of dependent industrial enterprises and more packets of unsalable shares. In addition, the remaining institutions were faced with an increasing demand for credit. The merger movement, which arose largely from the operations of the market, peaked in 1929 when the Credit-Anstalt für Handel und Gewerbe absorbed the Boden-Credit-Anstalt, after previously digesting the Anglo–Österreichische Bank in 1926. Yet it was no solution as the Credit-Anstalt itself crashed spectacularly in May 1931 (März and Weber,1983; Stiefel 1989). This, as is well known, sent out shock waves and exacerbated the international banking crisis of that summer. The whole Austrian economy, already strained by general depression, was plunged ever more deeply into crisis conditions.

The Austrian government and the Austrian National Bank mounted a rescue operation for the Credit-Anstalt, which by "socializing" the bank's enormous losses, both satisfied the foreign creditors and, after the fusion with the Wiener Bankverein, led eventually in 1934 to the creation of almost a *one-bank system*. As in Germany this state support was a state-aided reconstruction exercise, not the application of a conscious policy designed to nationalize the banking system. Under it, the debt burden of the insolvent banking system was shouldered by the government. Government financial guarantees indirectly also rescued the bank's industrial enterprises, as most of their debts were written off (Weber 1985: 345). The state became the majority shareholder in the Credit-Anstalt, which continued to function as the leading universal bank, although at a much reduced level. It headed a system that from 1934 was composed of three banks; the Viennese branch of a Czechoslovakian institution, the strong filial of the Prague Živnostenská banka, and the Länderbank, which was controlled by the Banque des Pays de l'Europe Centrale of Paris.

With its reconstruction, the Credit-Anstalt's management had to decide which of its enterprises to liquidate and which to finance with further credit (Mosser and Teichova 1991). The subsequent shrinkage of the banking system has been termed "Austrification," because the domestic industrial holdings were slimmed down and all the foreign holdings of the Credit-Anstalt were transferred to its foreign creditors (Stiefel 1983, 1989). Unlike in Germany, the bank was not reprivatized; the majority of its shares continued to remain in the hands of what ultimately became the Austrofascist state. By the time of the *Anschluss*, the Austrian banking system had resumed profitability, but was by then fully integrated into the German Reich.

III

Without a "lender of the last resort," universal banks were unable to cope with the crisis of the 1930s. The Great Depression marked an end to the form of mixed banking that had functioned since the 1880s. Across Central and Eastern Europe, the state was forced to intervene and mount rescue actions. Everywhere the losses of the big credit banks and their large industrial clients were "socialized" by direct state take-over, outright or through majority shareholdings. This did not, however, usher in socialism as Hilferding (1981) had expected; on the contrary, these actions succeeded in rescuing capitalism and buttressed highly concentrated structures within banking and industry.

In the case of Austria, universal banking had outlasted all changes. While banking organization after the *Anschluss* remained essentially unaltered except for the replacement of Jewish by German directors, banking operations were redirected to finance Hitler's war effort. During World War II, Austria was recognized as "the first victim of Nazi aggression" by the Allies (1943) and in the wake of Germany's defeat it recovered its independent status. After a decade of Allied occupation, Austria gained neutrality in 1955. The Credit-Anstalt was nationalized in 1946 to avoid being taken over as German property by the Allies. It has undergone partial privatization since 1957, leaving at least 51 per cent of its equity in the hands of the state.

It has functioned effectively as the leading financial institution in rebuilding the mixed economy of the Second Austrian Republic. Since 1989 the Austrian banks have shown vigorous interest in the recently opened investment opportunities in Central and Southeast Europe where – in historical context – their traditional market has been.

Seen in historical perspective, bank financing of industry in interwar Central Europe failed to engender capital accumulation or to support sustained economic growth. Empirical research into the financial and industrial history of Central Europe make it difficult to support the currently popular view that the former Communist countries must return to the "democratic governments and free market economies of 1938." By the 1930s, with the exception of Czechoslovakia, there was hardly a shadow of democracy left anywhere in Central and Southeastern Europe; nor did a free market economy exist anywhere at that time, including Czechoslovakia. If a lesson is to be learned from the period, the region's financial history suggests what to avoid rather than what to emulate.

NOTES

The author wishes to thank Leicester University Press for granting her permission to draw upon her chapter "Rivals and partners: Reflections on banking and industry in Europe, 1880–1938," in P.L. Cottrell, H. Lindgren and A. Teichova (eds.), *European Industry and Banking between the Wars: A Review of Bank–Industry Relations* (Leicester, London, New York, 1992). She also wishes to thank the Center for Humanities of Oregon State University, Corvallis, where she completed this paper during her Fellowship.

1 Universal banking also developed within the Scandinavian countries, which has given rise to a large literature; see especially: Lundström, 1986; Lindgren, 1987.

2 The research project: "Bank-industry relations in interwar Europe: Austria, Czechoslovakia, Hungary, and Sweden 1900–1939" began in October 1986. Those involved comprise: Elisabeth Boross (Monash University, Melbourne, Australia); Philip Cottrell (Leicester University, UK); Mats Larsson, Håkan Lindgren, Ragnhild Lundström, Jan Ottosson and H. Sjögren (Uppsala University, Sweden); Herbert Matis, Alois Mosser, Désirée Verdonk, and Fritz Weber (Economics University Vienna, Austria); György Ránki (until his untimely death in February 1988 – he is sadly missed by us all) and A. Pogány (Institute of History, Hungarian Academy of Sciences, Budapest); Dr. Vlastislav Lacina, Dr. Jan Hájek (Historical Institute, Czech Academy of Sciences in Prague), Dr. Jiří Novotný, Dr. Jiří Šouša (Archive of the Czechoslovak State Bank, Prague), Professor Jaroslav Pátek (Charles University, Prague); and A. Teichova (Business History Unit, London School of Economics and Political Science, and Girton College Cambridge, UK). The author wishes to express her warmest thanks to the Economic and Social Research Council (UK) for generously supporting the project.

3 Gerschenkron (1977: 45–84) unconvincingly tried to apply his approach to Austria.

4 P.L. Cottrell and I have discussed this particular period in other publications (Cottrell 1983a, b; Teichova 1979).

5 Allgemeines Verwaltungsarchiv, Vienna, BKA, Inneres Präsidium, Karton 67, Bankkomission: Die Tätigkeit der Bankkommission (1922–6).

REFERENCES

Compass, 1919, vol. I; 1925, vol. I.

Cottrell, P.L. (1983a) "Aspects of Western equity investment in the banking systems of East–Central Europe," in A. Teichova and P.L. Cottrell (eds.) *International Business and Central Europe 1918–1939*, Leicester.

Cottrell, P.L. (1983b) "Austria between diplomats and bankers 1919–1931," in G. Schmidt (ed.), *Konstellationen internationaler Politik 1924–1932*, Bochum.

Feldman, G.D. (1989) "Foreign penetration of German enterprises after the First World War," in A. Teichova, M. Lévy-Leboyer and H. Nussbaum (eds.) *Historical Studies in International Corporate Business*, Cambridge, Paris.

Gerschenkron, A. (1965) *Economic Backwardness in Historical Perspective*, New York.

Gerschenkron, A. (1977) *An Economic Spurt that Failed*, Princeton NJ.

Good, D. (1984) *The Economic Rise of the Habsburg Empire 1750–1914*, Berkeley.

Hilferding, R. (1981) *Finance Capital: A Study of the Latest Phase of Capitalist Development*, London.

Jindra, Z. (1957) "K rozvoji českého bankovního kapitálu před první světovou válkou," (The development of Czech banking capital before the First World War), *Československý časopis historický*, 5: 506–26.

Kernbauer, H. and Weber, F. (1986) "Multinational banking in the Danube basin," in A. Teichova, M. Lévy-Leboyer and H. Nussbaum (eds.) *Multinational Enterprise in Historical Perspective*, Cambridge.

Komlos, J. (1983) *The Habsburg Monarchy as a Customs Union*, Princeton NJ.

Kruk, M. (1977) "Macht als Aufgabe," in *Frankfurter Allgemeine Zeitung, Banken international*, (10 May): B15.

Lacina, V. (1983) "Živnobanka a její koncern v letech velké hospodářské krize (1929–1934)," (Živnobanka and its concern during the great economic crisis 1929–1934), *Československý časopis historický*, 3: 350–77.

Lacina, V. (1990) "Živnostenská banka před a během první světové války (1907–1918)," (The Živnostenská bank before and during the First World War 1907–1918), *Československý časopis historický* 3: 276–303.

Layton, W. and Rist, Ch. (1925) *The Economic Situation of Austria*. Report presented to the Council of the League of Nations, Geneva.

Lindgren, H. (1987) "Banking group investments in Swedish industry," *Uppsala Papers in Economic History*. Research Report 15.

Lundström, R. (1986) "Banks and early Swedish multinationals," in A. Teichova *et al.* (eds.) *Multinational Enterprise in Historical Perspective*, Cambridge.

März, E. (1968) Introduction to R. Hilferding, *Das Finanzkapital*, Frankfurt, Vienna.

März, E. (1981) *Österreichische Bankpolitik in der Zeit der großen Wende 1913–1923*, Vienna.

März, E. and Weber, F. (1983) "Commentary," in A. Teichova, and P.L Cottrell (eds.) *International Business and Central Europe 1918–1939*, Leicester.

Matis, H. and Bachinger, K. (1973) "Österreichs industrielle Entwicklung," in *Die Habsburgermonarchie 1848–1918. Die wirtschaftliche Entwicklung* Bd.I, Vienna.

Mosser, A. (1980) *Die Industrieaktiengesellschaft in Österreich 1880–1913*, Vienna.

Mosser, A. und Teichova, A. (1991) "Investment behaviour of industrial joint-stock companies and industrial shareholding by the Österreichische Credit-Anstalt:

Inducement or obstacle to renewal and change in interwar Austria," in H. James, H. Lindgren and A. Teichova (eds.) *The Role of Banks in the Interwar Economy*, Cambridge, Paris.

Nečas, C. (1987) *Na prahu české kapitalové expanze* (*At the Threshold of Czech Capital Expansion*), Brno.

Ránki, G. (1983) "The Hungarian General Credit Bank in the 1920s," in A. Teichova, P.L. Cottrell (eds.) *International Business and Central Europe 1918–1939*, Leicester.

Riesser, J. (1912) *Die deutschen Großbanken und ihre Konzentration im Zusammenhang mit der Entwicklung der Gesamtwirtschaft in Deutschland*, Jena.

Rosovsky, H. (1979) "Alexander Gerschenkron: A personal and fond recollection," *Journal of Economic History*, 39: 1009–13.

Rudolph, R. (1976) *Banking and Industrialization in Austria–Hungary*, Cambridge.

Stiefel, D. (1983) "The reconstruction of the Credit-Anstalt," in A. Teichova and P.L. Cottrell (eds.) *International Business and Central Europe 1918–1939*, Leicester.

Stiefel, D. (1989) *Finanzdiplomatie und Weltwirtschaftskrise. Die Krise der Credit-Anstalt für Handel und Gewerbe 1931*, Frankfurt am Main.

Teichova, A. (1974) *An Economic Background to Munich. International Business and Czechoslovakia 1918–1938*, Cambridge.

Teichova, A. (1979) "Versailles and the expansion of the Bank of England into Central Europe," in J. Horn and J. Kocka (eds.) *Recht und Entwicklung der Großunternehmen im 19. und frühen 20. Jahrhundert*, Göttingen.

Teichova, A. (1988a) *The Czechoslovak Economy 1918–1980*, London, New York.

Teichova, A. (1988b) *Kleinstaaten im Spannungsfeld der Grosßmächte. Wirtschaft und Politik in Mittel- und Südosteuropa in der Zwischenkriegszeit*, Vienna.

Teichova, A. (1989) "East–central and south–east Europe, 1919–1939," in P. Mathias, and S. Pollard (eds.) *The Cambridge Economic History of Europe* vol. VIII.

Tilly, R. (1986) "German banking 1850–1914: Development assistance for the strong," *The Journal of European Economic History* 15 (1): 113–52.

Weber, F. (1985) "Die Österreichischen Großbanken in der Zwischenkriegszeit," *Christliche Demokratie*, 4.

Wellhöner, V. (1989) *Grossbanken und Grossindustrie im Kaiserreich: Kritische Studien zur Geschichtswissenschaft*, Göttingen.

Winkler, H.A. (1974) *Organisierter Kapitalismus: Voraussetzungen und Anfänge*, Göttingen.

Wixforth, H. (1989) *Banken und Schwerindustrie in der Weimarer Republik*, PhD Dissertation, Bielefeld.

5

THE COLLAPSE OF STATE SOCIALISM

Causes and consequences

Ivan T. Berend

Stereotypes regarding the collapse of state socialism in East–Central Europe abound. The regimes were never legitimate, but rather imposed on the countries of East–Central Europe and collapsed when the Soviet Union could no longer keep them alive through force. They offered failed models, utopias that succumbed to harsh realities. Their peoples did not want to live in a lie, but in truth destroyed the hated regimes. They represented a system that declined and disappeared because it proved to be unreformable.[1]

To be sure, these statements have elements of truth. Major revolts and revolutions permanently challenged the Hungarian, the Czechoslovak, and the Polish regimes. Reforms involved half-hearted, half-measures, and in several cases failed entirely. Orthodox ideology and a kind of religious Communist fundamentalism created formidable obstacles to the required modernization.

The reality, however, was much more complex. In some of the cases state socialism was not forced upon the country, but was born from a genuine anti-Nazi resistance movement, civil war, and revolution near the end of World War II. The system that replaced right-wing fascist dictatorships followed the shocking years of the great depression and a most horrifying war. It promised a renewal from a sick interwar capitalism and in some cases gained a degree of mass support. Some of the regimes, although initially imposed by Stalin, later were able to achieve, at least temporarily, a certain legitimacy. Nationalism was an important instrument for this. Nationalist ideology directed against minorities or neighboring peoples assured mass support even for notorious dictators. Several factors provided legitimacy and even popularity for certain regimes, at least among the lower layers of the society. Rapid growth and development, a more evenly redistributed national income, greater social mobility and the destruction of a rigid social hierarchy, full employment and job security, a kind of "premature welfare state" that never existed before in these countries and in some rare cases a sort of (low level) "consumer society."

What then was the reason for the spectacular and universal collapse of state socialism in East–Central Europe at the end of the 1980s?

To answer this question, we have to uncover several different layers of a rather complex historical phenomenon. The first layer may be found in economic performance. If an impressive growth rate, a "catching up," and increased incomes at first provided some legitimization and acceptance, the decline began when these economic sources of support dried up. This did not happen all at once. The first stage at the time was not easily perceived and emerged near the end of the 1960s. At this point the benefits of the extensive import-substituting industrialization, the ruling economic policy in the region, were exhausted. The relative success and rapid growth in these backward, agricultural countries was mostly achieved. Surplus rural labor had fueled the transfer from lower to higher productivity branches, chiefly from agriculture and households to industry. Forced capital accumulation by means of a high investment rate was needed to create newer and better jobs. The model, which is more appropriate in backward countries than in advanced ones, worked until labor reserves were depleted and the second stage of import substitution, i.e., building up the investment goods or heavy industries led to a major restructuring. The second stage came at a very high price. Environmental destruction, technological backwardness, and a neglect of modern infrastructure had tragic consequences in the later decades. Some of the countries, especially Hungary and Czechoslovakia, realized the need for change. They sought to correct the severe mistakes of "extensive" economic growth based on utilizing surplus labor and replace it by "intensive" development based on increased productivity, i.e. technological development and rationalization. This new approach was emphasized in the preparation of economic reforms in both countries in the mid-1960s (Batt 1988).

Since "extensive" sources of growth had dried up, there was a general slowing down throughout East–Central Europe. As a consequence, the economies of the Council of Mutual Economic Assistance (CMEA) could not supply each other with all the products and modern technology that would continue to fuel economic growth. The degree of regional self-sufficiency decreased and the countries were forced to turn toward the world market. Overall, CMEA trade began to decrease from between two-thirds and three-quarters of total trade. In cases, especially Poland, Hungary, and Romania, the trade share of CMEA countries changed radically during the 1970s and 1980s, gradually dropping to 40–44 per cent (*International Trade Statistics Yearbook* 1988: 1044, 1990: 409–10). Trade on the world market, which was once marginal, now became an organic part of economic life.

This transformation had tremendous consequences. The Soviet model of forced, import-substituting industrialization was primarily based on national and regional autarchy. Only in this environment could it achieve impressive growth and major structural changes. These newly industrializing countries did not have to compete with more advanced economies in an open world market. For the relatively small countries national self-sufficiency was out of question. If the cut-throat world market gained an equal position in their trade with the closed, non-competitive CMEA market, they would be forced to export in competition, thus rendering the continuation of import-substitution impossible. A trade reorientation required the reshaping of the entire economic strategy, an export orientation took the place of import-substitution.

Recognizing the need for change occurred slowly: the first party resolution with the aim of replacing an import-substitution with an export-oriented strategy was made in Hungary in October 1977 (Berend 1990: 240–2). The new economic strategy, however, remained wishful thinking and was never implemented. Most other countries, however, never even recognized the need for a new strategy. But this was no time to hesitate. The 1973 oil crisis, and the second oil shock in 1980, revealed a gradually emerging structural crisis in the world economy that was being generated by a whole set of major technological changes. A kind of "creative destruction" along Schumpeterian lines hit the whole world economy, but especially the less-developed countries. The latter suffered from this destructive wave, but were unable to respond creatively on their own. Older leading sectors declined in the crisis, but new leading industries based on new technology failed to emerge.

The 1980s were devastating for those countries that could not adjust and restructure their trade and production. The consequences were surprisingly similar in Latin America and in East–Central Europe. State socialism, however, created a special, additional obstacle. The quasi-religious post-Stalinist ideology, the notorious equation of the Soviet model with socialism, and the rigid rejection of structural or even policy changes as revisionism or diabolic attempts to restore capitalism formed an unbreakable wall against change. In addition, the Soviet Union as a powerful police force watched, controlled, and for a long time blocked the road toward radical changes in East–Central Europe. The military intervention in Czechoslovakia in 1968 and the pressure on Poland that led to the introduction of the Martial Law in 1981 discouraged any effective adjustment in the region as a whole during this crucial time.

Although they were able to prevent adjustments in the region, the Soviets could not halt the erosion of the system from the mid-1970s. State socialism had lost all its previous advantages and modernizing dynamism. The most direct indicator of this erosion is the per capita growth of output, i.e., Gross National Product (GNP) or Gross Domestic Product (GDP). Most calculations, which strongly corrected official and, in all cases, highly distorted statistics clearly show that the "catching up" trend in East–Central Europe dramatically reversed around 1973. Based on Paul Bairoch's somewhat controversial data (Bairoch 1976: 307), the six East–Central European, state-socialist countries (Czechoslovakia, Hungary, Poland, Romania, Yugoslavia, and Bulgaria) had an average per capita GNP of 497 dollars in 1950 (in 1960 dollars), which represented 66 per cent of the 749-dollar European average. In 1973, the six countries had on average an income of 1738 dollars, more than three times higher than a quarter of a century before and 83 per cent of the European average.

Angus Maddison's newest estimates (Maddison 1990: 2, 6) place East–Central Europe in broad comparative perspective. Between 1913 and 1950 these countries comprised the slowest growing region of the world. Their average growth rate of 1 per cent per capita GNP remained behind the growth of the advanced European "core" countries (1.3 per cent), the non-European "core" countries (1.4 per cent), Latin America (1.4 per cent) and even Africa (1.2 per cent); only Asia had a slower growth (−0.1 per cent). In contrast, between 1950 and 1973, East–Central Europe could boast the best performance: its unprecedented growth rate of 3.9 per cent per capita surpassed the growth rate of the European and non-European "core" (3.8 and 2.2 per cent respectively), and was also better than the very rapid Asian (3.7 per cent) and less impressive Latin-American (2.5 per cent) and African (1.7 per cent) growth rates. According to these calculations, East–Central Europe almost quadrupled its interwar rate of growth after 1945 and achieved a moderate "catching up."

After 1973 this trend entirely changed. The countries of state socialism could not cope with the monumental structural crisis and lost their dynamism. According to the World Bank's figures (*World Tables* 1989–1990: 24–5) Hungary's annual per capita GDP growth of 6 per cent until the late 1970s, suddenly dropped to 1.6 per cent and 0.0 per cent in 1979 and 1980. Poland, strongly connected with its deep political crisis as well, had a −10.0 per cent and −4.8 per cent decline in 1981 and 1982. The growth rate of Yugoslavia, which previously had fluctuated, but was rapid, slowed to 1.2 in 1981, and 0.6 in 1982 and declined by −1.1 per cent in 1983.

Between 1973 and 1987 the annual economic growth of East–Central Europe dropped from 3.9 per cent to 1.9 per cent, the same rate as that of the European "core" but a much slower rate than the still high Asian rate of 3.7 per cent. By 1988 slow growth or stagnation had already turned into severe decline. Moreover, overall growth in the Western world reflected rather different patterns than in East–Central Europe. In the West there was a sharp decline from the mid-1970s to the early 1980s. That was the shock of adjustment, the "destruction" part of Schumpeter's "creative destruction." This adjustment led to a new prosperity from the early 1980s on.

In East–Central Europe decline was delayed because governments did not recognize the changes and for ideological reasons continued their previous economic policy of forcing rapid growth. The accompanying high rate of growth in foreign trade (in the mid-1970s exports as a per cent of GDP reached 48 per cent in Hungary, and 20–25 per cent in Poland, Yugoslavia, and Romania) ultimately created problems. The antiquated technology and obsolete export structure brought on by previous policies of import-substitution led to a permanent decline in the terms of trade. In the five years after the first oil shock, some of the East–Central European countries, e.g. Hungary, suffered nearly a 20 per cent decline, while others, e.g. Czechoslovakia and Yugoslavia, experienced a decline of around 10 per cent. Deterioration, however, continued in the 1980s and led to a drop of about 30–35 per cent in the Czechoslovak and Hungarian cases. In the early 1980s, therefore, some of the East–Central European countries had to export roughly one-third more for the same amount of imports compared with before 1973 (*Statistical Yearbook* 1990: 666). The continued forcing of rapid growth in the 1970s thus undermined the economies of East–Central Europe by creating an ever increasing trade deficit.

The trade deficit became a source of serious trouble in a double sense. First, the crisis gradually deepened and lengthened. Growth increasingly slowed down, and output ultimately stagnated and declined. In the crucial years of 1986–1989 the annual per capita GDP growth in Hungary was 0.9, in Poland 0.2, in Yugoslavia 0.5, and in Romania 0.7 per cent. In contrast, the OECD countries achieved an annual growth of 3.6 per cent in these four years. The gap between East–Central Europe and the advanced world, which had narrowed until the mid-1970s, began to widen. The major difference, however, was that East–Central Europe failed to adjust by restructuring; in Schumpeterian terms the destruction did not generate a creative response.

Secondly, the accumulated trade deficit required a financial solution. The countries that wanted to maintain their growth rate and standard of living had to turn to the international credit market from 1974 on. They surmised that they needed only stop-gap measures to bridge a few years of temporary difficulty before economic prosperity continued. This short-sighted policy had a disastrous backlash. On top of the structural crisis, a debt crisis emerged. By the end of the 1970s, Hungary, Poland, Romania, and Bulgaria accumulated huge debts of between 6 to 18 billion dollars each. From that time on, indebtedness became self-generating and accelerated in the 1980s. By 1990 net debt levels reached 41.8 billion dollars in Poland, 20.3 billion dollars in Hungary, and 9.8 billion dollars in Bulgaria. Although on a per capita basis, indebtedness was the highest in Hungary (2,585 dollars compared with 1,100 dollars in Poland, and 1,068 dollars in Bulgaria), Hungary remained the only country that was able to carry the tremendous burden with regular repayments. At the end of the 1980s total debt in Hungary was about twice as high as the value of exports, while in Bulgaria and Poland the corresponding figures three and five times respectively. Debt service at the end of the 1980s, consumed 40 per cent of Hungarian and 75 per cent of the Bulgarian hard-currency income from exports (*World Development Report*

1987: 239, 1988: 259, 1989: 211). High indebtedness bankrupted such East–Central European countries as Poland, Yugoslavia, and Bulgaria and forced them to ask for rescheduling. Indebtedness, furthermore, seriously hindered any adjustment to the crisis, because the 5–8 per cent of the GNP that drained out from the countries was not available for investment. Most of the new credits served repayment of the old ones. For example, from the more than 20 billion dollars of Hungarian debt, only about 4–5 billion dollars was actually invested in the economy.

What happened in East–Central Europe between the mid-1970s and the late 1980s was not unique. African growth declined from its already slow rate of 1.7 per cent between 1950 and 1973, to 0.3 per cent from 1973 to 1987, and Latin American growth decreased from 2.5 to 0.8 per cent in the two periods. The economies of Latin America showed other striking similarities to those of East–Central Europe. In the context of slower growth, they, too, experienced dramatic rises in their trade deficits and indebtedness. The total amount of debt in Brazil, Mexico, and Argentina was three to five times the level of exports, and the annual debt service consumed 50 to 62 per cent of export incomes in the late 1980s (Maddison 1985: 46–50).

Latin America and East–Central Europe show a common reaction to the structural crisis of the world economy. The consequences, including the political ones, reflected certain similarities as well. Economic crisis in both cases led to political crisis and, in the end, to the collapse of dictatorial regimes. A painful adjustment policy was introduced, with quite similar agendas including marketization and privatization.

The consequences in East–Central Europe were, however, even more far-reaching. State socialism was not just another form of dictatorship but was, even in its post-Stalinist form, a regime that ruled every sphere of life, including practically the entire economy. The deepening economic crisis undermined the transitory legitimacy of the regimes that they gained mostly in the 1960s and 1970s. The surplus income that had been redistributed by the state disappeared as economic growth vanished. The moderate but steady increase in living standards ceased, the welfare state lost its foundations, and the low but stable level of security provided by full employment – free medical and educational services – became uncertain. The emerging economic disaster gradually led to a complete crisis of the regime.

The climax arrived in the late 1980s when the external guarantor of the regime weakened and collapsed. State socialism, as Václav Havel rightly underlined (1985: 25), differed from a "regular" dictatorship, because its military strength did not rest on internal foundations but on the power of the Soviet Union. It was futile to question or challenge this situation, or to wait for any kind of internal explosion or foreign intervention. The over-ambitious Soviet expansionism during the reign of Leonid Brezhnev, however, met its Waterloo. The military strength and economic foundations of the Soviet Union were undermined by the erosion and decline of its economic model and economic power. The Soviet Union, in short, lost the cold war because it did not have the economic resources to keep up with a new technology that continuously transformed military technology and required ongoing, costly modernization. Mikhael Gorbachev had the ability to recognize this and the courage to draw the correct conclusion. He withdrew from Afghanistan and detached foreign policy from the ideology of the class struggle. The Brezhnev doctrine died in the late 1980s.

Combined with declining internal economies and eroding political power, the dramatic deterioration of external Soviet control undermined state socialism in East–Central Europe. Mass support dwindled. Perhaps even more important, the regime entirely lost the younger generations that kept away from the previously compulsory official youth organizations in the 1980s and failed to join the Party, e.g. in Poland and Hungary. In 1970 one-quarter of the members of the Polish Communist party was under the age of 30, but by 1985 its share declined to less than 7 per cent, and in Hungary its share was 7.5 per cent (*Rocznik Statystyczny* 1988: 34; *Adatok a Pártról* 1985: 12). The erosion of the system in the 1970s and 1980s was thus accompanied by an important generational change.

Pre-World War II generations survived the hardship of the Great Depression, the horrors of fascism, German occupation and war, and millions of families had to start a new life from scratch. As adults they went through the most frightening experience of the last years of Stalinism. These were the generations of the purges who had to worry about the sound of automobile brakes and the doorbell ringing at dawn. At one time or another, they experienced the euphoria that comes with liberation: liberation from the nightmare of war, liberation from deep peasant misery, from the isolation of an adobe hut stuck in the mud, from the backwardness of the East–Central European villages without electricity and one-class schools, from the abuses of minority status. They appreciated such basic achievements as having a proper diet, a secure job, low, but guaranteed levels of health care and pensions, or a new home where extended families no longer crowded together under one roof and washed-up from a tin basin. They had the excitement of having a modern bathroom with running hot water, of watching their first television broadcast, and of owning their first automobile. They felt privileged when allowed to travel abroad to see Paris and Rome. They welcomed the "gifts" of post-Stalinist liberalization, the wiping out of discrimination in university admissions, and a more tolerant cultural policy. These people knew in their bones that things had been much worse, and could be worse, and they were ready to make compromises to keep what they had. They accepted the limitations and cautiously avoided asking certain questions that were "uncomfortable" for the regime or challenged unquestionable taboos.

In contrast, those who were born after 1945 reached their twenties and thirties in the 1970s. A 30-year-old in the late 1980s was born in the late

1950s and began secondary school training in the early 1970s. The post-1945 generations had entirely different life experiences and expectations.

They were free from the fears of their fathers that were rooted in their pasts. The young accepted as normal that which the old regarded as a magnificent achievement. They longed for more and for something rather different: to gain more independence and freedom and to be rid of crippling mediocrity. They were attracted by the enticing life-styles, freedom, and affluence of the West. They wanted to make up their own minds and, unlike their parents, they very much liked to ask "delicate" questions and challenge taboos. The conforming behavior that seemed natural to the old ran counter to human nature according to the young. The younger generation was not happy with the East German two-cylinder Trabant and admired "real" Western cars. They often suffered under their bosses in their jobs, because half of the managerial positions were occupied by political appointees who lacked the appropriate education and qualifications. They suffered from the lack of mobility that characterized state-socialist regimes from the 1970s on when the industrialization drive slowed down. In short, the new post-war generations were alienated from the regime. They did not accept it as inevitable nor did they sympathize with the idea that it was better than what came before. They provided a reservoir of non-political apathy, but also a source of active opposition.

The erosion of state socialism unleashed all kinds of opposition to the regime. The revolts against existing state socialism took three major forms: the organized, militant mass movement most characteristic of Poland, the passive intellectual and moral resistance typical of post-1968 Czechoslovakia, and the "reform-from-within and from above" pattern, most successful in Hungary. Of course, these were often linked or even combined with each other from the mid-1950s on, as they gained momentum. In the changing internal and international environment of the 1980s, all three patterns were strengthened to an impressive degree, especially in Poland and Hungary. In contrast, the orthodox, non-reforming regimes in a horizontal chain from East Germany via Czechoslovakia and Romania to Bulgaria successfully resisted until the very last moment.

Historical events became quite dramatic in Poland. In the late 1970s, the availability of goods and services sharply deteriorated. When the government announced price increases on certain goods in the summer of 1980, strikes erupted and spread spontaneously like wildfire. In August the shipyards and ports of Gdańsk became the real center of the movement. On August 14 a strike committee was founded, headed by Lech Wałęsa, an electrician of the Lenin-shipyard. The agreements with the government recognized the existence of new unions as an "authentic representative of the working class." From mass resistance and open confrontation a peaceful revolution emerged (Garton Ash 1983). Its genuinely charismatic and talented leaders were religious workers and former Communists who had long ago become "dissident" intellectuals. Although basically uncompromising, they still knew the limitations of their power. As Bronisław Geremek, a historian and one of the heros of the Polish revolution, argued: the limits were provided by the movement of the Soviet tanks. The steadfast readiness of the Polish workers to struggle and strike, and the mature willingness of their leaders to participate in a political dialogue, led to the "self-limiting revolution," as Jadwiga Staniszkis (1984) called it, which promised a peaceful pluralization of the regime. The representatives of the new trade unions gathered in Gdańsk on 17 September and founded the united, nation-wide organization of "Solidarnosć." About three million people joined. In the stormy days of 1980–81, the Government turned towards reform, but the accepted plan (July 1981) contained an inconsistent set of idealistic proposals. The most precise part of it was the law on self-management. It was too little and too late. The Polish economy was already spiraling into decline and chaos. Wage increases fueled demand and generated a "shortage-spiral" that led to the total collapse of the market. Poland could not carry the burden of repayment of credits, and was the first among the indebted countries to ask for rescheduling. Crisis and decline became unparalleled (Mizsei 1990).

The chaotic situation became the arena of an ever-sharpening struggle for power. The rise of Solidarity alarmed the conservative wing of the party and the secret police. An open confrontation exploded after the Bydgoszcz incident in March 1981. Solidarity stopped negotiating with the government and prepared a general strike for 31 March. The party's Politburo declared on 22 March that the "foundation of the socialist system is in danger." The Soviet Communist party sent an open letter to the Polish party and accused it of retreating in the face of an "advancing counterrevolution." The letter also stated: "We will not desert the brotherly socialist Poland in trouble" (*Zyćie Warszawy* 1981).

On the other hand, Solidarity became radicalized as well. The "self-limiting Polish revolution" reached its end. In October 1981 several spontaneous strikes flooded the country, and the leadership of Solidarity, which struggled for the control of the movement, organized a general warning strike. Wałęsa himself spoke about an "unavoidable confrontation."

In the deepening crisis, the military wing of the leadership was strengthened. In February 1981 General Wojtech Jaruzelski, the minister of defense, became prime minister and soon took over the party leadership. As a consequence of permanent Soviet pressure, the preparation for a military take-over began.

On 11–12 December the National Committee of Solidarity gathered in Gdańsk. In the same hours Soviet army units were already mobilized. Jaruzelski did not hesitate to act: on 13 December the Polish army made its strange coup d'état, or more precisely, the Communist party with the help of the obedient army introduced martial law. Solidarity was outlawed and thousands of its activists arrested. Communication was cut off and the whole economy was taken under the control of the army.

The Jaruzelski putsch, however, did not introduce a "regular" military dictatorship. It was a bitter attempt of the party–state to get breathing space and, behind the shield of force, to introduce major reforms and consolidate the country's economic and political situation. Jaruzelski's ideal was János Kádár and the post-1956 Hungarian model. The party–military government immediately declared its commitments to the social contracts and economic reforms. Having destroyed the organized workers' opposition, the military government introduced a major price reform on 1 January 1982. Further major progressive reform steps followed, including institutionalized incentives to promote private and foreign investments and business activity. The belated Polish reform, however, could not work in this rather difficult situation. The government had to fail because it lacked legitimacy in the minds of the bulk of society, it was isolated by a Western boycott and burdened by high debts. János Kádár's "miracle" was not to be repeated in Poland.

A price-wage spiral generated accelerated inflation: from 6.7 per cent in 1979 it jumped to 101.5 per cent in 1982. The government consequently did not want to take the risk of an even more alienating hyperinflation, and reintroduced price controls. Several other steps counterbalanced the market-oriented reforms as well. Jaruzelski's government, in spite of certain temporary results, could not create an efficient economic system, and the country descended into a new crisis in 1986.

The rather benign military dictatorship, which was a desperate last-ditch attempt at party–state rule, could not and did not intend to use naked terror, especially since the second half of the 1980s when a different Soviet policy – the rejection of the Brezhnev doctrine and the introduction of glasnost and perestroika – came into existence. Because the monolithic rule of the party–state based on military power was only justifiable by the possibility and real danger of a Soviet military intervention, the military regime lost its last legitimacy and self-confidence. Gorbachev's opening was the final blow to the Polish regime, which was no longer able to justify its rule, even to its own elite. The party–military regime, put into power to provide breathing space, became the parting breath of Polish state socialism.

Events unfolded quickly. When new waves of strikes began in May and in August 1988, the government could only turn back to negotiations and bargaining. Secret talks had already begun in 1987, and Solidarity gradually returned to the scene. President Jaruzelski and prime minister Rakowski still hoped to retain some kind of shared power. The presumption of Soviet danger still did not disappear from the Polish minds, and Solidarity was ready for compromise. An uncertain party wanted to save the handle of the lost hatchet, and was thus ready to give a certain parliamentary role to Solidarity. The round-table talks led to a new compromise: the parties agreed to a semi-free election in June 1989, which allowed free elections for the less important upper house (the Senate), and assured 35 per cent of the seats for independent candidates in the Seim, the decision making parliament. The agreement also guaranteed a strong executive power in the hands of the Communist president.

The "good bargain," however, proved to be the last miscalculation of the party–state. The June election led to a landslide victory for Solidarity, which gained 99 of the 100 seats in the Senate and all the independent seats of the Seim. The humiliating defeat of the Communist party–state was completed. There is small wonder that it led to the appointment of Tadeusz Mazowiecki, the very first non-Communist prime minister of the region since 1947–48. His Solidarity-led government applied the so-called shock therapy to the economy. A total Solidarity take-over was only a question of time. The peaceful transformation of power took another two years and was crowned by the parliamentary elections in 1991.

Parallel with the Polish collapse, the same political avalanche occurred in Hungary between 1988 and 1990. If the Polish events were a consequence of an open confrontation between the Communists and the non-Communist opposition, the collapse of state socialism in Hungary shows a rather different pattern. There was no strong, organized mass opposition in the 1970s and 1980s. The confrontation occurred within the party, between the centrist–conservatives and the faction favoring "reform-from-within." The latter had a long and strong tradition in the country going back to Imre Nagy. Although his reform wing was defeated after 1956, many reformists remained in the party and started to play an important role again from the mid-1960s on. The breakthrough of the most radical reform in the region, however, was followed by a counter-attack against reform in late 1973, with the help of the Soviet, East German, and Czechoslovak parties. All the leading reformists, including Rezsö Nyers, Lajos Fehér, and prime minister Jenö Fock, were dismissed from the Politburo and Government. In face of increasing economic decline and indebtedness, the center of the party turned back to reforms at the end of the 1970s. A new price reform was instituted in two stages. The most significant new step of the early 1980s was the legalization of the "second economy," which in a subtle way granted a green light to grass-roots privatization. The private or semi-private firms (state owned but leased and privately run) in the "second economy" formed a dominant sector in the early 1980s and involved about three-quarters of active earners. In the mid-1980s about 80 per cent of construction output, 60 per cent of service output, one-third of agricultural production, and 15 per cent of industrial output were produced by private business – overall about one-third of the GNP.

In April 1984, the autonomy of firms was guaranteed by introducing elected company councils and the election of top managers. The monopoly of the National Bank was abolished and a two-level banking system was introduced in 1987, as well as a modern value added taxation of the firms and a comprehensive, progressive personal income tax (Berend 1990: 259–90).

The reform breakthroughs of the 1980s, although impressive, were still unable to create a flexible market economy. The Hungarian reform remained the "most radical half-measure." In the crisis situation, permanent state interventions worked against the reform. The government did not risk unpopular measures. It continuously subsidized deficit-producing firms in order to avoid bankruptcies, tried to keep full employment, and at least slow down the decline in the standard of living. The crisis was not solved and the inevitable, dramatic measures were postponed.

The militant reformers in the intelligentsia and radical party reformers gained new strength and inspiration from Gorbachev's glasnost and perestroika from the mid-1980s on. They felt that the door had at last opened and that the strongest obstacle to further reform had disappeared. It became more and more visible that the aging and strongly sclerotic secretary general Kádár and his old centrist–conservative guard were the real impediment to radical reforms. The reformists, moreover, realized that without an institutionalized change in the monolithic political structures, ongoing radical reform was impossible. From the early 1980s, the need for political reform and a major revision of obsolete ideology was clear. The reform wing was activated and became more aggressive. Besides Rezsö Nyers, the living symbol of reform, Imre Pozsgay, an agile and ambitious new reform leader, emerged and championed democratization. The Pozsgay group sought to secure an agreement with a strengthening opposition. It is true, as William Echikson argues, that "the few dissidents who existed in 1987 Hungary found it hard to fill a private coffeehouse" (Echikson 1992: 427). They, however, expressed the disappointment of the majority of the population, and became more radical. In remote Lakitelek on 27 September 1987 a meeting, inspired by the populist opposition, brought together representatives of different opposition groups. The opening speech was delivered by Pozsgay who stressed that ". . . it is time to work out . . . comprehensive and radical reform, including ownership relations . . . and political relations . . . [The reforms up to now] remained actions of an enlightened absolutist power circle . . . We have to go beyond this concept . . . The barriers have to sweep away first in the political arena . . ." Pozsgay criticized the party–state system and suggested a constitutional change by introducing a true constitutional state with a legislative role for the parliament, with local self-government, and with a referendum system on major national issues to create a new "national coalition" (Pozsgay 1991: 39–41). The "reform-from-within" opposition took control and went far beyond its previous, more limited agenda. The pressure to hold an extraordinary party congress (two years before its regular time) became strong, and in May 1988 a nation-wide party conference was held and swept away the entire "old guard," including János Kádár and the majority of his Politburo. Leading reformers, Rezsö

Nyers and Imre Pozsgay, replaced them in the Politburo, and one-third of the Central Committee was changed. The victory of the reform wing was not total, however. The key position of secretary general was filled by the pragmatic conservative Károly Grósz. Some other transition figures also remained on the stage. The party conference, nevertheless, declared the goals of mixed public/private ownership, a market economy, political pluralism (without clarifying what this meant), and a constitutional state.

There were a series of "minor turning points." Secretary-general and prime minister Grósz was replaced by the unambiguously and radical reform-oriented government of Miklós Németh and by a collective "quadriga" of party leaders (Nyers, Pozsgay, Németh, and Grósz). In February 1989 the Central Committee debated a reassessment of the 1956 revolution. Against the traditional label of "counter-revolution," it accepted the idea that it was a genuine people's uprising that emerged against the Stalinist Hungarian regime and because of an immediate Soviet military intervention, "the uprising became a fight for national independence . . ." (Berend 1989: 32). The revised view of 1956 heralded a dramatic change. Indeed, the same session of the Central Committee approved the ideas of a multi-party system and of free elections.

Opposition groups, which had not been able to play a decisive role up to that point, were now legalized and began to form dozens of new parties. The Smallholder and Social Democrat parties of the interwar era were reorganized, the Hungarian Democratic Forum emerged from the Lakitelek gathering, and liberal democrats founded both the Free Democrat Alliance and the Federation of Young Democrats. Round-table sessions with impressive participation levels increased the momentum for further changes. A formal opposition began to play an important role from that time on.

The "reform-from-within" opposition which had practically taken over the government became more active. The Németh government introduced radical deregulation and cleared the road for private enterprise: limitations on employees in private business were abolished and privatization began, including open invitations to foreign investors. Price and import liberalization promoted marketization. The parliament abolished the "peoples republic" and reestablished the Hungarian republic, with essential changes in the constitution. Freedom of press was guaranteed. In the Spring of 1989 the government ordered the destruction of the "Iron Curtain" at the Austrian border and soon opened Hungary's borders to tens of thousands of East German refugees.

In the summer, the leader of the 1956 revolution, Imre Nagy, as well as his comrades executed with him in 1958, were reburied. Three weeks later, on the very day that the Hungarian Supreme Court announced Imre Nagy's full legal rehabilitation, János Kádár died. "Shakespeare would not have risked such a crude tragic irony" (Garton Ash 1992). The two burials emotionally and symbolically closed a historical period. Kádár's Hungarian Socialist

Workers party did not survive its founder for long. It abolished itself in October 1989, with its reform majority creating the Hungarian Socialist party on a social democratic platform. An undisturbed free election was held in March 1990. The idea of "reform-from-within" and the reform wing of the party tried to transform the system and create a democratic, pluralistic socialism, but instead they promoted the collapse of socialism. A well-structured opposition dominated the political arena, and a coalition of right of center parties formed the new government. The peaceful reform–revolution, or as Timothy Garton Ash called it, the "refolution," was completed.

The Polish and Hungarian collapse in 1988–89 had a penetrating impact all over East–Central Europe. Regimes were totally discredited: both bitter military solutions (Polish Martial Law) and methodical, even partially successful reforms (such as the Hungarian ones) had failed and led to spectacular collapses. An accidental event was enough to have a "domino effect." When Hungary opened her borders to the East German refugees, tens of thousands cascaded into the country. Endless demonstrations flooded Leipzig and Berlin and in November 1989 the Berlin Wall physically collapsed.

As the collapse of the Bastille in Paris two hundred years earlier symbolized the end of European feudalism, the collapse of the Berlin Wall meant the end of state socialism. Czechoslovakia, a hard-line country with a passive intellectual resistance, immediately followed. The country, where a traditional "Svejkian" passive resistance was reckoned as a "national characteristic," whose people neither resisted Nazi occupation nor fired a shot against invading Warsaw Pact troops in 1968, suddenly experienced endless mass demonstrations and open resistance. The small but highly moral and important opposition of Charta 77, which emphasized a non-political but humanistic–moral trend, suddenly emerged as an alternative political force and its humanist–idealist leader, Václav Havel, became a genuinely charismatic leader. The turning point came on 17 November, with the biggest demonstration of post-1968 Czechoslovakia. About 30,000–50,000 young people, mostly students, organized a peaceful demonstration to celebrate the fiftieth anniversary of the death of Jan Opletal, the Czech student martyr of the Nazi occupation, to protest against oppression and actively support the ideals of freedom and truth. The young people thus took up the banner of the opposition, but changed its methods and tactics by going to the streets. The demonstration was attacked with unprecedented brutality by the riot police, but in the next few days tens of thousands protested in Prague, Bratislava, and Brno. The police were not used again. On 20 November, and again on 21 November, 200,000 people demonstrated in Prague and heard Václav Havel in the heart of the city. On 23 November 300,000 people flooded the streets of Prague while 50,000 gathered in Bratislava to hear Dubček for the first time in 21 years. On 27 November a general strike took place in the cities all over the country. In those stormy days a united opposition, the Civic Forum, was founded on the rock-solid basis of Charta 77. By their existence and high moral status, the opposition and its leaders gained tremendous importance and were automatically recognized as true leaders and representatives of the people.

It is worth mentioning that during these revolutionary days, Tadeusz Mazowiecki, Solidarity's prime minister, paid his first official visit to Moscow and signed a joint statement on 27 November. It repeated prime minister Ryzhkov's word: the Soviet Union "does not impose its recipes . . . on anyone and respects the right of each nation to freedom of choice." Gorbachev, in his toast at the official banquet, proclaimed: "It might surprise some people that I wish you success" (*Radio Free Europe* 1989: 14–15). The Czechoslovak Communist party, which sought to make concessions to the people by replacing first Jakes and then seven other members of the Politburo, at last gave up and agreed to all the demands of the opposition. The Federal Assembly modified the constitution and eliminated the leading role of the Communist party. A coalition government was appointed, followed in early December by one comprised of an opposition majority. After the resignation of Gustav Husak on 29 December, Václav Havel was elected president of the republic.

Bulgaria and Romania followed in a few weeks (Frankland 1990: 297–333). In two years Yugoslavia exploded, Albania successfully revolted and even the Soviet Union abolished state socialism and itself.

Living in the present and still lacking a proper historical distance on the era, it is certainly too early to try to evaluate the consequences of the collapse of state socialism in East–Central Europe. The initial euphoria and hope regarding a united, free and prosperous Europe and a just new world order based on cooperation as opposed to confrontation, and the belief in a huge "peace dividend" at the end of the cold war, are all evaporating in a surprisingly short time. A historian cannot predict the future, but may try to recognize long-term historical trends in the present and demonstrate some alternatives implicit in them.

The transition to a private, free market economy and parliamentary democracy has begun in East–Central Europe. Free elections were followed by the development of a more differentiated political arena, and freedom of the press and human rights are assured. A new legal and institutional framework, following the Western pattern, is in the making. A difficult and painful transition had its initial success in Hungary, Poland, and Czechoslovakia. Macroeconomic stabilization, a prerequisite of successful transition, had also some important results. There are still no hyperinflations in the region, and a genuine, grassroots privatization led to the foundation of millions of small and medium size private firms. The availability of goods and services has improved as well. A part of the large state-owned companies have already been sold, and there is some important foreign investment in potential leading sectors. Political and economic ties with the Western world are developing impressively. There is a possibility that the Western rim of East–Central Europe, led by the Hungarian–Czech–Polish "triangle" (some newly created countries may join them) would gradually create the conditions for a piecemeal integration to the European Community.

Other parts of East–Central Europe have less opportunities and more problems. The Yugoslavian multinational state has disintegrated. Unsolvable minority questions have already led to civil wars and further turmoil may come. Macroeconomic stabilization has not been brought to several countries and there is a strong popular resistance against market prices and the inevitable price increases. There is little tolerance toward social inequalities and a great suspicion regarding private business. Transition is a painful and slow process and the majority of the population has lost its security and previously acquired living standards. There is a strong resistance against accepting the East–Central European countries in the European Community and a lack of interest in offering a kind of Marshall Plan to help them ease the transition. Because of chaotic economic circumstances and political uncertainties, capital investment is limited and often motivated by a desire for achieving quick profits without long-term investment. A high inflation rate (between 30 and 500 per cent), steeply declining production and national income, increasing poverty, a double-digit unemployment rate and a rapid disorganization of a previously existing social safety net have jolted these societies. An entrepreneurial elite is emerging and skillful speculators are exploiting the situation. Social differences are increasing sharply, and many of the ugly features of early capitalism have appeared. There is a deep disappointment in the society. If economic improvement is delayed, and if conditions worsen for some years to come, people may lose their hope and the present social discontent may turn into a hotbed of bitter revolt.

The forces that are ready to act are already present. Extreme nationalism, conservative autocratism, an increasing role of the church along with an effort to reconnect it with certain state functions, right-wing populism, xenophobia, and anti-semitism are appearing in the vacuum created by the collapse of Communism. These trends appear elsewhere, but are marginal in most European countries. However, further humiliation, economic decline, and disorder might give impetus to their spread. Border and minority questions that have been unsolvable in this "belt of mixed population" are already unleashing irrational emotions and armed rebellions. They are reinforcing each other and might lead to an endless threat of local conflicts and civil wars.

Discredited state socialism may be easily replaced by other kinds of extremism and authoritarianism.

In this scenario, the European Community would remain an exclusive club. East–Central Europe, or the greater part of it, would be integrated into Europe as the periphery of the advanced core. It would supply the EC with cheap labor and certain products, while staying at a much lower income level as a subordinated economy with an increasing gap compared with the West. An "economic iron curtain" might survive and separate East and West. East–Central Europe's interwar right-wing march and post-war left-wing adventure may become an historical detour that began and ended on the European periphery.

In reality, both the optimistic and pessimist scenarios may be realized in one or other areas of East–Central Europe. In either case history "matters:" because the same forces that led to the failure of modernization along Western lines in the nineteenth century and caused the collapse of an anti-Western modernization attempt in the twentieth century, might generate new revolts in the next century. History may repeat itself because failed attempts at modernization may have a strong backlash and could push the pendulum towards the other extreme.

To break through from peripheral backwardness in the age of a demanding structural crisis is one of history's most difficult tasks. Only a few of the best prepared countries, those that already have a higher level of economic development, a favorable educational and cultural environment, and more developed market institutions have a well-founded hope of accomplishing this.

NOTES

1 An old East European joke expressed it in the following way: Under capitalism, governments collapse but the system remains; under socialism, governments remain but the system collapses.

REFERENCES

Adatok a Pártról [Data on the Party]. (1985) Budapest.

Batt, J. (1988) *Economic Reform and Political Changes in Eastern Europe. Comparison of the Czechoslovak and Hungarian Experiences*, London.

Bairoch, P. (1976) Europe's gross national product: 1800–1975," *The Journal of European Economic History*, 5: 243–340.

Berend, I.T. (1989) "Történelmi utunk" [Our historical road]. Statement on the causes of the existing situation by the Working Commission. *Társadalmi Szemle*, Különszám (Special edition), Budapest.

Berend, I.T. (1990) *The Hungarian Economic Reforms 1953–1988*, Cambridge.

Economic Survey of Europe in 1989–1990 (1991), New York.

Echikson, W. (1992) "Bloc buster," in L.H. Legters (ed.) *Eastern Europe. Transformation and Revolution, 1945–1991. Documents and Analyses*, Lexington, MA, Toronto.

Frankland, M. (1990) *The Patriot's Revolution. How East Europe Won its Freedom*, London.

Garton Ash, T. (1983) *The Polish Revolution. Solidarity 1980–1982*, London.

Garton Ash, T. (1992) "The last funeral" (from: The magic lantern), in L.H. Legters (ed.) *Eastern Europe. Transformation and Revolution, 1945–1991. Documents and Analyses*, Lexington, MA, Toronto.

Havel, V. (1985) "The power of the powerless," in J. Keane (ed.) *The Power of the Powerless: Citizens against the State*, London, Melbourne.

International Trade Statistics Yearbook 1986. (1988) vol. I, New York.

Maddison, A. (1985) *Two Crises: Latin America and Asia 1929–38 and 1973–83*, Paris.

Maddison, A. (1990) *Measuring European Growth: The Core and the Periphery*, Paper presented at the International Economic History Congress, Leuven, Belgium.

Mizsei, K. (1990) *Lengyelország. Válságok, reformpótlékok és reformok* [*Poland. Crises, Reform Substitutes and Reforms*], Budapest.

Pozsgay, I. (1992) Beszéd Lakitelken [Speech in Lakitelek] 27 September 1987 in the meeting on "A magyarság esélyei" [The chances of the Hungarians], *Társadalmi Szemle*, 2.

Radio Free Europe Research. (1989) 14 (50), 15 December.

Rocznik Statystyczny [*Statistical Yearbook*] *1988*. (1989) Warsaw.

Statistical Yearbook 1987. (1990) New York.

World Development Report 1987,1988,1989. (1987–9) Washington.

World Tables 1989–90. (1990) Washington.

˙ycie Warszawy. (June 11 1981) Warsaw.

6

THE RISE AND FALL OF YUGOSLAV SOCIALISM

A case study of the Yugo Automobile Enterprise 1954–92

Michael Palairet

During the 1950s and 1960s the Yugoslav economy grew rapidly, at roughly 6.6 per cent per annum between 1955 and 1971. In the 1970s growth decelerated, giving way by the early 1980s to secular decline.[1] Performance since 1978 looks particularly dismal when expressed in terms of output per worker, because employment expanded between 1978 and 1988 by 2.4 per cent per year.

The present literature on the performance of the Yugoslav economy is heavily orientated to the macroeconomic approach. This chapter, in contrast, attempts to throw light on the deterioration of the Yugoslav economy by studying the business history of a large manufacturing enterprise, the Zavodi Crvena Zastava, Yugoslavia's dominant automobile manufacturer. The performance of its automobile factory at Kragujevac in Serbia, when measured in terms of the number of cars leaving its production lines, closely shadowed the performance of the economy as a whole (see Figure 6.1). While the growth phase was based on the expansion of home market output, the deterioration at Zastava from the late 1970s was associated strongly with a drive to generate sales in hard currency. I argue that the role assigned for Zastava as a hard-currency earner undermined the enterprise, and that the resource waste entailed by this effort significantly worsened Yugoslavia's deep-seated economic crisis.

ZASTAVA AUTOMOBILES – AN HISTORICAL OVERVIEW

The Zastava automobile factory was established in 1954 within a run-down armaments works in downtown Kragujevac. Fearing closure for lack of orders, its management diversified into civil production (ZCZ 1973: 55; CZ 1 February 1980: 4). Cars seemed the most promising diversification, for there was plenty of pent-up home demand. Zastava failed to win the support

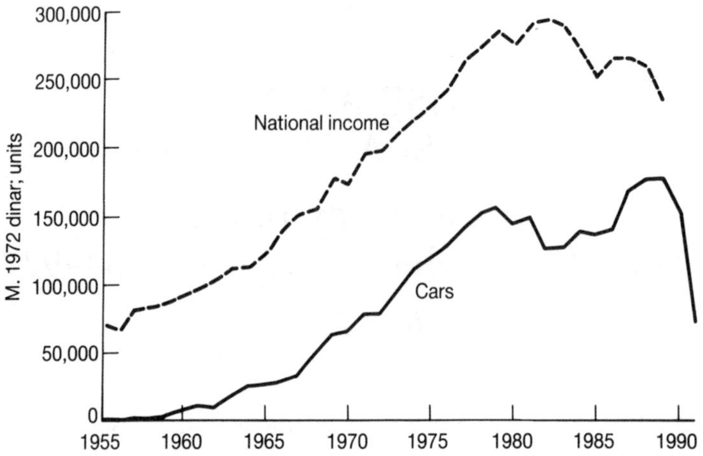

Figure 6.1 Adjusted national income and Zastava car output 1955–91

of the planners for car building, but the management secured a start-up investment by FIAT, under a contract of August 1954.[2]

In 1955 Zastava got a new boss, Engineer Prvoslav Raković, a first-rate manager who was determined to develop this small semi-mechanized operation into a fully fledged assembly plant (ZCZ 1973: 58). He did it in the face of unremitting obstruction by the planning apparat, which did not deem cars an appropriate product for building socialism (Miletić 1966). In 1959 Raković persuaded FIAT to invest 30 million dollars in a projected new factory, with capacity to produce 32,000 cars a year, mainly FIAT 600s, but (in defiance of the planners) with floorspace capable of producing 80,000. Production was transferred to the new factory in 1962 (ZCZ 1973: 61–4). Raković's foresight was vindicated because rising real incomes in Yugoslavia meant that Zastava had no problem selling its fast rising output.

In the mid-1960s, priorities changed throughout the Communist bloc; the Soviets and Poles began building large new auto plants. As the automobile industry had now won the socialist stamp of approval, Zastava received funding to boost its production capacity to around 80,000 cars. A further wave of expansion doubled capacity by 1972 to provide for the assembly of the new Z-101, a hatchback FIAT-128, designed at Turin at Raković's urging (Giacosa 1979: 290).

The Z-101 was built from much the same components as the FIAT sponsored Soviet Zhiguli (Lada) and the Polish 125P (Sedgwick 1974: 302–9; ZCZ 1975: 57–60). The idea, which was justified by events, was to enable the mutual exchange of components between the Soviets, the Poles, and the Yugoslavs that would yield scale economies in component costs. So Zastava became a major component supplier for Poland and the Soviets. The enterprise took payment in Ladas and Polish Fiats, which it sold on its home market.

Raković's longer-term aim (Phase 3) was to push capacity to 500,000 vehicles by 1977, establishing Zastava as a large-scale assembler of cars for export to COMECON markets, taking payment in components (CZ 16 November 1971). Phase 3, with FIAT backing and Soviet cooperation, was not "grandomanic," but a means of exploiting Yugoslavia's bridging position between East and West. In retrospect, it offered Zastava's only chance of long-run viability as an independent entity. It was not to be. Raković's "managerial" stance and ill-disguised contempt for the apparatchiks led to his sacking in late 1974. Milenko Bojanić, a party hack with no industrial experience, got the top job. Phase 3 was buried. The existing arrangements with Poland and the Soviets, although designed to minimize hard currency outlays by all participants, by no means extinguished them, because the component suppliers still had to import raw materials, rather than use low-grade inputs from domestic sources.

Besides this, Zastava was sliding inexorably into hard-currency debt. So too was the Yugoslav government, which borrowed recklessly during the oil crises of the 1970s to ward off recession. So the authorities exerted increasing pressure on Zastava to boost export sales to hard currency markets, and to surrender a rising proportion of its exchange earnings. A high-cost import substituter was to be turned by command into an internationally competitive car maker.

Unfortunately, neither the obsolescent Z-750 nor the workaday Z-101 were easy to export and a serious assault on Western markets required an up to date subcompact to meet both domestic and European tastes and pockets. Zastava therefore got FIAT to design a derivative of the 900cc FIAT-126. This vehicle was to emerge as the YUGO-45 (Micić 1983: 14–15). A new wave of investment accompanied the YUGO-45 program, to provide for a projected annual output of the new model that would build up to 125,000 units by 1985 (CZ 28 November 1980).[3] The YUGO began to roll off the production lines in November 1980. It was badly built, like all Zastava's cars, and bottlenecks of every kind limited output. Its sales abroad were disappointing. But by late 1982, Yugoslav goods cheapened in terms of hard currency, because the Planinc government continuously devalued the dinar at the behest of the International Monetary Fund (IMF), so as to force international payments into equilibrium. Yugoslavia's apparently low production costs attracted attention from foreign businessmen, who failed to take into account the inelasticity of supply from this still dangerously overheated economy.

In 1984, the lure of cheap supplies led Armand Hammer's Occidental to broker a swap of 500 million dollars in oil and hides against Zastava's

YUGO cars. The cars would be imported by Malcolm Bricklin, a flashy, fast moving "business visionary," with a patchy track record as a sports car importer (BW 11 February 1985). The original deal fell through (Lampe *et al.* 1990: 122–3) but Bricklin went ahead and set up a company, YUGO-America Inc. to mount a YUGO sales drive in the USA. The plans were ambitious: in a few years, it was projected, the American market would take the equivalent of Zastava's entire production. Moreover, the sales drive would require Zastava to diversify its output and bring forward new models. One of these, YUGO-Kabrio, a cheap and cheerful 8,000-dollar convertible, would be developed in cooperation with Bricklin, who promised to assist with financing. A further model, later unveiled as Florida, would establish Zastava in the 1400cc saloon class.

The YUGO-America contract was hailed in Yugoslavia as the deal of the century, which would pour billions of dollars into Yugoslavia's empty treasury. Bricklin became the hero of the hour, an industrial titan of infallible sagacity. Despite the scarcity of investment funds in Yugoslavia, Zastava was granted the finance for the YUGO-America project, and for development of Kabrio and Florida, although it had to accommodate its new commitments within the existing works.

By early 1988, the YUGO sales drive was turning sour. Bricklin sold his interest in YUGO-America to a syndicate that refinanced it with junk bonds. The business collapsed late in 1988, when its inventory was pawned to a loan shark (AN 27 March 1989: 1, 20; February 1989: 51). Zastava diverted its output to the home market, where runaway inflation encouraged customers to snap up all the cars offered. But exchange stabilization in January 1990 caught it with hideous debts, unable to sell much abroad, and burdened by grotesque overmanning. Devoid of liquidity, it was defaulting on its financial commitments long before the rupture with the northern republics paralyzed the plant for want of supplies.

In short, from the 1970s on, pressure for export earnings led Zastava into four strategic decisions: to develop the YUGO-45; to export the YUGO in bulk to the USA; to develop the Kabrio for export; and to move up-market with Florida. We will argue that each of those decisions was to hemorrhage resources out of Zastava.

THE ZASTAVA SUPPLY SIDE

As a protected supplier of an overheated home market, Zastava rarely curtailed production because of slack demand. Home customers waited 3–6 months for delivery after paying a hefty deposit. Supply bottlenecks posed the sole restraint upon output. Zastava seldom managed to produce cars uninterruptedly or in volume close to capacity. Partly because of these supply bottlenecks, the quality of the cars it manufactured left much to be desired.

In public Zastava usually blamed its production difficulties on its "proverbially inert" component suppliers. Relatively few components were made in-house. Even the engines were bought in from the "21 Maj" factory in Belgrade (DMB). In the early years Zastava and DMB depended on non-specialist suppliers, which regarded the manufacturing of small production runs for Zastava as an unremunerative chore (Rep. sekretarijat 1964: 33; Mikuz 1965, 35). The Soviet tie-up in the early 1970s ought to have solved this problem, but did not. A number of dedicated suppliers were established as Zastava subsidiaries in southern Yugoslavia, but these proved at least as erratic as any outside supplier (Palairet 1992) and delivery bottlenecks continued unfailingly to interrupt production at Kragujevac.

Supply disruptions were not always the fault of the component makers because they remained heavily dependent on imported materials. Since Zastava was a notoriously slow payer, they frequently lacked hard currency to pay their own bills, and were therefore unable to procure materials.

Even more production than was lost through failures of the supply chain was foregone through Zastava's internal weaknesses. These included breakdowns, line stoppages, and sloppy workmanship. Two fragments of data, for 1966 and 1983, indicate the sources of production losses.

In the final quarter of 1966, production losses were equivalent to 66 per cent of actual output. Of these losses, 69 per cent were attributed to shortcomings within the factory, mainly in the machine shop, which suffered repeated breakdowns, and shortages of appropriate cutting and drilling equipment (ZCZ 1967: 119). For 1983 losses were expressed in terms of unutilized machine-hours. In that year, 45.9 per cent of those theoretically available machine hours were lost after allowing for maintenance. But only 15 per cent of these losses were attributable to supplier problems (Kragujevac 2000: II, 53).

This admittedly fragile evidence indicates that Zastava was plagued by "internal weaknesses" even in the prosperous 1960s, but that they subsequently worsened, while the external supply chain, though persistently unsatisfactory, improved over time. The problems of 1983 were by no means transient. In 1988, the management blamed most of its losses on "problems in the car factory itself." Having mentioned "equipment faults because of bad quality repairs," it inveighed against "desertion of work, lines starting late at the beginning of a shift, early leaving of work, [and] frequent smoking breaks" (CZ 17 February 1988: 1).

There is now a consensus among Yugoslav economists that the system of self-management agreements, imposed on enterprises with increasing vigor in the 1970s, was the root cause of the subsequent deterioration in productivity. There is no shortage of evidence to support their case. Referring to Zastava, Professor Milan Ilić identifies the mismatch of labor skills to jobs as a serious source of inefficiency (Ilić 1987). Curiously enough, when I put this argument to Engineer Raković , he retorted: "I never had any problems

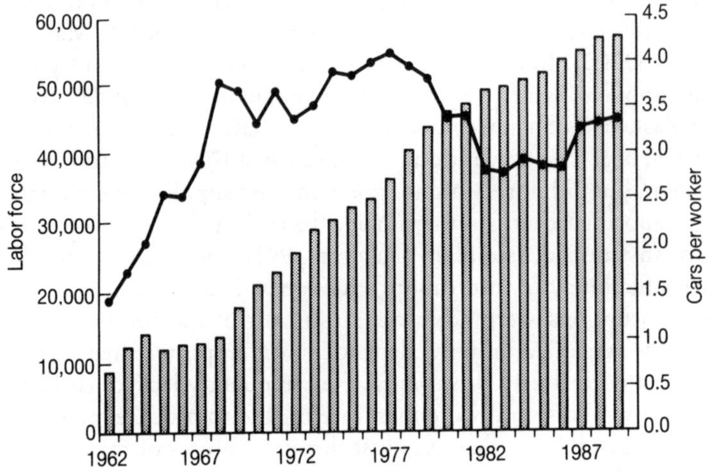

Figure 6.2 Zastava labor and productivity 1962–87

with self-management. I always explained what I wanted to do to the workers' council. Then we carried it out energetically. My successor [Bojanić] didn't know how to handle people . . ." But then Raković's managerial style, effective though it was, cost him his job. Bojanić was the type of person the Party wanted to run industry. What it got was management incapable of maintaining basic discipline.

Figure 6.2 shows just how seriously productivity deteriorated between 1977 and 1982.[4]

Productivity figures of this type are, however, only a very crude performance indicator, since they resulted also from over-recruiting at the behest of the political authorities. But this decline took place concurrently with a surge in investment and with mounting enterprise losses, both of which required huge infusions of external resources that went to waste. I will show that both unrequited investments and trading losses were caused by Zastava's attempts to break into the international automotive market.

THE NEW VEHICLE PROJECTS

Each new vehicle project – the Z-101 in 1970–2, YUGO in 1979–80, and Florida in 1986–8 – was associated with a massive wave of investment. Figure 6.3, from a study by the Kragujevac town planners (Kragujevac 2000: III, 79), shows that between 1965 and 1983, little investment went into the Kragujevac factory except during these two waves. Subsequent data are

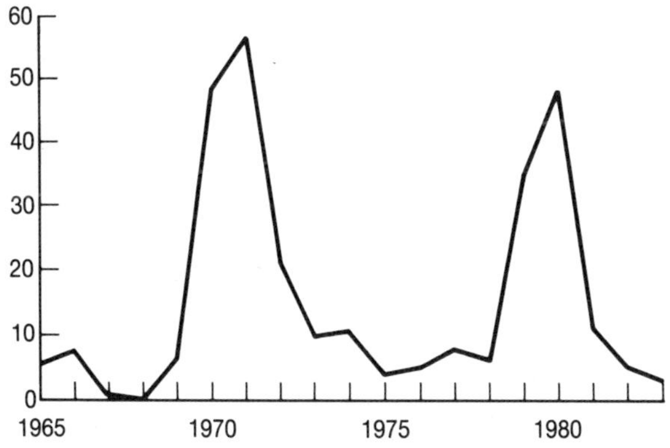

Figure 6.3 Fixed investment at Zastava as per cent of Zastava's social product 1965–80

lacking for the period of the YUGO-America and Florida projects, but in 1986–8 Zastava enjoyed another boom in investment, "the envy of every Yugoslav work organization" (EP 28 December 1987: 17).

Most equipment acquired for the Kragujevac factory was purchased abroad: 52.5 per cent of outlays over the period 1965–83 were for imported equipment, 12.3 per cent for equipment of Yugoslav origin and 32.7 per cent for construction work (Kragujevac 2000: III, 78). The sums involved rose steeply as each program superseded the last. Equipment imports in 1971–2 amounted to 574 million dinars (about 35.7 million dollars) and in 1979–80, 2.38 billion dinars (about 126 million dollars) (Kragujevac 2000: IV, 29). These sums take no account of investment undertaken by suppliers. The outlay (including local purchases) associated with the Florida program, was projected in June 1987 at 183 billion dinars (about 238 million dollars) (EP 22 June 1987: 38). But Florida was to encounter unexpected hold-ups, and in 1988 Zastava admitted that investment in the project exceeded 400 million dollars (CZ 27 July 1988; EP 13 November 1989: 34).

As investment in equipment other than for these projects was relatively small, expansion in capacity was confined to the project periods. Capacity leaped from around 80–90,000 vehicles in 1968–71 to 170,000 for 1972–9, and to 220,000 in the early 1980s. The output trend shows no corresponding discontinuities. It stagnated between 1971 and 1972, then rose steadily to 1979, and then declined to 1983 (see Appendix). Clearly the pay-off period associated with the investments of 1970–72 was very long, and for those made since 1978, infinite.

This was because the enterprise was unable to utilize its new machines quickly to turn out new models in economically efficient runs. Unlike a

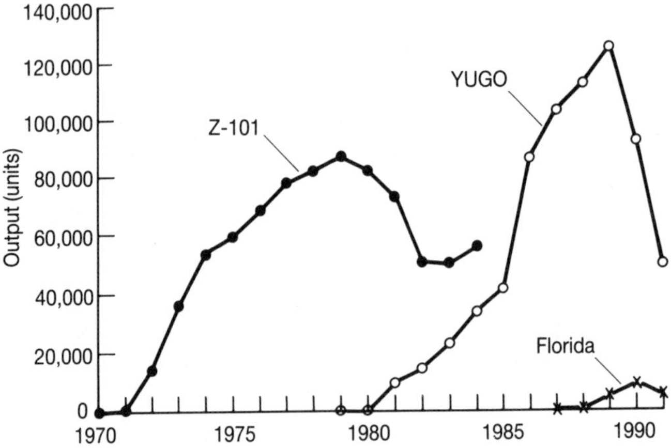

Figure 6.4 Zastava output of new models 1971–91

Western automobile manufacturer, which tries to maximize output of its new models as soon as they are offered to the public so as to capture the premium associated with the new good, Zastava expected to take several years before it could offer its new models in volume. By then any novelty they possessed for the export market had evaporated – and with it any hope of a premium that might recoup the investment outlays. This is shown in Figure 6.4.

With the Z-101, the curve is relatively steep, probably because FIAT supervised the introduction and implementation of the new technology. Even so, capacity utilization dropped spectacularly for several years. But with the YUGO-45, matters were different. FIAT designed the car to specifications that were heavily influenced by Kragujevac, and was not permitted to develop the production technology. Zastava proudly strove for "a high level of technological emancipation," and developed the technology in-house, even building some of its own machines (EP 20 April 1981: 19).

The YUGO-America program did not require a new vehicle, though the YUGO-A (YUGO-GV) had a larger (1116cc) engine than the 45, and eventually accommodated some 500 design changes (850 according to YUGO-America) to meet American tastes and compliance standards (CZ, 24 February 1988; 7 December 1988). The YUGO-GVs sent to the USA are included in the figures shown for the YUGO model as a whole. They account for the 1986–7 surge in the production trend.

As Zastava was not allocated funds to extend the factory, floorspace was released for a new line to build for YUGO-America by closing down production of the Z-750 (EP 13 January 1986: 33). The decision came even though the car was still selling in substantial volume (33,200 in 1984, the last year of full production) and unlike the newer projects, was probably still yielding a profit. The new line, separate from the existing YUGO line, was needed in order to produce to American quality control specifications (AN 17 December 1984: 3).

Some of the design work behind the GV model was carried out in association with Bricklin's engineers, but once more the development technology was handled in-house. No FIAT co-operation was invited and FIAT warned Zastava not to commit itself to this project (EP 9 June 1986: 14). Zastava attributed FIAT's attitude to the project to its own misfortunes on the American market, and to jealousy lest Zastava might succeed where FIAT had failed. FIAT's skepticism was shared by numerous "doubting Thomases" whose reservations were ritually excoriated by Zastava's management during the early stages of the venture. The production plans for YUGOs destined for the USA were ludicrously optimistic. When they failed (see Table 6.1), Zastava blamed Bricklin for unrealistic demands, but it had nevertheless assented to them by contract (CZ 3 July 1985).

Table 6.1 The YUGO-American program: Cars exported to the USA

Year	*Planned*	*Actual*
1985	35,000	9,894
1986	76,000	35,959
1987	102,000	57,832
1988	172,000	25,784
1989	218,000	18
1990	272,000	2,633

Source: Miladin Simović, "Automobili: izazovi prekretnice," EP 16 January 1989: 16.

The scale of investment associated with the YUGO-America project is difficult to gauge because it merges in time with the Florida project, but it was doubtless substantial. 1986 investment in which the "YUGO-A" – the export car – took a "dominant place" was budgeted at 68 billion dinars (over 160 million dollars). Heavy purchases of automated Japanese equipment were made (EP 14 September 1987: 18). The wisdom of these purchases may be doubted, for although automation would have reduced quality defects, it was hugely capital intensive, and inappropriate for a car maker paying 0.59 dollars per hour (3 per cent of the Detroit rate) for underemployed labor. On Zastava's puny production runs, its use could not fail to swell the burden of overhead costs.

When the Florida project was launched in 1982, FIAT refused to cooperate, and warned Zastava of the folly of undertaking it (CZ 19 October 1988). Zastava's bosses say FIAT feared "Florida" might offer serious competition to the FIAT-Tipo. The car was therefore developed in Kragujevac to avoid buying in licenses, although the styling was put out to Giugiaro's Ital Design in 1983 to ensure international acceptability (CZ 1 April 1987). Giugiaro's work was completed in 1985, but Zastava shelved the project, for lack of resources. It was resurrected in 1986 in response to YUGO-America's call for new models. Thereupon Zastava tried to organize the production technology at breakneck speed, accommodating Florida assembly within an existing YUGO line. The car should have been ready for the market in 1987, but production was deferred till October 1988, when the first Florida rolled off the line with much ballyhoo. It was less ceremoniously abandoned, for the vehicles fell short of marketable quality (EP 13 February 1989: 34). Even a restart in 1989 yielded a mere trickle of vehicles. To date large-scale production seems as remote as ever.

Zastava's other innovation, the 1300cc Kabrio, designed in association with Bricklin's YUGO-America, also proved more troublesome than expected. This was a cut down YUGO-GVX with an imported, powered roof. But it required new tools for 300 positions, and hit engineering problems in machining to tolerances that would let the roof seal fit accurately (CZ 11 May 1988). Zastava's outlays on the Kabrio were inflated by a project to set up a research department in Detroit (EP 22 September 1986; CZ 25 March 1987: 4). This was linked to a mystery firm called JUBBU, which was charged with producing special tools, probably of Japanese design.[5]

YUGO-America had undertaken to invest 5 million of 20 million dollars needed to provide these tools for Zastava to assemble the roof (CZ 27 July 1988), but it defaulted on payment and Zastava ended up having to find all the money itself. Output of 14,000 units was planned for 1988 (EP 16 January 1989). Kabrio entered production in May, in the presence of the American ambassador, who took it for a test drive (CZ 1 June 1988). No harm befell him, but production was promptly abandoned. The roof would not lift properly, and there were "also some smaller faults" (CZ 27 July 1988). In 1989 42 Kabrios were made, none in 1990 (MIJ 1990, 1991). The hold-up was connected with the non-arrival of tools and components from undisclosed sources. A few Kabrios were built for the Italian market in 1991 (Automobil 31 May 1991).

PROFIT AND LOSS

No realistic figures exist for the surpluses and deficits run by Zastava. Such as they are, published figures exaggerate profitability. For 1954–74 they show a consistent trading surplus to 1972, although Yugoslav accounts do not make adequate provision either for capital costs or for depreciation.

They are also compiled according to historic cost, and so tend to magnify inventory gains. It is noteworthy, however, that in 1973 the figures had to be massaged by "internal realizations" to disguise a severe trading loss (ZCZ 1975: 61). Cash flow was far less healthy, and each investment surge related to new models wrecked the liquidity of the enterprise, since the new models were so slow to build up sales.

After Raković's fall in 1974, his management was blamed implicitly by his successor Bojanić for the heavy burden of interest and of foreign credits that the enterprise had to carry. He alleged that the rate at which funds were turning over had slowed, bills stood unpaid, and Zastava's credit standing had plummeted (CZ 23 October 1974). Over the next few years he repeatedly expressed concern over low and falling levels of accumulation, although up to 1979 the accounts were claimed to have shown a nominal surplus. But Bojanić admitted in 1979 that the surplus was only achieved by writing off equipment over fourteen years, rather than over the seven Zastava considered appropriate, and that much of the depreciation provision was being used to pay old debts (CZ 13 February 1980). Rocketing interest charges the following year – up 77 per cent on 1979, which reflected the YUGO investment program under way, left 1980 "a year we would rather forget" (CZ 26 December 1980). However, 1981 was worse, because the opening of the YUGO line caused the number of cars in unfinished inventories to jump from 5,000 to 13,000. These vehicles stood in the factory yard awaiting missing components. As a rule less than half the cars that left the line were complete. Any pretense of profitability was abandoned. A loss of 770 million dinars was reported for the first half year, and around 1400 million for the period January–September (about 40 million dollars). "Illiquidity was felt as it never had been in earlier years" (CZ 25 December 1981). Bojanić thereupon departed for a softer job.

Losses persisted. Further deficits were reported for 1982, and Bojanić's successor Radoljub Micić warned at year-end that hard currency debt had mounted so severely that only "enormous export growth to the hard-currency area" could restore solvency. He wanted an export surge of 47–8 per cent which would raise the proportion of output to be exported to around 40 per cent (CZ 29 December 1982). Of course, his targets were missed by huge margins, new foreign credits were not forthcoming, and components arrived only intermittently because Zastava was unable to meet its suppliers' need for hard currency (CZ 28 December 1983). Liquidity remained at crisis levels. Small wonder therefore that the enterprise now pinned its hopes on the YUGO-America project, for by the end of 1984, resources were lacking even for maintaining equipment. Once again problems would have to be solved by "the explosive growth of exports" (CZ 26 December 1984).

The government was so eager for the American program to succeed that a large amount of credit was placed at Zastava's disposal. For a time, the position of Zastava's accounts may have improved because inflation was destroying its domestic debt with gratifying speed, but this was merely socializing its losses on a grand scale. At YUGO-America, Bricklin knew that the YUGO-GV had to be marketed as an "econobox" at the very bottom of the American market. So he posted a list price of 3,990 dollars. To ensure himself a hefty profit, he drove a hard bargain with Zastava, which the latter ought never to have agreed to, but did probably under political coercion. The price Zastava received was never disclosed officially, but is claimed to have been "a little over half the retail price of 4,000 dollars," f.o.b. Bar Harbor (EP 9 December 1985). This estimate looks optimistic. In 1987 the average export price of Zastava cars destined for hard currency markets was 1,993 dollars (CZ 2 February 1988).

As soon as the project was unveiled, Congressman Hertel of Michigan claimed that the price of the YUGO-55 (YUGO-GV) "indicates either massive subsidies or the use of slave labor" (AN 15 October 1984). This was followed by allegations made by Croat nationalists that each car carried a 450-dollar export subsidy and violated US anti-dumping laws (AN 8 February 1988). The accusation was indignantly denied, but subsidies were undoubtedly received though their value was unstable. In June 1986, Zastava complained that "at the start of the American market, the price of the YUGO had included significantly higher federal and republic stimulations which are now lacking" (EP 2 June 1986: 33). Then, in September, Zastava was awarded a 14 billion dinar export subsidy (EP 29 September 1986: 36). The award was based on a planned export volume of 83,000 cars, so it was then equivalent to 427 dollars per car. The Yugoslavs knew they had no cause for worry about American laws because of the protection they enjoyed from highly placed friends.

Even with this subsidy, the car cost far more to build than it earned, and the cost had to be borne through cross-subsidization and by enterprise losses. In mid-1986, Zastava, despite the subsidy, received 487,000 dinars (1,161 dollars) less for cars exported to the USA than it earned from similar models sold at home (EP 30 June 1986: 16).

Not surprisingly, Zastava reported a quarterly loss of about 7 million dollars in early 1986 (EP 19 May 1986: 37). Since prices on cars sold domestically did not fully offset export losses, YUGO-America was costing an internal subsidy of 1,100 dollars per unit plus, most likely, an external subsidy of around 400 dollars. If we allow a further 250–500 dollars for qualitative differences, then each YUGO-GV exported received a subsidy of around 1,800 dollars, or a total of 240 million dollars in all, between 1985 and 1988. The venture contributed a roughly similar sum in dollars to Yugoslavia's international accounts, but a more ruinous way of earning them would be hard to devise.

Small wonder that Zastava was soon complaining that the American customer was being absurdly pampered and that the program caused more trouble than it was worth. In early 1987 it threatened to back out, unless it were given a bigger subsidy. The response was a stern warning from Branko Mikulić, federal prime minister, that the YUGO-America program was sacrosanct, and that serious consequences would befall Zastava if it abandoned it (EP 2 February 1987). This induced the firm to continue exporting, but to provide fewer cars for YUGO-America than the latter demanded. The loss that Zastava had to bear on the American deal caused it to push part of the burden back on its suppliers. And as they consequently missed delivery dates, they had to be kept in line by the "declared support of . . . the organs" (EP 27 April 1987). The reaction of both Zastava and its suppliers to loss-making business was to curtail production, which was an important reason for YUGO-America's collapse into insolvency, although blame also resided at the American end.

The collapse of YUGO-America should have put an end to an expensive, resource-destructive venture, but Zastava and GENEX rushed to refinance the venture and run it themselves. The puny volume of exports this generated led to new losses, and eventual liquidation.

Florida, even on the optimistic projection of a 50,000 unit a year production run, would have lost money on a heroic scale. Allowing a 7-year payback, an outlay of 400 million dollars would have added about 2,000 dollars of overheads to variable costs in forming the ex-works domestic market price of the vehicle, which in spring 1991 was set at 165,000 dinars (12,200 dollars).[6] But as the vehicle was only built in nominal quantities, the investment can be regarded as an unrequited write-off; so too was whatever sums were sunk into Kabrio.

CONCLUSIONS AND PROSPECTS

Until the mid-1970s, Zastava traded as a closed-market, import substituter; it probably balanced its books while achieving impressive gains in productivity, which were passed back to the domestic consumer. Thereafter, it was all downhill. Although it is impossible to calculate the overall extent of the losses run by the Zastava automobile factory since the late 1970s, more or less identifiable costs include the subsidies and losses on the YUGO-America program, which I estimate at around 240 million dollars. To that we should add the investment write-off on Florida of over 400 million dollars. Allowing for losses on the development of the YUGO and the Kabrio and the losses borne by Zastava's tied suppliers, the overall loss arising from all of Zastava's export-led ventures may be around 1 billion dollars. Zastava's *dohodak* (value added minus depreciation) in 1985 amounted to 43 billion dinars or 170 million dollars (ZD 1986: 15), so it is probable that the firm destroyed resources at least as fast as it added value. Of course, these export-driven ventures were not the only source of losses. An enterprise that in 1989 had seen worker productivity fall by 18 per cent from the 1977 peak could hardly fail to lose money, even if it added nothing to its net capital stock.

Ilić correctly stresses the deterioration in manpower and plant utilization during the 1970s in explaining the long-run worsening of Zastava's performance. I argue, however, that the post-1978 commitment to internationalizing sales was of primary importance. Zastava had to be deployed as a foreign exchange earner to requite part of the import bill that its inputs and investment entailed. But it was vainglorious to imagine that the export drive could be mounted on a "Yugoslav" trademark; or that Zastava was competent to develop its own production technology for the YUGO; or that it could "conquer" the American market at a profit with a narrow range of downmarket vehicles; or that it could storm a ruthlessly competitive world market in the 1.3–1.4 litre saloon class with its in-house home-built Florida, when neither its component suppliers nor its engineers were equal to the task of assembling it in bulk. As for the Kabrio program there were elements that raise ethical questions. After the abandonment of Raković's Phase 3, the only way Zastava could have exported profitably would have been as a tied supplier to an international major – presumably FIAT. This would have required that Zastava's managers accept a close supervision of its affairs.

The experience of the only other significant assembler in Yugoslavia, IMV of Novo Mesto in Slovenia is instructive in this respect. IMV (now REVOZ) started up in 1955 to assemble Audi kits, switched in 1969 to assembling for Austin–Morris, and in 1972 to Renault (Kiković 1978: 36–40). Between 1977 and 1990 its annual output fluctuated between 26,000 and 49,000 cars. In 1978, it made huge misguided investments and, like Zastava, fell subsequently into acute distress (EP 23 November 1987). It was then converted to an anonymous Renault plant, ensuring itself reasonable long-term prospects (EP 27 February 1989: 30); it is now 51 per cent owned by Renault (EP 16 March 1992: 29).

But Zastava resisted an analogous deal with FIAT. Instead, it wanted FIAT to refinance the enterprise in return for a bigger share in the business, and to provide components that Zastava could no longer obtain from or through Croatia. Zastava would make payment in YUGOs. But it was unrealistic for Zastava to imagine it could salve its inordinately inflated pride as an independent producer, and go on selling internationally under its own logo. The deal was not attractive for FIAT, which did not particularly want to bail Serbia out economically at the expense of Croatia. Moreover, Zastava had lost its erstwhile attraction as a bridgehead into COMECON (EP 9 April 1990) and its cars had departed significantly from the FIAT standard (EP 20 January 1992). But some kind of deal was essential for Zastava, and before sanctions were clamped on Serbian exports, it tried to get FIAT to sell its 18 per cent interest to Volkswagen. Volkswagen would then close its small but profitable assembly plant at Sarajevo and "organize its own production at Kragujevac" (EP 17 February 1992: 12). The Sarajevo works was thoughtfully bombarded to impress on VW the advantages of the alternative location.

In the meantime, Zastava's very survival became problematic when it lost its privileges in Yugoslavia's main car purchasing provinces, and was starved of supplies from them. In December 1991, production was down to 20 per cent of plan, and since then the plant has only worked intermittently. The enterprise was so broke it could only import its sheet steel against advance payment (EP 24 February 1992: 35) and for months had been paying its increasingly mutinous workforce mainly in its own IOUs (EP 30 December 1991: 92). Exit would be unthinkable politically, but the plant could hardly have a permanent role to play as the workhouse of the Šumadija. The top managers left in droves. To the workers they looked like rats abandoning a sinking ship (EP 20 January 1992: 13).

At the risk of drawing a sweeping inference about Yugoslavia's development problems from the experience of a single enterprise, I suggest the following hypothesis. Yugoslavia fell into economic decline when the bill for the import of industrial technology outran the export base provided by primary products, tourism and remittances, and when the deficits could no longer be covered by new borrowing. This forced the country to include technically sophisticated manufactures within its export base, in the face of serious comparative disadvantage, and therefore at a massive loss. A survey in 1987 indicated that 78 per cent of all Yugoslav products exported into hard currency markets fetched a lower price than on the home market and that 22 per cent earned less than 60 per cent of their home market price (EP 10 August 1987: 27). Costly imported inputs and equipment were being converted into low grade or obsolescent output, so Yugoslav products on export markets could only be sold at 25–30 per cent under the market (EP 13 November 1989). This led to ruinous enterprise losses, as Zastava's experience testifies. From this followed crippling hard currency debt, tumbling living standards, and the gradual deterioration of the country's capital stock.

NOTES

Thanks are due to Engineer Raković, Ljubiša Todorović, and Gera Vuletić for interviews, and to Milan Ilić, Miladin Simović and Kurt Bayer for information and criticism. The project was funded by the Nuffield Foundation.

1 See trends in (adjusted) national income, Yugoslav concept, in Appendix series, p. 109 below.

2 When Zastava moved into automobile manufacturing, it did not abandon the production of weaponry and also produced machine tools. But by 1985 vehicles accounted for 91.2 per cent of its income. This included light commercial vehicles, 9,957 units that year compared with 136,000 cars, which were built together with armaments in the downtown factory, not in the auto plant (ZD 1986: 15).

3 Actual production in 1985 was 41,274.

4 Since employment series are obtainable only for the group as a whole, commercial vehicles are included with cars in the graphic. In 1978 vehicle production accounted for 88.7 per cent of ZCZ output.

5 References to JUBBU appear in EP 23 March 1987 and 16 January 1989. Interviewing Zastava's finance director in June 1991, I asked about the research institute in Detroit. He linked this to the Kabrio, and mentioned JUBBU, without prompting, as an independent American firm; 50 percent of JUBBU was bought up by YUGO-America in 1989. The affair is treated with unexplained secrecy.

6 Auto Kuća Zastava spring 1991 pricelist.

REFERENCES

AN: *Automotive News*.
Automobil: Belgrade.
BW: *Business Week*.
CZ: *Crvena Zastava* (works newspaper). Kragujevac.
EP: *Ekonomska Politika*. Belgrade.
MIJ: *Motorna industrija Jugoslavije*. (annual).
ZD: *Zastava danas*. (annual). Kragujevac.

Giacosa, D. (1979) *Forty Years of Design with FIAT*, Milan.

Ilić, M. (1987) "Nesklad izmedju stvarne i potrebne kvalifikacijone strukture radnika u industrije i njegove implikacije na zaposlenost," *Ekonomika udruženog rada*, 11–12.

Kiković, L. (1978) *Tržište automobila u Jugoslaviji. Ekonomska i sociološka studija o proizvodnji i tržišnoj tražnji automobila*, Belgrade.

Kragujevac 2000. (1986) I-IV. Skupština opštine Kragujevac, (March).

Lampe, J.R. Prickett, R.O. and Adamovich, Lj.S. (1990) *Yugoslav American Economic Relations since World War II*, Durham, SC.

Lydall, H. (1989) *Yugoslavia in Crisis*, Oxford.

Micić , R. (1983) "Značaji i uloga Crvena zastava u društvenom ekonomskom i tehničko-tehnološkom preobražanju i razvoju Srbije i Jugoslavije," *Zastava*, I (1 October).

Mikuz, M. (1965) "Uticaj tržišta na razvoj motorne industrije kod nas," *Simpozijum na sajmu motora i motornih vozila*.

Miletić, M. (1966) "Istorijat i perspektivni razvoj industrije drumskih vozila u Jugoslaviji," *Simpozijum na sajmu motora i motornih vozila*, Belgrade.

Palairet, M. (1992) " 'Ramiz Sadiku:' A Case Study in the Industrialization of Kosovo," *Soviet Studies*, 44: 5.

Republički sekretarijat za industriju SR Srbije. (1964) *Perspektivni mogućnosti plasmana putničkih i lakih teretnih vozila i razvoj proizvodnih kapaciteta Zavoda "Crvena zastava" u periodu 1964–72 god*, Mimeo, 13 January, Belgrade.

Sedgwick, M. (1974) *FIAT*.

ZCZ (Zavodi Crvena Zastava) Fabrika automobila, sluzba na ekonomiku. (1967) *Analiza poslovanja fabrika automobila i ocena njenog ekonomskog položaja u 1966 godini*, Kragujevac.

ZCZ. (1973) *Od topa do automobila 1853–1973*, Kragujevac.

ZCZ. (1975) *Dvadeset godina proizvodnje automobila*, Kragujevac.

APPENDIX

Time series data for Figures 6.1–6.3.

Year	*National income*		*Zastava production*	*Capacity*	*Output*		
	Official	*Adjusted*			*Z101*	*YUGO*	*Florida*
1955	73,057	70,206	445				
1956	68,964	66,624	424				
1957	85,255	81,664	1,935				
1958	87,155	82,872	1,686				
1959	101,957	85,957	3,428				
1960	110,047	91,557	8,191				
1961	115,608	96,475	10,995				
1962	119,026	102,627	10,561				
1963	132,958	111,864	18,912				
1964	148,034	111,927	25,960				
1965	152,354	122,233	26,748	33,688			
1966	164,406	139,348	29,022	38,644			
1967	165,270	150,852	34,466	64,786			
1968	170,697	154,116	49,920	81,171			
1969	187,153	175,929	64,346	86,603			
1970	198,022	173,027	67,207	75,769	0		
1971	214,416	193,719	79,334	91,716	508		
1972	221,096	196,562	80,069	183,644	14,293		
1973	216,752	209,867	96,434	172,821	36,163		
1974	235,659	219,612	111,553	170,050	53,573		
1975	261,849	229,049	119,559	170,070	59,799		
1976	268,609	241,114	128,543	170,030	68,632		
1977	293,230	261,382	141,904	170,149	77,869		
1978	313,517	271,442	151,989	177,973	82,146		
1979	336,723	282,541	157,118	180,181	87,112	0	
1980	343,461	272,859	144,466	220,223	82,090	36	
1981	350,608	289,456	149,110	220,251	73,204	9,715	
1982	344,510	292,371	126,256	187,046	50,533	14,414	
1983	340,272	285,924	127,306	219,872	50,288	22,738	
1984	349,189	269,301	138,112		55,995	33,392	
1985	353,125	250,157	136,383		47,068	41,274	
1986	368,093	263,615	139,891		33,731	86,492	
1987	356,970	264,198	168,495		30,231	103,157	0
1988	354,211	241,915	176,362		25,519	112,453	37
1989			177,359		27,391	124,913	4,749
1990			153,017		19,385	91,827	8,905

Cols 2 and 3: official and adjusted national income (Yugoslav concept) in million constant 1972 dinars. Adjusted national income (col. 3) eliminates spurious "official" growth created by inventory accounting malpractices. See Madžar's revision procedures explained in appendix to Lydall (1989).
Cols 4–8: Zastava car factory output and capacity, units.

Sources: Zastava car factory output: MIJ: 1966–92. Capacity estimates are derived from data on percentage of capacity use in Kragujevac 2000: II, 72.
Output figures are smaller than claimed officially, because the latter includes 35,275 cars imported annually between 1976 and 1990 from Poland and the Soviet Union.

7

THE TRANSITION TO MARKET ECONOMIES

Lessons from Hungary and the case for pessimism

Scott M. Eddie

INTRODUCTION

Converting a command economy to a market economy is a reconstruction problem easily on the same scale as that faced after a major war. After four to seven decades of a vast social experiment, the former Communist states of Central and Eastern Europe confront problems of economic transformation unprecedented even after wars, because they find themselves devastated in some unique ways:

First, not only was the economic system shattered, but so was the institutional infrastructure. What remained was a personal and capricious legal system inimical to the operation of a market economy. The rigidities and imperatives of planning forced people routinely to break the law to meet the plan objectives. Thus anyone in a decision-making position could be prosecuted as a criminal at any time, fostering a system of client–patron relationships very similar to the "service-protection contract" characteristic of feudalism (Bloch 1941). Even if a new system of laws could be built overnight, a culture of abiding by the law cannot.[1] No amount of foreign aid can overcome this fundamental problem.

Second, pervasive state ownership of property hinders transition in two principal ways:

(a) Because everyone, and therefore no one, owned the means of production, responsibility for the consequences of decisions could be diffused into nothingness or "bucked up the line" – indeed, avoidance of decisions and responsibility for them was developed into an art form by the *apparatchiki*. Since so many of the same people are in the same positions despite the formal collapse of Communism, we cannot expect that they will act markedly differently in the future. One of the most disturbing results of the lack of accountability has been environmental degradation – especially in the ex-Soviet Union, Czechoslovakia, East Germany, Poland, and Romania – on a scale unimaginable even from the "dark satanic mills" of the nineteenth century. A lesser, but currently very pressing, consequence is the inability to sell goods on the world market because their quality is so poor: even much of the military hardware is crude and prone to breakdown.

(b) Property rights are ill-defined, and governments, possessing the vast bulk of productive assets, are far too involved at even the micro-levels of economic decision-making. The conflict between the government's interest and the demands of privatization is all too evident.

Third, the very mentality of the labor force has been transformed: generations have learned that the head that stuck up above the crowd risked being lopped off. Success on the job came more as a result of whom one knew than from what one accomplished, or how hard one worked. The quiet life was provided under the motto "They pretend to pay us and we pretend to work." Doing just enough to avoid attracting attention became the prime motivation of most of the workforce, at least in their employment in the socialist sector.

Even previous wars did not wreak this kind of destruction, nor litter the socio-political landscape with so many unexploded economic mines. Like Hitler's Viennese flak towers in a physical sense, so the socialist fortifications of Budapest, Prague, or Warsaw in an economic sense: They cannot be torn down without inflicting intolerable damage to surrounding structures. The familiar dilemma of having to keep giant money-losing state enterprises afloat to prevent massive unemployment and possible unrest is only the most glaring example of this.

With these warnings about non-comparabilities, it is now time to examine the historical record. Rather than continue to deal with these countries as a group, I have chosen Hungary as an illustrative case. Her comprehensive economic restructurings after the two world wars illustrate well the lessons emphasized in the theme of this conference, and will thus form a major focus of the present paper.

1918–39

Hungary's experience with a relatively unfettered liberal market economy was brief: It could be said to have begun in 1849 after the defeat in her insurrection against Habsburg rule, and to have flowered during the era of the Dual Monarchy (1867–1918). But the good ship Dualism foundered on the jagged rock of the "nationalities problem" – an obvious historical parallel to the situation in many of the countries of the former Soviet Union – and the Habsburg empire disintegrated during the Great War. At the peace treaties, the victorious powers stitched together the patchwork of the so-called "successor states." The "Austria" and "Hungary" that emerged from this redrawing of the map of Europe were mere remnants of their former selves. Table 7.1 sketches the dimensions of the new Hungary compared with the former Kingdom of Hungary.

World War I marked a watershed in government intervention in the economies of Europe, and Hungary was a part of this trend. Because it had such a drastic restructuring to do (more than any other country, with the possible exception of Austria), the demands for, and public willingness to accept, government action were very strong. After the war, residual Hungary faced massive economic disruption: severe wartime destruction of productive capacity, transport chaos exacerbated by Romanian confiscations and removal of railway rolling stock, shortages of raw materials and fuels, even local food shortages. To reach old, former domestic markets now required crossing new (sometimes hostile) international frontiers. Credit-financed war expenditures had already set inflation in motion (Table 7.2).

Reconstruction, economic reorientation, and the yearning of a war-weary population for a return to normality put demands on the Hungarian government that far exceeded its resources. Ever-increasing deficits were covered by printing money, and inflation turned into hyperinflation.

As in Austria, the League of Nations' "financial reconstruction" of Hungary (begun in 1923) halted inflation and led to the introduction of a new currency, the *pengő*, in 1925. In the same year a new, higher, and more elaborate tariff was partly an attempt to stimulate greater balance in the domestic economy, partly a retaliation for the increased agricultural tariffs levied by Austria and Czechoslovakia. By the late 1920s, despite some small efforts to reduce barriers in trade agreements signed with her neighbors, Hungarian agriculture and industry were barely able to surpass pre-war production levels: In the peak year of 1929, industrial production was only about 12 per cent above the pre-war level (for the post-1922 territory of Hungary). These signs of recovery were suddenly effaced by the onslaught of the Great Depression.

Hungary's agriculture had to contend with a precipitous fall in prices: by 1933 wheat sold for three-fifths, rye for one-half, and corn for only one-third of its 1929 price. Production held up, but farm incomes, both nominal and real, declined rapidly with the severe deterioration in agriculture's terms of trade. Industrial production declined 25 per cent, and employment 30 per cent, from 1929 to 1932. Capital goods production sank to only 55 per cent of its 1929 level, as the inflow of foreign capital, vital to both monetary stabilization and industrial reconstruction, ceased almost overnight.

The Hungarian government acted forcefully: it suspended payment of all foreign debts and introduced controls on all foreign transactions. Higher tariffs, some outright import prohibitions, and export subsidies were introduced. Other countries enacted similar "beggar-thy-neighbor" policies, worsening the depression. Monetary policies, especially competitive currency devaluations, further exacerbated the problem.[2]

Germany stepped in to exploit the situation. Hjalmar Schacht's plan to

Table 7.1 Dimensions of the new Hungary compared with the former kingdom

	Kingdom of Hungary	*Post-1919 Hungary*	*Post-1919 territory as % of pre-1919 territory*
Territory (thousand km^2)	325	91	28
Population (millions)	20.9	7.5	36
in agriculture	13.5	4.2	31
in mining	0.21	0.09	41
in industry	3.36	1.52	45
in commerce	0.72	0.35	48
in other occupations	3.12	1.37	44
Railways (thousand km)	22.1	8.36	38
Roads (thousand km)	49.4	17.5	35

Source: "A háború előtti Magyarország statisztikai adatai a megmaradt és elveszett területek szerint reszletezve [Prewar Hungarian statistical data detailed according to remaining and lost territories], *Statisztikai Szemle* [*Statistical Review*] 1923, nos 7–8: 288–306.

Table 7.2 Weekly cost of a minimum standard of living[a]

Date	*Crowns*	*Percentage increase over 31 July 1914*
31 July 1914	42.68	
31 Dec. 1915	80.92	89
31 Dec. 1917	189.90	346
31 Dec. 1919	904.36	2,016
31 Dec. 1921	2,485.50	5,723
31 Dec. 1922	11,786.63	27,883

[a] Based on a worker's family of five members, as calculated in Jenő Dálnoky-Kováts (1923) "Az életszínvonal alakulása" [The trend of the standard of living], *Közgazdasági Figyelő* [*Economic Observer*], vol. II: 59.

have the agrarian countries of Central and Eastern Europe help finance Germany's rearmament was set into motion with the signing of a trade treaty with Hungary in January 1934. The offer by Germany was tempting: it would buy stated quantities of grains and animal products at prices above prevailing world market prices; for this the exporters would earn credits at the *Reichsbank*, which they could use to buy German manufactured goods and, to a very small extent, even some hard currency. Other countries followed Hungary into this system, and then Germany simply dragged its feet on delivery of German goods, using the resulting import surplus to free domestic resources for use in the Nazi military build-up.

Trade and production responded quickly: Already by the end of 1934 Germany's share of Hungary's foreign trade was twice its 1929 level, and Germany accounted for more than half of both imports and exports by 1939. Increasing economic dependence on Germany was accompanied by increasing political pressure from Germany. Hungary entered World War II on the German side, suffering German occupation in 1944, then Soviet occupation in 1945.

1945–91

The post-World War II period can be divided into four phases: the transition from war economy to planned economy (1945–9); the command economy (1950–67); the "New Economic Mechanism," or "reform" period (1968–89); and the attempt to reintroduce a liberal market economy (1989ff.).

The transition period 1945–9

Hungary's loss of productive assets in the war has been estimated at roughly 4.3 billion 1938 dollars (about twice 1938 national income); only Poland and Yugoslavia, among the Eastern European countries, suffered more damage.

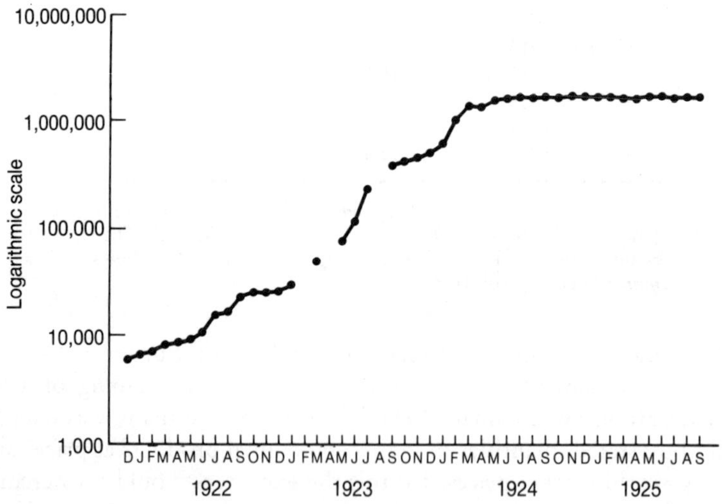

Figure 7.1 Cost of living index 1922–5
(1913–14 = 100)

After the end of the war, a spectacular hyperinflation destroyed the currency in a matter of months.[3] This time, however, stability was restored without recourse to the League of Nations and again a new currency was introduced: the *forint* became legal tender in August 1946.

The Communist party was a principal, then the dominating, force in the post-war coalition government that enacted a radical land reform in 1945, expropriating about one-third of the total area of Hungary. A three-year reconstruction plan was begun in 1947; all industrial enterprises with more than one hundred workers were nationalized in 1948, any with more than ten employees in 1949. This set the stage for the introduction of Soviet-style central planning on 2 January 1950.

The period of the five-year plans (1950–67)

Hungarian planning followed the Soviet model, with its emphasis on massive investments in heavy industry, restricted consumption, neglect of agriculture, use of "material balances," and so forth. It predictably recreated both the rapid initial growth and the characteristic mistakes of this system: monumental waste, shoddy goods, inappropriate output mix, collectivized and stagnant agriculture, artificial prices that gave no clue to relative scarcities.[4] The planning authorities had to employ more and more people to gather and process more and more information in an effort to correct observed problems. In consequence, the number of administrative employees per production worker more than doubled. The bureaucratization of the economy was in full swing.

Deviation from the Soviet model became imperative because of the uprising of 1956. Improved living standards for the working class received top priority, and inducements were to replace outright coercion in the planning system. Agriculture received more investment, compulsory deliveries were abolished, and some renting and selling of small plots was permitted. Collectives, which had dissolved in 1956, were to be reestablished, but without the crude force that had been used earlier. Begun in the winter of 1958–9, this drive brought a majority of the land (53 per cent) into collectives by 1960, a full three-quarters by 1965. The remaining one-quarter was roughly evenly split between residual private agriculture and state farms. In contrast to the original collectivization, re-collectivization did not cause agricultural output to fall.

The pattern in industry remained more conservative. The old plan was scrapped, replaced by only a three-year plan (1958–60). In 1961 Hungary returned again to a system of five-year plans. The actual mechanism of planning changed little, although some limited experiments were made: nine large firms were given independence with regard to exports and a portion of their imports, and Hungary introduced an explicit interest charge for investments in 1964. This latter had great symbolic value, but little economic impact, because (a) planning already had an interest rate, disguised as its inverse, the payback period, and (b) the chosen rate was artificially low.

Living standards did not grow as hoped: The annual average rate of 4.2 per cent in the 1957–67 period fell below that of the capitalist countries of Western Europe, so the gap between them and Hungary widened in both absolute and relative terms. The growth of agricultural output also lagged; by 1967 it showed only a 40–45 per cent increase over the very low levels of 1950. Planning remained rigid, and general dissatisfaction with the system was widespread.

A positive feature of János Kádár's "goulash Communism" was a steadily, if slowly, liberalizing political climate. In this climate open consideration of reforming the planning system was possible, and reform, which had been discussed and rejected by the inner councils of the Party in 1957,[5] now became a subject of public debate in learned journals and even in the (Party-controlled) newspapers. The result was the "New Economic Mechanism," introduced on 1 January 1968.

The reform period (1968–89): A critique of the reform

It is now commonplace to observe that reform efforts were doomed because the planning system was essentially unreformable. While that is almost certainly true, the Hungarian case cannot be cited as supporting evidence: Even though the Hungarians went further than anyone else in economic reform, their efforts failed not because they were foredoomed, but because they were so superficial and inessential. The debate was wide-ranging, but the actual measures adopted were mostly peripheral.

The economic reform debate had emphasized the cumbersome inflexibility of the command system and the uninformative nature of the price system in the system of planning. Accordingly, except in the most vital basic areas, resources were now to be allocated by "economic regulators,"[6] among which prices were to be most important.

Prices were divided into three categories: fixed, ceiling, and free. The prices of essential raw materials and basic foods such as bread and milk remained fixed and under central control; the prices of less essential items could fluctuate below centrally specified ceilings, while the third group of prices were to be set by supply and demand.

Over time, and especially for producers' goods, the government abandoned ceilings and allowed the role of "free" prices to expand. Consumer prices were freed to a very limited extent only, and the government engaged in extensive price subsidization, both to cushion fluctuations and to keep the prices of basic commodities low. Producers also depended on extensive subsidies to protect them from competition, a point to which we will return with some force.

Some restraints on agriculture were loosened: the production cooperatives were now free to engage in non-agricultural economic activities, and restrictions on private plots were relaxed in stages. Higher prices for farm produce were to increase farm incomes and to give incentives for greater production. Even the private non-agricultural sector was granted a little more freedom of operation.

Companies could now devote a limited share of their profits to an investment fund for their own use. These funds were to account for 57 per cent of total investment by 1970, but the goal was never reached nominally, let alone in practice.[7] Investment allocation remained completely under central control, even at the firm level.

Despite the superficial reports in the Western newspapers, with their headlines of "capitalism returns to Hungary," the goal was always to improve the functioning of the socialist economy and increase its share in total national output. Whatever incentives were given for private economic activity, the socialist sector was in the long run to expand relative to the private sector. Perhaps this ideological orientation explains the Hungarians' failure to deal with some of the most important macro- and microeconomic issues in their reform. In another paper, I offered the following summary analysis of the "curious, dual one-sidedness" of the reform:

> Prices in the *goods* market were gradually freed up, but *factor* prices . . . remained under tight control: Wages were kept artificially low, and the interest rate was never allowed to perform its market function of allocating investment funds. For all business intents and purposes, a market for land was not allowed to exist at all. Thus *all* the major components of value added entered into the calculation at artificial prices (or at no price at all). Hence the signals carried by the revamped price system merely shifted from being uninformative to being fundamentally distorted, especially given that prices were to be based on domestic costs, rather than on world price levels. . . . The price mechanism . . . was therefore flawed in its essence, and from the very start of the reform. The planners could not bring themselves to free up the factor markets. . . .
>
> Moreover, the signals sent *outside* the price system carried an anti-efficiency message: fear of unemployment led the government to prop up any and all money-losing enterprises. No big enterprise was, until very recently, allowed to go bankrupt. So even though profits were to be the yardstick of performance, they represented a marginal, rather than a fundamental, incentive. Even big losses would not cause an enterprise to "go under." The message was clear: Bonuses might depend on profits, but losses would never endanger the life of the enterprise or the jobs of its workforce; the relevant ministry would always provide a bailout. It was the carrot without the stick. . . .
>
> The measures undertaken as "reform" of the planning system were

> almost exclusively microeconomic. Indeed, the planners . . . seemed to ignore macroeconomic policy entirely, and tried to use only micro-economic "regulators" to deal with problems having a significant macro dimension, e.g., inflation. Conspicuously absent among the family of "economic regulators" were the interest rate and the money supply.
>
> The Hungarian government's approach to the interest rate was simply to legislate it, period. They may have thought that made no difference because the overall level of investment remained a command item. The question whether the interest rate or the size of the money supply should be the primary target of monetary policy had no meaning in Hungary: there was simply no concept of monetary policy at all. Indeed until rather recently they did not even know the size of the money supply, nor did they seem much concerned to find out.
>
> Fiscal policy was equally foreign to the economic reform.[8] Deficits in the government budget had nothing to do with fiscal policy; they were simply something that happened when the subsidy system got out of hand. This ignoring of macroeconomics was only much later repaired. . . .
>
> (Eddie 1990: 6–7)

I entitled this paper "A fraction of half of half a reform" because the New Economic Mechanism operated in only part of the goods market and not at all in the factor market, and because on the macroeconomic side it had only "willy-nilly fiscal policy and accidental monetary policy" (Eddie 1990: 7). It is not surprising that such a system did not solve the problems it was supposed to address, as data on the performance of the economy attest.[9]

The reform period: The performance of the economy

The following set of diagrams (Figures 7.2–7.7) presents summary data on the overall performance of the Hungarian economy and some of its important subsectors.

The data used for these figures are based on official Hungarian statistics which suffer from all the well-known problems: the Marxist concept of national income (Gross Domestic Material Product, hereafter GDMP) includes only material production and excludes services; output of private economic activity is significantly understated; prices used as weights for quantity indexes are problematical, since they are not true market prices;[10] there are unknown biases from the temptation to report what superiors wanted to hear, rather than what actually occurred, etc. But despite an increasing commitment to reform as the years after 1968 passed (with some reaction or hesitation in the mid-1970s), and therefore an increasing incentive to report favorable results, the New Economic Mechanism seems to

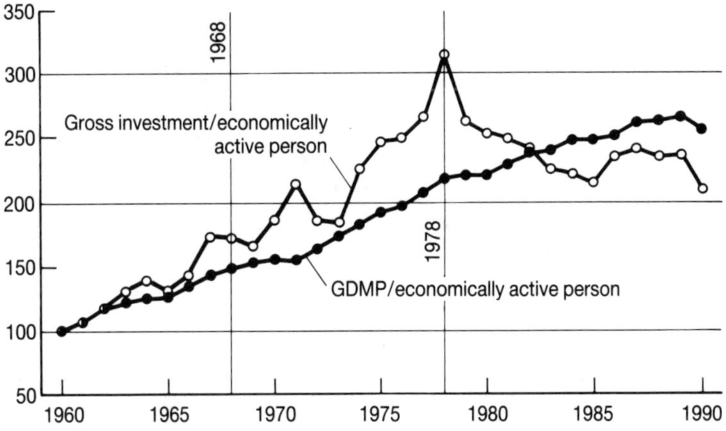

Figure 7.2 Investment and output per economically active person 1960–90 (1960 = 100)

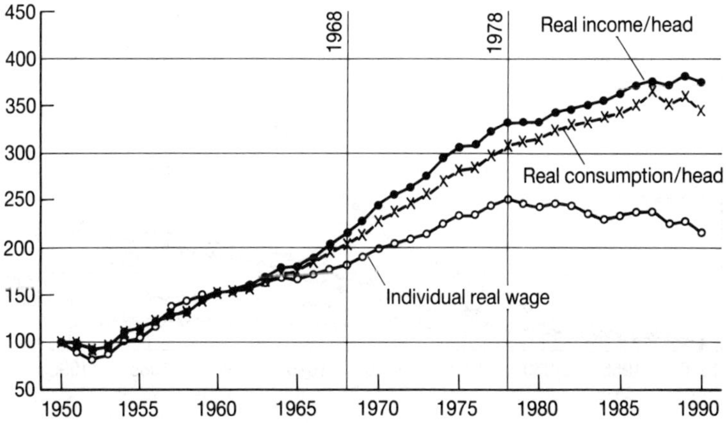

Figure 7.3 Real wage, real income, real consumption 1950–90 (1950 = 100)

have brought no improvement in indicators of macroeconomic performance. Even official data do not hide the poor performance since 1978, when reaction was overcome and commitment to the reform renewed and expanded. Given what we have seen above, this should be no surprise: despite the publicity, despite the obvious interest of the Western countries in seeing the Hungarian reform succeed, its extent was still simply too limited

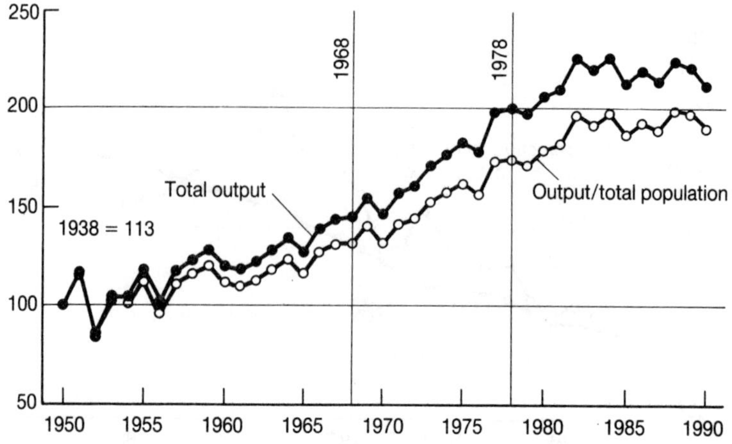

Figure 7.4 Index of agricultural output: total output and output per head of population 1950–90 (1950 = 100)

Source: *Hungarian Statistical Yearbook* (1990: 1, 9)

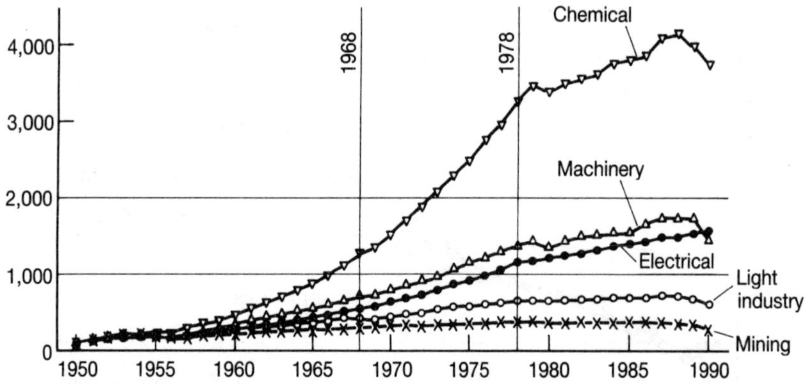

Figure 7.5 Gross output of selected branches of industry 1950–90 (1950 = 100)

Source: *Hungarian Statistical Yearbook* (1990: 5)

to be really effective. Here was a case where the degree of political liberalization clearly exceeded the degree of economic liberalization.

In Figures 7.2 and 7.3, the tendency toward over-investment, often noted in the reform debate, is clear in the 1968–78 period. The marginal capital/output ratio rose in this period: the growth in investment per worker exceeded the growth in output per worker.[11]

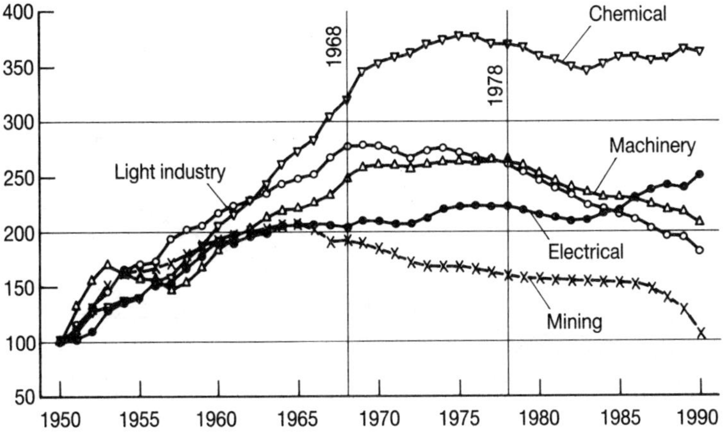

Figure 7.6 Employment in selected branches of industry 1950–90 (1950 = 100)

Source: *Hungarian Statistical Yearbook* (1990: 14)

Gross output per worker continued to rise, even when gross investment per worker declined after 1978. The growth paths of real income, the real wage, and real consumption per head began to diverge already in the early 1960s, but the divergence is dramatic after 1978, when the real wage actually declined while real consumption per head continued to rise. Here we see the result of wage controls and inflation, plus the Hungarian response: take on another job.[12] Thus the growth in output per worker appears to be the result primarily of an increase in hours worked, not in overall productivity. In this light, the post-1978 performance of the New Economic Mechanism looks even worse than it did at first glance.

Figures 7.4–7.7 show overall performance indexes for agriculture and selected branches of industry. Immediately noticeable is the leveling-off of agricultural output and output per head after 1968, which stands in contrast to the general image that agriculture received particular attention, and derived particularly great benefits, from the post-1968 reform. Increases in some industrial branches, particularly the chemical, electrical, and machinery industries, were spectacular during part of the post-war period. Employment in the selected industrial branches had already peaked in the 1960s, except for chemicals and the electrical sector, and employment increased after 1978 only in the electrical branch. The growth rate of all indexes, with the exception of those of the chemical branch, declined after 1968, and there are absolute declines in the level of productivity after 1988 or 1989 in all these branches.

Since the fall of the Communist government in Hungary, perhaps the

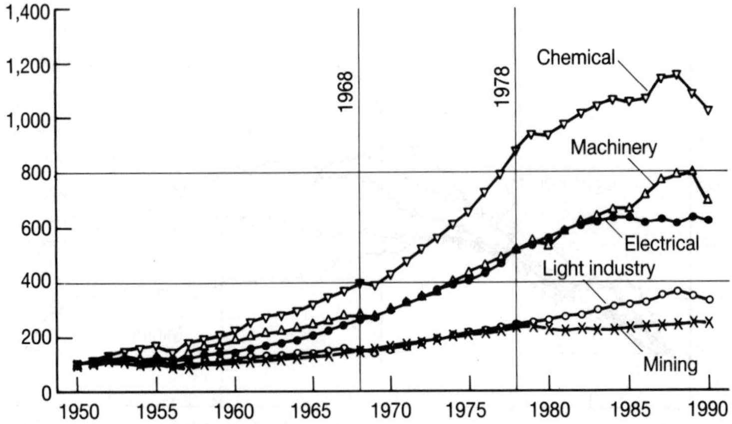

Figure 7.7 Output per worker in selected branches of industry 1950–90 (1950 = 100)

Source: *Hungarian Statistical Yearbook* (1990: 5, 14)

number one topic of conversation among the citizenry has been the rate of inflation, which currently hovers in the range of 25–30 per cent per annum. Yet inflation is not a new phenomenon. Despite the apparently firm control exercised over prices under the five-year plans up to 1968, inflation has been a more or less permanent feature of the Hungarian economy since World War II, with the notable exception of the 1960s.

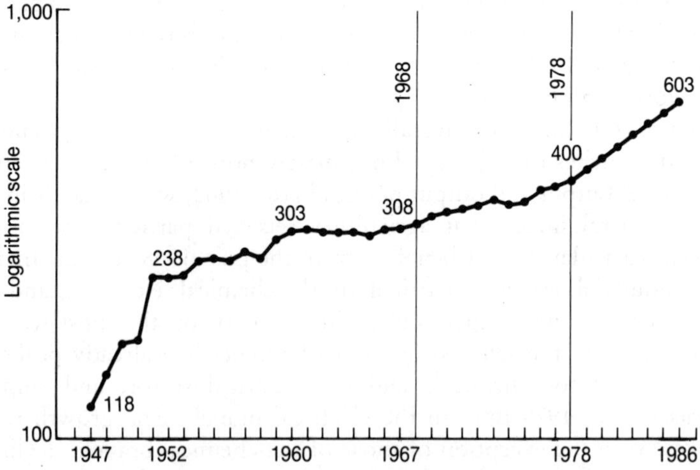

Figure 7.8 Implicit GDMP deflator 1947–85 (1946 = 100) Calculated from data in Huszti (1987: 223)

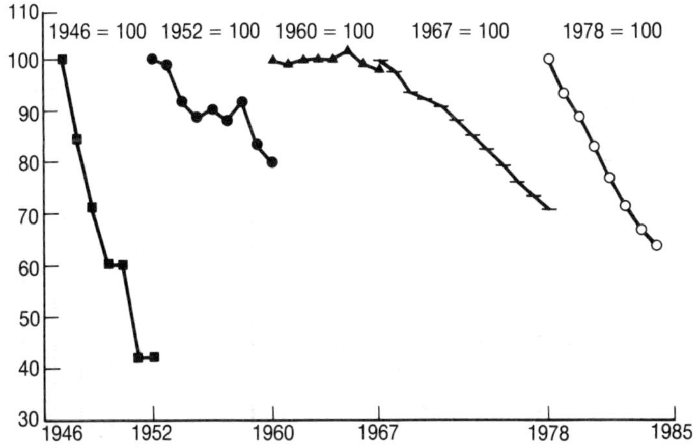

Figure 7.9 Decline in purchasing power of the forint, 1946–85 based on implicit deflator of gross domestic material product

Source: Huszti (1987: 221)

Taking Huszti's (1987: 36) subperiods, we can see the decline in the purchasing power of the Hungarian forint clearly in the data of Figure 7.9: The relatively stable prices of much of the early plan period gave way to persistent, if relatively slow, inflation from the end of the 1960s, and the rate of decline of purchasing power accelerated after 1978.

While inflation has accelerated further since 1985, the present problem did not suddenly appear with the collapse of Communism. Asztalos *et al.* (1987: 12–13) put the roots of inflation in the 1973–8 period, when Hungary incurred large foreign debts, ironically in an attempt to insulate itself from world-wide inflation. Figure 7.10 shows the growth of the convertible currency portion of that debt.

A Communist system has, somewhat paradoxically, a built-in inflationary bias: A country that has no capital market has, in practice, no non-inflationary way to finance government deficits. All deficits in Hungary were covered by printing money. The change that we now observe is thus merely a change in degree, not in kind: the deficits have grown larger, but even with a nascent capital market, money creation still remains the only way to finance these deficits.

It should be emphasized here that the Hungarian government deficit is not the same sort of deficit as understood in Western market economies. The Hungarian deficit also included, very importantly, the losses of state enterprises.[13] Thus enterprise losses were, and are, covered by printing money. Because of the fear of widespread unemployment, these enterprises were, until recently, not allowed to fail. The more economic reform exposed these

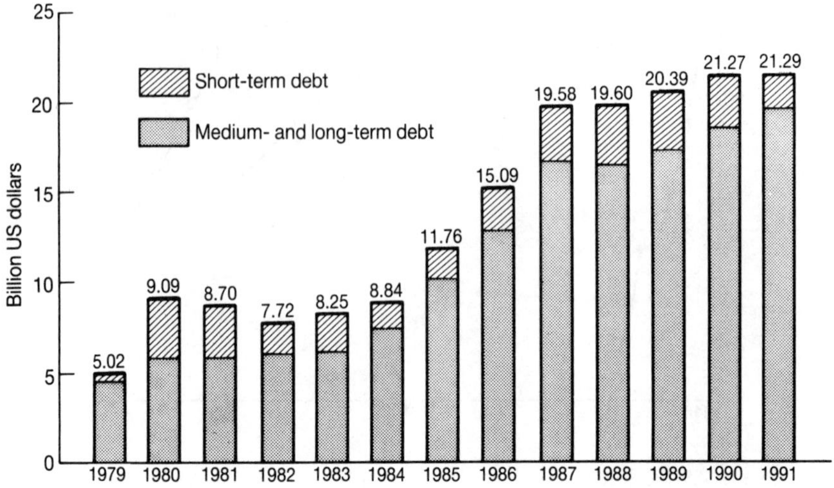

Figure 7.10 Hungarian external debt in convertible currencies 1979–91 (billions of US dollars on 31 December (November 30 in 1991))

Source: *Hungarian National Bank*

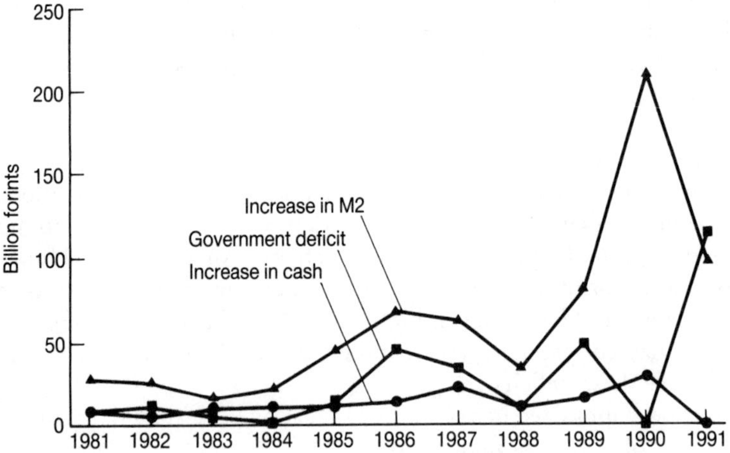

Figure 7.11 Government deficits and money supply 1981–91. Cash, M2: increase over previous year

Source: *Hungarian National Bank*

enterprises to competition, the larger their losses and the government deficit became. In this way, too, the government lost control over the size of its deficit,[14] and consequently over the money supply as well. Here the partial nature of economic reform was not merely problematical, it was downright pernicious. The failure to include and integrate a macroeconomic policy with the New Economic Mechanism was not simply an oversight, it guaranteed inflation.[15]

For a long time the Hungarian government did not even publish data on the money supply, and the suspicion exists that they neither knew nor cared about its magnitude. In consequence, Figure 7.11, showing the relationship between the government deficit and increases in the money supply, begins only with 1980. It would be very desirable to take the data back at least another twenty years, but this is not currently possible without further research.

The close correspondence between the size of the deficit and the increase in the money supply (M2 definition) is clear up to 1989. In the last two years, however, the increase in the deficit and the increase in the money supply have gone in opposite directions. An explanation for this phenomenon is difficult to find. Inflows of direct foreign investment, which have increased considerably in 1990 and 1991,[16] may account for some of this. The speculation is that the investment that flowed in during 1990 was largely converted into forints and actually invested in productive enterprise,[17] while that which came in during 1991 was largely held in idle foreign-currency balances or used simply for speculation in foreign exchange. The government's own figures on the money supply are inconsistent; it is not clear whether they include tens of billions of forints held by the postal system.

Whatever the explanation for this phenomenon, the basic point remains: so long as there is no well-developed domestic capital market, the Hungarian government will either have to limit its expenditures to a level that can be sustained by tax revenues or it will have to face the wrath of inflation-weary voters. Hungary does not have available the instruments of finance that Western governments take for granted. The only currently available way to finance deficits, including those of state-owned enterprise,[18] is money creation – either directly or indirectly through foreign borrowing. This means that privatization is not merely a short-term panacea on the revenue side, it is one of the main keys for controlling the deficit and thus the money supply.

LOOKING BACK TOWARD THE FUTURE

When regarding the present economic transition in light of past ones, it might be tempting at first to draw the parallels with 1849, a post-war transition not covered here. Peasant emancipation had given the majority of the population political freedom and had redefined property rights.

A feudalistic, hierarchical system had to give way to a more free-market system, although many of the old elite were still in charge; a new legal code was introduced at a single stroke. But there the parallels end. Hungary was then a country three times its present size, and member of a common market more than twice that again. It had neither its own currency nor control over tariff policy; the transition took place under occupation by a foreign army. Finally, its economy was not saddled with an outmoded, unproductive industrial sector.

The current situation of Hungary, and of most of its neighbors in the former "fraternal socialist camp," most resembles the situation of the early 1920s. In Hungary's case, the main parallels lie in the widespread destruction of capital (both physical[19] and human), the requirement to reorient international trade entirely, the burden of hard-currency debt largely borrowed to finance consumption (the equivalent of reparations in the post-1918 period), the threat of hyperinflation, and the re-emergence of ethnic conflicts with its neighbors.

The major differences from 1920 lie in the current need to rebuild a legal system and a capital market conducive to free-market activity, and the absence of concerted international efforts to assist in stopping inflation. Above all, the solution of the 1920s – increased government intervention in the economy – has become the problem of the 1990s. Therefore, while it might at first be tempting to look to the 1920s for guides to what to do in the 1990s, that could only be done selectively, and with great care. The Hungarian government and by extension the other governments in the area must, in my opinion, now concentrate on building the legal infrastructure, reestablishing property rights and the accountability that goes with them, and gaining the respect of the citizens for the rule of law.[20] But even success along these lines, as I shall argue later, is unlikely to guarantee success in the transition to a market economy.

The experience of the former German Democratic Republic should give all other former socialist countries of Central and Eastern Europe pause. Instant integration into the rich and powerful West German economy has produced not prosperity, but misery. It has exposed the grave flaws *and the long-term economic legacies* of the former system with merciless clarity, and to a greater or lesser extent, Hungary and her neighbors share these same problems. Let us enumerate the major issues:

1 Reconstruction from the ravages of Communism requires massive investment,[21] but until property rights are definitively clarified, investment of all kinds will be seriously impeded. While the German case may be extreme in this regard – nearly every potential Western investor who hesitates cites not knowing who owns what or what the investor will own after putting the money in as the reason for holding back – Hungary shares many of these problems, particularly in the agricultural sector.

2 Simply installing a legal code appropriate to the functioning of a market economy is not enough. If it were, East Germany would now be on track to prosperity instead of being a sink of unemployment, despair, and social unrest. Many pundits think that Hungary, having made the greatest progress in changing its legal code step-by-step even before the collapse of Communism, has therefore a good chance of successful continuation. That view is, in my opinion, overly optimistic; even when it has the requisite legal apparatus, the other problems remain.

3 Taken as a whole, the existing stock of industrial plant has no significant value; on balance the value may well be negative. For example, the issue of who shall bear the costs of the environmental clean-up inherent in the take-over of former GDR industries has further stifled investment in the industrial sector, and will certainly hold back foreigners in other countries as well. In most countries the state is saddled with ownership and still regards plant and equipment as assets. Moreover, so does the general public, so that giveaways are seen as political scandals rather than as liberation from an albatross. Piecemeal privatization means that the few viable enterprises go first, and over time the government's "assets" become increasingly burdensome because there are no profits available to offset losses. The state hangs on in the vain hope that when the worldwide recession is over, Western investors will appear to buy these enterprises for convertible currency. Giving these enterprises to the general public would defuse the political opposition to privatization and take the pressure off the state budget, but that solution is hardly even talked about in Hungary. So when these enterprises become an unbearable burden, it will not result in large private losses but rather in political crisis.

4 Ethnic homogeneity is no guarantee against severe social strains. "The devil makes work for idle hands," and when 40 per cent of the hands are idle, as they are in eastern Germany or in some urban ghettoes in the USA, anti-social gang activity is virtually certain to occur. This is not simply an eastern German problem; in every country there are some convenient scapegoats on which the mob can take out its frustration.[22] So even in Hungary, and even in the Czech Republic, if unemployment gets out of hand, German-style riots could occur. But even more instructive is the "Ossi" vs. "Wessi" ("Eastie" vs. "Westie") tension in Germany. Relations between the two groups have been thoroughly poisoned by the events and policies following unification, and we need look no further than the American South to see how long resentments engendered by feelings of having been treated unfairly can persist.

This look at history suggests a highly pessimistic outlook, both short-term and long-term. In the short term, Hungary and her neighbors will have to cope with their severe monetary and fiscal problems on their own (only Russia will receive a currency-stabilization loan), yet their hands are mostly tied by the lack of a developed domestic capital market. These countries are poor, and domestic savings could finance only a tiny fraction of necessary infrastructural and other investment, yet foreign investment in significant amounts is not forthcoming now, nor is it likely to come even when the world economy recovers.[23] So even if they manage to clarify property rights and produce an appropriate legal code, which are absolutely essential first steps, they will still have to depend on their own resources for growth for a long time to come. And if those resources (or the will to direct them to reconstruction) prove inadequate, as has been the case even in the rich country of Germany, debilitating social problems could arise. Many people understand this instinctively, and are trying to get out while the getting is good. Emigration of the young, the energetic, and the enterprising can only exacerbate the problem. There seems little chance of escape from the vicious circle.[24]

NOTES

The author is grateful to the Centre for Russian and East European Studies of the University of Toronto for financial support.

1 Friedrich Hayek, an Austrian philosopher much in vogue these days in the former Soviet bloc, contends that a system of laws grows "spontaneously" over a long period of time and is transmitted through culture and tradition. Thus to attempt to create a functioning system of laws *de novo* from nothing is to attempt the impossible (Hayek 1973–81, especially vol. I: 64–5, 101–6, and vol. II: 59). I owe this reference to my colleague, Richard B. Day.

2 Hungary never officially devalued the pengő, but the export bonus was effectively a devaluation of the currency.

3 On 1 August 1945 the cost of living index without rent stood at 117; it was nearly 28,000 by 19 December of the same year. Whereas 8,200 *pengő* bought a dollar on 12 October 1945, it took 128,000 to buy a dollar on 15 December (Büky 1947: 324.)

4 Indeed, since 1951 there were two prices for many goods, "production" prices and "consumption" prices, often unrelated to each other, let alone to any concept of cost or value.

5 For an account of the post-1956 reform proposals, see Berend (1988).

6 These regulators – introduced, modified, and expanded from time to time after 1968 – included such things as taxes on the wage bill and fixed assets, price supports, export subsidies, profits taxes, wage regulation, and interest on current assets.

7 An apparent 39 per cent of investment coming from individual companies in 1968, and 43 per cent five years later, masks the degree of central control still exercised through "informal" means. "According to some estimates independent company investment hardly accounted for a sixth of investment on the whole" (Berend 1990: 23).

8 This is curious, since – with the bulk of exports and imports pre-determined on essentially a contract barter basis, and with very strict control on imports from hard-currency areas – Hungary did not face the same degree of uncertainty in macroeconomic planning that a capitalist country with the same share of GNP

going into the foreign sector would have. Despite its openness as expressed by this ratio, the Hungarian economy could have been treated more like the closed economy of the simple Keynesian model.

9 In 1991, according to preliminary figures released by the Hungarian Central Statistical Bureau, Gross Domestic Product actually declined some 7–9 per cent, compared with 1990, including a 19 per cent fall in industrial production (*Magyar Nemzet* [*Hungarian Nation*], 19 February 1992: 9).

10 Perhaps, from this point of view, indexes based on a year in the remote past (1950) are not so bad as one might automatically assume. Since the five-year plans began only in 1950, 1950 prices might still have been close to true scarcity prices. The question then becomes whether, from a scarcity point of view, 1950 could in any way be regarded as a "normal" year.

11 Unless, of course, an increasing share of gross investment went into sectors whose output is not included in GDMP.

12 Since the Hungarian population actually declined, it is unlikely that the labor force increased during this period, so the entire increase in labor input must have been in the form of increased hours of work by existing members of the labor force. "By the late 1980s, about half the work force had at least two jobs" (Marer 1992: 13).

13 Government expenditures and revenues were normally 60 per cent or more of their measure of the GDP (Borbely 1991: 4).

14 Because money income is "inflexible downwards," and a positive balance of payments is necessary for servicing external debt, and "domestic utilization has to be moderated," argues Huszti (1987: 28), the government's inability to curb deficits led to the fall in the rate of investment. Translated into simple national income accounting, that says that $S = (X - M) + (G - T) + I$. If S is stable, the export surplus stable or rising, and the government deficit rises, investment must fall.

15 Indeed, Marer argues (1992: 9) that this kind of partial reform, particularly because it led to loss of control over the money supply, in fact "may have hastened the collapse of the system."

16 The Central Statistical Bureau reports that 5,693 enterprises "with foreign interests" operated in Hungary in 1990, and 10,335 in 1991.

17 The inflow of capital into mixed ventures in 1990 was more than triple the (relatively low) level of 1989, and it was heavily in small- and medium-size investments: 20 per cent of the total dollar value of foreign investment in 1990 was in amounts under one million US dollars, and a further 30 per cent in amounts between one and five million US dollars (Söjtöry 1991:14).

18 The round robin of credit among enterprises that Hungarians call "standing in line" (*sorbanállás*) is not a source of net credit.

19 If the capital–output ratio is conservatively estimated at 4:1, and if popular estimates that 50 per cent of the current capital stock is useless because it is rundown, outmoded, or badly designed and built, then this implies damage to the physical capital stock of the same relative order of magnitude (twice national income) as from World War II.

20 In this regard Czechoslovakia, or at least the Czech Republic if the country splits, may have the best historical tradition upon which to build.

21 Not just in directly productive plant and equipment, but especially in infrastructure, and most especially in housing. Besides sadly neglecting older buildings, East German and other governments also put up vast estates of substandard buildings that will soon have to be abandoned or torn down. Hungary's record in

housing, while poor by Western standards, was well ahead of that of most of her socialist *confrères*.

22 Already one hears the resentment of ethnic Hungarian refugees from Transylvania. Also, Croatian and Bosnian refugees could become burdensome if the Hungarian economy takes a real nosedive.

23 Looking at world demand for investment and the world supply of savings, Streissler (1990, part 2: 43) argues that the increase in German investment in Germany could well take up more than the entire increase in available world savings.

24 This is particularly true if Marer is right: "Perhaps the most damaging legacy is the inherited mindset of the population. The *political system* destroyed or prevented the emergence of a civil society. . . . *Central planning* made enterprise managers depend on the authorities for most things. The *welfare state* obviated the need of individuals and households to become self-reliant" (Marer 1992:9) (emphasis in original).

REFERENCES

Statistical Review. (1923) "A haboru előtti Magyarország statisztikai adatai a megmaradt és elveszett területek szerint részletezve" [Prewar Hungarian statistical data detailed according to remaining and lost territories], *Statisztikai Szemle* [*Statistical Review*] 7–8: 288–306.

Asztalos, L. *et al.* (1987) *Infláció és pénzügyek Magyarországon* [*Inflation and financial affairs in Hungary*], Budapest.

Berend, I. (1988) *Gazdasági útkeresés* [*Searching for an economic path*], Budapest.

Berend, I. (1990) "Plan and market in the Hungarian model," paper presented to the Xth International Economic History Congress, Leuven, Belgium, August 1990.

Bloch, M. (1941) "The rise of dependent cultivation and seigniorial institutions," *The Cambridge Economic History of Europe*, vol. I.

Borbely, L. (1991) "Allamháztartás a gyorsuló infláció időszakában" [Public finance in the period of accelerating inflation], Budapest: Gazdaságkutató intézet [Institute of economic research], January.

Büky, J. (1947) "A pengővaluta pusztulása" [Ruination of the pengő currency], in G. Márkos (ed.), *A közgazdaság évkönyve* [*Yearbook of the economy*], Budapest.

Dálnoky-Kováts, J. (1923) "Az életszínvonal alakulása" [The trend of the standard of living], *Közgazdasági Figyelő* [*Economic Observer*], II.

Eddie, S. (1990) "A fraction of half of half a reform: Hungarian economic experience after 1968," Report presented to the Xth International Economic History Congress, Leuven, Belgium, August 1990.

Hayek, F. (1973–81) *Law, Legislation, and Liberty*, Chicago.

Huszti, E. (1987) *Antiinflációs útkeresés – monetáris politika és gyakorlat Magyarországon* [*Seeking an anti-inflationary path – monetary policy and practice in Hungary*], Budapest.

Marer, P. (1992) "Economic transformation in Central and Eastern Europe," paper prepared for the Council of Foreign Relations symposium "Making Markets: Economic Transformation in Eastern Europe and the Post-Soviet Republics," New York City, February 1992.

Söjtöry, P. (1991) "A külföldi működő tőke résztvétele a vállalkozásban" [Participation of foreign operating capital in enterprise], *Gazdaság és Statisztika* [*Economy and Statistics*] 3(5) (October).

Streissler, E. (1990) "Deutschland, Deutschland über Alles?" Part 1: *Wochenpresse* no. 14 (6 April): 48–53; Part 2: *Wochenpresse* no. 15 (13 April): 42–5.

8

THE AUSTRIAN SOCIAL PARTNERSHIP

A model for Central and Eastern Europe?

Anton Pelinka

Prague, Cracow, Budapest, Zagreb, and Vienna have a common history as urban centers in the former Habsburg empire. But the collapse of the empire in 1918 seemingly destroyed many bonds of Austro–Hungarian commonality. The trend accelerated especially after 1945 when the small republic of Austria became a Western democracy, and the other successor states became part of the Communist world. In 1989 the Iron Curtain came down, the walls crumbled, and Central and Eastern Europe became – in a certain way – reunited, especially with the prospect of Westernization in the former Communist countries. The unity remains problematic, however, because with the exception of Austria, the region consists of struggling new democracies and comparatively weak economies.

In many respects, Central and Eastern Europe after 1989 is experiencing the return of history. Ethnic conflicts, the same force that many regard as responsible for the decline of the Habsburg empire, are back (Kann 1950; May 1965). In the search for solutions, some of the ideas developed before 1914 may be helpful, e.g., the social democratic approach (Mommsen 1963). It seems, however, that the solution of 1919, which involved establishing smaller states in the Paris peace treaties, seems to be the post-1989 solution as well. Instead of promoting multi-nationalism and inter-ethnic compromise, nation-building is the recipe for smaller ethnic groups. The multiplication of new nation-states like Slovenia, Croatia, Slovakia, Moldova, Belorus, and Macedonia implies a decline of predictability and a probable increase in violence on an international scale, much as it did after 1918 (Elias 1987: 127–133).

But there is also a potential lesson of history for post-Communist democracies: the post-1945 stabilization of Austria through certain political mechanisms, called "Proporzdemokratie" (Lehmbruch 1967) or "consociational democracy" (Lijphart 1977: 25–52). After World War II, Austria was in a similar situation as its Eastern neighbors are in now. It became Westernized by following a distinctive path; it developed democracy around the institutions of its social partnership. The social partnership fostered democracy, but placed certain limits on political competition; it promoted a competitive economy, but placed certain limits on the market. The major political parties competed for votes, according to the rules of liberal democracy; but they cooperated within a grand coalition for more than two decades. Business and labor, in cooperation with the major parties, established a network of social partnership, beginning with the agreements on wages and prices between 1947 and 1951, and continuing under pressure from Austria's "economic miracle" with the founding of the Joint Commission on Wages and Prices in 1957.

The social partnership evolved according to the neo-corporatist principle of tripartitism. Three partners – a democratically elected government, labor unions and employers' associations – were linked in a triangular, formal institutional structure. Is there a lesson to be learned from the Austrian experience? Is the Austrian experience with social partnership of any importance for Central Europe today? Can Austria "export" its political knowledge about dealing with economic crisis in the early stages of democracy?

POST-1945 AUSTRIA AND POST-1989 CENTRAL AND EASTERN EUROPE: PARALLELS AND DIFFERENCES

In 1945 Austria once again became an independent country. The three anti-fascist parties declared independence on 27 April 1945 – less than two weeks before the end of World War II in Europe. Independence and democracy were thought to be one and the same: The declaration of independence included a clear reference to reestablishing a democratic republic (Bluhm 1973: 46–72).

Between 1945 and 1955, Austria was in a unique situation. It was liberated by the allies from German occupation, yet was occupied by the same allies, which meant that it was treated like the other liberated countries and like Germany at the very same time. Being occupied during the cold war meant that Austria would be affected by East–West conflicts. Austria and its democratically elected, pro-Western government had to deal with both Soviet and Western troops on Austrian territory (Bischof and Leidenfrost 1988). In combination with the domestic trauma produced by the Civil War of 1934 (Gulick 1948: 1266–362), a climate of compromise and consensus drew together both the two major parties and labor and business.

After 1989, the former Communist countries in Central and Eastern Europe changed dramatically from one-party rule to competitive democracy and from centrally planned to market economies. In Yugoslavia, this transition of political and economic regimes was also combined with the break-up of the Yugoslav federation due to ethnic rivalries. In a different and less direct way, the regime transition in Czechoslovakia also led to the dissolution of its federation. But in all the other cases – Poland, Hungary,

Romania, Bulgaria, and Albania – transition had nothing to do with the issue of national independence and sovereignty. Transition was and still is a political and economic process, not a national one.

This already shows what the Austrian case after 1945 and the Central European cases after 1989 do and do not have in common. In Austria, the combination of regime transition and national independence was not linked in the same way, if at all. In the Austrian case, regime transition and national independence were more-or-less the same; Austria became an independent, sovereign state and established a Western-style democracy. In the post-Communist world, regime transition has, in principle, nothing to do with the question of national independence. Whereas Austria had to achieve a national identity, the former Communist countries are able to draw on their existing national identity, which was not broken through Communist rule. Even if the *de facto* independence from the USSR must be seen as an aspect of national sovereignty, the pure existence of a Czech or Polish or Hungarian nation was never in doubt.

Another difference has to do with the economy: Austria, as a former occupied part of Hitler's Greater German Empire, did not have to change from a centrally planned economy to a market economy (Hiscocks 1953: 69–80). Despite its high level of state intervention and its status as a war economy, the Austrian economy after 1945 had to transform from a German-dominated market economy to a uniquely Austrian market economy.

But there is an important economic parallel: Austria in 1945 and Central Europe after 1989 started capitalism without capital and without capitalists. In the former socialist countries, the organization of the economy in principle prevented private ownership of the means of production. Without private capital, there were by definition no capitalists.

In post-1938 Austria, the economy was completely directed from Germany – either by the state (like the Hermann Goering enterprises) or by privately owned capital. Austrian capital played only a small role. Between 1938 and 1945, Austria was on the periphery of the Greater German Empire. Liberation from Nazi rule after 1945 left Austria a market economy without established economic centers, which previously were in Germany, and without German capital. Building a market economy was a political goal, but capitalists, eager to move their investments into this economy, were missing. In this respect, post-1945 Austria and the post-Communist countries have much in common.

In both cases, rebuilding the economy required opening the country to foreign capital, and/or developing domestic capital. In post-1945 Austria, it was not, at least in the beginning, private foreign capital that became the focal point. It was the attempt by the Soviet Union to take over formerly German property as part of the compensation package after the end of the war (März and Szecsi 1981). To fight this kind of foreign take-over, the two leading non-Communist parties in Austria passed the nationalization acts in 1946 and in 1947. Here broad-based nationalization of property had a distinct anti-Communist flavor.

Nationalizing the most important industries and the leading banks was a way of securing economic independence, not a vehicle for building any kind of "socialism" (März and Szecsi 1981: 127ff.). But this policy cannot be exported to the former socialist economies because their industries and banks were already nationalized. Nationalization in socialist economies lost any possible credibility; it is seen as a pillar of a system that has to be destroyed in order to transform socialist economies into market economies. Because nationalization is – for understandable reasons – in complete disrepute, this part of the Austrian post-1945 experience cannot provide guidelines for post-1989 Central Europe.

Capitalism without capital and without capitalists in the post-cold war era has to be seen in the context of a rather strongly developed capitalist world economy, especially in Western Europe. This points to another difference with post-1945 Austria. At the end of World War II, Western European capital was not eager to move eastward. Central and Eastern Europe today can count on such an interest. Thus, it is more correct to refer to the present situation as one of "capitalism without domestic capital and without domestic capitalists" because foreign capital and foreign capitalists are likely to move in. Also, there is no doubt that public opinion in the former East bloc states generally favors such movements, in contrast to the Austrian mood in 1945 and 1946, which opposed the Soviet grip on formerly German property in Austria. In the case of Central and Eastern Europe today, nationalization is a reminder of a system almost everybody wants to overcome. In the case of post-1945 Austria, nationalization was a pragmatic move to secure domestic political control over the most important economic assets.

The lessons from Austria's experience with changing property ownership after World War II seem ambiguous. By contrast, lessons from its experience with corporatism are much clearer. In comparative analyses of neo-corporatism in post-1945 Europe, Austria has the strongest of the "strong corporatist" systems, ranking even ahead of Germany and Sweden (Lehmbruch 1982).

Neo-corporatism in post-1945 Europe is best seen as a blend of liberal democracy and institutionalized cooperation in all economic and social affairs. Neo-corporatism leads to a degree of political influence on the economy and on industrial relations that is not within the traditional pattern of a capitalist market economy. But it is not inconsistent with capitalism, either. Neo-corporatism is built on the existence of the class conflict, especially between employers and employees, i.e., between capital and labor (Schmitter and Lehmbruch 1979).

The former East bloc countries may profit from studying the Austrian experience with corporatism for two reasons. First, the Austrian variation of neo-corporatism, its social partnership, is a response precisely to the challenge of capitalism without capital and without capitalists. Because capital and capitalists were considered comparatively weak in post-1945 Austria, a system of institutionalized compromise looked especially useful to employers. In the absence of privately owned, Austrian large-scale industry, small entrepreneurs, manufacturers, and tradespeople were strongly interested in a permanent deal with labor and the unions.

Second, Austria did not have the institutional framework for a corporatist network in 1945: the basic institutions had to be established from the beginning. It lacked a central employers' organization and a central labor organization that could fulfill the prerequisites for a corporatist system. Corporatism did have some roots in pre-1938 Austria (Talos 1985). Its institutions could be built on specific traditions, e.g., the tradition of social reform that was rooted deeply in Austria's political catholicism and the pragmatic attitude demonstrated after 1918 by the Austrian Social Democrats (Pelinka 1981: 1–4). But all the necessary institutions had to be created during the first years of the Second Republic.

In short, the Austrian experience demonstrates that corporatism can be a reasonable response to the challenge of capitalism without capital and without capitalists and suggests the possibility of starting corporatism without an already existing institutional framework.

PREREQUISITES OF THE AUSTRIAN MODEL

Austria's social partnership is built on two structural prerequisites. First, the basic economic interests are organized in highly centralized and monopolistic institutions; the Austrian Federation of Labor (*Österreichischer Gewerkschaftsbund*) represents labor and of the Federal Chamber of Commerce (*Bundeskammer der gewerblichen Wirtschaft*) represents capital. These two bodies are integrated along with the government into the corporatist network according to the rules of tripartitism (Katzenstein 1984, 34–83), but each must speak with one voice. There must be only one government policy, only one employers' policy, and only one labor policy.

Second, the organizations representing business (Federal Chamber) and labor (Austrian Federation of Labor) are autonomous, i.e., independent from political parties and from government. But this independence is limited. Indirect linkages synchronize the separate policies of the social partners and of the political parties to avoid the possibility of paralysis between parties and parliament on one side and interest groups and social partnership on the other. The linkage results from integrating suborganizations of the major political parties (*Fraktionen*) into the major economic interest groups (Pelinka 1989). As a consequence, the Federation of Labor and the Federal Chamber stand above political partisanship, but they *de facto* are dominated by unionists attached to the SPÖ or by business elites attached to the ÖVP.

Centralization and autonomy are important because they provide flexibility to the institutions of social partnership. But both have costs. Centralization can strain democratic principles and autonomy can lead to institutions that lie beyond the constitution and its control mechanisms.

The consequence of centralization can be seen by comparing differences among labor unions in Europe with respect to their impact on policymaking. The more centralized unions are integrated into corporatist tripartitism, the more they are part of the political decision-making, and the more they are responsible for the political outcomes. Centralization generates a consensus that efficiency is a priority and so centralized economic interest groups that are interwoven into the tripartite system do comparatively well with respect to promoting economic growth as measured by GNP growth rates, and industrial peace as measured by strike frequencies (Katzenstein 1984: 239–57).

These outcomes require a related factor. The broad consensus on social and economic goals and policies requires not just the cooperation of business and labor, but also an active role by government. Here public opinion and political parties enter into the picture.

Social partnership demands moderation from its partners with respect to the main economic issues: the ownership of the means of production (private vs. public), state intervention into the market, and the distribution of income and property. In the context of traditional positions taken by European political parties and interest groups, that means that the left and labor must not be too socialistic; they must accept an economy and a society based on capitalistic rules. It means that the right and business must not be too capitalistic; they must accept some welfare policies and state intervention.

In the Austrian case, the two major political parties fulfilled this requirement of moderation. The left was dominated by Social Democrats, who oriented the SPÖ toward the political center; the Communists did not play any important role after they left the cabinet in 1947. The right was dominated by conservatives who shaped the ÖVP much more after the French MRP (Mouvement Republicain Populaire) than after purely conservative parties (Skalnik 1972). The Austrian left abstained from policies directed toward a centrally planned economy and from advocating any changes beyond the principles of a market economy. The Austrian right was never really tempted by the idea of destroying the welfare state.

But moderation cannot be isolated from its context. What was moderate in Austria in 1945 or 1950 may not be moderate in Austria in 1990 or in Czechoslovakia and Hungary in 1992. Moderation is a functional concept that requires a balance between two political trends, usually defined as "right" and "left;" the mutual acceptance of political legitimacy by groups ("pillars," "camps") around those two trends; political pragmatism instead of ideological fundamentalism (Lipset 1960); the ability to integrate followers within each camp according to traditional ideologies (Pelinka 1989: 21–3); and the ability to transform ideological traditions into pragmatic compromises.

CASE STUDY: TRIPARTITISM IN CZECHOSLOVAKIA, 1989–92

Among all post-Communist countries, Czechoslovakia was in a unique position after 1989 as the only one with a democratic tradition (1918–39, 1945–48). It was also, along with the German Democratic Republic, the most industrialized country in Central Europe. That is the reason why Czechoslovakia, before its break-up on January 1, 1993, is an especially interesting case for analyzing the potential for corporatist trends in post-Communist systems.

On October 3, 1990, representatives of the Czech government, the labor unions, and the employers' association constituted the "Council of Economic and Social Associations" (CESA).[1] This council existed on two different levels[2] – on the level of the two (Czech and Slovak) republics and on the federal level. The federal level formed a kind of second stage above the republic level, which consisted of the first and most important bodies – the Czech CESA and the Slovak CESA. On both levels, seven members represented each of the three partners so the CESA consisted of 21 members. Each side could invite up to four advisers to participate in the meetings. The CESA worked either in plenary sessions or through committees that prepared materials for the decisions CESA had to make.

The most important feature of CESA that gave it a clear corporatist quality was its decision-making process. Each side had to speak with one voice because it had only one vote. Within CESA, only three votes were possible, all decisions required all three votes, and each of the three "partners" had veto power. Although the Austrian experience was not used consciously as a model, the rules seem to come directly from the Austrian "Joint Commission on Wages and Prices" – with the significant difference that in the Austrian case government representatives have no voting rights (Marin 1982: 50–3). But the necessity of reaching unanimous decisions – or to reach no decision at all – links the Czechoslovakian model of tripartitism to the Austrian one. Both have in common an understanding of political decision-making that departs from the majority rules of representative democracy.

The main task faced by CESA at the beginning was to pass a "general agreement," which is a legal, not a political document. It binds the different partners by political consent, not by the threat of legal sanctions. The "general agreement," too, operated on two levels – the republic and the federal level, which means that CESA had to formulate three "general agreements" – one for the Czech republic, one for the Slovak republic, and one for the federal republic.

The federalist structure of CESA from 1990 on suggests optimism about the future of tripartitism now that the Czech republic and Slovakia have become independent states. The fate of social partnership in Czechoslovakia was not bound to the existence of federal institutions. Social partnership, after its very cautious beginnings, can survive and develop on the republic level even though it dissolved at the federal level.

The agenda for the Slovak CESA in the first half of 1991 gives a good example of how tripartitism worked in Czechoslovakia:[3]

January: four meetings, all dealing with different aspects of the "general agreement" (for Slovakia), with the finalization of the agreement and with the signing of this agreement.

February: one meeting, fifteen specific topics including social security, housing, heating, income tax, wage development, and unemployment.

March: one meeting, thirteen specific topics including energy policy, privatization, the environment, state decrees concerning financial privileges, tax reform, and price regulations.

April: one meeting, six specific topics, including privatization as well as changes in the general agreement for 1991.

May: one meeting, eight specific topics including social security and the draft of a bill dealing with minimum income and wage increases in response to inflation in the second quarter of 1991.

June: one meeting, fifteen specific topics including privatization and drafts of bills dealing with taxation, social security, and reimbursement for wages lost after illness.

For the rest of 1991 and for the first half of 1992 both Slovakia's CESA and the Czech CESA followed the established pattern: usually one meeting per month that covered a broad agenda of very different topics.

The minutes of the Czech CESA meetings, unlike the Slovak CESA, also include results of meetings, for example, whether proposals were accepted, accepted with certain exceptions or with suggested changes, or postponed for further consultations. Only for the general agreement (signed, as in the Slovak case in January 1991), was there a decision to sign.

The range of possible responses indicates the linkage between the constitutional institutions (represented by the government) and the corporatist "partners". Tripartitism in Czechoslovakia, as in Austria, did not substitute for parliament and the executive branch; it supplemented the rules and institutions set forth by the constitution.

CESA's agenda clearly demonstrates that its main initial purpose was to establish the basic rules for the social and economic order in the post-

Communist era. The government used CESA as an advisory body to gauge the responses of labor and business with respect to decrees and bills.

CESA can be compared with the five agreements on wages and prices, signed in Austria between 1947 and 1951 by the coalition government, labor, and business (März and Szecsi 1981, 129) because it was not established by law, but by voluntary agreement of key interest groups and its decisions had political consequences but no legal basis. In both cases – Austria from 1947 to 1951 and Czechoslovakia in 1991 and 1992 – the tripartite institutions developed basic political rules by consensus. Both cases followed the pattern of "consociational democracy." (Lijphart 1977: 25–52). But the agenda of CESA in 1991 also demonstrates an extremely broad range of interests that included all fields of social and economic policy.

Guido Baglioni (1990: 13ff.) identifies three types of industrial relations systems in contemporary Europe: the constitutional, the consultative, and the deregulatory. Corporatism belongs to the consultative type, but it also has some constitutional aspects. "Reaganomics" and "Thatcherism" are contemporary versions of the deregulatory type that fits best into a market economy, free of government intervention. The constitutional type is more-or-less the antithesis: the main rules regulating industrial relations are generated by the institutions of a centrally planned economy. The consultative type lies somewhere in between as a kind of synthesis.

Czechoslovakia's CESA clearly follows the consultative pattern. Its tripartitism was based on voluntary agreement, not on legal rules, and the representatives of both labor and employees cooperated with the government, but were not part of it. But Czechoslovakia still had to develop strong centralized unions and strong centralized employers' associations. In Czechoslovakia, as in all former Communist countries, remnants of the old Communist organizations competed more-or-less openly with other unions while others, like the Polish Solidarity, were part of the anti-Communist struggle of the past. The employers' associations, too, lacked the traditions of professional centralized organizations.

One other factor, the party system, must be considered because it suggests the difficulties of any simple transfer of the Austrian experience to Czechoslovakia. The party system in post-1989 Czechoslovakia was highly decentralized. In post-1945 Austria, the party system was highly centralized. But as I discuss in the next section, a decentralized party system is not unique to Czechoslovakia; it is a factor that influences (and minimizes) the chances of social partnership in all former Communist countries.

CENTRAL AND EASTERN EUROPE: PUBLIC OPINION AND THE PARTY SYSTEM

There is no doubt that the former Communist countries are plagued by inflation, unemployment, the problems typically dealt with by corporatism.

Although the argument that corporatism can successfully fight inflation and unemployment is not undisputed, it is at least plausible. In the immediate post-1945 period, Austria faced these twin economic problems. The five Wage–Price Agreements (1947–51) were a corporatist response. In the late 1940s, holding down inflation was a goal in itself in Austria and economic growth started on a larger scale only in the 1950s. Since then, controlling inflation and unemployment have typically been highest on the social partnership agenda.

In the former Communist countries, there is now great concern over inflation and unemployment. A 1991 study organized by the Paul Lazarsfeld Society in cooperation with the Institute of Conflict Research, both based in Vienna, underlines this. The following tables summarize the results of public opinion polls in Austria and in the former East bloc countries: Bulgaria, Czecho–Slovakia, Poland, Romania, and Hungary.[4] Table 8.1 demonstrates the growing public concern in former Communist countries over inflation; Table 8.2 indicates concern over the political consequences of inflation; and Table 8.3 shows the already substantial fear of unemployment.

Table 8.1

Question: "Which problems are the two most important the government has to face?" (two answers possible) (percentage of total respondents)

	A	*BG*	*CS*	*PL*	*RO*	*HU*
Inflation	18	25	22	35	70	63
Unemployment	59	58	51	71	36	61
Crime	37	51	45	31	16	27
Privatization	10	12	11	9	20	7
Minorities	12	7	8	1	6	4
"Nomenklatura"	[a]	12	15	13	11	3
International relations	12	2	3	7	6	4
Social security	37	27	37	23	24	18
Taxes	13	4	6	8	9	9

N= (A)1,954 (BG)1,002 (CS)1,034 (PL)1,193 (RO)1,000 (HU)1,019

[a] not included in Austria

A: Austria; BG: Bulgaria; CS: Czechoslovakia; PL: Poland; RO: Romania; HU: Hungary

The outcome of the study is quite clear. Public opinion may be more than ready to accept the creation of political instruments that would control inflation and fight unemployment. Corporatism, e.g., in the shape of an Austrian-style social partnership, might be accepted with open arms.

But public opinion is not enough to bring about effective corporatist arrangements; the proper political framework is also needed. Besides having to centralize the basic interest groups (labor unions and employers' associ-

Table 8.2

Question: "Next year, demonstrations on the streets will be possible because of . . . ?" (for both items, "yes" is a possible answer) (percentage of total respondents)

	A	*BG*	*CS*	*PL*	*RO*	*HU*
Prices	26	69	67	78	84	81
Unemployment	68	82	74	89	86	84

N= (A)1,954 (BG)1,002 (CS)1,034 (PL)1,193 (RO)1,000 (HU)1,019

A: Austria; BG: Bulgaria; CS: Czechoslovakia; PL: Poland; RO: Romania; HU: Hungary

Table 8.3

Question: "Are you afraid of losing your work place?" (percentage of total respondents)

	A	*BG*	*CS*	*PL*	*RO*	*HU*
yes, very	4	34	21	22	19	29
yes, a little	12	34	42	33	44	34
no	82	31	27	34	37	26
no answer	3	1	10	11	0	10
N =	982	510	678	531	538	581

A: Austria; BG: Bulgaria; CS: Czechoslovakia; PL: Poland; RO: Romania; HU: Hungary

ations), the party system has to be shaped according to some minimal conditions. There must be concentration within the party system and a balance among the leading parties.

Corporatism is fostered by political balance. Indeed, the need to compromise provides the initial incentive for building consociational structures. Corporatism profits from a small number of independent political actors. For example, the smaller the number of relevant political parties, the easier it is to compromise. The best possible precondition is a perfect two-party system with no permanent majority for either party. That Scandinavian, especially Swedish, corporatism is not based on such a perfect two-party system may explain that Swedish post-war corporatism has been ranked number two in strength behind the Austrian case (Lehmbruch 1982).

The Austrian case illustrates the importance of these conditions. The first free, that is competitive, elections after independence resulted in both concentration and balance in Austrian politics. In the 1945 parliamentary elections, ÖVP and SPÖ together captured 94.4 per cent of the votes, with the difference between these two leading parties being 5.2 percentage points.

The outcome was an almost perfect balance. The (Christian Democratic, conservative) ÖVP, linked with business, and the (Social Democratic) SPÖ, linked with labor, were almost forced to look for compromise. Compromise was also promoted by the international situation; the beginning of the cold war made it more urgent and therefore easier in occupied Austria. From the beginning, the Second Republic was characterized by a highly centralized and extremely balanced party system.

Just the opposite case is true for the former East bloc countries today. In 1990, free elections took place – in Poland at the presidential level, in the other countries at the parliamentary level. But as the results of Table 8.4 clearly indicate, there is almost no concentration and no balance. Hungary has balance, but no concentration. Romania and Slovenia have concentration, but no balance. Compared with the Austrian experience in 1945, the best conditions for social partnership are in Bulgaria where concentration and balance in the party system are high.

There is not much chance for improving this situation in the short run. The elections after 1990, the first year of democracy, actually brought a decline of party concentration – the Polish (1991) as well as the Czech and Slovak (1992) parliamentary elections provide special examples of this trend. Consensus-building organizations that are rooted in the anti-Communist democratic improvements, like Solidarity or Civic Forum, get split up under the conditions of free political competition. With the obvious exception of the rebirth of ethnic sentiments, there are no strong traditional trends in the former Communist countries.

The emerging democracies of Central and Eastern Europe need social compromise to build consensus around economic reconstruction. The people and their leaders are aware of the need, but lack a political system with the proper preconditions. Communist rule eroded the basic roots that could have created those preconditions – a strong, moderate, unified left and a strong, moderate, unified right. The surprising lack of success faced by social democratic parties in all countries is one aspect of this erosion. "Socialism" still seems to be synonymous with Communist dictatorship. In the aftermath of this dictatorship, any democratic form of socialism – even created out of anti-Communist opposition – seems to be tainted. The weakness of the left corresponds with the decomposition of the right. Communist dictatorship did not allow the survival of pre-Communist democratic traditions with a "bourgeois" origin.

SUMMARY AND CONCLUSION

Post-1945 Austria and the post-1989 former East bloc states have strong social and economic parallels. Fighting inflation and unemployment and building a stable market economy and a welfare state were priorities in both.

But the political systems differ markedly. Post-1945 Austria had from the

Table 8.4 Competitive elections in Central Europe 1990: The two strongest parties or candidates

Bulgaria (Bulgarian Socialist Party, Union of Democratic Forces)	
combined	83.3%
difference	10.9%
Czecho-Slovakia (Civic Forum + Public Against Violence, Communist Party)	
combined	59.6%
difference	32.4%
Slovenia (Demos, Party of Democratic Renewal)	
combined	72.0%
difference	38.0%
Hungary (Second ballot) (Hungarian Democratic Forum, Union of Free Democrats)	
combined	46.1%
difference	3.3%
Poland (Wałesa, Tyminski) (presidential elections, first ballot)	
combined	63.1%
difference	16.9%
Romania (National Salvation Front, Democratic Union of Hungarians)	
combined	73.5%
difference	59.1%

Source: All data are based on Weilguni, W., Suppan, A., Heuberger, W. and Koch, K. (1991) *The Elections of 1990 in Central, Eastern and Southeastern Europe*, Vienna: Österreichisches Ost- und Südosteuropa-Institut.

very beginning a strong party system that was both centralized and balanced. In the Austrian case, the unique political culture of the "camps" survived the years of Nazi rule to shape the creation of a strong party system and a system of strong economic interest groups. The survival of this political culture provided the legacy for building the social partnership in Austria after 1945.

By contrast, the four decades of Communist rule in Central and Eastern Europe almost completely eroded pre-Communist political culture and political traditions. It left no legacy to use as the backbone for the institutional arrangements of corporatism. Of course, such institutions can be built, as the example of CESA in Czechoslovakia shows. But it is at least arguable that without the necessary political prerequisites corporate institutions will not have the same consequences in the newly emerging democracies as they did in Austria after 1945.

NOTES

1 All the information about CESA is based on data provided by L. Brokl and Z. Mansfeldova, Institute of Sociology, Czechoslovak Academy of Sciences, as part of a joint research project in cooperation with the Department of Political Science, Innsbruck University, and the Institute of Conflict Research, Vienna.

2 The difference between the federal and republic level mirrors the constitutional crises the new democracy in Czechoslovakia had to face.

3 1991 was the first year CESA was working.

4 See the unpublished papers: Haerpfer, C. (1992) *Neue Demokratienbarometer*, Research Paper. Vienna. See also Rose, R. and Haerpfer, C. (1992) "New democracies between state and market," in *Studies in Public Policy*, 204. Centre for the Study of Public Policy, University of Strathclyde, Glasgow.

REFERENCES

Baglioni, G. (1990) "Industrial relations in Europe in the 1980s," in G. Baglioni and C. Crouch (eds.) *European Industrial Relations*, London.

Bischof, G. and Leidenfrost, J. (eds.) (1988) *Die bevormundete Nation. Österreich und die Alliierten 1945–1949*, Innsbruck.

Bluhm, W.T. (1973) *Building an Austrian Nation*, New Haven.

Elias, N. (1987) *Engagement und Distanzierung*, Frankfurt.

Gulick, C.A. (1948) *Austria from Habsburg to Hitler* 2 vols, Berkeley.

Hiscocks, R. (1953) *The Rebirth of Austria*, London.

Kann, R.A. (1950) *The Multinational Empire* 2 vols, New York.

Katzenstein, P.J. (1984) *Corporatism and Change*, Ithaca.

Lehmbruch, G. (1967) *Proporzdemokratie*, Tübingen.

Lehmbruch, G. (1982) "Introduction: Neo-corporatism in comparative perspective," in G. Lehmbruch and P.C. Schmitter (eds.) *Patterns of Corporatist Policy-Making*, London.

Lijphart, A. (1977) *Democracy in Plural Societies*, New Haven.

Lipset, S.M. (1960) *Political Man*, New York.

Marin, B. (1982) Die Paritätische Kommission, Vienna.

März, E. and Szecsi, M. (1981) "Austria's economic development, 1945–1978," In K. Steiner (ed.) *Modern Austria*, Palo Alto.

May, A.J. (1965) *The Hapsburg Monarchy, 1867–1914*, Cambridge.

Mommsen H. (1963) *Die Sozialdemokratie und die Nationalitätenfrage im habsburgischen Vielvölkerstaat*, Vienna.

Pelinka, A. (1981) *Modellfall Österreich? Möglichkeiten und Grenzen der Sozialpartnerschaft*, Vienna.

Pelinka, A. (1989) "Decline of the party state and the rise of parliamentarianism," in A. Pelinka and F. Plasser (eds.) *The Austrian Party System*, Boulder CO.

Schmitter, P.C. and Lehmbruch, G. (eds.) (1979) *Trends Toward Corporatist Intermediation*, London.

Skalnik, K. (1972) "Parteien," in E. Weinzierl and K. Skalnik (eds.) *Die Zweite Republik*, vol. 2, Graz.

Talos, E. (1985) "Zur Entwicklung und Entwicklungsdynamik kooperativ-konzertierter Politik in Österreich," in P. Gerlich *et al.* (eds.) *Sozialpartnerschaft in der Krise*, Vienna.

Part IV

THE STATE AND STRUCTURAL CHANGE

9

THE YUGOSLAV ECONOMY FROM AMALGAMATION TO DISINTEGRATION

Failed efforts at molding a new economic space 1919–91

Ivo Bićanić and Marko Škreb

INTRODUCTION

Understanding the disintegration of Yugoslavia in 1992 requires taking the long view. We do so by analyzing the Yugoslav economy at two levels. First we survey the repeated attempts to mold, create, and control the Yugoslav economy through various institutional forms of centralization and then we consider Yugoslavia's long-term economic performance: growth rates of national income and employment and patterns of interregional trade.

We argue that from the very beginning tensions were built into the centralized economic system of Yugoslavia. These tensions resulted from very different levels of development in the newly amalgamated regions, which led to asymmetric effects of centralized policy, different trade orientation of the regions, and the inability of the center to act as an honest broker of regional interests. Initial and later attempts to promote growth and manage crises through economic centralization and state dominance compounded the tensions. Yugoslavia went through a sequence of varied centralized economic systems that did not deal adequately with continuous pressures for decentralization and the devolution of economic power; the only two attempts to create a decentralized economy were short-lived. In the context of these institutional problems, the Yugoslav economy performed poorly. Its relative position on the European development scale did not change and modern economic growth failed to moderate the pattern of short growth bursts and subsequent economic crises. In addition, interregional trade shows that an integrated economy was never built.

The most important building block of Yugoslavia's disintegration in 1992 evolved during the late 1980s. When the socialist economies faced their final crises and the transition to post-socialist development started, the pressures for disintegration were too strong. Individual regions sought "go-it-alone" policies and at least five new states emerged. Disintegration is not yet complete as the "Wars of the Yugoslav Succession" which began in the early 1990s, continue.[1]

THE AMALGAMATION OF 1918: CREATING A NEW ECONOMIC SPACE

The political climate of post-World War I Europe favored a re-drawing of Europe's boundaries. At the Paris peace conference, the Austro–Hungarian Empire was carved up with Yugoslavia emerging as one of the newly formed successor states. From an international point of view unification seemed to satisfy the dominant political interests, whose roots can be traced to the mid-nineteenth century, yet cover over important differences regarding the constitutional organization of the new state.[2]

Whereas the political underpinnings of unification in 1918 seemed beyond doubt, the economic foundations were never clearly identified, despite frequent political demands to that effect. From an economic point of view, the new state of Yugoslavia was merely an amalgamation that did not automatically bring unity. The constituent regions differed greatly with respect to levels of development, institutional structures, and legal and business traditions. Yet, their economic structures were quite similar; they were mainly agrarian economies with surpluses of livestock often competing for the same export markets. Trade links were insignificant and direct rail links were non-existent (see Bićanić 1972).

The first economic task after amalgamation was to create the common economic institutions needed to promote interregional economic links. This meant creating a new monetary system from five separate currencies and a new fiscal system from twelve separate tax systems, plus implementing a new tariff and foreign trade system. What emerged was the first in a sequence of government economic interventionist policies aimed at introducing a "grand design," in this case a "liberal capitalist Yugoslav economy." These policies were based on modifications of the centralized pre-World War I institutions of the Kingdom of Serbia. In essence the new economic system produced a small étatist autarchic economy that exported agricultural products and raw materials. Internally undeveloped markets facilitated the dominance of overt or covert government-brokered deals.

The time horizon of the transition path varied. The internal convertibility of other currencies to the Serbian dinar was completed by 1925, but monetary stability was achieved only by 1931 and it took over 20 years for the National Bank to reorganize (Mirković 1964). A uniform tax system was proposed in 1922, but not passed until 1928. The first balanced budget was passed in 1925, yet it was incomplete, so that landmark seems to have come only in 1934 (Lamer 1936). The Serbian tariff system of 1904 was adapted in 1925, but its basic approach (protection and autarchy) was not changed;

indeed the level of protection increased (Kukoleča 1941). A uniform system of railway tariffs was introduced as late as 1925 favoring links within the country, thus attempting to redirect trade flows.

The policies of amalgamation had important regional consequences, which resulted in the initial disappointment over amalgamation among the more developed northern regions. First, internal exchange rates, the redistribution of inherited government debts, and an agrarian reform led to major redistribution of wealth. Second, the new national boundaries and rail tariff policies changed trade relations between Slovenia and Croatia on one side and their previously well established markets in Austria and Hungary on the other side. Third, increasing economic interventionism and centralization, especially after the St. Vitious Day Constitution of 1921, reduced autonomy and the Austrian and Hungarian state administration with its Eurocentrism was replaced by a Balkan one. Fourth, industrial policy in the new system was biased against the industrial and financial sectors of Slovenia and Croatia and in favor of new industries in other parts of the country. This dissatisfaction was further increased by later economic policies that continued the biases of the policies implemented during the amalgamation.

SHIFTING POLICY REGIMES, 1918–91

The amalgamation achieved during the 1920s was the first step in creating an integrated national, i.e. Yugoslav, economy. Creating a Yugoslav economy was a difficult task not only because it involved influencing long-term trends, but also because of the different meanings that could be and were attached to the term "Yugoslav economy." Thus, the same policies could be seen as either promoting and accelerating growth or retarding and decelerating it.

As has been pointed out, the amalgamation itself quickly become contentious. Bitter political battles were fought as different parties strove for their vision of Yugoslavia and the Yugoslav economy. There were multiple lines of conflict over policy decentralization vs. centralization, market orientation vs. government interventionism, and international competition vs. autarchy. During the whole period those issues were debated but no coherent combination could be put together. The debate lies outside the scope of our chapter. Here we are concerned only with the extent to which government policies led to economic integration. We judge the success of policies with respect to their influence on interregional trade, interregional disparities in income, and interregional inequalities in the distribution of economic power.

Three types of policies influence economic integration as defined above; those dealing with the division of power between the central government and local governments, those designed to promote growth, and those aimed at managing crisis. Of course, during Yugoslavia's 73-year existence these policies tended to cluster and overlap. They appeared alone or in combination. Between the amalgamation of 1918 and the disintegration of 1991 eight policy clusters can be identified. The first cluster coincided with the initial amalgamation policies described above and lasted from 1920 to 1925. It called for new internal transport links and new tariff systems. It protected the domestic market, while centralizing economic policy decisions and reducing regional autonomy. After initially high growth rates, which some attribute to the synergistic effects of unification and others to the European post-war boom in agricultural exports, came the first of Yugoslavia's economic crises in 1924 with the collapse of agricultural exports.

The second, more complex cluster involving the "first grand redesign" of Yugoslavia came with King Alexander's dictatorship in January 1929 and inspired economic policies into the early 1930s. This cluster led to further centralization and growth promotion through *ad hoc* government decisions. It required eliminating economic dualism by completely reorganizing the economy along lines that gave the state complete control and eliminated other independent decision-makers in the economy, especially those in the more developed northern regions. Private banks were intentionally bankrupted, while the government organized foreign trade, began to manage firms directly, and oversaw increasing cartelization. Although designed for the crises of the late 1920s, it was implemented only after 1930 during the great depression in Yugoslavia. Centralized crisis management failed to achieve its goals. The Yugoslav economy suffered crises that were even deeper than its neighbors (Vučo 1968) and lasted longer than many other European countries. Furthermore, the government failed to be an honest broker of diverse regional interests and, as it was accountable only to the king, its policies led to the misuse of discretionary power and business scandals (Bićanić 1988).

The third cluster includes the only growth-promotion plan designed in the interwar period. It was devised by Milan Stojadinović in 1935 as part of his successful election campaign. Following the elections, the Stojadinović government implemented the plan from 1935 to 1939. It favored industrialization with steel as a leading sector and called for using domestic raw materials, import substitution, and protection through regulating foreign trade and import tariffs. Public works were to improve transport and communications and facilitate electrification. In implementing the plan, the state went even further in building a "dirigiste" system. It fostered military spending and bilateral trade agreements. This second step toward centralization coincided with economic recovery that can be tied convincingly to trends in the world economy and especially Germany, Yugoslavia's main trading partner and source of foreign capital (Dimitrijević 1958). But by bringing an even greater inequality in the distribution of economic power, it failed to diffuse regional tensions, which were increased further by dissatisfaction over biased decisions and corruption at the federal level.

The failure of extreme centralization to solve any of the economic or political issues led to the fourth cluster; the "Second Redesign of Yugoslavia," which started in 1939. Long drawn-out negotiations centered mainly on political issues, but also led to a significant redistribution of economic power. Regional boundaries that reflected historical and national criteria were established. Together with political devolution this involved fiscal independence as a first step. But the redesign went no further than establishing one regional unit (Banovina Hrvatska) and was abruptly stopped by the country's disintegration in 1941 during World War II.

A return to the centralizing trend of the interwar period, but along somewhat different lines, came with the introduction of centralized planning and a command economy in 1947 and marks the fifth cluster. The cluster had a growth promoting motivation. To a large extent, industrialization was to proceed along the same lines as in the 1935 plan; expanding steel and electrification, using domestic resources, and fostering import substitution. Through a very high ratio of investment spending to GDP, the program implied a large welfare sacrifice. External events, the 1948 break with Stalin, and a lack of internal coherence in the system led to changes in the incentive structures, but did not decentralize investment or reduce party control. Microeconomic efficiency was encouraged by the introduction of worker self-management in 1950, decollectivization in agriculture, and increased incentives. Also, the production of consumer goods assumed greater importance. The high growth rates of the late 1950s can probably be attributed to these changes, to the prolonged gestation period of investment projects, and to foreign aid (Bićanić 1990). By the early 1960s, the slack in the centralized economy was exhausted and the latent economic crisis began to appear in earnest.

The sixth cluster dealt with this crisis beginning in 1962. It was initially based on increasing microeconomic efficiency by means of expanding both self-management and markets, but its failure led to more radical reforms in 1965. Together with further efforts to increase efficiency, the reforms phased out (until 1972) the centralized allocation of investment, but without decentralizing economic policy or decreasing the leading role of the Communist party. When the reforms started endangering the power of the party in 1968 and did not seem to be managing the crisis effectively, the government rolled back market incentives and indirectly re-imposed centralization (Bilandžić 1985; Rusinow 1974).

A seventh cluster of policies that started in 1972 and lasted through the 1970s included another grand redesign of Yugoslavia. There was a major devolution of economic power; decisions at the federal level were to be reached by consensus and republics achieved considerable fiscal independence. The goal was to expand the efficiency gains of self-management through the "associated labor paradigm," which was a mechanism for avoiding and replacing markets by "economizing through consensus." The cosmetic approach to decentralization and devolution meant that the central government retained its dominance in monetary, exchange rate, and price policy and the central party apparatus maintained its hold over all important economic decisions. During the entire period, Yugoslavia imported capital via foreign loans and workers' remittances. However, when foreign lending ceased in the early 1980s, the accumulated economic difficulties plunged Yugoslavia into the deepest and longest economic crises of its 73-year history (Bićanić 1988).

The final cluster of policies that was adopted during the 1980s offered neither a redistribution of power between the center and the republics nor growth promotion policies. Instead, it concentrated on stop-gap measures (usually some administrative controls) and successive reforms of self-management as a kind of new socialism that would provide an institutional remedy for the crisis. In its final form in 1989 this implied a "grand redesign" of socialism; self-management was restricted and private entrepreneurs were put on equal footing with the socialist sector. None of these efforts had any lasting influence as the economy slid further into recession. By the end of the 1980s, living standards and real wages approximated those of the mid-1960s.

As our brief survey shows, centralizing decision-making provided the main vehicle for creating a Yugoslav economy, overtly through one-man or one-party dictatorship or indirectly through "state dirigism" or "economizing through consensus." These policies did not promote long-term economic growth nor did they deal successfully with the crises they attempted to solve. Furthermore, they were implemented by a succession of governments with no accountability. This spawned behind the scene deals, the growth of an unofficial economy, the dominance of political considerations, and regional bias in policymaking. Yugoslavia thus never evolved into a modern state. The continuous pressures for devolution and decentralization led to a shifting sequence of relatively short-lived policy clusters. As a result, Yugoslavia remained near the bottom on the European development scale and did not begin to catch up. The long-term failure to manage crises, when coupled with the unstoppable shift to post-socialist development, incited go-it-alone national policies and ultimately disintegration.

UNSUCCESSFUL CREATION OF A SINGLE ECONOMIC SPACE

The disintegration of Yugoslavia started in the early 1990s. But arguably Yugoslavia had never managed to function as a well integrated, unified economy. The final disintegration clearly demonstrates that the amalgamation which started in 1918 was not successful. We offer three sets of economic data which in our opinion support this argument. The data show clear evidence of long-term inefficiency in Yugoslavia's economy, of substantial economic differences among its republics, and of loose links among its republics.

Long-term inefficiency

Scholars have analyzed economic growth in subperiods of Yugoslavia's 73-year history, but have not looked at its performance over the period as a whole. Here we take the long view by focusing on the behavior of two variables: national income per capita (NI/pc) and employment (Emp.). Long-term series for NI/pc and Emp. (excluding data before 1923 and from 1940 till 1946) appear in Figure 9.1. (See Appendix for a description of the data and methodology.)

The growth of NI/pc was above the linear trend from 1923 till 1933 (obviously reflecting the great depression) and was below trend until 1972. From 1972 to 1989 NI/pc grew above the long-term trend. The long-term growth rate of NI/pc was a respectable 2.2 per cent (see Table 9.3 in the Appendix), indicating that the average Yugoslav was roughly four times richer in 1991 than in 1923. But this result was obtained while the growth rate of labor productivity was negative, and strongly oscillating from year to year (see Table 9.3 in the Appendix). This dichotomy (rising NI/pc and falling NI/Emp.) can be explained by the very fast increase of employment relative to national income. Self-employed peasants are not included in the labor force statistics so the sharp increase in the number of workers (average rate of growth 3.7 per cent) is most likely due to the transfer of workers from the agricultural to the industrial sector. Due to lack of data, we could not explore this phenomenon more closely. Therefore, the evidence of falling labor productivity must be interpreted with great caution.

But other data provide further evidence of inefficiencies. Bajt (1989) estimates that Yugoslav social product could have been twice as high as it was in 1980, had the efficiency of investment in Yugoslavia been similar to that of comparable countries (Greece, Turkey, Spain, Portugal) from 1960 to 1980. Finally, as mentioned, Yugoslavia's relative position on the European development scale has remained unchanged.

Therefore, the Yugoslav economy was inefficient in the sense that relatively high growth rates were achieved only through rapid increases in the non-agricultural labor force, i.e., sectoral shifts, and large-scale, unproductive investment, a development pattern that could no longer be sustained and which resulted in the deep economic crisis of the 1980s (see Figure 9.1 and Table 9.3). Because no solution was forthcoming, economic inefficiency contributed to Yugoslavia's disintegration and the unfortunate conflicts that followed.

Persistent income inequalities

The republics were the key political units of Yugoslavia, yet they displayed very different levels of economic development. Despite all political and economic efforts to diminish the differences through special investment

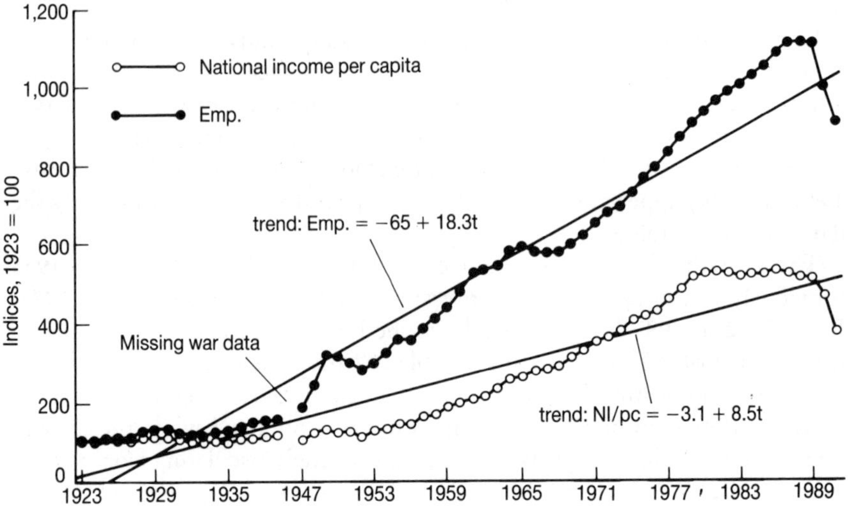

Figure 9.1 Long-range trends 1923–89. Constant prices 1938

Source: Computed from Table 9.3 Emp.: Employment (number of employed persons, mid-year) NI/pc: National income per capita

funds and subsidies for the less developed regions, they not only remained large, but even increased over time. The republics with social product per capita (SP/pc) below the average in 1955 were still in the same position in 1988. The ratio of SP/pc between the most developed (Slovenia) and the least developed republic (Macedonia) increased from 2.67 in 1955 to 3.1 in 1988. If the then Autonomous Province of Kosovo is included, the range increases from 1:4 in 1955 to 1:8 in 1988 (see Table 9.1).

The share of less developed republics in social product has barely changed, with a notable fall in the share of Bosnia and Herzegovina. In short, regional differences, which must have been huge in the interwar period (when comparable data do not exist), remained large after World War II and subsequently widened.

Loose interregional links

At the time of amalgamation in 1918, the Yugoslav regions traded almost nothing with each other. For example, Croatia traded less than 1 per cent of its exports to Serbia and Serbia traded less than 1 per cent of its national product with Croatia (Bićanić 1972). Yugoslavia most likely remained a relatively loose federation in economic terms after that. Interrepublic flows for certain declined after 1968 (when good data became available) through the late 1980s (see Table 9.2).

Table 9.1 Economic indicators: Comparison of republics (Yugoslavia = 100)

Republic	*SP/pc*		*C/Emp.*		*GI/pc*		*Share SP (%)*		*R-SP*
	1955	*1988*	*1955*	*1988*	*1955*	*1988*	*1955*	*1988*	*1955–88*
Bos-Herz	80	65	107	94	100	67	14.4	12.7	4.6%
Croatia	120	129	100	110	100	133	26.7	25.5	4.6%
Montenegro	80	71	49	137	200	67	1.8	2.0	5.0%
Macedonia	60	65	68	75	100	67	5.2	5.7	5.2%
Serbia	80	88	93	87	100	100	37.6	37.5	5.1%
Slovenia	160	200	124	137	200	233	14.3	16.6	5.2%

Source: Computed by authors from *Statistical Yearbook of Yugoslavia* (SYY), various years

SP/pc: Social product per capita
C/Emp: Capital–Labor ratio
GI/pc: Gross investment in fixed assets per capita
Share SP: The share of social product of republics in total Yugoslav social product (%)
R-SP: Average yearly rate of growth of social product from 1955 to 1988.

The republics exchange less than one-quarter of their output with each other (the exception is Montenegro at 26.3 per cent) and all are increasingly dependent on their own domestic market. From Table 9.2 one can see that the share of goods and services sold to other republics has declined in the time period analyzed for all republics with the exception of Macedonia. On the other hand, the share of goods and services sold within republics (comparing 1967 and 1987) have increased for all of them without exceptions. Exports have increased their share in the total amount of goods and

Table 9.2 Sold goods and services (%)

Republic	*Within rep.*		*To other rep.*		*Exports*		*St. disc.*[a]	
	1968	*1987*	*1968*	*1987*	*1968*	*1987*	*1968*	*1987*
Bos-Herz	61.7	69.5	29.1	19.7	7.4	9.5	1.8	1.3
Croatia	65.1	68.6	21.6	19.1	10.1	10.8	3.2	1.5
Montenegro	56.8	59.8	32.0	26.3	8.8	10.0	2.4	3.5
Macedonia	65.6	66.5	22.7	23.5	8.9	9.2	2.8	0.8
Serbia	66.5	76.2	17.4	14.8	14.0	8.7	2.1	0.3
Slovenia	60.0	62.9	27.5	22.2	10.7	13.4	1.8	1.5

Source: compiled from Grubišić, 1990.

Within rep.: sold goods and services within republic (%)
To other: sold goods and services to other republics (%)
Exports: exported goods and services outside Yugoslavia
St. disc: statistical discrepancy

services sold (exception Serbia). The dynamics of trade indicates that republics preferred selling goods and services either abroad or within their "frontiers" and not to other republics. Similar loose links can also be seen in interrepublic investment flows. Burkett and Škegro (1988) present data that show weak interrepublic economic ties and no trend in changes in the level of integration. In spite of all attempts to create a unified market, which reflected more political slogans than economic means, Yugoslavia remained from the economic point of view "a fractured federation." It is, indeed, very difficult clearly to define what is a unified economy. But, the above mentioned arguments taken together, combined with the fact that the Yugoslav economy has disintegrated, lead us to believe strongly in our (admittedly arguable) statement that the Yugoslav economy remained an amalgamation of regional economies throughout its history.

THE DISINTEGRATION OF THE YUGOSLAV ECONOMY

The crises of the 1980s led to widespread debate on three issues that are now tied to discussions of Yugoslavia's disintegration: the role of self-management and socialism, the balance sheet of Yugoslavia's regional economic development, and the role of decentralized decision-making in crisis management.

With respect to the first issue, most observers pointed to the inefficiency of socialism by citing the social losses it involved and the costs of achieving its goals. They did not identify self-management as such as the main culprit, but did point out problems in the specific form (Associated Labor) it took. Two official blueprints were published and at the end of the 1980s the legal and institutional structure started changing. Each step in the changes was increasingly radical as the crisis continued and politicians began to recognize the need for more deep-rooted changes. Discussions ended with significant restrictions on self-management, equalization of all forms of ownership, i.e., private and socialized, a multi-party system, and a call for "new socialism." Thus, the taboos concerning socialism and the role of the party were attacked from the mid-1980s.

Several important published papers pointed out failures in Yugoslavia's regional development. Even Slovenia, the most developed region, lagged increasingly behind comparable regions in Austria and was not developing as fast as it could. And it was claimed that Serbia's growth was dropping below the Yugoslav average, which meant that Serbia was falling behind the developed regions and becoming increasingly similar to the less developed regions. In addition some claimed that there were major redistributions of income from Serbia to the developed regions. Here Serbia agreed with the less developed regions, which pointed out that government-regulated prices of energy and raw materials led to a shift in the terms of trade against less developed regions and thus a regional redistribution of income. Finally (in terms of trade) Croatia argued that the government-regulated foreign trade system was biased against it and that it experienced the most restrictive macroeconomic stabilization policies. These discussions from the mid-1980s further broke down taboos that had prevented these kinds of interregional comparisons in the name of Yugoslav "brotherhood and unity."

Debate on the third issue often overlapped with the other two but centered especially on the relative merits of confederalist approaches to consensus decision-making and more centralized crisis management policies. One particularly vocal view argued that the mixture of federalist and confederalist solutions in the 1974 constitution were directly responsible for Yugoslavia's disintegration and for its inefficient economic policy and that a redesign of the country was needed along more centralized lines. Opposing views defended the existing decision-making arrangements and pointed out that trends toward weaker interregional links could be explained more convincingly by alternative explanations, chiefly the crisis itself and the system of self-management. Discussions on the demands for a grand redesign of Yugoslavia did place the important issue of redistributing economic power into the limelight.

Thus by the early 1990s all three underpinnings of the Yugoslav economic system were under discussion and review: the system of self-management, the distribution of economic power, and the very purpose of the economy. The inability to find any acceptable solution to the continuing economic crisis marked the economic sources of the go-it-alone policies that were used by each republic to find its own appropriate transition path, which ultimately led to Yugoslavia's disintegration.[3]

The final disintegration of the Yugoslav economy (and of Yugoslavia) into its successor states came with the international recognition of Croatia and Slovenia in January 1992. Already by the end of 1992, the economies of the successor states of Yugoslavia were different in terms of institutions (privatization laws, monetary systems, fiscal systems, etc.) and structural features (level of development, dominant sectors, inflation and disequilibrium, etc.). The disintegration of the Yugoslav economy was so complete that the trade links established during the previous 73 years have been almost completely cut. This is a consequence of the Wars of the Yugoslav Succession, whose brutality will most likely generate an economic climate that is not conducive to reestablishing these links in the foreseeable future.

APPENDIX

Methodological explanation of data

Data for NI, and NI/pc, for the period till 1939 are taken from Stajić (1959). This is the sole source of national income data measured in constant prices

Table 9.3 Macroeconomic indicators in Yugoslavia 1923–91 – prices 1938 (no data for period 1940–6)

No.	*Year*	*NI*[a] *mil.din.*	*NI/pc din.*	*Emp. (000)*	*Pop.(000) mid-year*	*Unemp. (000)*	*Lab.pr. din.*
1	1923	34,470	2,775	619	12,422		55,670
2	1924	36,515	2,896	612	12,607		59,664
3	1925	40,147	3,138	643	12,796		62,483
4	1926	38,709	2,981	664	12,987		58,282
5	1927	37,624	2,854	709	13,181		53,048
6	1928	41,079	3,071	781	13,378		52,573
7	1929	43,471	3,202	824	13,577		52,745
8	1930	43,062	3,125	817	13,780	10	52,727
9	1931	42,071	3,009	780	13,982	14.5	53,962
10	1932	38,333	2,705	742	14,174	14.2	51,695
11	1933	38,945	2,710	714	14,369	17.7	54,551
12	1934	40,398	2,774	775	14,566	16.5	52,125
13	1935	39,271	2,659	803	14,767	18.7	48,914
14	1936	44,885	2,998	873	14,970	22.1	51,437
15	1937	45,122	2,947	924	15,311	26.1	48,830
16	1938	48,476	3,151	961	15,384	23.6	50,462
17	1939	50,988	3,269	973	15,596	23.8	52,426
18	1947	45,795	2,921	1,167	15,679		39,242
19	1948	54,688	3,439	1,517	15,901		36,050
20	1949	60,384	3,743	1,990	16,133		30,344
21	1950	55,455	3,393	1,944	16,346		28,526
22	1951	58,453	3,524	1,843	16,588		31,716
23	1952	51,491	3,065	1,734	16,798	45	29,695
24	1953	61,418	3,603	1,836	17,048	82	33,452
25	1954	63,110	3,651	2,005	17,284	76	31,477
26	1955	72,110	4,116	2,215	17,519	67	32,555
27	1956	70,122	3,965	2,216	17,685	99	31,643
28	1957	81,047	4,538	2,392	17,859	116	33,882
29	1958	82,270	4,566	2,552	18,018	132	32,238
30	1959	95,715	5,255	2,730	18,214	162	35,061
31	1960	102,632	5,577	2,972	18,402	159	34,533
32	1961	108,390	5,824	3,242	18,612	191	33,433
33	1962	111,815	5,942	3,318	18,819	237	33,700
34	1963	125,210	6,580	3,390	19,029	230	36,935
35	1964	139,496	7,257	3,608	19,222	212	38,663
36	1965	141,819	7,297	3,662	19,434	237	38,727
37	1966	153,031	7,790	3,583	19,644	258	42,710
38	1967	156,365	7,881	3,561	19,840	269	43,910

Table 9.3 Continued

No.	*Year*	*NI*[a] *mil.din.*	*NI/pc din.*	*Emp. (000)*	*Pop.(000) mid-year*	*Unemp. (000)*	*Lab.pr. din.*
39	1968	161,890	8,083	3,587	20,029	311	45,133
40	1969	175,628	8,691	3,706	20,209	331	47,390
41	1970	187,194	9,189	3,850	20,371	320	48,622
42	1971	202,105	9,823	4,033	20,574	291	50,113
43	1972	210,601	10,137	4,210	20,775	315	50,024
44	1973	220,939	10,539	4,306	20,963	382	51,310
45	1974	239,414	11,312	4,514	21,164	449	53,038
46	1975	248,125	11,614	4,758	21,365	540	52,149
47	1976	257,708	11,946	4,925	21,572	635	52,326
48	1977	278,219	12,774	5,148	21,780	700	54,044
49	1978	297,142	13,522	5,383	21,974	735	55,200
50	1979	318,299	14,359	5,615	22,167	762	56,687
51	1980	325,352	14,587	5,798	22,304	785	56,115
52	1981	329,764	14,675	5,966	22,471	809	55,274
53	1982	331,487	14,640	6,104	22,642	862	54,306
54	1983	327,492	14,361	6,222	22,805	910	52,635
55	1984	333,121	14,505	6,355	22,966	975	52,419
56	1985	334,410	14,462	6,516	23,124	1,040	51,321
57	1986	346,221	14,876	6,716	23,274	1,087	51,552
58	1987	341,962	14,603	6,866	23,417	1,081	49,805
59	1988	335,810	14,250	6,884	23,566	1,128	48,781
60	1989	337,827	14,260	6,876	23,690	1,196	49,131
61	1990	308,999	12,978	6,188	23,809	1,303	49,935
62	1991	250,290	10,457	5,631	23,934	1,499	44,449
R		3.3	2.2	3.69	1.08		−0.36

Source: Čobeljić (1959) *Yugoslavia 1918–1988*, *SYY*- various years *Index* No. 12/1991

NI:	National income
NI p/c.	National income per capita
Emp.:	Employment (number of employed persons, mid-year)
Pop.:	Population (mid-year estimations)
Unemp.:	Unemployment
Lab. pr.:	Labor productivity = NI/Emp.
mil. din.:	Millions of dinars (year indicated in table)
din.:	Dinars
R:	Average growth rate for 1923–91 (no data 1940–6). All growth rates are computed as average annual geometric growth rates (in per cent).

for the above mentioned period. Almost all researchers in the field quote him (see Mirković 1964; Čobeljić 1959 etc.). Data for population, unemployment and employment for this period are taken from the publication: *Yugoslavia 1918–1988* (1989). The number of employed people is taken from this publication (see the publication for further explanations). Unfortunately many sources report different numbers of workers. For example: Mirković 1964; Vučo 1968; Kukoleča 1941 have different numbers for employed workers than those reported in our work. As there were no reliable central labor statistics at that time, these studies based their estimations mostly on the figures obtained from numerous insurance companies. To make data on employment more comparable with those after 1947, we have used statistics from the publication of the Federal Statistical Bureau: *Yugoslavia 1918–1988* (1989).

Employment data do not take into account self-employed peasants before and after World War II. Unemployment data are also taken from the publication *Yugoslavia 1918–1988* (1989). There are no data before 1930; reported data are end-of-year figures. Apparently, unemployment was much higher in the period 1930–39 than the data show because large groups of unemployed people did not register themselves (Mirković 1964). Thus, the unemployment rate is grossly underestimated for this period.

For the period 1947–91 all the data are taken from three sources: *Statistical Yearbook of Yugoslavia* – various years, *Yugoslavia 1918–1988* (1989) – which uses mainly the same data as the statistical yearbooks and for the last three years (1989–91), the monthly publication of the federal statistical bureau *Index*:12/1991. As no absolute numbers are available we have made estimates based on index numbers for the relevant years. For 1991 we could use only indices for January–November 1991. Unemployment data are not available before 1952. There are no data from 1940 to 1946 due to World War II. The tricky part was to combine and compute the long-term series. We have done this only for national income. Čobeljić has given data for national income up to 1956 in 1938 prices. On the basis of overlapping data in 1972 and 1938 prices for the years from 1947 to 1956 we have computed the *average deflator* for 1972/1938 to be 1.05, and we have computed all data for national income from 1957 until 1991. Great caution is recommended when comparing unemployment data for 1930–9 for the post-1945 period, because the interwar data are rough estimates only.

In Figure 9.1 we have computed linear trend polynomials for Employment and NI/pc. for the whole period 1923–91 (without data for World War II).

The resulting equations are:

For employment data and t = 1 . . . 62 , where t – years

$$(\text{Emp.})t = -\ 65.1314 + 18.3457\ t\ (0.4896)$$

$R = 0.959 \qquad \text{SE of Y est.} = 68.99$

For NI/pc data and $t = 1 \ldots 62$

$(NI/pc)t = -3.1239 + 8.49194\,t\,(0.4155)$

$R = 0.87436$ (SE of Y est. = 58.56).

NOTES

Views expressed here are those of the authors and do not necessarily represent views of the National Bank of Croatia.

1 The Yugoslav state frequently changed official names. It was unified as the Kingdom of the Serbs, Croats, and Slovenes in 1918, it modernized its name in 1919, became the Kingdom of Yugoslavia in 1929, the Democratic Federal Yugoslavia in 1943, the Federative National Republic of Yugoslavia in 1947 and the Socialist Federative Republic of Yugoslavia in 1963. For simplicity we will call it "Yugoslavia," regardless of the time period concerned.

2 The details of the unification are outside the scope of our chapter. For an account see Banac (1984).

3 The other sources were political considerations and the start of economic transition to post-socialist development throughout Europe.

REFERENCES

Aerst, E. and Milward, A.S. (eds.) (1990) *Economic Planning in the Post-1945 Period*, Lueven.

Bajt, A. (1989) *Samoupravni oblik društvene svojine*, Zagreb.

Banac, I. (1984) *The National Question in Yugoslavia*, Ithaca.

Bićanić, I. (1988) "The fractured economy," in D. Rusinow (ed.) *Yugoslavia: A Fractured Federalism*, Washington.

Bićanić, I. (1990) "The failures of post-war Yugoslav planning," in E. Aerts and A.S. Milward (eds.) *Economic Planning in the Post-1945 Period*, Lueven.

Bićanić, R. (1938) *Ekonomska podloga hrvatskog pitanja*, Zagreb.

Bićanić, R. (1972) *Economic Policy in Socialist Yugoslavia*, Cambridge.

Bilandžić, D. (1985) *Historija Socijalističke Federativne Republike Jugoslavije – glavni procesi*, Zagreb.

Burkett, J. and Škegro, B. (1988) "Are economic fractures widening?," in: D. Rusinow (ed.) *Yugoslavia: A Fractured Federalism*, Washington.

Čobeljić, N. (1959) *Politika i Metodi Privrednog Razvoja Jugoslavije*, Nolit, Belgrade.

Dimitrijević, S. (1958) *Strani kapital u privredi bivše Jugoslavije*, Belgrade.

Grubišić, M. (1990) *Međurepublički promet robe i usluga od 1968 do 1987*. Analize i prikazi – 73. Zavod za Statistiku, Zagreb.

Kukoleča, S. (1941) *Industrija Jugoslavije 1918–1938*, Belgrade.

Lamer, M. (1936) *The Development of Foreign Capital Investment in the Balkans*, Washington.

Mirković, M. (1964) *Ekonomska historija Jugoslavije*, Zagreb.

Rusinow, D. (1974) *The Yugoslav Experiment*, London.

Rusinow, D. (ed.) (1988). *Yugoslavia: A Fractured Federalism*, Washington.

Stajić, S. (1959) *Društveni proizvod i narodni dohodak Jugoslavije u stalnim cenama 1938*, Belgrade
Vučo, N. (1968) *Agrarna kriza u Jugoslaviji 1930–34*, Belgrade.
Yugoslavija 1918–1988 – Statistički godišnjak. Savezni Zavod za Statistiku, Belgrade.

10

STRUCTURAL CHANGES IN POLISH AGRICULTURE 1918–89

Janusz Kaliński

INTRODUCTION

Poland belongs to the group of industrialized countries, yet agriculture still plays a large role in its national economy. In the early 1990s, some 27 per cent of total employment was in agriculture, while this sector's share in the national income was 15 per cent (*Rocznik Statystyczny* 1991: XXIV–XXV). Together these two indicators demonstrate the low efficiency of Polish agriculture, which is one of the factors that accounts for both the slowing down of growth in the national economy and the falling living standards of the population.

A central problem of Polish agriculture is its backward agrarian structure, which is dominated by small peasant farms that have little contact with the market economy. The scattered nature and small size of the farms follows from the way nineteenth-century reforms were implemented, the lack of radical agrarian reform in the interwar period, and the policies of the Communist governments, which aimed at socializing agriculture.

THE PERIOD 1918–44

In 1918 the new Polish state inherited a highly diverse system of farming households. On the one hand, there were great estates (*latifundia*) that accounted for a considerable proportion of farm land. On the other hand, peasants holding small plots suffered from a permanent shortage of land. In 1921 18,916 farms over 100 hectares (ha) (of which 1,964 were over 1,000 ha) held some 45 per cent of arable land. Among the greatest landowners were the families of Zamoyski, Radziwill, and Potocki. Meanwhile, one million peasant farms under 2 ha owned a mere 2.8 per cent of arable land. The incomes on these farms did not provide subsistence to peasant families, which forced them to seek extra wages, chiefly from seasonal jobs (Mieszczankowski 1960: 224).

In addition, the small farms, even those with up to 5 ha, usually did not require full use of the peasant family workforce. The result was large numbers of workers who could not find full employment on the land and who were a burden on the rural community. The size of the rural population thought to be redundant in agriculture had been estimated at 2.4 to 4.5 million people (Landau and Tomaszewski 1991: 11). These people could not be employed in industries or services due to the low level of industrial and urban development in the country. Nor could the problem of "surplus labor" be solved by emigration. As a consequence, the disguised unemployment restricted demand for manufactures and, in general, hampered economic growth.

The agrarian reform in 1925 sought to improve the agrarian structure. Its core was confined to parceling the public estates and those private estates that exceeded 180 ha. In the eastern provinces (*voivodships*), which contained the greatest latifundia, the size of land holdings was limited to a maximum of 300 ha, while in industrialized estates (a farm with its own brewery, sugar factory, etc.) it reached 700 ha. It was assumed that 200,000 ha would be parceled each year (Mieszczankowski 1983: 77).

In practice, the law was not strictly applied. Until 1938 some 2,655,000 ha of land were parcelled out, mainly that owned by the landed gentry. As a result of this agrarian reform, the total acreage of landed estates decreased by 16 per cent, while that of peasant farms increased by 13 per cent. The parceling created 154,000 new farms and increased the size of 503,000 old ones. The average area of the new farms reached 9.8 ha, while the average size of the existing farms increased to 2.1 ha (*Mały Rocznik Statystyczny* 1939: 71).

Table 10.1 shows the changes in the structure of peasant farms under the agrarian reform. Contrary to the intentions of the authorities, there was a rise in the share of the smallest farms (under 5 ha) and a decline in the share of the larger ones (over 10 ha).

Table 10.1 The structure of peasant farms according to their size 1921, 1938 (%)

Farm size (hectares)	*1921*		*1938*	
	Farms	*Area*	*Farms*	*Area*
<2	29.3	5.4	30.7	5.9
2–5	32.9	21.6	33.8	23.1
5–10	24.9	33.3	23.9	33.7
10–20	10.4	26.4	9.5	25.6
>20	2.5	13.3	2.1	11.7
Total	100.0	100.0	100.0	100.0

Source: Historia Polski w liczbach. Zeszyt 2. Rolnictwo. Lesnictwo. (1991) Warsaw: 194.

The agrarian reform did ease the land shortage among the peasantry, but it did not improve the size structure of their farms. The partitioning of peasant property was not stopped, despite its adverse economic and social effects. The growing agrarian overpopulation and inefficiency of small farms was a special burden on the country. The governments of Poland in the interwar period were aware of the problem and tried, especially after the great depression, to improve conditions for the peasants by instituting measures aimed at lifting the fiscal burden on agriculture, at improving the relationship between farm prices and the prices of industrial goods, and at creating new jobs in industries located within areas with substantial surplus labor. But these measures did little to improve the situation in agriculture and consequently Poland failed to advance among European countries.

The idea that structural changes in agriculture were a necessary factor for economic progress was supported by Polish émigrés who had contacts with the Polish exile government in London during World War II. They favored a continuation of agrarian reforms that would generate larger family farms. Also, they planned a further parceling of state farms, which included land belonging to Germans and to collaborators with the Germans during the war, and estates exceeding 50 ha in size (O co walczy naród polski 1944: 9). The land gained from parceling was to be used to create new farms of 8–15 ha and to increase the size of petty farms. These changes would increase the efficiency and intensity of farm production and indirectly increase rural demand for industrial products. The resulting industrialization would modernize the economic and social structure of the country.

Generally, the war years brought about even more radical views on the need for structural changes in agriculture. Most economists and politicians, whether they had emigrated, or stayed in the occupied country, or were associated with the exile government in London, were unanimous about eliminating the great estates and developing small-farm agriculture. They were backed by Polish Communists in the Soviet Union, who also demanded that the thirst for land be quenched by parceling large farms into small and medium-sized peasant farms. They were motivated less by the need to rationalize the agrarian structure and more by the desire to appeal to the poorest rural classes. They hoped to gain support for Communist slogans and pave the ground for the future collectivization of agriculture (Kumoś 1983: 160).

The period of occupation was marked also by actual changes in the structure of agriculture. In the territories occupied by the Soviet army in 1939, the private farms were liquidated and their land passed into the collective farms and state farms. After 1941 German agricultural policy was extended to the eastern territories, which meant forming large colonial farms there. In the Polish territories included in the Third Reich, Germans deported Poles and fused farms under 5 ha into larger units, which were then passed over to German colonists. Until 1942 Germany confiscated 897,000

Polish farms containing more than 8 million ha. The confiscation of land in the rest of occupied territories was on a lesser scale. Among the most spectacular actions taken by the German occupiers was the dislocation of the population in Zamojszczyzna, which lost 12,000 farms to the German colonists. In other regions confiscations resulted from German sanctions or from the economic ruin of the smallest farms, which were incapable of meeting the high taxes and levy of agricultural products (Jastrzębowski 1946: 293–8).

While the smallest farms were fused, the parceling of the large estates, which had started already before the war, was stopped. The estates either became German property or were managed by Germans. According to the plans of the occupation authorities, they were never to be returned to their previous owners nor were they to be partitioned further. Overall, occupation policy led only to a decline in the number of the smallest farms.

THE COMMUNIST ERA AFTER 1944

In the post-World War II era, the structure of farms was determined by territorial changes, agrarian reforms, and policy aimed at socializing the agricultural sector.

The change in borders after the Yalta Conference reduced Poland's area from 390,000 to 312,000 km^2. The area of farm land decreased by 14 per cent and that of pastures and meadows by 31 per cent. The eastern territories, where the greatest estates were concentrated before the war, were now within the boundaries of the Soviet Union. In the former German lands, the western and northern territories, large Junker estates and farms that were usually larger than in central Poland changed hands. After deportation of the Germans, these changes allowed for the resettlement of Polish peasants from the overpopulated central provinces and from land taken over by the Soviet Union. Some of the rural resettlers made their homes in the numerous war-destroyed towns on the Oder and found employment in non-agricultural trades (Piskozub 1987: 262).

The territorial changes, which were favorable from the viewpoint of building industrial potential and economic infrastructure, together with heavy war losses, contributed to a considerable reduction in overpopulation of the Polish countryside. Of course, a complete solution to that problem depended on progress in industrial and urban development.

When the Communists took over, they began to implement their own political and socio-economic policies. One of the first acts was the decree of 1944 relating to agrarian reform, which was complemented in 1946 by the decree on the agrarian system and settlement. These applied in particular to the "Regained Lands" and the former free town of Gdańsk, territories within German boundaries prior to 1939. The former German territories, the land held by war collaborators, as well as estates exceeding 50 ha in area (in the western provinces of pre-war Poland those over 100 ha) were used to set up the State Land Fund. This land was then divided among small peasants, tenants, and farm laborers in order to create new farms or supplement the area of existing farms up to the standard size of 5 ha per average family. The size of allocations in the west and the north were higher, since more land was always available there (Słabek 1986: 38)

Implementing agrarian reforms in the lands included in Polish territory prior to 1939 resulted in parceling some 2.4 million ha by the end of 1949 (mainly latifundia). Some 347,000 farms were formed and 254,000 existing farms were enlarged. The actual area of the farms created through reallocation of land differed from the standard size adopted in the decree on agrarian reform. The average area of the new farms reached 5.4 ha, and the size of additional lots for existing farms reached 1.9 ha.

In the land integrated into Poland in 1945, some 3.7 million ha of farm land were allocated for re-settlement purposes; 467,000 farms were formed, with an average area of 7.9 ha per farm, mainly in the 7–15 ha bracket.

Overall, 6.1 million ha were parceled among 1.1 million families. These peasant-farm owners accounted for 57.4 per cent of allocations, farm laborers for 25.0 per cent, and landless peasants for 14.3 per cent. A small proportion of the lots (2.7 per cent) passed into the hands of gardeners, craftsmen and as allotment gardens (*Rolniczy rocznik statystyczny* 1945–65: 115). The effects of World War II and of the parceling and re-settlement on the agrarian structure are presented in Table 10.2. Between 1939 and 1949 the number of the smallest farms (those under 2 ha) decreased considerably, as did, to a much lesser extent, the number of farms ranging between 2–5 ha. One unquestioned achievement was the rise in the number and area of medium-sized and large farms (5–20 ha). This was accompanied by a drop in the number of the largest estates (20–50 ha), which resulted from the changing borders.

Table 10.2 The structure of peasant farms according to their size 1938, 1950, 1960, 1970, 1987 (%)

Farm size (hectares)	*1938*		*1950*		*1960*		*1970*		*1987*	
	No.	*Area*	*No.*	*Area*	*No.*	*Area*	*No.*	*Area*	*No.*	*Area*
<2	30.7	5.9	25.9	4.9	32.8	6.3	33.4	6.1	29.6	5.5
2–5	33.8	23.1	31.3	20.1	30.4	21.7	28.4	19.9	27.6	15.8
5–10	23.9	33.7	30.8	41.9	26.1	39.5	26.1	38.5	25.2	31.3
10–20	9.5	25.6	10.7	26.2	9.7	26.8	8.7	21.6	10.7	22.5
>20	2.1	11.7	1.3	6.9	1.0	5.7	3.4	13.9	6.9	24.9
Total	100	100	100	100	100	100	100	100	100	100

Source: Historia Polski w Liczbach. Zeszyt 2. Rolnictwo. Lesnictwo. (1991) Warsaw: 194.

Officially, the Communists boasted about the effects of agrarian reform and stressed the favorable impact of the larger role of medium-sized farms, and the more restricted role of the smallest and largest farms. Some economists, e.g., Poniatowski (1965: 58), however, thought that it was a mistake to restrict parceling to 6.0 million ha because 3.0 million ha more could have been used for this purpose instead of being turned over to state-owned farms or placed in the State Land Fund. According to Poniatowski, the land fund should have been used to boost the size of existing farms, which would have generated better economic effects than creating new farms that were not self-sufficient. This form of parceling was suspected (not without grounds) of leading towards further collectivization of agriculture.

Despite its positive tendencies, the agrarian reform did not change the unfavorable structure of family farms, which has not been modified even by the formation of large state-owned farms, and the few agricultural cooperatives that were spontaneously organized by the farmer–settlers. In 1949, the public sector in agriculture embraced 2.2 million ha of land, and its share in total farm land reached 11 per cent. Among 13,400 public farms, 47.4 per cent averaged under 50 ha while 44.5 per cent exceeded 100 ha.

Altogether, there were some 10,300 farms in the country exceeding 50 ha (including 3,300 private ones), i.e., only 0.3 per cent of all the farms. They occupied 2.3 million ha of ground, which made up 11.4 per cent of their overall area. Meanwhile, the dwarf farms (under 2 ha), like before the war, covered 1.0 million ha, while the small ones (up to 5 ha) covered 3.8 million ha (*Rocznik Statystyczny 1949*: 53).

Retaining over 57 per cent of dwarf and small farms and devoting only a quarter of the overall farm land to reform meant continuing low productivity in Polish agriculture and its extensive development based on surplus labor. Radical improvement, according to the Communist authorities, depended on further changes in the size of farms, transformation of the system, and the migration of manpower from the countryside into towns.

After 1949 the structure of farms reflected the political determinants of the agrarian reform of 1944. It brought about the liquidation of the gentry and deprived ethnic minorities of their land. Allocations of land to poorer peasants made them politically neutral in the uneven struggle for a democratic Poland, which continued until the late 1940s. From an economic point of view, the effects of this reform can hardly be regarded as favorable; retaining a large number of too small farms created a considerable problem for the future once the need to intensify agricultural production became apparent. It should be remembered that under the difficult post-war conditions, e.g., the lack of capital, small farms increased their productivity fairly quickly, making use of their own labor reserves and the assistance provided by the United Nations Relief and Recovery Administration. By 1949 total agricultural output reached 95 per cent of the level attained between the wars; given the smaller population, the level in per capita terms exceeded the years 1934–38 by some 28 per cent (Markowski 1955: 53).

In the long run, the domination of the private sector in agriculture could not be tolerated by the Communist system. In spite of a reluctance in some circles of the party leadership to embark on the path of transforming the ownership patterns, the collectivization of agriculture became an issue early in 1948, as it did in the other states of the East bloc. Contrary to early promises that collectivization would be voluntary and gradual, it soon adopted forms seen earlier in the Soviet Union. Political, administrative, and police pressure were used to encourage collectivization. The results, however, were by no means dramatic; by the end of 1955 some 9,076 cooperatives were established, covering 1.9 million ha of land, a mere 9.2 per cent of the total farmland area (Kaliński 1988: 166–201). Official policy gave priority to forming collective farms on land given for re-settlement and left over after parceling, so most collective farms sprang up in western and northern provinces. Collectivization was least advanced in old villages in southern and central voivodships, which showed the great determination of peasants to maintain private property in contrast to the other countries of East bloc, where collectivization had a considerably larger following.

A slightly larger role in the socialization of agriculture was played by the state-owned (public sector) farms. They formed on lands belonging to Germany before the war in the west and north of the country. Up to 1955 6,185 state farms formed, embracing an area of 3.1 million ha, approximately 12.4 per cent of the entire farmland (*Statystyka rolnictwa 1946–1957*: 175).

At the same time, policy sought to weaken and eliminate private ownership. The class-oriented agrarian policy undermined wealthier peasants, who were suspected of being sympathetic to restoring capitalism. Family-owned farms were refused credits and the right to purchase machinery and equipment. In addition, they made compulsory contributions in money and kind to finance industrial development. Selling land was, in practice, precluded. Thousands of peasant farms disappeared, giving rise to a mass migration of young people from the countryside, while also undermining prospects for individual husbandry.

The compulsory collectivization of agriculture and the elimination of the wealthier peasants led to a drastic change in the structure of private farms. The share of dwarf farms (under 2 ha) rose by 11 per cent, and of the small ones (2–5 ha) by 7 per cent. At the same time the share of the largest farms fell by 23 per cent, that of large ones (10–20 ha) by 20 per cent and that of medium-sized (5–10 ha) by some 7 per cent.

In the mid-1950s there were only 29,300 private farms greater than 20 ha in size. Together with the state-owned and cooperative farms, there were only 45,200 large farms out of 3 million total farms (*Rocznik Statystyczny 1956*: 150). These large farms were the only ones capable of intensive production. Yet their potential for this has to be viewed critically given the depreciation in their technical equipment and diminishing supply of skilled labor that ultimately led to the ensuing breakdown in agricultural production in the early 1950s.

One social consequence of the deteriorating agrarian structure and forced industrial development of the country was the emergence on a large scale of "peasant-workers." These people lived in the countryside tending their small plots of land, while simultaneously supplementing their meager agricultural incomes with wages earned in urban occupations. Their number reached 126,000 in the 1950s.

Political changes in Poland after fall 1956 forced a change in the government's approach to agriculture, in particular with respect to collectivization. It allowed the cooperatives to be dissolved and in a wave of "liquidatory fever" in late 1956 the number of cooperatives fell to 16 per cent of the level recorded in December of the previous year (Kaliński 1988). This amounted to a drastic defeat of Communist doctrine in rural Poland.

Indirectly admitting its failure, the Communist party in 1957 announced a new agricultural policy that allowed for the free development of family farms without abandoning collectivization as a foundation for building the socialist system. This time, however, the authorities were hoping for the gradual emergence of collective farms by developing various kinds of productive and commercial associations, especially the so-called "farmer's circles." The press referred to the policy as an "indirect socialization of agriculture" because the authorities were still dedicated to supporting state-owned farms. The new agrarian policy favorably affected the peasant attitudes toward individual husbandry. There was hope for the acceptance of family farms by the Communist authorities, regardless of their size. The lifting of economic burdens on the peasants by the state also created better prospects. Compulsory contributions in kind were cut and taxes were lowered. Credits for private farmers were increased and the right to use them was extended to wealthier peasants with more than 12 ha of land. Investment in farms increased considerably and included the purchase of land besides the construction of buildings and barns. From fall 1956 until late 1958 peasants purchased 465,000 ha of land and rented another 846,000 ha from the resources of the State Land Fund alone (*Rocznik Statystyczny 1959*: 188).

The large-scale dissolution of farm cooperatives and increased sales of land moderately affected the size structure of family-owned farms. Until 1960 the share of large farms (between 10–20 ha) increased slightly and the percentage of the largest ones held steady. Nevertheless, the share of dwarf farms (those under 2 ha) increased due to the fusion of the small and medium-sized farms imposed by more liberal turnover in land. The new agrarian policy stopped further increases in the size of the public sector in agriculture. After the disaster of 1956, the number of cooperatives changed very little in the period 1957–60. As old cooperatives dissolved, new ones formed. The number of state-farms fell slightly, while their average land area rose slightly. The state policy towards peasant farms in the 1950s was decidedly restrictive. The policy was liberalized after 1956, however it continued to produce a deteriorating size structure (see Table 10.2).

After 1949 the percentage of farms over 5 ha fell drastically as did their share in the total farmland area. There was further disintegration of peasant plots, as expressed by the rise in the number and area of dwarf farms. In fact, the unsuccessful policy of collectivizing agriculture along with its discrimination against private ownership brought about considerable backwardness in the country's agrarian structure. It eliminated the potentially positive effects of both the agrarian reforms of 1925 and 1945 and the policy of resettling the western and northern territories. In 1960 the role of the dwarf farms was greater than in 1921 while, at the same time, the percentage of the larger farms, i.e., those exceeding 10 ha, was smaller. They made up a mere 10.7 per cent of the total number of private farms, which was less than in the interwar period.

The small number of large private farms, as well as the chronically inefficient "public farms," restricted productivity growth in Polish agriculture. As a consequence, from the mid-1950s imports of corn and fodder were covering the growing deficit of domestic production in relation to the needs of consumption. These imports reached the level of 2.5 million tons in the early 1960s (Olszewski 1964: 249). In order to curb this burden on the balance of payments, the authorities decided to apply state policy to the peasant farms and continue the policy of socializing agriculture.

Since the early 1960s, the state directed its basic economic assistance to private agriculture through "farmer's circles" and credit cooperatives. At the same time it promoted private husbandry in farmers' cooperatives. Not without pressures from the Kremlin, which was dissatisfied with the considerable size of the private sector in Polish agriculture, the state aimed at fully collectivizing agriculture by 1980.

The authorities attempted in many ways to increase the share of "nationalized farms" in total farm output. They tried to put the considerable proportion of land belonging to the State Land Fund to productive use and to take over private farms that were on the verge of collapse and deprived of young manpower by offering financial and technical assistance. At the same time, the authorities adopted administrative measures designed to accelerate the disintegration of peasant farms through a legal ban on parceling medium and small plots, which thereby restricted land sales and the inheritance of farm land (Adamowski and Lewandowski 1970: 182). All the actions that discriminated against the peasantry and were carried out through the State Land Fund were not capable of stopping the parceling of farmland. Estimates suggest that the annual increase in the number of farms reached 0.5–1.5 per cent (Szemberg 1969: 91).

In the 1960s the number of dwarf plots was still increasing at the cost of small ones. State support to larger farms, which produced much-demanded corn and specialized in industrial crops, led to increases in the number of medium-sized and large farms (see Table 10.2). These farms were in a better economic situation, which enabled them to purchase land and investment.

Preferential state policy with respect to farms in the public sector permitted structural changes that were further reinforced by their ability to use land belonging to the State Land Fund. As they were still mismanaged, however, this had no impact on productivity. Increases in the overall volume of farm output continued to depend on the private peasant farms, which were suffering from a shortage of capital.

Consequently, in the late 1960s the inadequate supplies of farm produce, especially meat, gave rise to a leap in prices and increased social discontent. In December 1970 this dissatisfaction turned into bloody workers' riots, which were suppressed by police and the army (Czubiński 1992: 424). The riots on the Baltic coast brought about a change in the Communist government, as well as policy changes that aimed at visibly improving the living standards of the population.

In agriculture the new policies sought to increase productivity, especially in cattle raising. In addition, they abandoned the system of preferences given to collective farms. The purchase prices dictated by the state were raised, compulsory contributions in kind were lifted, taxes were lowered, and land sales were made easier. Peasants were also allowed to rent land from the State Land Fund. These actions helped the peasant farms, particularly the larger ones, which further polarized the farm structure. The better-off peasants, who were oriented to specialized production, were becoming economically stronger, while the number of dwarf farms fell, as these were not market-oriented and responded poorly to economic stimuli (Mazurkiewicz 1979: 77).

Meanwhile the demographic situation in the countryside became more complex with the outflow of young people to towns. The number of people with by-employment who had trouble subsisting on their undersized farms and could not find housing in the cities was increasing (Ostrowski 1989: 23).

In spite of these adverse conditions, the early 1970s brought about a visible increase in farm output, particularly in livestock raising. The main factors behind this increase were both the growth in productivity in private farms and growing imports of fodder for livestock raising. The favorable situation in agriculture, particularly in the socialized sector, once again prompted the Communist regime to push for the full socialization of agriculture. This time cooperatives were to grow through the decline of dwarf farms and farms without heirs, and through the retirement pension scheme implemented in 1977, which encouraged peasants to turn their lands over to the state in return for alimentary allowances. These lands could not be purchased by individual peasants because they were to be used for extending the size of cooperatives and state farms. This was done despite their low productivity, which was far below that achieved in the private sector (Strużek 1982: 258).

Not surprisingly, this policy of transforming agriculture brought about another breakdown in farm output. Already in place in the late 1970s, the policy deepened further under martial law, where economic sanctions precluded, among other things, using credits to finance fodder imports. This forced Polish authorities to impose food rationing, which was designed to prevent further price increases, but led instead to a rise of the black market for food. The policy also caused incomes among the rural population to grow and a further polarization in farm structure. These effects were reinforced by the policy aimed at increasing the country's self-reliance in food that was launched by the military authorities (Mazurkiewicz 1982: 22).

The events and trends discussed above had considerable impact on the structure of peasant farms after 1970 (see Table 10.2). For the first time since the agrarian reform of 1944, the share of farms under 10 ha, especially dwarf plots, in the total area of arable land decreased. This was the result of an overall decline in the number of farms (by 16 per cent from 1970–87), a decrease in the area of arable lands available for farming, and the accelerated growth of land in the socialized sector. The relative decline of small farms might have had favorable results because it produced large farms that were owned by individual families, relatively well-equipped in capital and labor, and oriented towards specialized commodity produce. But it came at immense social and economic cost, as farms owned by peasants disintegrated.

After 1970 agricultural policy favored the socialized sector by giving it preferential access to land, credits, and supplies of imported capital. Between 1970 and 1989 the number of cooperatives doubled to 2,200 farms and their average size rose from 242 to 387 ha. The number of state farms also doubled to 2,523 farms, and their average size rose more than three-fold to a level of 3,277 ha in 1989.

Despite the liberalization of government policy, the share of the public sector increased slightly from 22.7 in 1955 to 23.8 in 1989. Accordingly, the "peaceful methods" of the 1960s and 1970s were much more successful in socializing agriculture than in the days of terror and open struggle against the peasantry that characterized the early 1950s. Nevertheless, the output of farms in the public sector, particularly those owned by the state, was modest despite their size (most of them exceeded 1,000 ha) and their access to various facilities extended by the authorities. The share of the public sector farms in domestic farm output reached 18.7 per cent. Comparing the data on its share in farmlands with its share in agricultural output demonstrates the shortcomings of socialist agriculture.

The data also prove that despite their economic weakness and uncertain future, private farms were still much more efficient. In 1989 they used 13.5 million ha or 71.7 per cent of all land, which was scattered among 2,143 family farms, of which 58 per cent were under 5 ha (*Rocznik Statystyczny*

1990:322). In most cases, they were insufficiently equipped with machinery and tools, still applied traditional farming methods, were deprived of appropriate commercial and servicing infrastructure, and, on the whole, were incapable of covering the domestic demand for foodstuffs.

Transformations in the size structure of land in the whole of Polish agriculture, which were inadequate in the period between the wars, failed to occur after 1944. The agrarian reforms that were conducted with varying intensity and aimed at socializing agriculture increased the average size of family farms but decreased (compared with 1939) the role of large farms in the supply of farm produce. This is confirmed by data on the average size of peasant farms. In 1950 it reached some 5.2 ha, subsequently declined and regained its 1950 value in 1978. It was only in the last decade of Communist rule that the area of an average peasant plot increased, to 7.2 ha by 1989 (*Rocznik Statystyczny 1990*: 329).

In the Polish context, this increase in the average size of peasant farms by a mere 2 ha (see Table 10.2) over almost four decades indicates stagnation in the size structure of landholding in private agriculture. Compared with the countries of Western Europe, the pace of change was decidedly slower in Poland (Kowalczyk 1991: 104). This demonstrates that Polish agriculture was mishandled by Communist governments. The low efficiency of large socialized farms, as well as the disintegration of private farms, are the fundamental causes behind the insufficient growth in agricultural output and its profitability.

In 1918–89, the reasons producing the structural problems of Polish agriculture were the low level of industrialization, the lack of outlets for agricultural production, and the shortage of capital. All these problems are still there and are producing an important challenge for the new democratic government. The necessary transformation will take a long time and will depend on the rate of growth and the rate of integration of the Polish economy with the world market.

THE POST-1989 TRANSFORMATION

The program of democratic changes and radical economic reforms inaugurated in 1989 charged agricultural policy with the very difficult task of adapting the ownership and land structure of agriculture to the requirements of a market-oriented economy. Both of these tasks are extremely difficult and would require successful solutions to complex social questions besides specific economic measures.

Since socialization in Poland had been less widespread than in other countries of Eastern Europe, it is possible to privatize the inefficient state and cooperative farms in a relatively short time. At the same time it is much easier to split up cooperatives, as their members in most cases have still retained their private buildings and are capable of reconstituting their former family farms. It is also feasible to carry out rapid privatization of cooperative manufacturing and services, which require relatively small capital to operate.

Privatization of state farms seems much more difficult, particularly of the largest ones located in the western and northern territories. Their privatization is further obstructed by shortages of domestic capital and by little interest on the part of their employees, who are disinterested in buying out often severely indebted enterprises. Further parceling into smaller farms is obstructed by a lack of appropriate infrastructure as well as by the lack of technical equipment and machinery needed to cultivate smaller plots. Apart from the mode of privatizing, serious social problems arise because new ways of making a living have to be found for the employees of the former state farms.

It is still not fully recognized what social effects are being brought about by the necessary structural transformation of landholding, which in Polish conditions means increasing the average size of the smallest farms. The transformation has to be carried out by privatizing the state-owned farms, but the spatial mismatch in demand and supply for land should also be taken into account. Most state farms are located in western Poland while greatest demand for land is in central and eastern Poland.

According to specialists, it is necessary to create some 400–600 thousand modern farms over 30 ha each that would act as the driving force in Polish agriculture. In the meantime, the experience of 1990–91 points to the very slow progress in creating such farms and to their small average size (4 ha). The reasons are the rapidly rising price of land at rates faster than the rate of inflation and the poor financial condition of the farmers (Ostrowski 1992: II).

In turn, the increase in peasant lots at the cost of the smallest farms might give rise to further tensions on the labor market as thousands of people would inevitably have to find their way into non-agricultural occupations. Many may have to find employment in insufficiently developed services and rural trade, yet most of them will certainly count on jobs in the cities, where high unemployment rates are already a burden.

Transforming the structure of landholding of farms, which is necessary for increasing and rationalizing farm production, requires a multi-directional approach – raising capital, shaping incentives for increasing the size of peasant farms, developing services and trade in rural areas, reviving rural self-government, as well as adapting industrial production to the new demand generated by agriculture and the agricultural processing sector. Successful restructuring depends not only on proper economic policy by the Polish government, but also on the external environment, especially the timing and nature of European integration.

REFERENCES

Adamowski, Z. and Lewandowski, J. (1970) *Rolnictwo polskie w dwudziestopięcioleciu*, Warsaw.
Czubiński, A. (1992) *Dzieje najnowsze Polski 1944–1989*, Poznań.
Jastrzębowski, W. (1946) *Gospodarka niemiecka w Polsce 1939–1944*, Warsaw.
Kaliński, J. (1988), "Collectivization of agriculture in Poland (1948–1955)," *Acta Poloniae Historica*, 57.
Kowalczyk, S. (1991) *Rolnictwo, rozwój – struktura*, Warsaw.
Kumoś, Z. (1983) *Związek Patriotów Polskich. Założenia programowo-ideowe*, Warsaw.
Landau, Z. and Tomaszewski, J. (1991) *Gospodarka Drugiej Rzeczypospolitej*, Warsaw.
Mały Rocznik Statystyczny 1939. (1939) Warsaw.
Markowski, S.(1955) "Rozwój produkcji rolnej w Polsce Ludowej," *Ekonomista*, 1.
Mazurkiewicz, E. (1979) *Podstawowe problemy polityki rolnej w PRL*, Warsaw.
Mazurkiewicz, E. (1982) *Rolnictwo i gospodarka żywnościowa*, Warsaw.
Mieszczankowski, M. (1960) *Struktura agrarna Polski międzywojennej*, Warsaw.
Mieszczankowski, M. (1983). *Rolnictwo II Rzeczypospolitej*, Warsaw.
O co walczy naród polski. (1944) *Deklaracja Rady Jedności Narodowej*, Warsaw.
Olszewski, H. (1964) *Problemy równowagi bilansu zbozowego w Polsce*, Warsaw.
Ostrowski, L. (1989) *Problemy społeczne wsi polskiej*, Warsaw.
Ostrowski, L. (1992) "Nie ma urodzaju na farmerów," *Rzeczpospolita* (13 July).
Piskozub, A. (1987) *Dziedzictwo polskiej przestrzeni*, Wrocław.
Poniatowski, J. (1965) "Uwagi o ustroju rolnym," in *Dylematy gospodarki polskiej*, London.
Rocznik Statystyczny 1949. (1949) Warsaw.
Rocznik Statystyczny 1956. (1956) Warsaw.
Rocznik Statystyczny 1959. (1959) Warsaw.
Rocznik Statystyczny 1990. (1990) Warsaw.
Rocznik Statystyczny 1991. (1991) Warsaw
Rolniczy rocznik statystyczny 1945–1965 (1965) Warsaw.
Słabek, H., Kaliński, J. and Landau, Z. (eds.) (1986) "Reforma rolna," in *Gospodarka Polski Ludowej*, Warsaw.
Statystyka rolnictwa 1946–1957. (1946–1957) Warsaw.
Strużek, B. (1982) *Rozwój socjalistycznych form gospodarki rolnej w Polsce*, Warsaw.
Szemberg, A. (1969) "Przeobrażenia struktury agrarnej chłopskiego rolnictwa," *Nowe Drogi* 7.

11

THE POLITICAL ECONOMY OF AGRICULTURE IN CZECHOSLOVAKIA 1899–1992

Daniel E. Miller

Since the Candlelight Revolutions of 1989–90, the fragile new democracies of Central Europe and the Balkans have been struggling to survive and thrive. In addition to social, economic, and ethnic difficulties that could contribute to instability, a multitude of parties crowds the political spectrum of each state and confuses the electorate. Apart from restrictions and modifications to proportional representation, the sheer number of parties increases the potential for political atomization. The Czech and Slovak Federated Republic from 1989 to the end of 1992 was typical in this regard. In the election of 1990, over one hundred parties were registered, although only twenty-three parties and coalitions appeared on the ballot. Four groups entered the House of the People, and five were elected to the House of Nations, the two chambers which comprised the Federal Assembly, while four gained representation to the Czech and seven to the Slovak National Council.[1] By 1992 the number of parties expanded to nearly one hundred and twenty, and in June of that year forty-one parties and coalitions participated in the parliamentary elections – nearly double the number of the 1990 contest. Eleven groups sent representatives to the House of the People, and twelve entered the House of Nations. Eight parties were sent to the Czech and five to the Slovak National Council.[2] In each case, with the exception of the Slovak National Council, the total of parties and coalitions in the parliaments doubled or even tripled. The increase can be construed as an indicator of voter frustration over politicians' handling of economic recovery, ethnic relations, and other matters. Popular discontent definitely explains the poor showing of certain groups originating from Civic Forum and Public against Violence, the Czech and Slovak organizations that had been prominent in the 1989 revolution.

Several issues facing the electorate pertained to agriculture, including privatization and price supports, and these were articulated by several agrarian parties that spoke for interest in the countryside. Given the strong tradition of agricultural politics among the Slovaks and Czechs in the latter years of the Habsburg Monarchy and during the First Republic (1918–38), a practical consideration is whether current parties have any ties with previous political organizations that once served rural needs.[3] An examination of the evidence will demonstrate that although issues and responses of the Czechoslovak agrarian movement before 1938 are similar to those of politicians representing the countryside since 1989, there is little continuity in leadership and organization between the agrarian politics of the past and the parties of the present. Aside from ethnic cleavages, the only direct connection with the past are ideological, and they are tenuous. For the most part, the similarities that exist are largely products of agrarian politics in a multiparty parliamentary system.

I

Czech agrarian politics began in the latter half of the nineteenth century, when estate owners and wealthy farmers became distraught with the lack of attention political parties paid to rural interests. By the 1890s several agricultural organizations and small parties emerged, but the nucleus of a unified movement came from the Czech Agrarian party (Česká strana agrární), established in 1899. The overriding concern of the Agrarians was to maximize agricultural profits. Their strategy was to promote economic organizations and financial institutions, pass legislation to improve the business climate, and pursue an active role in political affairs. Through the work of its energetic chairman, Antonín Švehla (1873–1933), the party established a number of interest groups to serve the needs of sugar beet growers, dairymen, hops and flax growers, and many more. The party was also linked with the cooperative movement, including thousands of savings and loan associations, known as *kampeličky*, and hundreds of non-credit agricultural cooperatives for production, purchase, and distribution. The Agrarians were also involved in non-economic groups, including the *Dorost* (Youth) organization established in 1906–7 and associations uniting various professionals.[4]

The efforts of Švehla and the Agrarians to organize the countryside and promote its interests had their dividends. First, there were successes at the ballot box. With the institution of universal male suffrage in the Austrian half of the Monarchy in 1907, the Agrarians became the strongest Czech party in the *Reichsrat*. After the 1909 local elections, they had the largest party in the Bohemian Diet. The Agrarians took advantage of their electoral strength by participating in the political system: at the highest level Karel Prášek (1868–1932) served as the Czech minister in the Max W. von Beck government of 1907–8, and Švehla became the chairman of the Bohemian Diet in 1911. The second measure of the party's success was its rapid growth. Over the years, the party experienced steady increases in its membership, reporting 91,194 members in nearly 2,500 local organizations as of January 1914 (Česká strana agrární 1914: 31). The party press, comprised of its daily *Venkov* (*Countryside*) and a host of other papers, reached nearly every member. Švehla could indeed boast that "the countryside is one family" (Frankenberger and Kubíček 1931: 106).

II

From the republic's founding in 1918 until the Munich *Diktat* of 1938, agricultural politics continued to be influential in Czechoslovakia. In 1922 the Czech Agrarians merged with their Slovak counterparts, who maintained some organizational uniqueness, to form the Republican Party of Agriculturalists and Small Farmers (Republikánská strana zemědělského a malorolnického lidu). The party also began an affiliate political group in Ruthenia. Republican strength came largely from villages and small towns, home to the country's agriculturalists, then roughly 26 per cent of the economically active population.[5] The party was involved in every level of politics, but it gained the most visibility through the National Assembly and the cabinet. After 1920, when a split occurred in the Social Democratic party, the Republicans had the largest party in parliament. They attained the peak of their power in the election of 1929, when they won 15 per cent of the vote and captured 46 of 300 seats in the Chamber of Deputies.[6] The Republicans were the only party with the distinction of serving in every political cabinet until 1938. Beginning in 1918, Švehla led the party in a broad coalition and then a center-left government under the Social Democrats. The Republicans later entered the cabinet of Foreign Minister Edvard Beneš (1884–1948), who then had no party affiliation. After 1922 Švehla led three governments: two broad coalitions and a center-right alliance. He also created and represented his party in the extra-parliamentary *Pětka*, or Committee of Five, comprised of the largest groups of the National Assembly (the Republican, Social Democratic, National Socialist, Czech Populist, and National Democratic parties), which provided leadership for the cabinet and the National Assembly. After illness forced Švehla to resign in 1929, Republicans continued to participate in cabinets and serve as the prime ministers until the end of the republic. At first Švehla's center-right government continued, but it was soon replaced with a broad coalition of socialist, minority, and conservative parties that survived in one form or another until September 1938.

Parallel to the Republican party's growing strength at the polls during the interwar years was its intensified involvement in rural economy and society. The party cultivated its ties with the cooperatives, which became more powerful when the Central Union of Agricultural Cooperatives united with eleven other Czech, German, Slovak, Ruthenian, and Polish federations to form the Centrokooperativ. By 1935, there were well over 6,000 credit institutions, most of which were *kampeličky*, and more than 5,000 non-credit ventures, such as processing and production, purchasing and sales, or machine and elective cooperatives.[7] Party leaders often served on the boards of large agricultural processing plants, seen at the time as a civic responsibility to help improve the economy rather than a conflict of interest. One example was Viktor Stoupal (1888–1944), a crucial conservative figure in the Republican party, who had an estate and interest in twenty distilleries and twenty-five sugar refineries.[8]

Another Republican success was the land reform, enacted in 1919 as a political compromise to divide great estates inherited from the Habsburg Monarchy.[9] While the Social Democrats talked of creating more small farms and of confiscating estates, conservative Republicans sought to preserve estates up to 1,000 hectares (ha) and compensate owners for any losses.[10] In the end it was decided that estates over 250 ha of land or 150 ha of arable land would be divided and partial compensation would be given to the owners. Although most of the land was destined for sale to farmers with dwarf, small, and medium-size plots, some went to the state, and a number of so-called remainder estates of approximately 150 ha were created to insure the continued profitability of agricultural processing facilities and other agro-industries. The bureaucracy that implemented the reform was the Land Office. Although it was outside the government but responsible to the cabinet in hopes of keeping it apolitical, most of its personnel were Republicans. Despite some corruption, partiality, and political awards (benefiting Republicans and adherents of other parties), the reform was successful. By 1938, with plans for further reforms being discussed, 1.8 million ha of land was distributed, mainly to those with holdings less than 100 ha (Pavel 1938: 35). Those benefiting from the reform were grateful supporters of the Republican party and the republic.

After the land reform, Republican concern focused on agricultural parity. Like other states in Central Europe and the Balkans at the time, Czechoslovakia suffered from a scissors crisis. The ratio of the agricultural wholesale price index to the industrial products and raw materials index had fallen to 0.81 by 1923. Agricultural prices improved in the next three years but did not close the gap significantly: 0.89 in 1924, 0.87 in 1925, and 0.88 in 1926 (from Průcha *et al.* 1974: 503). Agriculturalists were in dire financial straits in another way, as net receipts per ha declined from 1914 to 1922 and again after 1924 (Brdlík 1938: 41). Moreover, agricultural indebtedness was mounting, increasing in the Czech provinces nearly two-and-a-half times from 1918 to 1924 (Lacina 1978: 165). The Republicans saw higher tariffs as the solution to the problem of agricultural prices, which was a popular approach among their constituents, but not among supporters of the Social Democrats and the National Socialists who did not wish to see the cost of food escalate. Hoping to please the socialists, the Republicans in October 1924 helped introduce unemployment insurance and pensions. Not until June 1925, after months of polemics, did Švehla push through a tariff increase and a sliding tariff with the help of the National Socialists but in opposition to the Social Democrats. His disregard for the wishes of any party in the cabinet was unusual, but this was an act of desperation, the consequence of which was the demise of the coalition (Miller 1989: 266–85). With disparity in relative prices large, agricultural profits declining, and indebtedness increasing, the Republicans instituted a high fixed tariff in October 1926, with the help of the Czech Populists, during the formation of Švehla's third government. As a further price support, a Grain Monopoly was instituted in 1934 to purchase and sell imported or exported grain, fodder and flour (Feierabend 1964).

Although Republicans could boast that they won the trust of agriculturalists from the Šumava Mountains in southern Bohemia to the Tatry Mountains in northern Slovakia, they could not claim that they were solidly united. The party faced some minor splits in the 1920s, but more complicated and distracting were the internecine struggles between the moderates and conservatives. The moderates under Švehla appealed to those who supported the farmers and peasants, the land reform, and generally agreed with the moderate-left politics of those around President Tomáš G. Masaryk (1850–1937) and Edvard Beneš, known simply as the *Hrad* (Castle). The conservatives followed the leadership of Karel Prášek (1868–1932) until the mid-1920s and then František Staněk (1867–1936). They were largely comprised of agro-industrialists, financiers, wealthy landowners, those uncomfortable with the moderates' mass appeal, and enemies of the *Hrad*. In the late 1920s, distinctions between the moderate and the right wings began to blur because of death or illness in the leadership of the moderate camp, the unifying effect of the Great Depression, and the desire of all party members for higher agricultural tariffs. Since the land reform was then an accomplished fact, it no longer served as a bone of contention, also fostering coherence within the party. Finally, the Sudeten German problem of the 1930s helped to unite the ranks of all major parties. Nevertheless, many old personal rivalries remained, especially over cooperation with the *Hrad*.

Despite their popularity, the Republicans did not monopolize agrarian representation in the National Assembly. In predominantly rural Slovakia, the strongest party after 1920 was Hlinka's Slovak People's party (Hlinkovej slovenskej l'udovej strany), which was first under the leadership of Father Andrej Hlinka (1864–1938) and then Msgr. Jozef Tiso (1887–1947).[11] Although the party had a clerical orientation and promoted Slovak autonomy, its constituents were mostly small farmers and peasants. In Ruthenia, the poorest region of the republic and nearly exclusively agrarian, the Communists were strongest.[12] Among the Czechs, appeals to the rural population other than those emanating from the Republicans had mixed success, but parties depended upon some rural votes, especially the Czechoslovak Populists.[13] Many wealthy agriculturalists rallied around the small National Farmers' Union (Národní rolnická jednota), led by a former Republican who allied with the conservative National Democrats. There were also several agrarian fringe parties.

Although the Republicans attracted some non-Slavic votes, most German and Magyar farmers and peasants supported their own political organizations. The German agrarian party was known as the *Bund der Landwirte* (BdL). Under the leadership of Franz Spina (1868–1938), it was the second strongest German party in Czechoslovakia (after the German Social Democratic party) until the 1935 success of Konrad Henlein's (1898–1945) fascist *Sudetendeutsche Partei*.[14] Spina was a driving force behind the so-called activist movement, which brought Germans into the National Assembly in 1920. In 1926 he and a German Christian Socialist entered Švehla's third cabinet, and Spina was the only German to remain in all succeeding governments until the Munich disaster. Like the Republican party, the BdL was active in organizing a German cooperative movement, which was comprised of twenty-four locals.[15] Six months before the Munich Agreement, the BdL merged with Henlein's party, and Spina went into retirement. The Hungarian National party (Magyar Nemzeti Párt) represented Magyar agriculturalists. It sent one representative to the parliament after the 1920 elections and, because of minority guarantees, four deputies in 1929 and 1935.

Certain features characterize agrarian movements in Czechoslovakia between the two world wars. The agrarian parties were determined to participate in all levels of political life – from local government to the cabinet. To do so, they formed coalitions with other parties during elections, within the National Assembly, and in the cabinet. In the parliament, they were interested in reform rather than abrupt change, and to achieve their goals they were willing to compromise with each other and with non-agrarian parties on a variety of issues. Unlike some parties in other Central European and Balkan states that referred to themselves as agrarian but cared little for the countryside, agrarian parties in Czechoslovakia were truly concerned about rural society and economics, a mood which is reflected in their programs and actions. Finally, their number and structure reflected the ethnic divisions of the state.

The Munich Agreement of September 1938 and the collapse of representative parliamentary politics in Czechoslovakia ended this phase in the development of agrarian politics. The constitution was rewritten, and the new Czecho–Slovak Republic gave autonomy to Slovakia and Ruthenia. The Republican Rudolf Beran (1887–1954) formed a cabinet, but it was dissolved when German troops entered Czecho–Slovakia in March 1939. The state went through another partition: Slovakia became independent under Hlinka's Slovak People's party, which took on the trappings of fascism; Ruthenia was given to Hungary; and the Third Reich absorbed the Czech provinces, then known as the Protectorate of Bohemia and Moravia. The Republican party and all other parties were dissolved and politicians entered the Czech National Confederation (Národní souručenství), Hlinka's Slovak People's party, joined the underground, or fled abroad.

III

After 1945 what little remained of the fabric of agrarian politics was completely shredded. Political activity was restricted to parties of the National Front, which was under the leadership of the Communists. The Republican party, along with groups that participated in the National Confederation and those accused of collaborating with the Nazis, was forbidden from reorganizing, in accordance with the Košice Program of April 1945. Former Republicans found their way into other political parties. Most Czechs entered the National Socialist party, and Slovaks joined either the Democratic party (Demokratická strana), later renamed the Slovak Renewal party (Strana slovenskej obrody), or the Freedom party (Strana slobody). After the Communists came to power in February 1948, some former Republicans joined the Communist party as experts. Many of these were later victims of the show trials of the Stalinist era, as were some ex-Republicans who had abstained from public life.

The political structure of the Czechoslovak agrarian movement was completely dismantled as a result of the political changes between 1938 and 1948, while its economic features were destroyed in building socialism. All financial institutions, including the *kampeličky*, came into the hands of the state (Feierabend 1952: 58). Most of the non-credit cooperatives were merged into the Central Cooperative Council in July 1948. Later that year the Center for the Management of Agricultural Products brought the warehouse, dairy, alcohol, potato, and several other cooperatives under its control.[16] Finally, the process of socializing all land in the republic began in February 1949 with the law creating the Unified Agricultural Cooperatives, or cooperatives.[17] A smaller number of state farms equivalent to the Soviet *kolkhozy* were also created. By 1960 over 83 per cent of all agricultural land was in the hands of collective and state farms, a number which reached approximately 95 per cent by 1989.[18]

In socialism, there were to be no competing political interests, so there were no independent parties outside the Communist dominated National Front. Although three agricultural interest groups formed, all with some ties to the Republicans, they had relatively short lives: the Associated Union of Czech Agriculturalists (Jednotný svaz českých zemědělců) from 1945 to 1947, the Associated Union of Slovak Agriculturalists (Jednotný zväz slovenských rol'níkov) from 1945 to 1952, and the Association of Agriculturalists (Svaz zemědělců) formed by the cooperatives during the Prague Spring of 1968.[19] The minor role agriculturalists played in the events of 1968 provides some understanding of the mood of the countryside twenty years later. By and large, the electricity of the reform movement was not transmitted to the countryside, where the acceptance of collectivization and an appreciation for the economic stability it brought made inhabitants hesitant to advocate rapid change. One Communist party leader even stated in 1969 that "the cooperative farmers as a whole did not succumb to the hysteria generated by the news media last year and this year and that in general they represent a very important part of the sound forces of the (Communist) party."[20]

Although they had no permanent independent organization, agriculturalists did influence decision-makers in the party and the bureaucracy responsible for the five-year plan through the collectives, or the Jednotné zemědělské družstvo (JZD) and Jednotné rol'nícke družstvo (JRD). As of 1989 the members of JZD–JRD accounted for 72 per cent of all those employed in agriculture.[21] The importance of the JZD–JRD in the party and state can be seen in the career of its chairman before 1989, Pavel Jonáš (b. 1925). In 1972, Jonáš left his post as chairman of the central committee of the Union of Cooperative Farmers in Slovakia, a position he had since 1968, to become the chairman of the Union of Cooperative Farmers for the entire republic. He was a member of the Central Committee of the Slovak Communist party and a deputy and member of the chairmanship of the Slovak National Council from 1969 to 1971, and from 1976 he was a member of the Federal Assembly. Finally, from 1981 he was a candidate of the Central Committee of the Communist party.[22]

IV

By the time of the 1989 Candlelight Revolution in Czechoslovakia, dramatic transformations had occurred in the countryside. Conditions that existed during Švehla's time had vanished, and there was little desire to imitate the past. Hardly any private farms remained, and agricultural employees had replaced the peasants, farmers, and agro-industrialists. The total number of gainfully employed citizens in agriculture diminished from nearly 30 per cent in 1930 to 20.4 per cent, and nearly half the population lived in urban areas of over 16,000 inhabitants.[23] Moreover, attitudes toward farming changed. Agriculturalists now preferred the security of collective farms as opposed to private farms, in part because of the vast amount of capital investment and time independent farming required. According to a poll conducted in 1990, while over two-thirds of all agriculturalists favored privatization of agriculture, most were skeptical about its success. Only 7 per cent indicated an interest in becoming private farmers, and three-quarters wanted to continue working for cooperatives.[24]

When the leading role of the Communist party evaporated in 1989, a new era dawned for the countryside. As in the pre-1938 period, politics reflected agrarian concerns and demands, but the circumstances had changed. Free elections were scheduled for 8–9 June 1990, and a host of parties vied for votes in the countryside. Among those stumping in the rural districts were politicians from the old National Front. The Communist party played on the agriculturalists' concern over the fate of the cooperatives. The Slovak

Renewal party, which had claimed a large number of ex-Republicans after 1945, was quick to abandon its association with the Communists in 1989 and assumed its pre-1948 appellation. As the Democratic party, it ran on a platform of private ownership and directed its message to Eastern Slovakia.[25]

In addition to the previously established parties, interest groups that had existed within the socialist system – legitimate, semi-legitimate and illegitimate – came into the open as either parties or popular movements.[26] Given the extensive organization of the JZD–JRD and their economic importance before 1989, it is not surprising that this interest group produced a rather influential agrarian movement. During a congress of the JZD–JRD near Zlín in January 1990, delegates voted to form the Czechoslovak Agricultural party (Československá strana zemědělská, ČSSZ). The ČSSZ claimed to follow the tradition of Švehla and even named its newspaper *Venkov*.[27] The party program of December 1989 promised to serve the needs of all agriculturalists, including the collective farmers, food processing employees, and the handful of independent farmers.[28] Aside from its avowed ideological link with the Republicans, its attempt to represent all interests of the countryside, and its republic-wide organization, there were few similarities with the old Republican party.

The ČSSZ chairman became František Trnka, an assistant professor and economist with JZD–Slušovice, the most progressive and controversial collective in Czechoslovakia.[29] The party's economic program, which Trnka outlined in *Venkov*, displayed a willingness to consider alternatives for reorganizing agriculture. Trnka maintained that most JZD–JRD and state farms should be restructured as corporations or private concerns, with only a few divided into independent farms.[30] Before the election, the party presented the details of this plan as a third agrarian reform – to follow that of 1919–38 and the Communist-inspired reform after 1945. The proposal would have enabled farmers (exclusively Czechoslovak citizens) to rent land or purchase it at low cost, as long as it was used strictly for agricultural purposes.[31]

After talks between the ČSSZ and Civic Forum fell through, the ČSSZ entered an electoral coalition of eight parties known as the Alliance of Agriculturalists and the Countryside (Spojenectví zemědělců a venkova, SZaV). Of the four agrarian parties in the coalition, only the small Republican Party of the Czechoslovak Countryside (Republikánská strana československého venkova) had a significant number of Republican old-timers or their descenants.[32] The coalition's eleven-point program included the "renewal of the rights of land ownership" and "conditions of equal rights for all farmers."[33]

Like the SZaV, other agrarian parties entered electoral coalitions. The Free Farmers' party (Svobodná rolnická strana) also claimed to be the heirs of Švehla, but in contrast to the ČSSZ it supported private agriculture and the abolition of collectives. It joined with the Catholic Czechoslovak Populist party (Československá strana lidová) and its broader alliance, the Christian and Democratic Union (Křesťanská a demokratická unie). Civic Forum (Občanské fórum) included two parties to attract voters from the countryside: the Agrarian Party of Civic Forum (Agrární strana občanského fóra) and the Party of the Czech Countryside (Strana českého venkova), centered in southern Bohemia and concerned with ecological and cultural issues.[34] There were only two small agrarian parties that did not enter coalitions and did not appear on the ballot.[35]

The new election law required parties to receive at least 5 per cent of the vote in one republic to enter the Federal Assembly. The same number applied for election to the Czech National Council, although it was lowered to 3 per cent in Slovakia to accommodate minorities. The victors in the election, Civic Forum and its Slovak counterpart, the Public against Violence, sent 170 deputies to both houses of parliament out of 300. Other winners were the Communist party in both republics (47 seats), the Slovak Christian Democratic Movement (40 seats), the Association for Moravia and Silesia (16 seats), the Slovak National party (15 seats), and the Hungarian Christian Democrats (12 seats).[36] Since most agrarian parties were associated with large parties or movements, it is impossible to gauge their success. Such was not the case with the SZaV, of which the ČSSZ was a dominant member. It did not gain the 5 per cent of the vote in either republic required to enter the Federal Assembly, but it was able to acquire at least 5 per cent of the votes in one or both of the chambers for half of the Czech districts: Central (which surrounds but does not include Prague), Southern, Western, and Eastern Bohemia. In Slovakia, the Alliance was unable to garner 5 per cent in any district for either race. It had an equally poor showing in the contest for the Slovak National Council, but it had more success in Bohemia, where it was able to gain a total of 4.11 per cent of the vote, once again from Central, Southern, Western, and Eastern Bohemia.[37]

Between 1990 and 1992 the political impact of the agrarian parties was minimal. The Christian and Democratic Movement in the Czech provinces did not take part in the coalition government, which limited the influence of the Free Farmers' party. The agrarian parties within Civic Forum seem to have had no dramatic effect on policy formation, but the lack of information on their activity make definitive statements impossible. The chairman of the ČSSZ, Trnka, was able to score a small victory, although a short-lived one, when he was appointed deputy minister for the federal economy with responsibilities in agriculture in early July 1990. He was recalled later that month, charging that Civic Forum deputies resented his affiliation with the ČSSZ.[38]

Certain factors worked in favor of the ČSSZ in the first parliamentary period after 1989. The party had a number of important business contacts, such as Stanislav Labounek, the former chairman of the ČSSZ's Czech section. Because of his involvement in the establishment of the Agricultural Bank (Agrobanka) in January 1990 and its management, he resigned his party post in June.[39] The ČSSZ improved its ability to reach the rural inhabitants by transforming its weekly newspaper into a daily. The SZaV dissolved, but the ČSSZ became involved in a grouping with seven other groups not represented in the parliament – including the Social Democrats, the Czechoslovak Socialists, the Greens, and the Society for Moravia and Silesia – known as the *Octet*. The new coalition began a campaign of registering protests about Civic Forum's monopoly over the media, rising inflation and unemployment, dismissals of those who did not agree with Civic Forum policies, and the labeling as criminals of those who cooperated with the secret police but committed no crime.[40]

After talks about merging agrarian parties within the SZaV failed in the fall of 1990, the ČSSZ faced another challenge.[41] It underwent a friendly split in October 1990, when Slovaks left to form the Slovak Farmers' party (Slovenská rol'nická strana).[42] Given the pressures of nationalism, separate parties along ethnic lines were more in tune with the mood of the electorate. Furthermore, after the revolution the federal ministry of agriculture was discontinued in favor of separate ministries on the republic level. The intent was to have the government and the Federal Assembly supply overall direction for agriculture, leaving "management and development" to the republics.[43] This necessitated that agriculturalists focus their concerns on the republic levels, making the existence of a state-wide party less practical.[44]

The Agriculturalists' and Slovak Farmers' parties did rather well in the local elections of November 1990, considering that all parties ran independently without any minimum vote requirements. The ČSSZ received a total of 1.5 per cent of the votes and 2.5 per cent of all seats in municipal councils, and the Farmers' Movement in Slovakia won 3.2 per cent of all council seats. The Political Movement of the Members of Agricultural Cooperatives, also a former member of the SZaV, gained 2.1 per cent of the votes.[45] Although Civic Forum won in the Czech Republic, the Public against Violence came in second to the Christian Democratic Movement in Slovakia. The Communist party made another strong showing, winning 13.6 per cent of the council seats in Slovakia and 14.4 per cent in the Czech Republic. Its success reflected discontent with the parties in power over their failure to bring a speedy conclusion to the restructuring of the state and the transition to capitalism.

Between 1990 and 1992, a host of controversies and problems faced agriculturalists, only some of which were resolved. There were political squabbles, such as the dispute between Czech Minister of Agriculture Kubát, a non-political expert favored by Civic Forum, and Czech Prime Minister Peter Pithart, who disliked Kubat's performance. There was also an investigation into the affairs of Slušovice during the Communist era.[46] Important economic concerns were the huge surplus of agricultural goods that stockpiled in warehouses and government support for large agricultural firms rather than smaller ones.[47] In the summer of 1991, a land privatization law was passed, enabling those who lost property between 1948 and 1989 to reclaim it under certain conditions.[48] In December 1991 a law was passed on the privatization of cooperatives, the so-called transformation bill, which required members of collectives and the former property owners before collectivization to determine jointly whether enterprises will become a commercial or private firm or continue as a cooperative. The members and former owners were empowered to liquidate an enterprise either by vote or by failing to act within one year.[49]

Whether resolved or not, these and other agricultural issues were being tackled without any direct representation from a party that had the welfare of the countryside as its sole interest. As a result, the level of frustration in the countryside grew. In October 1991 before the transformation law was passed, demonstrations involving over twenty thousand farmers in Prague and Bratislava were held to protest high prices, reduced living standards, and the slow pace of agricultural reorganization.[50] After it was enacted, Trnka spoke against the measure, claiming that "chaos and confusion" will result from the inclusion of the former owners and discrepancies in the legislation.[51] Increasingly, rural voters perceived that they were not properly represented in a political system already tainted with the inability to solve ethnic disputes and rejuvenate the economy. Their anger was to be translated into political action.

To improve its standing at the polls, the ČSSZ, which had become known as the Agriculturalists' party (Zemědělská strana, ZS), formed the Liberal Social Union (Liberální sociální unie, LSU) electoral coalition with the Czechoslovak Socialists, the Greens, and other parties from the *Octet*.[52] The LSU registered as a political movement in late 1991 with Trnka was its chairman. It appealed to moderate voters, expressed a desire to represent the middle and lower classes, and was against the speedy road to capitalism of Václav Klaus and his Civic Democratic party.[53] In the 1992 election, the LSU gained 5.84 per cent of the votes to the House of the People, 6.06 per cent to the House of Nations, and 6.52 to the Czech National Council. Trnka entered the Federal Assembly to lead the LSU in opposition to the Civic Democrats and Christian Democrats, who formed a government in the Czech Republic.

Other parties claimed to represent the countryside in 1992, but most did not stand for election.[54] The only one to have some measure of success was the Free Farmer's party, which entered both houses of the Federal Assembly and the Czech National Council along with its associate, the Catholic Czechoslovak Populist party. The conservative Party of Czechoslovak Entrepreneurs, Tradesmen and Farmers attempted to build a constituency in the Czech countryside, but it failed to reach the 5 per cent threshold. Several other agrarian parties once allied with the ČSSZ and Civic Forum registered, but they either did not participate in the elections or did not play a prominent role in any coalition. Included in this group is the Agrarian Republican party (Agrární republikánská strana), created in January 1992 from the Republican Party of the Czechoslovak Countryside, former ally of the ČSSZ and claimant to the pre-1939 Republican party heritage.[55]

V

Some parallels can be drawn between the agrarian movement among Slovaks and Czechs before 1938 and since 1989, but they must not be overstated. At first glance, the environment in which agrarian parties currently are functioning has some resemblance to the past. Economic concerns prompted agriculturalists to unite and protect their interests in 1989 just as they motivated rural inhabitants from the late nineteenth century to 1938. Furthermore, agriculturalists of the post-1989 period are experiencing the effects of industrialization that began in the Habsburg Monarchy, especially in the Czech Republic, where a decline in the agricultural labor force complicated the recruiting efforts of Republicans before 1938 and agrarian parties after 1989. Even land reform and price supports are issues on the agendas of agrarian parties from both time periods. In fact, it can be argued that privatizing collective farms after 1989 is but another step in the continuing effort to reverse the injustices of land distribution that existed during the Habsburg Monarchy. Despite the similarities with the past, specific concerns of Slovak and Czech agriculturalists today are dramatically different from those of their predecessors because of drastic alterations in politics and agriculture between the two time periods.

To fully understand agrarian politics in the Czech Republic and Slovakia after 1989, one must begin with the premise that the agrarian movements' ties with the past have been torn. The parliamentary democracy of the interwar years, interrupted during World War II, was resumed with some changes in 1945. The Republican party, however, was not reestablished. After 1948, the Communists preserved parliamentary politics in form but not function, precluding the development of a new independent movement or the rebirth of an old organization specifically representing the countryside. Following the Candlelight Revolution of 1989, multi-party politics based on free elections and proportional representation resumed. Under these conditions, agricultural groups quickly emerged to enter the political fray, just as they did in the nineteenth century and afterward. With the possible exception of the small and ineffective Agrarian Republican party, these parties are creatures of the present rather than of the past.

Resemblances that can be detected in the agrarian movements before 1938 and 1989 afterward can be misleading. As in the years between 1918 and 1938, the parties of today have expressed a range of opinions regarding the problems facing agriculture, but all favor moderate changes and shun drastic measures that would disrupt agriculture. To achieve their ends, parties from both periods have worked to build broad constituencies, energetically organizing the countryside and participating in every level of public life. Finally, as in the days of Švehla, the agrarian parties after 1989 have formed alliances and mergers, ongoing processes, in order to secure a voice in the legislative process. Rather than indicating continuity with the past, these common characteristics demonstrate the reality of agrarian politics in a developed economy with a multi-party political system.

Differences between the pre-1938 and post-1989 agrarian movements are more dramatic, suggesting that the most significant features of current agrarian movement among Czechs and Slovaks are outgrowths of the 1948–89 period. The lack of an extensive or diversified agrarian political organization among Slovaks and Czechs today stems not only from the destruction of the Republican infrastructure but also from the inability of any group to develop that would compete with the Communists' monopoly of power after 1948. The new agrarian parties claim to have ideologies that place them to a greater or lesser extent in the shadow of the Republican party and Švehla, but such links are tenuous. The small parties that extolled the virtues of independent agriculture, as did the Švehla's Republicans, performed poorly at the polls. The collective farm experience has reduced the interest in small or medium-sized independent farms and has led to a desire on the part of most agricultural employees to maintain large agricultural enterprises. Most efforts to mimic Republican ideology, therefore, are aimed at identifying current agrarian parties with the successes of Švehla's party before 1938. The present weakness of agrarian parties at the polls may also be related to the legacy of the Communist era. At first, there was broad support for the leaders of the revolution, the Public Against Violence and Civic Forum, but that soon evaporated. In the Czech Republic, there was a growing desire to desocialize as rapidly as possible through a heavy dose of traditional liberalism and capitalism.[56] In Slovakia there was a different concern, a consequence of the depression in heavy industry. This dampened the Slovaks' enthusiasm for rapid progress toward a market economy and fueled the fires of nationalism, since it appeared to them that the Czechs were not sensitive to their plight. In this atmosphere, the concerns about agriculture in both republics seemed secondary at best, and agrarian parties had little hope of gaining a healthy share of the vote. The efforts of the ZS in the last two years to tackle broader economic and social issues within the *Octet* and the LSU, therefore, may improve its chances at the polls in 1994.

If one is to seek a connection with the past in the current agrarian movement in Slovakia and the Czech Republic that lends continuity to all three eras – before 1918, between the wars, and afterward – nationalism promises to be the most productive lead. After 1989 there were divisions along national lines in the agrarian movement within and among parties just as there were between the two world wars. This generalization is also true for other political groupings, including socialists and catholics. The basis for cleavages along ethnic lines is deeply rooted in the political cultures of both nations. Despite their ethnic similarities, Slovaks and Czechs had vastly different historical experiences that began when the Slovaks came under the Magyars in the ninth century and the Czechs established the Kingdom of Bohemia. Although both nationalities were components of the Habsburg Monarchy after 1526, the Slovaks remained under Hungarian domination, which ensured a different political, social, cultural, and economic development from the Czechs. Disputes between Czechs and Slovaks surfaced in the early years of the First Republic and were not resolved. The Slovaks believed that their association with the Czechs was strewn with pitfalls, and politics in Slovakia often centered around nationality rather than economic issues. Many Slovaks viewed independence as the best solution, but the Slovakia created as Germany's puppet state in 1939 collapsed with the retreat of the Third Reich's troops and never had an opportunity to evolve. Although politicians between 1945 and 1948 were determined to avoid the mistakes of the pre-1938 days, they had little time to complete their experiment. In the Communist era, there were few serious attempts to address the nationality question, especially at the institutional level, and the party worked hard at creating the illusion of consensus. Evidence of this half-heartedness is the ineffectiveness of the federated state structure that the Communists introduced after the Prague Spring. When the Communists fell from power, nationalism again become a pivotal issue. In this atmosphere, the viability of any unified Czech and Slovak party was tenuous, and the short life of the ČSSZ is a case in point. Moreover one might assume that a party concentrating on agricultural rather than on ethnic matters might not fair well in Slovakia at the polls. Such was the case in the federal elections of 1990 and 1992. In the Czech Republic and Slovakia, as with other successor states, nationalism is a bequest of the Habsburg Monarchy that can be discerned most readily.

Given the effects of World War II and the building of socialism under the Communist party, searching for direct ties to the First Republic or the Habsburg Monarchy other than nationalism and perhaps ideology would be analogous to the quest for the Holy Grail. The emergence of agricultural parties in Slovakia and the Czech Republic today is a logical result of the rebirth of pluralism in a participatory parliamentary democracy, the impact of failures in socialist economics, and the social concerns of rural inhabitants. Certainly the political culture of the Czechs and Slovaks as well as the symbolism of the old Republican party can blend together to help legitimize new agrarian parties, but these are the most tangible links with the distant past.

NOTES

I would like to thank Damon R. Cox of the University of West Florida for culling through some of the English references for this paper and Mary Hrabik Samal of Oakland University (Rochester, MI) for reading the first draft.

1 The Federal Assembly was bicameral, with each chamber having equal powers. The 150 deputies of the Chamber of the People were selected on the basis of population, and the 150 deputies to the Chamber of Nations were divided equally between the dominant nationalities. The Slovak and Czech republics had their own unicameral national councils.

2 For summaries of the political scene at the time of the 1990 elections, see Wolchick (1991:59–96); J. Pehe "The political spectrum," in *REE*, 9 March 1980: 12–15; J. Pehe "New political parties maneuver before election campaign," in *REE*, 20 April 1990: 17–21; J. Obrman and J. Pehe "Political organizations register for elections," in *REE*, 4 May 1990: 5–9; and J. Obrman "Civic forum surges to impressive victory in elections," in *REE*, 22 June 1990: 13–16. For the 1992 election, see (as), "Politické strany a hnutí" [Political parties and movements], *Lidové noviny* [*People's News*] (hereafter cited as *LN*), 2 March 1992: 5; 3 March 1992: 11; 13 March 1992: 11; "Parties, coalitions running in elections necessary," *Lidová demokracie* [*People's Democracy*], 15 April 1992, as quoted in *FBIS-EEU*, 17 April 1992: 9; J. Pehe "Czechoslovakia's changing political spectrum," *RFE/RL Research Report*, 31 January 1992: 1–7; J. Pehe "Czechoslovakia: Parties register for elections," in *RFE/RL Research Report*, 1 May 1992: 20–5; and J. Obrman "The Czechoslovak elections: A guide to the parties" in *RFE/RL Research Report*, 29 May 1992: 10–16.

3 I treated this question specifically in Miller (1992).

4 The best source on the early organizational efforts of the Czech agrarian movement is Frankenberger and Kubíček (1931). Information on the cooperatives may be obtained from *Třicet let* (1928).

5 *Manuel statistique*, 1934, Table II-12: 15–19. This percentage is low because it does not accurately reflect the role of women and children in agriculture. Over half of the entire population lived in towns of 2,000 inhabitants or less in 1930, which is a rough indicator of the number of those depending upon agriculture for a livelihood. See *Statistická Ročenka*, 1936, Table II-4: 6.

6 Election statistics for the interwar years appear in Buchvaldek *et al.* (1986: 631–2).

7 *Statistisches Jahrbuch*, 1938, Table V-77, cols 8, 9: 112–3. See also Spirk (1966: 20–21). I would like to take this opportunity to correct a statement found in Miller (1992: 41). I noted that there were 1,315 agricultural purchasing and sales cooperatives, 1,574 processing and production cooperatives, and 2,475 machine and electric cooperatives. The wording in the sentence leads the reader to believe that these organizations were part of the Republican dominated Centrokooperativ. In fact, they represent several different groupings of cooperatives. The machine and electric cooperatives also includes other miscellaneous groups.

8 *Památník věnovaný předsedovi Viktoru Stoupalovi*, n.d. A copy of the book is located in Státní archív Brno [State Archive, Brno], Inventory 483/62, Signature II-1.410.

9 In the pre-war Czech Crown Lands, Slovakia, and Ruthenia, 89.75 per cent of the holdings were between 0 and 10 ha and accounted for 25.37 per cent of the land; 9.96 per cent of the holdings were between 10 and 100 ha and accounted for 33.85 per cent of the land; and 0.29 per cent of the holdings were over 100 ha and accounted for 40.78 per cent of the land. The situation in the former Hungarian

territories of Slovakia and Ruthenia was somewhat worse than in the Czech Crown Lands. See Výkonný výbor Republikánské strany zemědělského a malorolnického lidu [Central Committee of the Republican Party of Agriculturalists and Small Farmers, VV-RSZaML], 1928–9: 654–5.

10 For the Social Democrats' proposal, see Textor (1923: 27). For the Republican proposal, see "Národní shromáždění československé republiky, 39. schůze plenární" [The National Assembly of the Czechoslovak Republic, 39th Plenary Session], *Venkov*, 27 March 1919: 2–3.

11 Hlinka's Slovak People's party received 6.9 per cent of the votes in the elections to the Chamber of Deputies in 1925 and 1935. In Slovakia in 1925, it received 34.3 per cent of the vote, while the Republicans came in second with 17.4 per cent. *Les élections à l'Assemblée Nationale*, 1925: 19.

12 In 1925 the Communists received 30.8 per cent of the vote in Ruthenia – over twice the amount of the Republican party. *Les élections à l'Assemblée Nationale*, 1985: 19.

13 At their height in 1925, the Czechoslovak People's party received 9.7 per cent of the votes and sent 31 deputies to parliament.

14 The BdL sent its greatest number of deputies to parliament in 1925, when it received 8.0 per cent of the votes.

15 *Statistisches Jahrbuch*, 1938, Table V 77: 113.

16 *Sbírka zákonů*, Law 187 of 21 July 1948 and Law 278 of 2 December 1948. See also Feierabend (1952: 74–7); Spulber (1957: 135).

17 Unified Agricultural Cooperatives are known as Jednotné rol'nícke družstvo (JRD) in Slovak and Jednotné zemědělské družstvo (JZD) in Czech. For the law that created the collectives, see *Sbírka zákonů*, Law 69 of 23 February 1949.

18 *Historická statistická ročenka*, 1985, Tables 11–9, 11–21, 11–22: 217, 224–5, and *Statistická ročenka*, 1990, Table 11–10: 297.

19 The Association of Agriculturalists was established during the VII JZD-JRD congress in January 1968 (Buchvaldek *et al.* 1986: 537). It was particularly cautious to deny any links to the Republicans (Skilling 1976: 589).

20 O. Švestka, *Tribuna* [*Tribune*], 8 October 1969, as quoted in Ulč (1974: 49).

21 *Statistická ročenka*, 1990, Table 11–8: 295.

22 *Malá československá encyklopedie*, 1986 ed., s.v. "Jonáš, Pavel."

23 Based on information found in *Statistická ročenka*, 1990, Table 1–1: 20–1; Table 4–4: 97–8.

24 *Die Presse*, 12 October 1990, as cited in Martin, P. (1990) "Agricultural reform," *REE*, 16 November 1990: 7. See also Greenhouse "Collective farms in Czechoslovakia score one success for communism," *New York Times*, 16 April 1990: D4; "Reforms alter the landscape of Czechoslovakia's farming," *New York Times*, 4 June 1991; T.N. Ash "East European agriculture at a crossroads," *RFE/RL Research Report*, 24 January 1992: 22–8.

25 Transcription of Prague Domestic Service on 21 May 1990, in *FBIS-EEU*, 21 May 1990: 22.

26 For a discussion of interest groups in the Soviet system which can be applied to Eastern Europe, see Skilling and Griffiths (1973). About the latent pluralism in Czechoslovak society during the period of Communist party domination, see H.G. Skilling "Czechoslovak political culture: Pluralism in an international context" (115–33), and D.W. Paul "Czechoslovakia's political culture reconsidered" (134–48) both in Brown (1985).

27 During the 1990 election campaign, the ČSSZ distributed a reprint of Karel Čapek's *Drobty ze Švehlových hovorů* [Fragments from the words of Švehla].

28 "Our documentation: Program declaration of the Czechoslovak Agrarian party"

Rudé právo [*Red Right*], 15 December 1989: 3, as quoted in *FBIS-EEU*, 22 December 1989: 25.

29 During the socialist regime, Slušovice was involved in a variety of unusual undertakings and experiments that were often considered to be nearly capitalist. After the Candlelight Revolution, the managers of Slušovice were accused of having been close to the old Communist leadership and dependent upon its funds. The collective has been associated with some controversial projects, including an ecologically questionable canal for the Vítkovické Iron Works. See M. Kovář "Slušovice: Příklad nebo mafie?" [Slušovice: model or mafia?], *Respekt* [*Respect*] 2–8 May 1990: 3. Trnka refuted connections between his party and the Communists in articles and radio broadcasts in late December 1989 and mid-January 1990, summaries of which appear in *FBIS-EEU*, 22 January 1990: 38–9. See also "Vážení čtenáři, vážení občané!" [Dear readers, dear citizens!] *Venkov*, 13 June 1990: 1–2. Despite attempts to deny allegations of cooperation with the Communists, the party did not submit its list of candidates for screening to determine if they had collaborated with the secret police, although only a total of ten parties did so. On this matter, see the transcription of the Prague Domestic Service radio broadcast in *FBIS-EEU*, 7 June 1990: 18. The congress which established the ČSSZ was actually held at the Slušovice JZD. See E. Staněk and E. Hoffmann "Agricultural workers have their own party: Delegates so far unable to agree on a name" *Rudé právo*, 15 January 1990: 1, as quoted in *FBIS-EEU*, 22 January 1990: 39.

30 Trnka, F. "Jde nám o svobodný a hodnotný život venkova" [In the interest of a free and profitable life for the countryside], ČSSZ literature reprinted from *Venkov*, n.d., but in the spring of 1990.

31 B. Jankovský and T. Smetana "Žádáme třetí pozemkovou reformu!" [We are asking for a third land reform!] Prague: ČSSZ, spring 1990 (photocopy).

32 The other two agrarian parties were the Political Movement of JZD Members (Politické hnutí členů JZD) and the Party of the Moravian Countryside (Strana moravského venkova). The other parties were the Movement of Pensioners for a Secure Life [Hnutí důchodců za životní jistoty], the Czechoslovak Party of Integration [Československá strana integrace], State-Wide Active Citizens [Celostátní aktiv občanů], and the Movement for the Equal Standing of Women [Hnutí za rovnoprávné postavení žen]. For the talks between Civic Forum and agricultural parties, see "An end to hopes for unity,?" *Zemědělské noviny* [*Agricultural News*] (hereafter cited as *ZN*), 12 March 1990: 1, as quoted in FBIS-EEU, 16 March 1990: 21. For information on the Republican party of the Czechoslovak Countryside, see M. Vanura "The Countryside is emerging from a period of darkness," *ZN*, 12 March 1990: 7, as quoted in *FBIS-EEU*, 16 March 1990: 23. The electoral alliance is discussed in "Electoral coalition of agrarians and countryside realized," *ZN*, 27 March 1990: 1, as quoted in *FBIS-EEU*, 10 April 1990: 27, and "Women join with 'Countryside'," *ZN*, 4 April 1990: 1, as quoted in *FBIS-EEU*, 10 April 1990: 28. The Republican Party of the Czechoslovak Countryside has *Brázda* [*Furrow*] as its newspaper – also the title of a Republican party journal between 1920 and 1942.

33 "Program spojenctví zemědělců a venkova" [Program of the alliance of agriculturalists and the countryside], 1990 campaign poster.

34 On these parties see "Přehled politických stran a hnutí" [Survey of political parties and movements], *SS*, 18 October 1990: 5; "A free farmers' party," *Pravda*, 2 April 1990: 2, as quoted in *FBIS-EEU*, 11 April 1990: 19; and "Free farmers go with us," *Lidová demokracie*, 2 April 1990: 1, as quoted in *FBIS-EEU*, 16 April 1990: 31. Civic Forum's counterpart in Slovakia, the Public Against Violence, was far less of an umbrella organization and contained no allied political parties.

35 The parties were the Independent Farmers' party (Nezávislá strana rolníků), which geared its orientation to the private farmers of eastern Slovakia, and the Socialist Agriculturalists' party (Strana socialistických zemědělců), which directed its appeal to north Bohemian voters. *Občanská beseda*, 1990; "Občanské fórum a volby 1990" [Civic forum and the 1990 elections] (photocopied leaflet); "Přehled politických stran a hnutí," *SS*, 18 October 1990: 5; *Spektrum 90*, 1990.

36 "Výsledky voleb do FS a ČNR podle jednotlivých krajů" [Election results for the Federal Assembly and the Czech National Council according to individual regions], *SS*, 12 June 1990: 4; "Volby do SNR" [Elections to the Slovak National Council], *SS*, 12 June 1990: 4; "Kandidáti do FS a ČNR, zvolení ve 2. skrutíniu" [Candidates to the Federal Assembly and the Czech National Council selected in the second scrutiny], *SS*, 14 June 1990: 4; and J. Obrman "Civic Forum surges to impressive victory in elections," *REE*, 22 June 1990: 13–16. A list of parties and coalitions that participated in the election appears in "Do voleb s trojkou!" [To the polls with number three!], *SS*, 20 April 1990: 1.

37 "Výsledky voleb do FS a ČNR podle jednotlivých krajů," SS, 12 June 1990: 4. The Alliance's minimal success did assure it government campaign funding.

38 "Jednotkou doby jsou i dny" [Days are also units of time] *Venkov*, 1 August 1990: 1, 7; "Nejde už jen o docenta Trnku!" [It's not only about Docent Trnka!] *Venkov*, 8 August 1990: 1; and ČTK [Czechoslovak News Agency] "Is Slušovice a thorn in the side?" *Hospodářské noviny*, 27 July 1990: 2, as quoted in *FBIS-EEU*, 31 July 1990: 12–13.

39 "Zasedal ÚV ČSSZ" [Meeting of the Central Committee of the ČSSZ] *Venkov*, 4 July 1990: 2. On the creation of the Agrobanka, see "A one-billion endowment," *ZN*, 11 January 1990, 1, as quoted in *FBIS-EEU*, 29 January 1990: 44.

40 ČTK, "They do not want a monopoly," *ZN*, 5 October 1990: 2, as quoted in *FBIS-EEU*, 12 October 1990: 15; transcription of ČTK report of 10 January 1991, as quoted in *FBIS-EEU*, 15 January 1991: 30; transcription of ČTK report of 31 January 1991, as quoted in *FBIS-EEU*, 1 February 1991: 15; transcription of Prague Domestic Service radio broadcast of 31 January 1991, as quoted in *FBIS-EEU*, 1 February 1991: 19; transcription of ČTK report of 21 February 1991, as quoted in *FBIS-EEU*, 22 February 1991: 23.

41 "Zasedal ÚV ČSSZ," *Venkov*, 4 July 1990: 2.

42 "Czechoslovak Agrarian party divided by agreement," *ZN*, 23 October 1990, as quoted in *FBIS-EEU*, 29 October 1990: 20.

43 O. Šnajder "Zemědělci budou mít zastání" [Agriculturalists will have their defence], *Občanský deník* [*Civic Daily*], 3 July 1990: 3.

44 Transcription of the ČTK radio release of 27 June 1990, as quoted in *FBIS-EEU*, 28 June 1990: 20, and "Nové orgány české republiky" [New organ of the Czech Republic] *Česká politika* [*Czech Politics*], 10 July 1990: 2.

45 P. Janyška "Co řekly volby?" [What did the election say?], *Respekt*, 5–11 December 1990: 4–5; P. Šavata "Jak dopadly volby" [How the elections turned out], *MFD*, 27 November 1990: 2; P. Šavata "Volby: podtrženo, sečteno" [Elections: underscored, totaled], *MFD*, 28 November 1990: 1–2; and P. Martin "New law on land privatization passed," *REE*, 19 July 1991: 14, (5).

46 Kubát's relationship to Civic Forum may be seen in *ZN* articles appearing in *FBIS-EEU*, 25 October 1990: 24. Kubát later became affiliated with the center-left movement that emerged from Civic Forum known as the Civic Democratic Alliance. See J. Štěpánek "Jen silácká gesta" [Only strong gestures] *MFD*, 11 May 1991: 1–2. Information on the Kubát-Pithart conflict may be found in J. Štěpánek "Jen silácká gesta," *MFD*, 11 May 1991: 1–2. Kubát accused Trnka of cooperating with Pithart in the assault, but there is no proof. See the Czechoslovak Broadcasting transcript of 16 July 1991, as quoted in *FBIS-EEU*, 17 July 1991:

13. Developments in the Slušovice case may be found in a transcript of a ČTK broadcast on 22 July 1991, as quoted in *FBIS-EEU*, 26 July 1991: 14; an interview with Kubát and Czech Interior Minister Tomáš Sokol by J. Subert, "Slušovice and Žák – Halftime," ZN, 1 August 1991: 1–2, as quoted in *FBIS-EEU*, 6 August 1991: 10–11; and "Cooperative claims government monitoring activity," ČSTK [Czechoslovak Press Agency] press release, 23 March 1992, as quoted in *FBIS*, 25 March 1992.

47 Agricultural surpluses are recounted in Z. Hoffmann "How to sell meat and milk?" *Rudé právo*, 20 June 1991: 2, as quoted in *FBIS-EEU*, 5 July 1991, 14, and in an interview of Slovak Agriculture and Food Minister Jozef Kresk by H. Hanku "Giving little is bad; giving much even worse," *Národná obroda* [*National Renewal*], 6 July 1991: 3, as quoted in *FBIS-EEU*, 10 July 1991: 19–21. Government favoritism for large firms is noted in Vačkář, "Několik postřehů," *Venkov*, 1 February 1992: 1–2.

48 For a summary of the land privatization law, see P. Martin "New law on land privatization passed," *REE*, 19 July 1991: 10.

49 "Federal government approves 'transformation law,'" *Národná obroda* [*National Renewal*], 16 November 1991: 2, as quoted in *FBIS-EEU*, 25 November 1991: 12–13; "Federal Assembly passes 'transformation bill,'" ČSTK press release, 21 December 1991, as quoted in *FBIS-EEU*, 23 December 1991: 5–7; and J. Štěpánkek "Družstva konečně jinak" [Cooperatives are finally changed], *MFD*, 16 November 1991: 1.

50 "Nahoře si dali vatu do uší" [Up above they put cotton in their ears], *Venkov*, 25 October 1991: 10; J. Štěpánek and P. Šporer "S cepem na Kubáta" [With the flail against Kubát], *MFD*, 25 October 1991: 1, and "Farmers demonstrate," *REE*, 1 November 1991: 27. The numbers of those participating were inconsistent in the reports.

51 "Agrarian party opposes law on cooperatives," ČSTK press release, 30 December 1991, as quoted in *FBIS-EEU*, 3 January 1992: 9.

52 For the origins of the electoral coalition, see the transcription of ČTK radio broadcast of 21 May 1991, as quoted in *FBIS-EEU*, 22 May 1991: 16, and J. Vačká "Několik postřehů" [Several opinions], *Venkov*, 1 February 1992: 1–2.

53 "Parties, movements, and coalitions for the parliamentary elections in 1992," *Hospodářské noviny* [*Economic Newspaper*], 21 April 1992: 9, as quoted in *FBIS-EEU*, 29 April 1992: 19; "Two electoral commissions – Two opinions about the Liberal Social Union," *Rudé právo*, 20 April 1992: 2, as quoted in *FBIS-EEU*, 6 May 1992: 13; "Liberal social union criticizes electoral commission ruling," and "Commission revises decision on Liberal Social Union status," as quoted in *FBIS-EEU*, 29 May 1992: 8 and 9.

54 Changes in the election law certainly discouraged smaller parties. See J. Pehe "Czechoslovak Federal Assembly adopts electoral law," *RFE/RL RR*, 14 February 1992: 27–30.

55 The list also includes the Farmers' Party of Slovakia, the Party of the Moravian Countryside, and the Political Movement of JZD Members, all of which separated from ČSSZ, along with the Agrarian party and the Party of the Czech Countryside, once with Civic Forum. For references to the parties in 1992, see note 3. For election results, see "Czech election results," ČSTK press release, 7 June 1992, as quoted in *FBIS-EEU*, 8 June 1992: 14–15; "Slovak results for Federal Assembly," Prague Federal 1 Television Network broadcast, 7 June 1992, as quoted in *FBIS-EEU*, 8 June 1992: 15–17; "Slovak Parliament results," Bratislava Rozhlasová Stanica Slovensko [Bratislava Broadcast Station, Slovakia] broadcast, 7 June 1992, as quoted in *FBIS-EEU*, 8 June 1992: 17; and J. Obrman "The Czechoslovak elections," *RFE/RL RR*, 26 June 1992: 13–19.

56 In many respects, economic conditions in the Wild East, as much of Central Europe and the Balkans is termed after 1989, resembles the USA during its period of rapid industrialization before the progressive era or England during the first industrial revolution. Opportunities are open to anyone with some money, fortunes are made or lost quickly, and there is little government regulation protecting investors or consumers.

REFERENCES

Česká politika [*Czech Politics*].
Mladá fronta dnes [*Young Front Today*] (cited as *MFD*).
New York Times.
Respekt [*Respect*].
Svobodné slovo [*Free Word*] (cited as *SS*).
Venkov [*Countryside*] (1906–1944).
Venkov [*Countryside*] (1989–present).

Brdlík, V. (1938) *A Short Survey of Agriculture in Czechoslovakia*, Prague.
Brown, A. (ed.) (1985) *Political Culture and Communist Studies*, Armonk, NY.
Buchvaldek, M. *et al.* (1986) *Československé dějiny v datech* [Czechoslovak History in Dates], Prague.
Česká strana agrární [The Czech Agrarian Party] (1914) *Sjezdová zpráva o činnosti české strany agrární v létech 1912 a 1913* [Report from the Congress about the Activity of the Czech Agrarian Party in the Years 1912 and 1913], Prague.
Federální statistický úřad [Federal Office of Statistics] (1985) *Historická statistická ročenka ČSSR* [Historical Statistical Yearbook of the ČSSR], Prague.
Federální statistický úřad, Český statistický úřad, Slovenský štatistický úrad [Federal Office of Statistics, Czech Office of Statistics, and the Slovak Office of Statistics] (1990) *Statistická ročenka české a slovenské federativní republiky, 1990* [Statistical Yearbook of the Czech and Slovak Federative Republic, 1990], Prague.
Feierabend, L. K. (1952) *Agricultural Cooperatives in Czechoslovakia*, New York.
Feierabend, L. K. (1964) "The Czechoslovak grain monopoly system," in M. Rechcigh, Jr. (ed.) *The Czechoslovak Contribution to World Culture*, The Hague.
Foreign Broadcast Information Service: Eastern Europe (FBIS-EEU).
Frankenberger, O. and Kubíček, J. O. (1931) *Antonín Švehla v dějinách československé strany agrární* [Antonín Švehla in the History of the Czechoslovanic Agrarian Party], Prague.
Lacina, L. (1978) *Zadlužení kapitalistického zemědělství v českých zemích v letech 1918–1938* [The Indebtedness of Capitalistic Agriculture in the Czech Lands, 1918–1938], Prague.
Malá československá encyklopedie [Small Czechoslovak Encyclopedia] (1986).
Miller, D. E. (1989) "Antonín Švehla and the Czechoslovak Republican Party (1918–1933), Ph.D. dissertation, University of Pittsburgh.
Miller, D. E. (1992) "The organization of farmers and peasants in interwar Czechoslovakia: The uses of experiences from the past," in J. R. Lampe (ed.) *Private Agriculture in Eastern Europe: Prospects for the 1990s and the Lessons of Prewar Cooperatives and Land Reforms*, Washington, DC.
Občanská beseda [Civic Society] (1990) Prague.
Památník věnovaný přesedovi Viktoru Stoupalovi k padesátinám úřednictvem hodonínské cukrovarské skupiny [A memorial volume dedicated to Chairman Viktor Stoupal on his fiftieth birthday from the officials of the Hodonín Sugar Refinery Company]. No publication information given.

Pavel, A. (1938) "Československá pozemková reforma" [The Czechoslovak land reform], in *Pozemková reforma* [*Land Reform*], May.
Průcha, V. *et al.* (1974) *Hospodářské dějiny československa v 19. a 20. století* [An Economic History of Czechoslovakia in the Nineteenth and Twentieth Centuries], Prague.
Report on Eastern Europe (REE).
RFE/RL Research Report.
Sbírka zákonů a nařízení republiky československé [Collection of Laws and Orders of the Czechoslovak Republic], Prague.
Skilling, H. G. (1976) *Czechoslovakia's Interrupted Revolution*, Princeton.
Skilling, H. G. and Griffiths, F. (eds.) (1973) *Interest Groups in Soviet Politics*, Princeton.
Spektrum 90: Nově vzniklé společenské, zájmové a profesní organizace, hnutí, sdružení, spolky [Spectrum 90: Newly Developed Societies, Interest and Professional Organizations, Movements, Associations, and Clubs] (1990) Prague.
Spirk, L. (1966) *Czechoslovak Agricultural Co-Operatives*, Prague.
Spulber, N. (1957) *The Economics of Communist Eastern Europe*, New York.
Statistisches Staatsamt (1938) *Statistisches Jahrbuch der Čechoslovakischen Republik*, Prague.
Státní úřad statistický [State Statistical Office] (1925) *Les élections l'Assemblée nationale en Novembre 1925*, Prague.
Státní úřad statistický (1934) *Manuel statistique de la république Tchécoslovaque*, Prague.
Státní úřad statistický (1936) *Statistická ročenka republiky československé* [Statistical Yearbook of the Czechoslovak Republic], Prague.
Textor, L. E. (1923) *Land Reform in Czechoslovakia*, London.
Třicet let české zemědělské družstevní práce [Thirty Years of Czech Agricultural Cooperative Activity] (1928) Prague.
Ulč, O. 1974. *Politics in Czechoslovakia*, San Francisco.
Výkonný výbor Republikánské strany zemědělského a malorolnického lidu [Central Committee of the Republican Party of Agriculturalists and Small Farmers, VV-RSZaML] (1928–1929) *Deset let práce republikánské strany zemědělského a malorolnického lidu v republice československé* [Ten Years of Work of the Republican Party of Agriculturalists and Small Farmers in the Czechoslovak Republic], Prague.
Wolchick, S. L. (1991) *Czechoslovakia in Transition: Politics, Economics, and Society*, London.

Part V

INTERNATIONAL ECONOMIC RELATIONS

12

GERMAN BANKS AND FOREIGN INVESTMENT IN CENTRAL AND EASTERN EUROPE BEFORE 1939

Richard Tilly

In the past few years scholarly speculation on the economic future of Central and Eastern Europe has been widespread. Historical analogies have also made their appearance. In Germany, analogies between post-1945 experience, including discussion of the Marshall Plan, and the contemporary situation are common. The parallels seem clear: then, as now, a strong need for foreign exchange to buy imports, and an extreme shortage of capital. In both situations, estimates of the required transfers vary, but neither the potential value of the transfers for the receiver, nor the importance of appropriate institutional changes in the receiver countries are in doubt.[1]

Whatever the merits of these analogies – and I believe they have some – a case can be made for widening the range of eligible historical experience. My candidate is the 1870–1914 period. In general, this was a period of unprecedentedly large capital transfers from rich economies to poor ones, a period in which transfers were frequently accompanied or soon followed by relatively rapid economic growth – both in the capital-exporting and capital-importing country. With some restrictions, that characterization applies to Germany – a major capital exporter of the period – and to the Eastern and Central European countries. The transfers were relatively large and had, on balance, unmistakably positive economic results.

Today strong interest and hopes are attached once again to German capital transfers into Eastern and Central Europe. It has been pointed out that Germany, a central European country, must have a "natural" comparative advantage in transferring know-how and capital into the former East bloc, and should be a major beneficiary of trade flows between West and East (Kantzenbach 1992: 100–1).

A quick look back into the nineteenth century shows that German trade and financial ties to Eastern and Central Europe were indeed relatively strong. However, a somewhat longer look at the pre-1914 experience reveals some striking contrasts. First, German capital exports to the region in this period arose from market-driven private investment. Contrary to popular opinion, German political leverage in this area was quite limited.[2] Today hopes are pinned on private capital, but the realities call for government-intermediated transfers tied to institutional reform and change moving toward stable market economies, which would then attract that private capital. Second, German capital flows to Eastern and Central Europe before 1914 were built on cooperation between stable banking institutions and stable governments in the region. It is thus worth posing the pre-1914 experience as a possibility that might grow stronger as political and institutional structures in the former East bloc countries stabilize, a possibility that must follow, rather than lead to initial institutional reform.

This chapter looks at German foreign investment in Eastern and Central Europe by focusing on the role of the banks and the capital market in the period following 1870. I interpret my results largely in financial terms, although politics receive some attention as well. I focus on portfolio investment, the purchase of foreign securities; and devote only a few paragraphs to the more prominent cases of direct investment. The chapter concentrates on pre-1914 experiences, since World War I put an end to Germany's capital exports, and, indeed, reversed the flow.

PRE-1870 BEGINNINGS

German bankers and their capitalist clients engaged in foreign portfolio investment even before outlets in German industry became important. The Napoleonic Wars occasioned unprecedentedly high government borrowing and peace introduced a corresponding increase in tradeable debt instruments. By the 1820s, nascent financial centers such as Frankfurt/Main, Berlin, Augsburg or Hamburg, reported considerable trading in Austrian, Russian, or Dutch government securities. By 1830, Berlin had security price tables published daily (including over a dozen foreign securities) (Brockhage 1910: 159, 162, 170). In subsequent decades this business continued to grow, supplemented by foreign railroad bonds even after domestic railroad building began to compete for bankers' services and for domestic savings. At the same time, the German banking sector grew and modernized. Private bankers, who dominated capital market transactions in this period, began linking investment banking techniques to their commercial credit operations; and they created joint-stock banks to widen their range of business opportunities, not least of all, to handle foreign investment projects better. The "financial revolution" of the 1850s and 1860s, about which so much has been written, was in large part a response to the possibilities of international investment banking, even in the German case (Cameron 1961; Landes 1956; Boehme 1966). Although the banks' domestic industrial business grew steadily and eventually came to dwarf their involvements abroad, foreign activities remained – particularly for the larger commercial banks – an integral part of business operations. Thus German banks had developed a tradition of foreign investment activity long before the 1870s, the period traditionally believed to mark the beginnings of the German economy's external expansion.

GERMAN FOREIGN INVESTMENT AFTER 1870: AN OVERVIEW

Systematic evidence on German foreign portfolio investment is available only for the period beginning in the 1880s. That is unfortunate, for the unsystematic evidence suggests relatively large flows for the 1860s and 1870s, particularly into Russian and Austro-Hungarian railroads.[3] Between the beginning of the 1870s and the end of 1913, German holdings of foreign securities rose from three or four billion marks to 23–25 billion marks.[4] German firms and capitalists also made substantial direct investments abroad in the period, the value of which is even less certain than that of portfolio investment, but must have been at least six or seven billion marks by 1913 (e.g. Kabisch 1982; Kellenbenz and Schneider in Levy-Leboyer 1979; Kerken 1925). These investments made Germany the world's third largest exporter of capital in 1913, well behind France with perhaps 36–40 billion marks and Great Britain with 82–84 billion marks. (See Cameron and Bovykin 1991: 13.)

Table 12.1 shows the geographic distribution of German foreign investment according to the standard picture. Note the approximate equality between European and overseas investment and the considerable weight of investment in the USA, which at times before 1914 represented the largest single block of German foreign holdings (Kabisch 1982; Wilkins 1991). The growing importance of Europe is no surprise; and as will be seen, it reflected mainly the attraction power of Eastern and Central Europe.

The time shape of German foreign investment is shown in Figure 12.1. estimates of new security issues indicate a clearly discontinuous pattern of foreign portfolio investment.[5] The incomplete information for the 1870s cited above suggests substantial annual fluctuation, but not the marked boom and bust of domestic financial activity that we associate with the Gründerzeit before 1873 and the Gründerkrise after 1873. In the 1880s new issues climbed sharply, falling off in the depression of the early 1890s and then rising again to new heights by 1897–8. The slackening off around 1900 was followed by the peak of 1905 induced by the Russo-Japanese War and the rather jagged upward movement after 1907.

PORTFOLIO INVESTMENT IN EASTERN AND CENTRAL EUROPE

German portfolio investment in Eastern and Central Europe over the 1870–1913 period took place against the background of the capital exports just

Table 12.1 The geographical distribution of German foreign portfolio investment 1897–1914 (billions of marks)

Regions	*New issues 1897–1906*	*New issues 1907–14*	*Estimated total foreign investment 1914*
Europe			
Austria-Hungary	7.1	5.5	12.5
Russia			3.0
Turkey			1.8
Balkan states			1.7
North America	4.0	1.1	3.7
Central America (inc. Mexico)	0.7	0.6	
South America	0.2	0.8	
Latin America	0.9	1.3	3.8
Asia	1.7	0.9	1.0
Africa		0.2	2.0
Total	13.7	9.0	23.5

Source: Feis (1915); Arndt (1915)

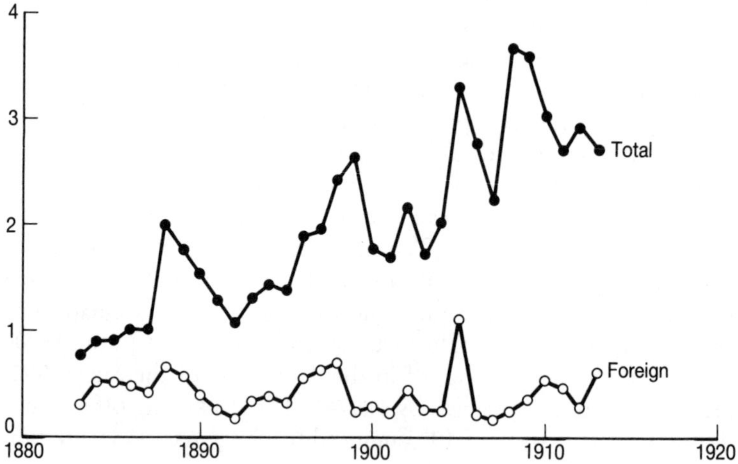

Figure 12.1 Total and foreign security issues in German capital markets 1883–1913 (in billions of marks)

described. Figure 12.2 and Tables 12.2–12.4 introduce the story's basic quantitative outlines. These numbers are estimates, of course, and their interpretation requires caution. As indicated earlier, they are based on data for new issues modified where possible by alternative (and better) sources.[6]

A few common features stand out. First, in all countries debt growth not surprisingly dominated foreign investment; equity was of small importance. In contrast, roughly one-third of domestic securities issued in Berlin in the early twentieth century were equities; and in the UK at this time, equities also played a more important role, even among foreign issues (Edelstein 1982: 138; Davis and Huttenback 1986). Second, and equally unsurprising, is the predominance of government debt. On closer examination, however, much of this category is accounted for by railroad finance (probably well over half). Railroads were thus, for all countries, the true main vehicle of capital imports. Third, most railroad securities marketed in Germany bore government guarantees, and both government and railroad securities frequently stipulated interest payments in gold or a gold currency. Fourth, the timing of this foreign investment into Eastern and Central Europe as a whole, was roughly correlated with that of German total foreign issues (see Figure 12.2), with troughs around 1890, 1900, and 1907, and peaks in the mid-1880s, late-1890s and 1902 and 1905. No clear correlation seems to have existed between the level and growth of economic activity and German foreign portfolio investment in the capital-importing countries.

I turn to the individual countries. Taken as a unit, the Habsburg Monarchy was Germany's largest debtor throughout the period. Within the

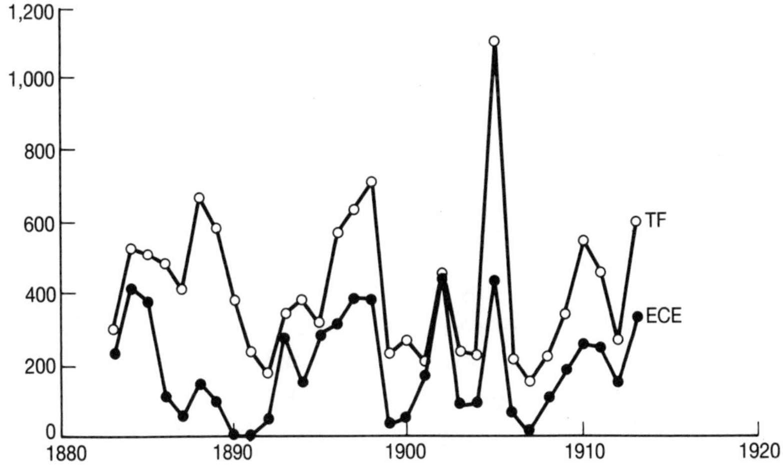

Figure 12.2 New issues of securities in German capital markets, total foreign (TF) and Eastern and Central Europe (ECE) 1883–1913 (in millions of marks)

Table 12.2 Estimates of German foreign portfolio investment in Eastern and Central Europe 1883–1913 (millions of marks, current prices)

Year	*Russia*	*Austria*	*Hungary*	*Balkans*[a]	*Total*
1883	66	72	74	19	231
1884	270	36	79	322	417
1885	174	94	81	20	369
1886	43	61	0	16	120
1887	5	43	0	0	48
1888	23	43	45	37	148
1889	7	52	0	36	95
1890	0	36	0	0	36
1891	0	25	0	41	66
1892	0	13	1	29	43
1893	0	89	177	23	289
1894	70	49	0	36	155
1895	129	90	42	32	293
1896	93	92	104	28	317
1897	240	3	143	3	389
1898	236	26	37	64	363
1899	0	17	18	0	35
1900	0	1	55	0	56
1901	148	26	0	0	174
1902	262	110	52	45	469
1903	5	73	1	10	89
1904	24	13	57	0	94
1905	308	11	7	109	435
1906	0	39	0	36	75
1907	0	0	5	12	17
1908	17	0	47	42	106
1909	128	15	14	38	195
1910	87	76	16	85	264
1911	107	49	97	0	253
1912	97	28	0	23	148
1913	49	110	73	102	334

Source: *Deutsche Ökonomist* (1883–1913); and text.

[a] Romania, Bulgaria, Serbia

Monarchy, the data point to the declining importance of Austria and growing weight of Hungary over time. Changes in the Monarchy's share of German foreign investment in Central and Eastern Europe reflect borrowing by the *Hungarian* government. Railroad and government finance dominated, although the heyday of capital imports came in the 1860s and 1870s. One final point about the Dual Monarchy is worth making; the tables do not reflect Austria's role as a source and intermediary of capital flows into Hungary. According to Komlos, Austria held over 60 per cent of Hungary's government debt as late as 1893 (Komlos 1983a: 164 ff.). This share then fell below the level of German holdings by 1913, although Austrian direct investments and holdings of securities in the private business sector were quite substantial. However, German investment in Austrian securities may have "released" Austrian funds for investment in Hungary. Moreover, there seems little doubt but that the "Austrian connection," which was intermediated by the Viennese Rothschild group, facilitated the flow of German funds into Hungarian securities.[7]

Czarist Russia is in some respects the most interesting case. It was one of Germany's largest debtors. Moreover, my figures do not reflect direct investment, e.g., by Silesian industry in Poland, which is included here under Russia.[8] Also the Russian series shows the most dramatic shifts, e.g., the massive sales and cessation of issues of Russian government securities following Bismarck's well-known decree (*Lombardverbot*) in 1887 and the war loan of 1905. Note the great weight of railroad securities; and here, as in the other cases, a substantial part of the proceeds of government loans did go into railroads. This is worth stressing, and for two reasons. First, in financing railroads, German capital made a significant contribution to Russia's economic growth. Government guarantees were indispensable initially, but not big enough to attract sufficient domestic capital so German financing of the railroads helped to mobilize the resources, and generate the revenues and export income that made foreign investment in Russia pay off (Matthesius 1905; Gregory 1979, 1982). Second, historians have not always appreciated how much German bankers and capitalists retained their strong interest in Russian foreign investments right up to 1914, despite the German–Russian split from 1887 on (Mai 1970: 165; Reininghaus 1973). Indeed, of the regions surveyed here, only Russia clearly received more funds in the second period than in the first.

The data for the Balkans have no surprises. Noteworthy is perhaps the

Table 12.3 German foreign portfolio investment in Eastern and Central Europe by type 1883–1913 (in millions of marks in current prices)

	1883–95		*1896–1913*	
Country	*Debt*	*Equity*	*Debt*[a]	Equity
Austria	528	131	423	86
Hungary	492	8	698	30
Balkans[b]	312	0	529	68
Russia	757	30	1,598	206
Total	2,098	169	3,248	390

Source: as for Table 12.2.

[a] Includes small amount of preference shares.
[b] Romania, Bulgaria, Serbia.

Table 12.4 German foreign portfolio investment in Eastern and Central Europe by recipient 1883–1913 (in millions of marks and in current prices)

Country	*State*	*City*	*Railroads*	*Private business*	*Total*	*Holdings as of 1913*
Austria[a]	535	117	513	222	1,387	2,305[b]
Hungary	903	101	53	168	1,225	1,720[c]
Balkans	735	60	39	85	919	1,630[d]
Russia	1,008	21	1,314	236	2,579	3,273[e]

Balkan Countries

Country	*State*	*City*	*Railroads*	*Private business*	*Total*
Romania	583	46		85	714
Serbia	89		8		97
Bulgaria	63	14	30[e]		107

Source: as for Table 12.2.

[a] Includes Bosnia–Herzegovina.
[b] Bartsch (1917: 19–21).
[c] Estimated using estimates in Feis (1915: 269); and *Der Deutsche Volkswirt* (1926/27 II: 181).
[d] Reininghaus (1973, Tables 11–19a); Anan'ich and Bovykin (1991).
[e] Betriebsgesellschaft der orientalischen Eisenbahnen.

same downward break around the turn of the century that occurs in the other series. Government borrowing apparently dominated more than was true of Russia or Austria–Hungary, although some of these borrowed funds, to be sure, financed acquisition of already existing private railroads. Notice the clear predominance of Romania as German client. This reflected German political hopes, but was also a legacy of earlier German involvement in the 1860s and 1870s, especially in railroad investment. Increasingly after 1895 interests in Romanian oil wholly explain the investments under the heading "private business." Only in the Balkans, significantly, did German investors hold a larger share of government debt than did their French counterparts. How much these capital exports contributed to Balkan development before 1914 is hard to say. Oil is a special case.[9] Otherwise, much depends on how government loans were spent and the burden they represented. Specialists seem skeptical that the results were positive (Lampe and Jackson 1982).

THE IMPORTANCE OF PROFIT EXPECTATIONS

The proximate cause of these substantial capital flows were bankers' profit expectations. That is largely a truism, of course, but it is worth mentioning because it calls attention to the key role of bankers and to the importance of commercial criteria in these foreign investments. Every foreign security issue or listing recorded in the German market was initiated and sponsored by a banker or group of bankers. This was a relatively small group. All of the security transactions discussed here involved no more than 39 different German financial intermediaries, eight of which accounted for about 70 per cent (by value) of these transactions. In a typical case, pre-placement negotiations focused on price and quantity as well as on which intermediaries would participate. In addition, provisions concerning whether funds were to be deposited in German banks or spent on German goods were frequently arranged.[10] The latter use was particularly characteristic of railroad and military loans. The small sample of "inside evidence" on placement agreements in the period suggests that bankers realized variable, if predominantly positive profits.[11] It also suggests that bankers took substantial losses from time to time, which explains why they frequently turned down business, mainly because of expected risks. In short, the judgement and expectations of a fairly small group of bankers were key factors in determining when and how foreign portfolio investment developed.

In the longer-run, however, bankers had to adapt to the willingness of the capital market to take foreign securities. The expected rate of return on foreign assets had to be competitive with domestic opportunities – allowing for liquidity, risk, and other attributes of the assets. I believe that it was. The evidence comes from an extensive sample of domestic and foreign securities traded on the German capital market in the 1870–1913 period.[12] Using information on the prices and yields of these securities, it is possible to estimate the rates of return German investors realized over the period 1870–1913. The estimates are summarized in Figure 12.3 and Table 12.5.

I use the "mean-variance" model of portfolio theory (the so-called capital asset pricing model, or CAPM). The long-term trend in returns on assets measures expected yields while fluctuations of these returns around that trend measures expected risks. Using the CAPM on the German data leads to the conclusion that foreign securities promised and yielded a significantly higher rate of return and higher risks than did comparable domestic issues. Using statistical analysis on the portfolio data, it is possible to "explain" the mean-yield differences among the various security classes through differences in their variances, i.e., their expected risk. In addition, these data permit us to identify a "bias" in the German capital market against foreign securities. Repeated tests that include a correction for differences between debt and equity securities show that a higher rate of return was required to induce investors to hold foreign securities than to hold domestic ones. These and related statistical tests lead to the following conclusions. First, the capital market was biased against foreign securities, but only weakly. Second, in the long run, the yields and risks of foreign securities show a tendency to decline. Third, the yields and risks among the different security

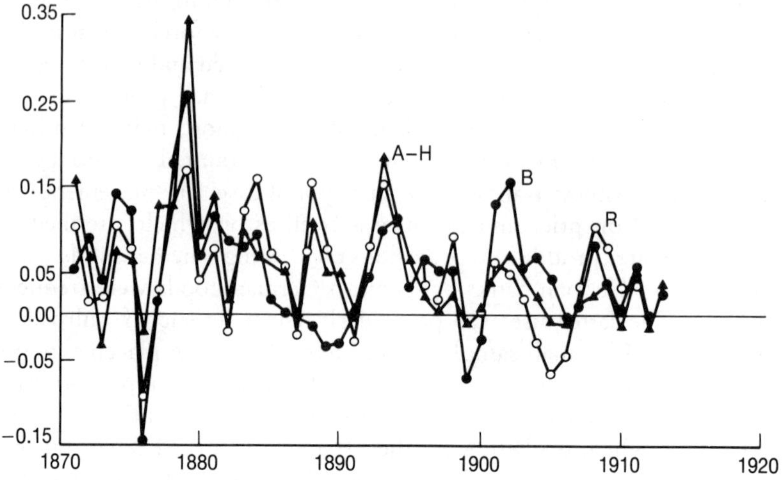

Figure 12.3 Annual rates of return on Eastern and Central European securities 1870–1913, price-deflated

A–H: Austria–Hungary; R: Russia; B: Balkans

groups converge. This supports the notion that the capital market became more integrated in the period and also that foreign portfolio investment was not undertaken at the expense of domestic investments, at least not in the dimensions some contemporaries believed.[13]

Viewing the 1871–1913 period as a whole, securities from Eastern and Central Europe should be seen as fairly typical of the entire German portfolio. The mean rates of return on Austro–Hungarian, Russian, and Balkan securities were above the average for German domestic ones, which is apparent from Table 12.6.

Correcting for the larger share of equity in domestic securities improves the margin in favor of these foreign assets (Row 3 compared with Rows 4–7). Moreover, these securities may have had useful portfolio diversification effects not captured by the mean returns. To the extent that the covariance of individual group returns with the overall market average and the distinction between debt and equity adequately reflects investor risks – and that is a basic tenet of the CAPM – one can distinguish between total returns and "risk-corrected" returns. On that basis German portfolio investments in Eastern and Central European did not include any unusual "winners" or "losers." In the long-run, this investment paid, although not by a large margin.

It may be somewhat ahistorical, however, to treat the entire period from 1870 to 1913 as a single unit. I opt here for a two-period division: 1871–91 and 1892–1913. Table 12.7 offers a useful point of departure, comparable with that of Table 12.6. The data show the continuing gap in favor of returns on foreign securities as opposed to domestic securities, which also applies to those of Eastern and Central Europe. The long-run decline in returns was generally greater for domestic securities than for foreign ones, so the relative gap widened.

Two features of these data deserve additional comment. First, when interpreting the gap in returns, it is necessary to consider risk. In this case, the increasing difference between the domestic and foreign standard deviations – one measure of the riskiness of returns – indicates the greater

Table 12.5 Average annual rate of return on securities traded in German capital markets 1870–1913, price deflated

Security group	*Mean*	*SD*
Domestic Banks	0.082608	0.129203
Domestic City Government, Debt	0.018105	0.031135
Domestic Industry, Equity	0.095400	0.193798
Domestic Industry, Debt	0.012402	0.032640
Domestic Mortgage, Bank Debentures	0.035824	0.034620
Prussian State Consols	0.033224	0.035983
Austria–Hungary, State, Debt	0.028612	0.060755
Austria–Hungary, Lottery	0.062843	0.074087
Austria–Hungary, Railroads, Debt	0.051639	0.058527
Austria–Hungary, Railroads, Equity	0.071757	0.178416
Russia, State, Debt	0.052936	0.063413
Russia, Railroads, Debt	0.049455	0.061252
US, Government, Debt	0.065340	0.080978
US, Railroads, Equity	0.093125	0.183257
South Europe, Government, Debt	0.065819	0.062389
South Europe, Government, Lottery	0.025029	0.078011
South Europe, Railroads, Debt	0.064011	0.073659
South Europe, Railroads, Equity	0.027190	0.071517
Near East, Government, Debt	0.060875	0.186780
Near East, Railroads, Debt	0.041449	0.044877
Near East, Railroads, Equity	0.070381	0.074997
Latin America, Government, Debt	0.078672	0.122737
Scandinavia, Government, Debt	0.038715	0.039039
Western Europe, Government, Debt	0.027559	0.033802
Western Europe, Lottery, Debt	0.027875	0.080446
Western Europe, Railroads, Debt	0.035402	0.068815
Western Europe, Railroads, Equity	0.094786	0.281940
Far East, Government, Debt	0.040452	0.032440
US, Railroads, Debt	0.038218	0.046677
Balkans, Government, Debt	0.026504	0.099504

Source: Author's calculations

SD: standard deviation.

Table 12.6 Mean annual rates of return on securities in German capital markets 1870–1913, price-deflated

Issuer	*Mean*	*SD*
All foreign	0.0704	0.0708
German domestic	0.0501	0.0595
German, debt	0.0341	0.0330
Austria–Hungary	0.0606	0.0664
Austria–Hungary, debt	0.0571	0.0529
Russia, debt	0.0512	0.0614
Balkans, debt	0.0523	0.0694

Source: See text and Tilly 1991a.

SD: standard deviation.

stability and smaller risk of domestic portfolio investment. Second, the experience of Eastern and Central European securities diverges over time. In contrast to the Russian and Balkan ones, the gap favoring Austro–Hungarian securities narrows. This pattern can be interpreted by considering returns and risk jointly. Assuming that investors seek an equilibrium trade-off between risk and return among available securities leads to the following interpretation: in the first period, Austria–Hungary had to offer German investors relatively high risk-corrected returns in compensation for other perceived risks, e.g., the risk that political instability might engender financial weakness in the context of international *Großmachtpolitik*, and the risk of repayment in depreciating currency (foreign exchange risk). In the second period, these risks appeared smaller: the Dual Monarchy had become Germany's principle ally, stabilized its finances after 1887, and moved

Table 12.7 Mean annual rates of return on securities in German capital markets, two periods 1870–1913

	1870–1891		*1892–1913*	
Issuer	*Mean*	*SD*	*Mean*	*SD*
All foreign	0.0856	0.0904	0.0560	0.0425
German domestic	0.0675	0.0693	0.0335	0.0400
German, debt	0.0451	0.0318	0.0237	0.0320
Austria–Hungary	0.0847	0.0765	0.0386	0.0456
Austria–Hungary, debt	0.0790	0.0518	0.0372	0.0456
Russia, debt	0.0631	0.0684	0.0398	0.0528
Balkans, debt	0.0557	0.0855	0.0489	0.0514

Source: See Text and Tilly 1991a.

SD: standard deviation.

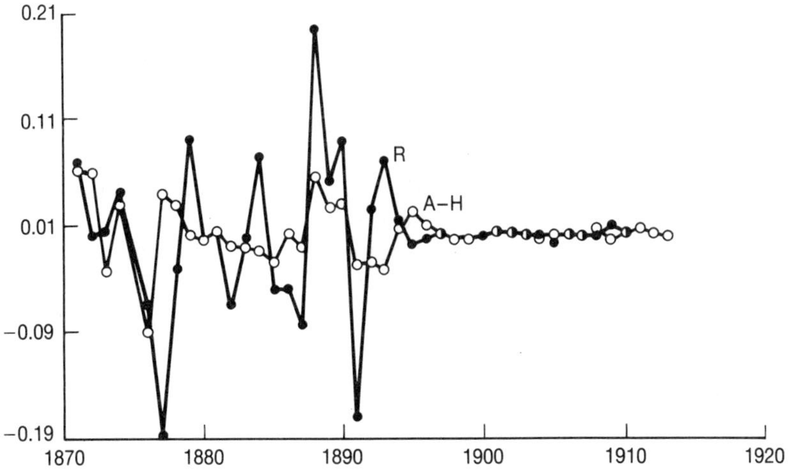

Figure 12.4 Annual rate of change of mark-ruble and mark–florin/crown exchange rates 1871–1913

A–H: Austria–Hungary; R: Russia

toward the gold standard in 1892. Of course, the fact that Austria repatriated a good share of its German-held debt in this period may also have helped.[14] The comparison with Russian securities is interesting in this connection. Given the increasing friction within German–Russian relations in the second period, it is surprising in retrospect that returns on Russian securities could fall as far and stay as close to those of Austrian–Hungarian securities as they did. Perhaps the explanation lies in the massive import of French capital – a relatively low-cost competitor for German investors – as well as in the adoption of the gold standard in the 1890s.

The gold standard played a crucial role. Russia, Austria–Hungary, and the Balkan countries all made the transition to the gold standard in the period, although the individual histories and the consequences differed. At the beginning of the period, exchange rate fluctuations were marked for both Czarist Russia and Austria–Hungary. Figure 12.4 presents an overview.

In both cases the stabilization of the exchange rate is striking. For both Russia and Austria–Hungary, exchange rate movements (marks per 100 ruble) and the rate of return on its securities traded in Berlin have strong positive correlations in the pre-gold standard era ($R^2 = 0.43$ in both cases), and much lower ones thereafter ($R^2 = 0.24$ for Russia and 0.10 for Austria–Hungary). Also, a strong positive correlation between the "surplus return" on Russian securities (defined as the difference between their returns and those realized on German domestic securities) and exchange rate movements exists (see Figure 12.5).

Perhaps the results reflect arbitrage in face of changed expectations about Russian debt.[15] Nevertheless, even in the Austria–Hungarian case, evidence suggests that exchange rate fluctuations influenced the links to the German capital market. Figure 12.6 makes the point: it reveals that the gap between paper (non-convertible) and gold-denominated Austrian *rente* closed only in the 1890s following the adoption of the gold standard.

Some additional evidence for both countries points in the same direction. John Komlos has compared differences between bond yields in Austria–Hungary and other important European countries and found an analogous pattern: no correlation between non-gold bond yields before 1892 and high positive correlations for the period thereafter. This interpretation specifically includes Germany as a foreign investor.[16] For Russia as a whole, Gregory's analysis of the 1881–1913 period suggests a strong positive connection between stabilization of the ruble on the gold standard in the early 1890s and aggregate net foreign investment thereafter. He compares interest rates in Russia and elsewhere (rather than yields) but the role of exchange rate fluctuations is the same as in the Austro–Hungarian case: they hinder the import of financial capital (Gregory 1979). To be sure, both cases have trouble accounting for the considerable foreign investments Germany made in these economies in the pre-gold standard era. Thus the argument cannot be based on *ex post* flows alone; it must be based on a comparison with flows that would have been forthcoming under an earlier or later shift to the gold standard. Nevertheless, this mechanism no doubt helps explain why the market position of Russian and Austro–Hungarian securities improved

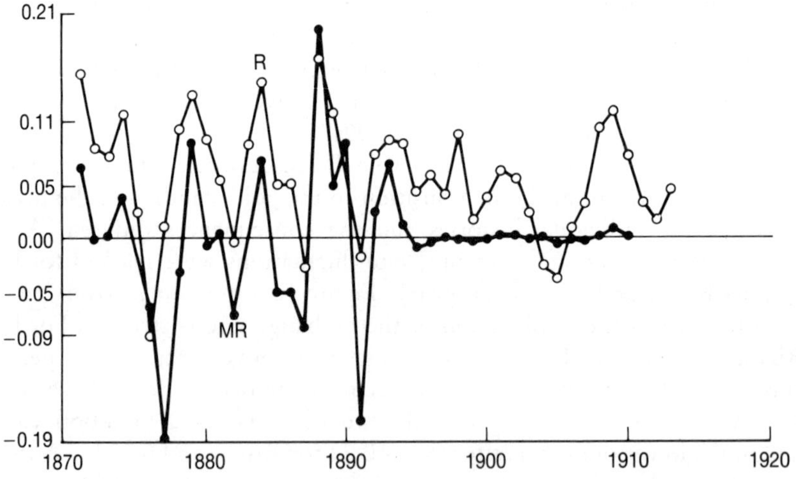

Figure 12.5 Annual nominal rates of return (R) on Russian securities in German capital markets and rate of change of mark–ruble of exchange rate (MR) in Berlin 1871–1913

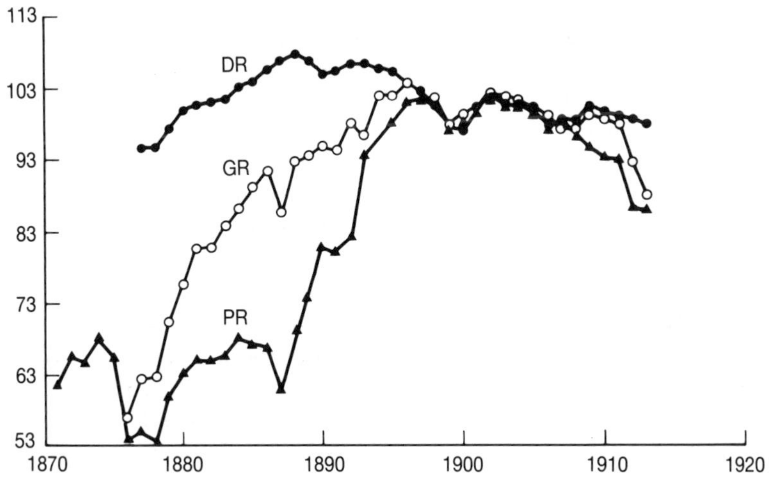

Figure 12.6 German and Austrian Government securities prices in the German capital markets 1870–1914

DR: German Reich 4% bonds; GR: Austrian gold-rente; PR: Austrian paper-rente

relative to German domestic ones in the period after 1892, a point made earlier.

The case of the Balkans is rather different. As soon as these countries had autonomous governments, they stabilized their currencies, and, barring a few exceptional phases, adhered more-or-less to hard-money rules from the 1880s on. In the 1890s they essentially became gold-standard countries. But this necessitated monetary policies that restricted credit and demand and was, according to Lampe and Jackson (1982), responsible for missed investment chances.[17] The question remains, however, whether the development of these countries in the 1890–1914 period would have been furthered by an alternative policy stance. With even less sound currencies, they would have remained more closed to the outside world, with less access to the French, German and Austrian capital markets than they actually enjoyed.

GERMAN BANKS AND INSTITUTIONAL PROBLEMS OF FOREIGN INVESTMENT

Intermediating foreign portfolio investment and realizing satisfactory rates of return were not automatic results of "market forces." The success of bankers in this activity required continuously solving institutional problems. They could be labelled "informational problems," but they were something more than that since conflicts of interest were also involved. Here I deal with three essential features of the banks' institutional strategy: 1) the development of closer ties to relevant institutions of the capital importing country; 2) the response to delinquent debt and default; and 3) the internationalization or "multilateralization" of portfolio investment.

Initially, German bankers built on their links with correspondent banks in the capital-importing countries, as seen in the Russian case. In many cases those links grew into quite long-term connections, occasionally leading to "intermarriage" as a kind of international partnership. This was the case, e.g., with the Warburgs of Hamburg and the Günzburgs of St. Petersburg. The connections were facilitated in the nineteenth century by the migration of German bankers to Russia, e.g. the Hamburger Kapherr (Mai 1970, 48–9, 64–73; Tilly 1991b). German bankers sought stronger positions, however. As the financial revolution swept across Europe in the 1850s and 1860s, German bankers attempted to obtain concessions from the Czarist government to establish large joint-stock promotional banks.[18] Though these specifically German projects were rejected, the Russian government did respond to the pressure created by the juncture of massive railroad building plans and relatively backward financial institutions. The response included an important decree in 1859 clarifying the rights of foreigners, and especially of Prussian citizens, to own land and other property in Russia, the founding in 1860 of a modern state bank whose aims included lending to private business, and concessions for the creation of joint-stock banks.[19] Noteworthy, too, was the founding of the Great Russian Railway Company in 1857 by an international group of bankers including the Berlin firm Mendelssohn & Co. The new company was more like a financial institution (a holding company) designed to attract foreign capital into Russian railroads than a railroad enterprise, and it clearly embodied the liberal aims and spirit of the period.[20] All told, between 1863 and 1873 over 40 new banks were reportedly founded, some of them fairly large and a few with substantial participation of German capital, e.g. the St. Petersburg International Commercial Bank, the St. Petersburg Discount Bank, and the Russian Bank for Foreign Trade.[21]

These institutions were no doubt important instruments for German financial penetration of Russian financial affairs, which is reflected in numerous financial operations involving the cooperation of Russian and German banks.[22] Penetration may also be seen in the strong interest taken by German banks in insuring representation on the board of directors of those banks. For example, the Deutsche Bank and its Viennese ally the Wiener Bankverein took up large amounts of newly issued shares of the Russian Bank for Foreign Trade in 1881 on the condition, which was granted, that two new board members be their "delegates" (Mai 1970: 156 ff.). Even after 1890 German participation in Russian banking continued to expand.

Direct German influence on Russian banking institutions should not be overstressed. If we are to believe recent Russian research, neither shareholding rights nor directorships held by Germans conveyed control over banking operations in Russia.[23] Nevertheless, increasing German participation in Russian banks since the 1890s could hardly have been justified by their dividends and capital gains alone, welcome though they were.[24] Even if significant influence over day-to-day operations was not attainable, positions in such banks undoubtedly provided useful information on the Russian financial world, and served as a kind of advertisement or calling card. Finally, top German bankers cultivated direct contacts with high government officials, especially when large-scale financial projects loomed.

Attempts by German bankers to forge closer links to the Austro–Hungarian financial world may be summed up, with only some exaggeration, in one word: "Rothschilds." Almost all large government loans of the period and most of the larger railroad projects involved German participation in connection with the Rothschilds or their group. German banks sought financial participation in some of the larger Viennese and Budapest banks with a view to obtaining more decision-making power over their operations and more influence in Austro–Hungarian affairs, in particular relative to the Rothschilds. Success in this respect was limited, or at least ambivalent. On the one hand, the German banks apparently never gained decisive control over any of the most important Viennese or Budapest banks, let alone dislodge the Rothschilds. The clearest case in point is the strong minority position attained by the Deutsche Bank in the Viennese Bankverein in the 1880s; which could not be converted to a majority one, despite considerable effort and money.[25] As Michel has persuasively argued, neither the Viennese financial elite, nor Viennese bourgeois public opinion, nor the government itself, would accept such a German takeover (Michel 1976: 239ff.). Nevertheless, German banks *did* play an important financial role here. Their efforts led to a widening of the Rothschild group in the 1860s and the 1880s, which somewhat diluted Rothschild influence. Moreover, the ties to Austro–Hungarian institutions helped the German banks secure abundant information on investment opportunities and risks. The Austrian financial environment was close enough to the German one that the German banks did not need to spend time studying the structure and translating rules. Finally, as we have seen, for most of the pre-1914 period the profits on Austro–Hungarian transactions were in themselves, considering the risks, satisfactory.[26] It is not clear that increased investment in institutional control – had it been feasible – could have significantly increased rates of returns.

An additional motive for a German presence in Austria–Hungary was its usefulness as a stepping stone to further investment opportunities in the Balkans. Quite a number of the projects and investments in these countries were organized via Vienna, Budapest, or both.[27] The point is worth stressing, since it now seems clear that German banks did not achieve significant penetration of the Balkans. Routine banking relations were apparently based on trade–finance links with correspondent banks. Direct entry came late and remained relatively modest. In Bulgaria a Berlin group led by the Disconto–Gesellschaft founded the Kreditna Bank in Sofia in 1905, but as Lampe and Jackson have said, it "did not play an important part in Bulgaria's financial history until the First World War" (Lampe and Jackson 1982: 227.) Moreover, the experience in Bulgaria may have set the pattern throughout the Balkans. "In Serbia," the same two authors write, "the Great Banks confined their influence to buying minority interests in several existing institutions," the most important of which was carried out by the Berliner Handelsgesellschaft in 1909 – probably in connection with a big government loan it was intermediating (Lampe and Jackson: 228).

Romania seems to have been the exception for German pre-1914 banking interests in the Balkans. As mentioned earlier, German capital had become heavily involved in Romanian railroads in the late-1860s and remained so for decades. A significant movement into banking came in 1890, as the Bank of Darmstadt joined with its Hungarian ally, the Hungarian Commercial Bank of Pest, to take a controlling interest in the Bucharest bank, Marmorosch, Blank et Cie (Kövér 1991: 330–2). The continued growth of the German stake in this bank, however, was probably related to its interest in Romanian oil, which explains the presence of German capital in other banks in the country. The Deutsche Bank's involvement derived, here as elsewhere, from its close association with the Viennese Wiener Bankverein. In 1890 the latter had founded a Hungarian bank, the Bank for Industry and Trade, which became involved in Romanian oil and, in particular with the leading Romanian firm, the Steaua Romana. The bank proved incapable of bearing the resulting financial burden and its liquidation in 1901 or 1902 brought the Bankverein on to the scene. The Deutsche Bank followed – and soon dominated (Seidenzahl 1970: 205–24; Pohl 1989: 86, 90 ff.; Brack 1977: 165 ff.). The Disconto–Gesellschaft had been active in Romania since the 1860s. In 1895, when Romanian law became more favorable for large-scale foreign exploitation of the country's petroleum resources, it founded, together with the private bankers, Bleichröder & Co. and Romanian capital, the largest Romanian bank, the Banca Generale Romana (Brack 1977: 164; Lampe and Jackson 1982: 262–4). The story of the industry's subsequent growth and of the fight between the Deutsche Bank and Disconto–Gesellschaft over its control has been told often and needs no repeating here.[28] It was, at least from the point of view of German investors until 1914 (or 1918), a story of commercial success related to bank entrepreneurship, a story with a strong political component, but still an exception in the history of German foreign investment in the region.[29]

The story of German foreign investment in the 1870–1914 period also contains some interesting chapters on the problem of delinquent borrowers and defaults and of banker responses to them. Even the relatively mature borrower, Austria, gave German lenders some headaches. These had to do with the Austrian railroads' obligation to redeem and service its bonds in marks in the 1870s and early 1880s. After the German Reich had been founded and went over to the gold standard, the Austrian railroad companies wished to satisfy their mark bondholders at an exchange rate between silver Gulden and gold marks that bondholders found unjust, if not to say, illegal because the silver price was plummeting at this time. Compromises were reached and the problem disappeared in the 1880s.[30]

Much more serious, however, were the problems in the Balkans. First on the list were the difficulties created by Romanian railroads in the 1870s. They derived from the grandiose railroad development plans of the "Railroad King" Bethel Henry Stroussberg.[31] Stroussberg had raised large sums of money by issuing bonds on the basis of concession rights obtained from the Romanian government, rights that implied revenue guarantees by that government per completed kilometer. Unfortunately, the money was spent before the railroad was close to completion, in part on projects other than the railroad itself. By 1871, Stroussberg was bankrupt. The Romanian government recognized some obligation toward Stroussberg's creditors, probably because their interests were organized and represented by a prominent Berlin bank, the Disconto–Gesellschaft, and by Bleichröder, which were close to the top of the Prussian government. The interim solution was a joint-stock company whose share capital of around 250 million francs corresponded to the old German bond claims plus some fresh funds needed to finish the railroad.[32] These new equity securities did not do too well, although the railroad was completed and began to operate. The Russo–Turkish war intervened and the treaty negotiations that followed also raised once more the issue of Romanian government obligations to these shareholders, this time at Bleichröder's urging and now in connection with the question of the status of Jews in the new Romanian state.[33] In the end the government purchased the railroad at a price that reportedly involved a 15 per cent write-off of investors' claims and a new Romanian government loan in 1881 (Münch 1932: 160–1).

The young kingdom of Serbia in the 1880s furnishes another instructive example. In this case, a German bank, the Berliner Handelsgesellschaft, operated as part of an international consortium. This consortium issued a Serbian loan of around 40 million francs in 1884. Serbia soon proved unable to service this debt, which was a heavy burden equal to total government revenues and carried an effective interest rate of 8.3 per cent per annum. Military defeat in a brief war against Bulgaria in 1885 contributed to a worsening of its financial situation. By 1886 the Berliner Handelsgesellschaft was already paying most of the German-held coupons so as to protect its own reputation and the market for Serbian securities; new loans helped to service the old. In 1889 the Handelsgesellschaft paid out of its own pocket over four million francs (the equivalent of around 3 per cent of its total assets!) on Serbian coupons. A satisfactory solution was first reached in 1895, when an international banking group (the Banque Imperiale

Ottomane, the Handelsgesellschaft, and the Österreichische Länderbank) negotiated the creation of an independent body, the so-called "monopoly administration," with special claims on Serbian tax revenues and debt-servicing responsibilities. Its board of directors, not surprisingly, also included representatives of the involved banks. Like the Turkish "Administration de la Dette publique Ottomane" on which it was modelled, the solution worked (Born 1988; Fürstenberg 1931: 287–9). From the bankers' point of view, it represented a successful response to a high-risk business operation.

The example just cited suggests the importance of the third strategy, internationalization. As a rule, substantial projects built on multi-national, rather than bilateral relationships. To some extent this followed from the business strategies of the banks themselves. Placing new securities posed less risk for German bankers if they could count on the cooperation of banks operating in the financial markets of other countries. In good times, such securities offered their holders greater liquidity and the possibility of arbitrage profits; in bad times, as we have seen, international consortia not only spread the risk more widely, but they had more political clout *vis-à-vis* debtors. This had its price, of course, for the formation of international consortia took time and effort, and placement profits had to be spread out across more institutions. It is therefore impossible to explain the internationalization of German foreign portfolio investment in terms of German bank strategies alone. Above all, the interests of the capital importers were crucial, too. They were likely to favor multinational issues, other things being equal. Also, since the German capital market was generally more expensive than its British, French or Dutch competitors in the 1870–1913 period, borrowers in Eastern and Central Europe could try to play off such markets against their German suppliers.

Other things were not equal, however. At any given time political alignments barred certain markets from consideration, while others could only become relevant after having been prepared for the task. The classic case is Czarist Russia. Estranged in the 1870s from Great Britain, up to then its principal lender, it became almost wholly dependent upon the German capital market until the late-1880s. As late as 1886, the London *Economist* described the German stock market boom in Russian securities as a kind of illusion, or "fiction" not simply because the "paper profits" had no sound basis in Russia's intermediate-term development prospects. The main reason was that German investors as a whole could not "realize" their profits because Russian securities no longer had an international market, neither in Britain nor in France.[34] In 1887, when Russo–German conflicts led to a break, Russia turned to France, which soon became its major source of foreign capital (Anan'ich and Bovykin 1991: 259; Reininghaus 1973).

Further examples of segmentation can be cited. Since the 1870s, for example, German capital dominated Austro–Hungarian business. Even when French participation could be assured, as in the Bulgarian loan of 1902, the status of the German market remained important for timing.[35] Nevertheless, despite alignments and barriers, multi-national connections remained vital. French, German, British, Dutch, and Belgian markets remained linked. Even Russia's switch to France actually involved the active cooperation of German bankers who were interested in selling off their investors' Russian securities without loss.[36] Such connections contributed to the integration of international capital markets. Relative shifts in demand and supply were swiftly communicated from one market to another. Different securities in different national markets could still be fairly close substitutes by means of international transactions so long as they had similar risk and return characteristics. Declining differences in yields and rates of interest suggest that such communication was improving toward the end of the pre-1914 period (See Homer 1963: 459–519; Komlos 1983a; Sommariva and Tullio 1987: Ch. 2).

SUMMARY AND CONCLUSIONS

In retrospect, Germany's foreign investments in Eastern and Central Europe in the 1870–1914 period were substantial. World War I put an end to this capital export. Not even the Nazi expansion of the 1930s really led to significant German financial penetration of the area. Analogy to present conditions thus builds on pre-1914 experience. In order to reflect on the relevance of this era for current problems in the region, it is necessary to return to some of the paper's concrete findings and arguments. The quantitative dimensions make a useful starting point. To speak of "substantial" foreign investments is to call for a standard. Aggregate German savings offer one. By my estimate they grew by over 2 per cent per annum 1883–1913, i.e., by more than estimated gross national product (GNP) (1.7 per cent) and also by more than total foreign investment.[37] To be sure, there were times when foreign investment absorbed a significant share of savings. Figure 12.7 depicts the temporal pattern. Note the high points in the 1880s, 1890s, and 1905 (mentioned earlier).

Also, German investments in Eastern and Central Europe represented a large and increasing portion of total savings. The all-time peak, however, was the 17 per cent share in 1884. Thereafter, the trend was downward. That is, foreign investments in this region were a growing segment of a relatively declining field of activity. Comparing that burden with current "guesstimates" of German savings "required" for Eastern Europe reveals in fact a family resemblance. Assuming (1) that German transfers and credits extended to the states of the former Soviet Union in 1990 and 1991 remain a continuing liability, and (2) that a Marshall Plan style approach to financing the reconstruction of the other six Eastern European countries would call for a German contribution of 50 per cent, the annual cost would be

50 billion marks, not quite 10 per cent of gross savings.[38] Like the 17 per cent cited for the 1880–1913 period, that is probably a maximum figure that subsequent economic growth could considerably reduce.

However, the numbers are perhaps more interesting for the questions they raise than for the results they suggest. Two relevant questions concern the financing and political sustainability of such flows. In the contemporary case, these are largely government transfers, dependent upon politics, including German domestic politics. Here, intra-German public sector transfers from West to East dominate and have been financed largely by new government borrowing. These have created inflationary and political pressures and calls for limiting government-sponsored capital exports. On the other hand, foreign policy goals include stable social and political conditions in Eastern Europe, and these speak in favor of ongoing capital exports. If such government-financed transfers could help stabilize social and political conditions and also improve the material infrastructure in Eastern Europe, private business investment might be encouraged there, and German business might be able to gain a greater share in the more attractive opportunities.

In the case of pre-1914 capital flows, as indicated earlier, such political arguments played almost no role. Capital exports were market-driven, intermediated by banks, and motivated by private profit expectations. At times these exports attracted public criticism. They fueled a "capital shortage" interpretation of Germany's economic situation and even led to direct political interventions.[39] Yet political considerations were only in very few instances a major force.

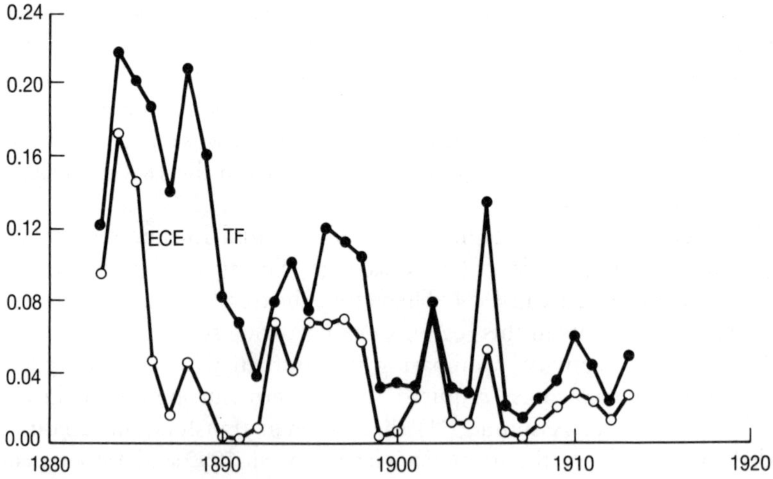

Figure 12.7 German new foreign issues as percentage of gross savings 1883–1913
TF: Total foreign issues; ECE: Eastern and Central Europe

At times the flows had considerable weight in the economies of the receiver countries. For Czarist Russia, net foreign investment financed an unusually large part of net capital formation and Germany's share accounted for roughly one-third of this. For the 1895–1913 period Germany alone contributed capital exports that corresponded to around 0.8 per cent of estimated Russian national income – 40 per cent of the new "Marshall Plan" goal. For the other countries I have not located comparable data, but in the immediate pre-war years the amount of German investment in Hungary was equivalent to about 1 per cent of national income; in Austria, the share was much less. The impact defies quick summary here; but at a minimum, the imports did free capital markets in the receiver countries for the financing of local enterprise. That is a positive result that also figures among currently held hopes about Eastern Europe (see Hartwig 1991).

Beyond such quantitative considerations lie a series of important questions concerning the role of institutions and institutional change, including the relations between economic and political development. Western market economies currently have an obvious interest in tying financial assistance to institutional change. Like the original Marshall Plan of the 1940s, contemporary discussions focus on this. They stress, for example, the need to open the economies by reducing restrictions on imports and improving the legal environment for foreign investment. Such modest aims, however, require purposeful state activity, and, as literature on transition points out, the state *is* the problem, not the solution. In these socialist economies the state was everywhere, while the private sector was small.

Transformation means reversing the proportions, altering the fiscal and monetary constitutions, in short recreating the market, albeit mixed economies of the West. But relying on political leaders and the state bureaucracies in these economies to bring about such change has frequently been tantamount to inviting them to dig their own graves. In the short run, at least, the need to introduce parliamentary democracy does not make change easier to implement. On the contrary, policies that shut down state enterprises and cut food and other subsidies disappoint some interest groups and disgruntle some voters, so politicians interested in re-election obviously have to take this into account. For this reason, some writers have suggested a reform constitution that would fix the reform agenda and place it practically out of reach of day-to-day politics (Hartwig 1991).

Agendas like these differ radically from the historical experience of the late nineteenth century. Bankers intermediating capital flows into Eastern and Central Europe did not have the means nor, with some exceptions, the will to push for institutional changes there. They did share with contemporary sources and intermediaries of capital exports an interest in strong states and political stability. For a quick characterization of bankers' views about the institutional conditions most propitious for a flourishing capital import business, the phrase "authoritarian capitalism" might come pretty close to the mark. The economy of Czarist Russia had no more than an important capitalist wing in this period (see Crisp in Sylla and Toniolo 1991). Yet it remained an attractive investment target through most of the period because its powerful central government guaranteed interest and principal on the lion's share of German–Russian loans, always paid promptly, and had large reserves of foreign exchange, held in part on deposit with banks in the principal Western European financial centers, to show commitment to stable relations.

Bankers, like other informed contemporaries, recognized Russia's social and economic backwardness and its potential political instability, but the scenario seemed too far in the future to serve as an effective deterrent.[40] When German political leaders attempted to use German financial power as an instrument to influence Russian foreign policy, as in 1887 or 1906, it either failed or backfired. Bankers themselves warned against such attempts (see Stern 1977: 439–43). In Austria–Hungary, institutions were sufficiently German-like to be accepted by German bankers. The one attempt made to make a change – the Deutsche Bank's attempt to create a large, German-controlled bank in Vienna in the 1880s – had to be abandoned. Hungary received ample support because it yielded attractive returns, despite criticism of its "anti-German" magyarization policies in the 1870s and 1880s.[41] In the Balkans a few attempts were made to shape and influence institutional arrangements, largely unsuccessful, or rather, only successful when the desired changes were limited to strictly commercial, clearly defined aims. The classic example involves Romania in the 1870s. When Bleichröder tried to exploit a strong creditor position and Bismarck's support to obtain equal citizenship rights for Jews in that country, he failed, so strong were nationalist and anti-semitic sentiment there; but he did gain Romanian acceptance of German financial claims.[42] Similar examples can be cited for Bulgaria and Serbia in the 1890s.[43]

To sum up: there are no easy lessons to be learned from the German foreign investments of the pre-1914 period for the present. They undoubtedly furthered economic development in Eastern and Central Europe. They were also accompanied by growing German economic weight in the region, as indicated by international trade flows and direct investment. In a few instances they led to German dominance, e.g. temporarily in Romanian oil; but usually competing interests, either German, French or other, limited that possibility. It seems highly likely that the flows and accompanying presence of the banks promoted institutional changes that favored industrialization, e.g., in banking practices and enterprise organization, although they are hardly quantifiable. There seems no reason to expect that such an experience could repeat itself. Considering the enormous political hurdles to be overcome, it seems certain that market-driven foreign capital flows – including German capital exports – will have no more than a minor direct role to play. Put differently, capital flows will only become important when the political bottlenecks have been overcome and stability insured.

NOTES

My chapter is based on a longer unpublished manuscript that is available on request.

1 In Germany, of course, interest has concentrated mainly on transforming the former GDR states. See Helmstädter (1991a and b); also informative and useful are the contributions in Wagener (1991).
2 Even at the end of the 1930s, despite Nazi expansion, which enlisted the help of German banks, German financial penetration of the area reportedly remained weak. See Teichova (1983: 104–5).
3 According to the *Deutsche Ökonomist*, 1885, German holdings of Austro-Hungarian and Russian securities in 1884 amounted to around 5.7 and 3.8 billion of marks respectively. A careful examination of Russian security issues going back to 1870 (by Reininghaus) yields a Russian figure of 808 million marks. Taking the same rate of growth for Austro–Hungarian securities, modified by the difference in information on new issues in the Berlin market (*Jahresbericht der Berliner Börse*) gives us a figure of around 2.5 billion marks for 1870. Further backward extrapolation of this rate through the 1860s would lead to implausibly low values by, say, 1862 or 1863.
4 These estimates derive from a number of works listed and discussed in Tilly (1991a: Appendix A).
5 These are estimates made by the *Deutsche Ökonomist*, a reputable business weekly, 1883–1913, of the share of foreign issues made in German markets and which presumably remained in Germany, at least for more than a moment. They are likely to be minimum estimates, if not underestimates of the initial placements. Strictly speaking, they cannot be aggregated to estimate the total stock of foreign securities over time (owing to repatriation, etc.); but they do indicate the movement of German demand for foreign securities over time.
6 One or two anomalies must be acknowledged. The *Deutsche Ökonomist* estimated German holdings of Austro–Hungarian securities in 1884 at around 5.7 billion marks, whereas the estimates made here for the 1883–1913 period add up to 2.6 billion marks and official statistics for 1913 to only 2.3 billion marks. See *Deutsche Ökonomist*, 1885; and Bartsch (1917: Table 3). For 1900 we have Komlos' estimate of German holdings of private Hungarian business securities of around 340 million marks, while the estimate made here for the 1883–1913 period is only 150 million. See Komlos (1983: 182).
7 This flow promoted, as well as reflected, the real forces driving Hungarian industrialization forward in the period: investments in social overhead capital, investments in manufacturing industry, and rising agricultural and industrial productivity (Komlos 1983: 162–213; Ránki 1983: 57–62; Eddie 1968, 1983).
8 According to Pustula (1989), this direct investment amounted to around 67 million marks by 1913.
9 On this see Brack (1977); and Pearton (1971). I return to this topic briefly below.
10 Examples of both of these are cited, for example, in Carl Fürstenberg (1931) for Russian and Serbian loans.
11 Evidence taken from the participation of the private banking firm Bethmann (Frankfurt/Main) on ten placements shows an average profit rate of 4.85 per cent per annum in addition to interest. This and other evidence, however, identify the market price as the crucial determinant.

12 The indicator used to measure returns in my paper has several characteristics which require comment. First, it includes capital gains, presumably an important motive for acquiring securities. Second, the series on returns used here was constructed using the assumption of repeated one-year holding periods and consumption of annual income by investors. Average returns here thus correspond to the arithmetic mean; the geometric means employed by other scholars, e.g., by Edelstein (1982), implies asset accumulation patterns which are unrealistic. Third, the indicator is price-deflated, using the private consumer goods price index (1913 prices) of Hoffman *et al.* (1965: Table 148). Nominal returns are used in a few instances where comparison requires them. As Figures 12.3 and 12.4 show, however, the nominal and real series have almost identical temporal patterns; prices do not seem to have dominated the series. Fourth, the analysis of the series uses covariances of the returns with the market average as risk indicator, rather than the own standard deviations of the returns. This implies portfolio construction by investors encompassing all securities, which may be unrealistic. The two magnitudes are related, to be sure (r = 0.69 for 30 security classes, 1871–1913), but the matter requires further thought. Fifth, the market average used here is a weighted average with the following weights:

(a) foreign securities: 0.30 (each foreign security group has equal weight);

(b) domestic securities: 0.70, distributed as follows:

(1)	Banks	0.16
(2)	City Government	0.05
(3)	Mortgage Bank Debentures	0.16
(4)	Prussian State Consols	0.28
(5)	Industrial equity*	0.30
(6)	Industrial debt*	0.05

* Distributed evenly across three industrial subgroups

These weights correspond roughly to estimated assets held in Germany between 1900 and 1913. They overstate the share of equity held in the earlier years (though probably not in the 1870s) and understate the share of government in these years. Experimentation with alternative weighting schemes suggested that the mean-variance comparisons were not terribly sensitive to such variation, but the question merits further attention. In that sense, the results reported here are provisional.

For the full distribution of observed and predicted returns for the 34 security groups see Tilly (1991a: 6, Appendix B).

13 See the contemporary debate discussed in Witt (1970), esp. 143–52.

14 If one accepts the *Deutsche Ökonomist*'s estimate for 1884 of German holdings: 5.7 milliard marks. See note 6.

15 There is some evidence on this point. See, e.g., Yeager (1972) and Annual Reports of *Älteste der Kaufmannschaft zu Berlin*, 1872–1913.

16 Particularly for Hungary, which, according to Komlos (1983a), attracted much German capital from 1893 on.

17 Lampe and Jackson (1982: 205–8, 212–20). I could not find a series on exchange rates between marks and Balkan currencies but the literature also mentions fluctuations in gold premia, which raised the cost of international transactions involving these countries, even as late as 1908 (e.g. in Romania). Report, German Consulate Bucharest to German Foreign Office, 12 September 1908, RDI, 15.01 No. 2051, Bundesarchiv Potsdam.

18 On Hansemann's efforts in this respect see *Festschrift Disconto-Gesellschaft*: 1901, 53–4.

19 On this besides Mai (1970); Anan'ich and Bovykin (1991: 130). The first director of the new State Bank was a "court financier" by the name of Stieglitz.

20 This company experienced difficulties and became dependent on government credit. See Anan'ich and Bovykin (1991).

21 In addition, one should mention the presence of Silesian capital in Polish banks and Hamburg capital in Baltic coast banks. See Mai (1970).

22 Anan'ich and Bovykin (1991) provide direct information on about 30 new issues that illustrates this point, 1871–1906.

23 Anan'ich and Bovykin (1991: 145, 154–5) where, among other things, cultural assimilation of German expatriates in banking is mentioned. These expatriates became more Russian than the Russians, their loyalties shifting accordingly.

24 The average return on the shares of the Russian Bank for Foreign Trade, 1882–1913, e.g., was 8.33 per cent per annum. See also Mai (1970: 210–12).

25 According to K. Helfferich (1921–3), George von Siemens sought to parlay German influence in the Bankverein into control over it and over another large Viennese bank, the Länderbank, an operation which involved acquisition of a large block of shares of the latter. On this see Helfferich 1921–3, II: 169 ff. and *London Economist* (1887: 13).

26 See Tables 12.6 and 12.7.

27 Examples are the Deutsche Bank involvements of the 1880s in Romania and Bulgaria, see Helfferich (1921–3, III: 4, 9). See also Kövér (1991).

28 See besides Brack (1977) and Pohl (1989) also Pearton (1971).

29 Differences of opinion prevail on the extent to which German banks successfully developed the industry. Lampe and Jackson (1982: 263–4), strike a skeptical tone. Chandler (1990), on the other hand, sees the Steaua Romana as prototypical of the positive entrepreneurial and organizational activities of German banks.

30 In the 1870s and early 1880s, in addition, German investors and bankers were complaining about uncertainty with respect to government interest guarantees and tax exemptions for the securities of private railroads which were candidates for nationalization. The *Älteste der Kaufmannschaft* (1872–82) in its Reports on the Berlin stock exchange, repeatedly mentions the investor uncertainty related thereto. See also Matis (1972: 294) and *The Economist* (1881: 1017).

31 On Stroussberg see Stern (1977: ch. 14); and of course Stroussberg himself (1876).

32 On this, H. Münch (1932: 148–63); W. Däbritz (1931: 232–5). An Austrian railroad company, the Staatseisenbahngesellschaft, was empowered to complete construction and operate the road.

33 On this see the fascinating account by Fritz Stern (1977: ch. 14).

34 *The Economist*, 1886, cited in: *Deutsche Ökonomist*. 30 October 1886.

35 For example, the Austro–Hungarian business was tied for most of the period to the German market, the French only occasionally opening up to it.

36 On conversion operations of Hansemann and French banks see Münch (1932: 198–204).

37 My estimate of gross savings amounts to adding an estimate of depreciation to the Hoffmann (1965) estimates of net investment, government sector saving, and net foreign investment.

38 These numbers were collected from the IWD (Informationsdienst des Instituts der deutschen Wirtschaft) 30 May 1991, 22 August 1991, 6 February 1992 and 5 March 1992.

39 For example, in the 1890s when the government investigated stock exchange practices and enacted a somewhat restrictive regulatory law.

40 An interesting discussion of this aspect of Russian Loans took place among the Leadership of the Deutsche Bank in 1905–6. The project was not realized, apparently because of its risk. Deutsche Bank Archiv, Frankfurt/Main, S3127: Russische Anleiheverhandlungen 1905–6. For an assessment in the 1880s see *Deutsche Ökonomist* 1884: 962.

41 See the sharp criticism of the *Deutsche Ökonomist* 1884: 130.

42 This story has been well told by Fritz Stern (1977: Ch. 14).

43 The background of the Bulgarian "Tobacco Loan" of 1902 offers an interesting example of German bankers' control difficulties. Interesting material on this episode is in the Bethmann Archiv (V 57), Stadtarchiv Frankfurt/Main. See also Helfferich (1921–3, III: 7–12). For Serbia, see also text, and Born (1988).

REFERENCES

Anan'ich, B.V. and Bovykin, V. (1991) "Foreign banks and foreign investment in Russia," in R. Cameron (ed.) *International Banking 1870–1914*, New York.

Arndt, P. (1915) "Wesen und Zweck der Kapitalanlage im Ausland," *Zeitschrift für die gesamte Staatswissenschaft*, N.F. 6, Leipzig.

Bartsch, F. (1917) *Statistische Daten über die Zahlungsbilanz Österreich-Ungarns vor Ausbruch des Krieges*, Vienna.

Berend, I. and Ránki, G. (1974) *Economic Development in East–Central Europe in the 19th and 20th Centuries*, New York.

Boehme, H. (1966) *Deutschlands Weg zur Großmacht. Studien zum Verhältnis von Wirtschaft und Staat während der Reichsgrüdungszeit, 1848–1881*, Cologne.

Born, K.-E. (1988) *Internationale Schuldenkrisen des 19 Jahrhunderts*, Abhandlungen der Akademie der Wissenschaften und der Literatur, Mainz.

Brack, U. (1977) "Deutsche Erdölpolitik vor 1914. Eine Fallstudie zu den Problemen der Marktbeherrschung und Staatsintervention im Wilhelminischen Deutschland." Dissertation, Universität Hamburg.

Brockhage, B. (1910) "Zur Entwicklung des preußisch-deutschen Kapitalexports. 1. Teil: Der Berliner Markt für ausländische Staatspapiere 1816 bis um 1840," in G. Schmollers and M. Sering (eds.) *Staats- und Sozialwissenchaftliche Forschungen*, 148, Leipzig.

Cameron, R. (1961) *France and the Economic Development of Europe*, Princeton, NJ.

Cameron, R. (1991) *International Banking 1870–1914*, New York.

Chandler, A. (1990) *Scale and Scope: The Dynamics of Industrial Capitalism*, Cambridge, MA.

Däbritz, W. (1931) *Gründung und Anfänge der Diskonto-Gesellschaft*, Berlin.

Davis, L. and Huttenback, R. (1986) *Mammon and the Pursuit of Empire. The Political Economy of British Imperialism 1860–1912*, Cambridge, MA.

Disconto-Gesellschaft, *Die Disconto-Gesellschaft 1851 bis 1901. Denkschrift*, Berlin.

Eddie, S. (1968) "Agricultural production and output per worker in Hungary, 1870–1913," *Journal of Economic History*, XXVIII: 197–222.

Eddie, S. (1983) "Agriculture as a source of labor supply: Conjecture from the history of Hungary, 1870–1913," in J. Komlos (ed.) *Economic Development in the Habsburg Monarchy in the Nineteenth Century: Essays*, New York.

Eddie, S. (1989) "Economic policy in Austria-Hungary, 1867–1913," in P. Mathias and S. Pollard (eds.) *Cambridge Economic History of Europe*, vol. VIII, Cambridge.

Edelstein, M. (1982) *Overseas Investment in the Age of High Imperialism: The United Kingdom, 1850–1914*, London.

Feis, H. (1915) *Europe, the World's Banker*, New Haven.

Fürstenberg, H. (ed.) (1931) *Carl Fürstenberg: Die Lebensgeschichte eines deutschen Bankiers, 1870–1914*, Berlin.

Gerschenkron, A. (1962) *Economic Backwardness in Historical Perspective*, Cambridge, MA.

Gregory, P. (1982) *Russian National Income, 1885–1913*, Cambridge.

Gregory, P. (1979) "The Russian balance of payments, the gold standard and monetary policy: A historical example of foreign capital movements," *Journal of Economic History* XXXIX: 379–99.

Habedank, H. (1981) *Die Reichsbank in der Weimarer Republik*, Berlin.

Hallgarten, G. W. F. (1963) *Imperialisms vor 1914* 2 vols, Munich.

Hartwig, K.-H. (1991) "Reformen der staatlichen Finanzwirtschaft: Zu den neuen Funktionen staatlicher Haushaltspolitik", in K.-H. Hartwig and J. Thieme (eds.) *Transformationsprozesse in sozialistischen Wirtschaftssystemen*, Berlin, Heidelberg.

Helfferich, K. (1921–3) *Georg von Siemens. Ein Lebensbild aus Deutschlands großer Zeit* 3 vols, Berlin.

Helmstädter, E. (1991) "Wann kommt das Wunder in der DDR?," in *Kommentare zur Wirtschaftspolitik*, Münster.

Helmstädter, E. (1991) "Neue Bundesländer als Industriestandort," *List-Forum*, 17.

Hoffmann, W. *et al.* (1965) *Das Wachstum der deutschen Wirtschaft seit der Mitte des 19. Jahrhunderts*, Berlin.

Homer, S. (1963) *A History of Interest Rates*, New Brunswick.

Kabisch, T. (1982) *Deutsches Kapital in den U.S.A.*, Stuttgart.

Kantzenbach, E. (ed.) (1992) *Die Wirtschaftliche Neuordnung Europas – Erfahrungen und Perspektiven*, Berlin.

Kellenbenz, H. and Schneider, J. (1977) "Les investissements allemands en France, 1854–1914", in Levy-Leboyer, M. (ed.) *La position internationale de la France. Aspects economiques et Financiers XIXe-XXe siecles*, Paris.

Kennedy, P. (1988) *The Rise and Fall of the Great Powers: Economic Change and Military Conflict from 1500 to 2000*, New York.

Kerken, G. (1925) "Die deutsche Kapitalanlage im Ausland vor Kriegsausbruch 1914," Dissertation, University of Giessen.

Klebba, W. (1920) *Börse und Effektenhandel im Kriege unter besonderer Berücksichtigung der Berliner Börse*, Berlin.

Kövér, G. (1991) "The Austro-Hungarian banking system," in R. Cameron (ed.) *International Banking 1870–1914*, New York.

Komlos, J. (1983a) *The Habsburg Monarchy as a Customs Union*, Princeton, NJ.

Komlos, J. (ed.) (1983b) *Economic Development in the Habsburg Monarchy in the Nineteenth Century: Essays*, New York.

Lampe, J. and Jackson, M. (1982) *Balkan Economic History, 1550–1950*, Bloomington.

Landes, D. (1956) "Vielle banque et banque nouvelle: La revolution financière du dix-neuvième siècle," in: *Revue d'histoire moderne et contemporeine*, III (Juillet-Septembre).

Mai, J. (1970) *Das deutsche Kapital in Russland, 1850–1914*, Berlin.

Matis, H. (1972) *Österreichs Wirtschaft 1848–1913. Konjunkturelle Dynamik und gesellschaftlicher Wandel im Zeitalter Franz Joseph I*, Berlin.

Matthesius, O. (1905) "Russische Eisenbahnpolitik im 19. Jahrhundert," in *Archiv für Eisenbahnwesen*, 72–118.

Michel, B. (1976) *Banques et banquiers en Autriche au debut du 20e siècle*, Paris.

Münch, H. (1932) *Adolph von Hansemann*, Berlin.

Pearton, M. (1971) *Oil and the Romanian State*, London.

Pohl, H. (1989) "Die Steaua Romana und die Deutsche Bank, 1903–1920," in Deutsche Bank (ed.), *Beiträge zu Wirtschafts- und Währungsfragen und zur Bankgeschichte*, No. 24, Mainz.

Pohl, M. (1977) *Deutscher Kapitalexport im 19. Jahrhundert. Emissionen, Banken, Anleger bis 1914*, Frankfurt/Main.

Pustula, Z. (1989) *Deutsche Kapitalbeteiligungen in der Schwerindustrie des Königtums Polen, 1856–1914*, Unpublished conference paper, Münster.

Ránki, G. (1983) "On the economic development of the Austro–Hungarian Monarchy," in J. Komlos (ed.) *Economic Development in the Habsburg Monarchy in the Nineteenth Century: Essays*, New York.

Reininghaus, W. (1973) "Der deutsche Kapitalexport nach Russland, 1870–191," Unpublished Diplomthesis, Münster.

Seidenzahl, F. (1970) *100 Jahre Deutsche Bank*, Frankfurt/Main.

Sommariva, A. and Tullio, G. (1987) *German Macroeconomic History, 1880–1979*, London.

Stern, F. (1977) *Gold and Iron: Bismarck, Bleichröder, and the Building of the German Empire*, New York.

Strousberg, B. H. (1876) *Dr Strousberg und sein Wirken. Von ihm selbst geschildert*, Berlin.

Sylla, R. and Toniolo, G. (eds.) (1991) *Patterns of European Industrialization: The Nineteenth Century*, London, New York.

Teichova, A. (1983) "The Mannesmann Concern in East Central Europe in the interwar period," in A. Teichova and P. Cottrell (eds) *International Business and Central Europe 1918–1939*, New York.

Tilly, R. (1991a) "German banks and foreign investment in Eastern and Central Europe before 1939," unpublished manuscript.

Tilly, R. (1991b) "International aspects of the development of German banking," in R. Cameron (ed.) *International Banking 1870–1914*, New York.

Tomaszewski, J. (1983) "German capital in Silesian industry in Poland between the two world wars," in A. Teichova and P. Cottrell (eds.) *International Business and Central Europe 1918–1939*, New York.

Treue, W. (1972) "Das Bankhaus Mendelssohn als Beispiel einer Privatbank im 19. und 20. Jahrhundert," in C. Lowenthal-Hensel (ed.) *Mendelssohn Studien. Beiträge zur neueren deutschen Kultur- und Wirtschaftsgeschichte*, Berlin.

Wagener, H.-J. (1991) "Anpassung durch Wandel. Evolution und Transformation von Wirtschaftssystemen," *Schriften des Vereins für Sozialpolitik*, 206, Berlin.

Wilkins, M. (1991) "Foreign banks and foreign investment in the United States," in R. Cameron (ed.) *International Banking 1870–1914*, New York.

Witt, P.-C. (1970) *Die Finanzpolitik des Deutschen Reiches von 1903 bis 1913*, Lübeck, Hamburg.

Yeager, L. (1972) "Fluctuating exchange rates in the nineteenth century: The experiences of Austria and Russia," in R. Mundell and A. Swoboda (eds.) *Monetary Problems of the International Economy*, Chicago.

13

AUSTRO-HUNGARIAN TRADE AND THE ECONOMIC DEVELOPMENT OF SOUTHEASTERN EUROPE BEFORE WORLD WAR I

Roumyana Preshlenova

Among the most far-reaching factors for the Balkan states' economic development before World War I was their decisive turn to Europe after decades of Ottoman rule. By the time most Southeastern European countries emerged as newly independent states in 1878, a core and a periphery had formed on the European continent.[1] The periphery comprised the Scandinavian countries, the Iberian peninsula, Italy, the Balkans, the eastern part of the Habsburg Monarchy and the Russian empire. Its most significant feature was the "lack of spontaneous domestic forces, adequate for a transition along the lines of the industrial revolution" (Berend and Ránki 1980a: 61–2, 1982: 113). The powerful and expanding Northwestern European core produced an unprecedented challenge for the rest of Europe. Despite its relative backwardness and weakness, the periphery began to change as a result of complex interactions between domestic factors and external influences emanating from the innovative European core. This chapter explores the role of Austro-Hungarian trade in the economic development of the pre-1914 Balkan states and traces the implications for the current economic transformation of the region.

THE GENERAL OUTLINES OF ECONOMIC DEVELOPMENT IN SOUTHEASTERN EUROPE

The interaction of internal and external factors affected economic development on the periphery differently, depending on geopolitics, resource endowment, and historical and economic legacies (Gerschenkron 1962: 31–51, 353–64; Lampe 1975: 56–85). Also important was the legislative framework of economic development. In the newly independent Balkan states this framework was based more or less on Western European models, as was usually the case with developing countries before 1914 (Galanter

1966, 153). The Balkan countries oriented themselves toward the advanced European states, which embodied prosperity and potential sources of aid for the lagging periphery (Stokes 1980: 63). The interaction between internal and external forces in the Balkans (Black 1966; Crampton 1989) was extremely complicated and painful. In general, it reflected a striving to catch up to the more advanced and usually industrialized countries (Janos 1989: 337 ff.). An exception in this respect was the Ottoman empire, which introduced only isolated elements from Western Europe, chiefly the military organization and technology it needed to postpone its dissolution (Sugar 1976; Petrosian 1976).

A wide variety of links to the rest of the continent both provoked and promoted the far-reaching economic and social transformations on the European periphery before 1914. Many of these ties lie beyond economic analysis and are not susceptible to measurement (Kuznets 1966: 285–6). It is therefore not easy to evaluate the transitions in these countries using evidence only on the pace of economic change.

Between 1878 and 1914, population, agricultural production, railroad networks, industry, foreign trade, and national income grew considerably in Southeastern Europe. Yet these changes, although impressive, reflected a very low starting level. Also, the Balkan states remained heavily agricultural with an output per capita among the lowest in Europe. Their economic development proved less successful than elsewhere on the periphery, e.g., in Scandinavia, Hungary, and Italy and failed to exceed even the most backward regions of the Habsburg empire. Their predominantly small-scale industry still could not satisfy the domestic demand for consumer goods, not to mention investment goods such as machinery. Some, especially Romania, and to a lesser extent Serbia or Bulgaria, performed relatively well, while others like Turkey and Montenegro lagged considerably behind.[2]

There are different explanations for this relatively poor performance. Among these are the legacy of Turkish rule, the scarcity of natural resources, and the lack of domestic and foreign capital, entrepreneurship and a skilled labor force. Also, to these should be added an educational system geared to promoting nationalism, an insufficient internal market, and the poor condition of the state finances.[3]

However, during the period under review the Balkan states did not lag hopelessly behind. On the eve of World War I, rough approximations of income per capita indicate close to 250 francs for Serbia and Romania and 200 francs for Bulgaria against 400 francs for Hungary, between 700 and 800 for the Czech lands, and nearly 1,000 for Germany (Lampe and Jackson 1982: 160–1). During the late nineteenth century, the Balkan states began to take, although with a delay, the "ascending path open to all" (Lampe 1989: 177). They changed insufficiently, but irreversibly.

Admittedly the two most important channels for the transformation were foreign investments and international trade (Berend and Ránki 1980a: 63).

By the end of the nineteenth century, one-tenth to one-third of the Balkan gross national product (GNP) passed through foreign trade. This was enough for the region to begin experiencing West European business cycles. The tendency toward greater parallelism in the fluctuations of industrial and agricultural prices in the two regions facilitated trade between them (Berov 1985: 33–7) and assisted the spread of changes from Western Europe to the Balkans.

The link between economic development and foreign trade in the Balkans is evident from Bulgarian data. On the eve of the Balkan wars, capitalist agriculture was predominant in the hinterland of the great export centers, where the largest proportion of agricultural machines and workers were concentrated (*Ikonomika* 1989: 330). Bulgaria depended almost completely on machinery imports from the advanced trading partners.[4] Also, the Bulgarian industries depended to a great extent on imported raw materials as well – in 1911 27.2 per cent of all raw materials were imported.[5] Although industrial production was growing, the industrial sector could not meet even half of the domestic consumption. However, the share of domestically produced industrial goods did improve over time: 1896 – 13 per cent; 1901 – 23 per cent; 1911 – 43 per cent (*Ikonomika* 1989: 346).

TRADE WITH AUSTRIA–HUNGARY

Trade between Austria–Hungary and the Balkans deserves special consideration because the Dual Monarchy was one of the region's most important trading partners. A systematic treatment is necessary for reconciling the two opposite views: one stressing the civilizing impact of trade on the Balkans and the other emphasizing imperialistic exploitation. Austro–Hungarian trade with Southeastern Europe is the subject of some research (Grünberg 1902; Grunzel 1892; Schwaighofer 1900; Stojanoff 1914; Djordjević 1962; Müller 1979), but unresolved issues remain. This chapter tries to provide a more balanced framework for approaching the issue.

After the political changes in Central Europe between 1848 and 1867, Austro–Hungarian diplomacy logically shifted to the Balkans partly to offset the empire's failure to gain hegemony in Central Europe. This does not represent a radical turn in the Monarchy's foreign policy. Because it included sizeable territories that were geographically, ethnically, and culturally related to the Balkan peninsula, the Habsburg Monarchy always had to take the region into account. However, under the new circumstances this necessity attained a much greater importance. Austria–Hungary's declining role in the European balance of power, as well as the claims of the Balkan nations for independence as the Ottoman empire weakened, called for economic activity in the region rather than for direct military expansion. That is why Habsburg foreign policy tried to maintain the territorial status quo as long as possible through economic penetration of the region. The

Austro–Hungarian claims were officially declared and later regulated in the Berlin Congress (1878), in the 1897 agreement with Russia, in treaties with Italy, in the Triple Alliance, and in the 1887 Mediterranean agreements with Great Britain and Italy. Nevertheless the empire could hardly prevent political and economic competition (Palotás 1980; Jelavich 1969: 140–2; Bridge 1972; Sosnosky 1914; Carlgren 1955; Fellner 1960; Tamborra 1986).

Economic as well as political considerations shaped foreign policy in the Balkans. The Dual Monarchy's weakening position as a great power in international affairs coincided with its relative economic decline (Diószegi 1970: 363–6, 394; Gross 1973: 14; Battaglia 1917). Recent research in economic history has thrown considerable light on Austria–Hungary's relative economic backwardness, which was so often emphasized by contemporaries and later by historians. In general the research shows that the Habsburg Monarchy experienced modern economic growth beginning in the 1820s and 1830s, but that it was less pronounced than in England and Germany.[6] After a period of about five decades when the economic gap between Austria–Hungary's "core" (the early industrializing regions) and its "periphery" (the eastern agricultural regions) was widening sharply, economic integration acted to reverse the regional differentials.[7] By 1913 the degree of economic unity and regional income convergence achieved by the Habsburg empire compared favorably with that of several contemporaries (Good 1984: 125 ff., 237–41, 246). Despite these undeniable positive results, especially in the last pre-World War I decades, its relative economic backwardness as a whole appears to have intensified from the Napoleonic period to World War I.[8]

Some features of the Austro–Hungarian pattern proved especially significant for the empire's penetration of Southeastern Europe. The Dual Monarchy remained the only great power without colonies, which may explain its greater interest in the Balkans compared with contemporaries. Also, the overwhelming share of commodity trade was with its neighbors, chiefly Germany. During the period under review, approximately 60 per cent of Austria–Hungary's total imports and nearly three-quarters of its exports were accounted for by neighboring countries, including the Balkans.[9] The Balkans as a whole shared second place with Great Britain in aggregate Austro–Hungarian foreign trade behind Germany, which remained the leading partner up to World War I.

Another pattern is the sizable economic gap between Austria and Hungary, which persisted despite rapid growth in Hungary. On the eve of World War I, Hungary's economy was still essentially agricultural; the primary sector employed two-thirds of the labor force and produced close to the same share of the national product (Komlos 1983: 113–4, 212; Good 1984: 139). This situation had two very important consequences for economic relations with the Balkans. The accelerated growth in the eastern part of the Monarchy attracted sizable capital investments from Austria. By facilitating the flow of capital, the Hungarian government played a more active role than it did by promoting nascent domestic industries (Komlos 1983: 154, 162). Reflecting the relatively large interregional flow of capital within the empire, Austria–Hungary was a relatively modest capital exporter.[10]

Another consequence of the time lag between the beginning of modern economic growth in Austria and Hungary was the relatively high degree of complementarity between the two parts of the Monarchy. In the close association between Austria and Hungary, the traditional exchange of Hungarian foodstuffs for Austrian manufactured goods is, broadly speaking, clearly reflected in its patterns of foreign trade.[11] The complementarity of the Austro–Hungarian economy provided a favorable basis for the return to protectionism, which preserved markets inside the customs union for Hungarian agricultural goods and Austrian manufactured goods. Protective import duties were introduced in 1878 and gradually raised until 1906 (Eddie 1977: 330). Austrian industrialists and later Hungarian large landowners launched a strong protectionist movement to insulate the customs union against the industrial imports from more developed European countries and grain and livestock from Russia and Southeastern Europe (Good 1984: 141, 226–31; Matis 1971, 175; Paulinyi 1973, 584–8; Matlekovits 1891, 1901: 10). This cooperation was inherent in the Compromise of 1867, which officially set down the right of Austria and Hungary to make decisions and influence the Monarchy's common affairs, including foreign trade policy (Paulinyi 1973: 567–72; Brusatti 1967: 137).

The return to protectionism in Austro–Hungary was not an isolated event, but a natural response to trends in European commercial policy since the late 1870s. Free trade policy on the continent was replaced in several waves by a kind of neo-mercantilism that lasted up to World War I. The exceptions were Great Britain, with the largest colonial empire in the world, as well as Sweden, Netherlands, Finland, Belgium, and Turkey, which retained moderate, chiefly revenue-raising import taxes (Bairoch 1976: 53, 117 ff.; Pollard 1981: 254–5, 259, 264; Issawi 1980: 74).

There were, of course, other factors behind protectionism in Austria–Hungary (Peez 1892: 9–10). Perhaps the most important were the duties imposed on a wide range of agricultural products in Germany after 1881 (Eddie 1977: 332). Grain imports, which had flowed into Europe in the 1870s thanks to the enormous rise of production and the parallel lowering of transportation costs by approximately 75 per cent, began to decline after reaching their peak in the late 1870s. At the same time, wheat production and grain exports in Eastern Europe increased (Sieveking 1905: 128–30). Tariffs against agricultural products were joined with restrictions on livestock imports and transit. The latter measures, which diffused eastward from Britain in order to prevent the dissemination of cattle pestilences (Matlekovits 1891: 38–9; Peez 1892: 176, 192), affected not so much overseas trade, but agricultural exporters such as Hungary, Romania, Bulgaria, Serbia, and Russia.

Germany's turn to agrarian protectionism and its refusal to conclude a trade agreement with Austria–Hungary from 1877 to 1891 opened an "epoch of undeclared tariff war" (Grunzel 1901: 72) that gradually drew a response in Hungary. The more systematically tariff protection was imposed in Europe, the more quickly Austria–Hungary adopted analogous measures. In particular, German policy regarding livestock imports from Hungary guided Austro–Hungarian policy on livestock imports from Serbia, and Romania. Also, the duties Germany imposed on Hungarian grain were to match the duties imposed by Austria–Hungary on grain from Russia, Serbia, and Romania. Such attitudes were not surprising, if we consider that Germany was willing to grant concessions for Austro–Hungarian livestock imports only on condition that the Dual Monarchy modified its veterinary system and undertook effective measures against Romania and Russia (Matlekovits 1891: 78). Thus, Hungary was driven to secure the customs union market and to some extent its own export interests by prohibiting livestock transit and imports from Russia, Turkey, Bulgaria, and Romania (Matlekovits 1901: 66–7).

The degree of protection in the Austro–Hungarian tariffs as measured by the ratio of customs revenue to the value of imports was not very high. This ratio grew from 4.63 per cent in 1879–82 to 6.99 per cent in 1883–7, fell to 6.60 per cent in 1888–1906 and grew again to 7.09 per cent in 1907–13. Measured *ad valorem*, tariff rates were on the order of 18 per cent, which was not a high level compared with other European countries or to the interwar period. They were somewhat higher than Germany, but equal to France and Italy (Good 1984: 227–8; Eddie 1980: 244–6).[12] While the 1906 tariff doubled the duty on grain, the ratio of total customs revenue to the value of imports after the 1906 tariff was enacted, increased only by 0.5 per cent. Yet the protectionist policy in the Dual Monarchy contributed to the improvements in the Hungarian terms of trade after 1900 (Eddie 1977: 341–4; Berend and Ránki 1980a: 550).

The response of the Balkan countries to the European trend toward agrarian tariff protectionism matched the Austro–Hungarian policy. Different Balkan states had different opportunities for an independent foreign trade policy. Some acquired this right when they became independent states; Greece in 1830, and Serbia and Montenegro in 1878. Others obtained it to a certain degree prior to independence, Romania in 1875 and Bulgaria in 1889–90. The Ottoman empire was bound not to undertake any changes in tariff policy without the agreement of the great powers, i.e., it had no independent trade policy at all. Greece, Montenegro, and Turkey promoted their industries neither through "administrative" protection on the Hungarian pattern, nor through protectionist tariffs.[13]

On the other hand, Romania, Serbia, and Bulgaria reacted to the protectionism of Austria–Hungary by raising import duties on items that were the most important among Austro–Hungarian exports to the region. Thus, they did not use tariffs simply to protect their nascent domestic industries. They hoped to establish a basis for trade negotiations that would later permit them to gain concessions in return for reducing duties on some of their especially important articles.

In negotiations with Austria–Hungary in 1875, Romania established its first tariff levels at 4–20 per cent *ad valorem* rates. But for a number of Austro–Hungarian export articles like sugar, paper, candles, soap, simple fabrics, leather, wine, and alcohol, rates were set at 15–20 per cent *ad valorem* (Antonescu 1915: 39–43). The Romanian tariff from 1886 aimed explicitly at protecting nascent domestic industries. Rates for some import duties reached 180 per cent *ad valorem*, especially when Romania followed Germany and Austro–Hungary in imposing tariffs amounting to 100–200 per cent *ad valorem* on imports from countries that failed to treat Romanian goods according to the most-favored-nation clause (*Istorie* 1979: 188; Jinga 1975: 30). This policy, coupled with the industry promotion law from 1887, marked the decisive turn toward protecting domestic industries in Romania (Antonescu 1915: 105–8 and note 78).

Several factors led to a five-year tariff war (1886–91) that harmed both countries – the refusal of the Dual Monarchy to allow unconditional access to Romanian livestock, the Romanian demand for duty-free imports of goods that competed with Austro–Hungarian articles (grain, flour, livestock, among others), the Austro–Hungarian desire for duty-free imports of fifty articles included in the Romanian program of industry promotion but, above all the reluctance on both sides to make any concessions (Bindreiter 1976: 258–61; Antonescu 1915: 64, 82–8, 99–105; Grünberg 1902: 72 ff.). The tariff war introduced a prolonged cooling in Romanian and Austro–Hungarian trade relations, which for nearly two decades afterwards proceeded only on the basis of the most-favored-nation clause. It also brought about a reduction in the volume of trade, which, measured as a share in each other's overall trade, did not recover until the end of the period (Table 13.1). Romanian exports shifted to England, Belgium, and the Netherlands, i.e., to markets that were not surrounded by high tariffs, had a relative stable demand for raw materials, and were accessible by sea. Livestock lost its importance as an export item because the new markets lay rather remote for its transportation. To a certain degree, Germany supplanted the Dual Monarchy as an export market for Romania (Table 13.1).

Bulgaria acquired *de facto* the right to conduct trade policy independently from the Sublime Porte after concluding agreements in 1889–90 with Britain, Austria–Hungary, France, Italy, Switzerland, Belgium, and Germany, although they in fact reduced duties on imports from Bulgaria (*Istoria* 1983, 176–7; Svrakov 1935–6: 16). Later, the Dual Monarchy gradually agreed to the Bulgarian request to raise its import duties partly for fiscal and partly for

Table 13.1 Foreign trade of the Balkan countries with main trading partners: trade shares 1886–1911 (%)

	Austria–Hungary		*Germany*		*France*		*England*		*Belgium*		*Turkey*	
	X	*M*	*X*	*M*	*X*	*M*	*X*	*M*	*X*	*M*	*X*	*M*
Romania												
1883–5	34.6	43.8	1.3	13.9	7.4	8.1	36.1	20.4	2.1	1.7	5.1	4.0
1886–90	7.2	18.2	3.5	28.1	7.4	8.5	54.0	26.8	10.8	5.2	3.3	3.0
1891–5	11.9	23.9	18.8	28.8	3.0	8.5	33.5	22.1	19.5	5.0	4.4	3.6
1896–1900	20.4	28.4	5.2	27.7	2.7	7.0	18.4	19.6	37.1	3.4	4.7	4.1
1901–05	13.1	27.1	7.1	28.5	3.3	5.8	8.6	16.8	42.5	2.0	2.7	3.6
1906–10	9.7	24.6	6.2	33.9	6.5	5.5	9.9	15.4	29.5	3.1	4.7	3.6
1911	9.1	24.1	4.8	32.3	7.1	6.2	8.1	15.0	38.1	4.9	3.0	2.4
Bulgaria												
1886–90	5.8	30.1	0.8	4.9	21.7	5.3	15.5	28.6	1.2[a]	2.4[a]	43.1	14.4
1891–5	3.7	35.8	14.2	10.9	20.3	4.2	17.1	21.0	2.7	1.8	28.6	12.2
1896–1900	7.6	28.1	13.1	12.6	11.5	5.3	22.3	23.1	9.4	3.6	25.9	11.2
1901–05	9.7	27.2	8.8	14.8	6.1	6.1	16.4	17.5	25.2	2.5	19.5	14.2
1906–10	7.1	26.3	12.1	17.1	6.1	6.5	11.6	16.2	18.5	4.0	29.1	13.8
1911	5.7	24.2	12.4	20.0	6.0	12.5	13.1	15.1	29.1	2.5	15.8	8.0
Serbia												
1886–90	86.9	68.3	1.6	5.0	2.0	1.6	0.4[b]	10.3[b]	—	0.8	5.3	2.5
1891–5	88.4	59.3	3.1	9.2	0.7	1.1	*	12.1[c]	0.1[c]	1.0[c]	4.9	5.5
1896–1900	86.6	54.8	6.1	14.7	0.6	2.9	—	10.9	0.1[d]	0.6[d]	3.0	4.3
1901–05	85.7	58.3	5.2	13.3	0.5	2.6	0.7[e]	8.9[e]	1.2	0.8	2.8	3.8
1906–10	26.2	32.7	24.5	33.0	3.0	3.5	1.1	12.2	14.6	1.5	15.7	5.5
1911	41.4	41.1	24.7	27.2	3.3	2.7	0.1	8.2	5.3	—	10.3	3.3

Table 13.1 Continued

	Austria–Hungary		*Germany*		*France*		*England*		*Belgium*		*Turkey*	
	X	*M*	*X*	*M*	*X*	*M*	*X*	*M*	*X*	*M*	*X*	*M*
Greece												
1887–90	17.1	13.9	3.0	3.6	23.3	8.7	36.9	16.8	—	—	6.9	14.9
1891–5	17.9	13.4	4.2	7.2	12.5	8.1	37.3	28.2	—	—	7.3	13.5
1896–1900	16.2	11.2	6.4	8.1	9.8	8.9	31.7	24.2	—	—	7.0	10.4
1901–05	22.1	13.8	7.6	8.8	10.3	8.2	26.7	21.2	—	—	6.4	10.1
1906–10	15.2	12.2	9.5	9.4	8.3	7.0	26.0	21.5	—	—	5.0	8.6
1911	17.0	13.8	11.3	7.5	9.9	5.7	24.1	23.6	—	—	3.5	5.2
Turkey												
1886–90	8.6	19.4	0.3	0.2	32.4	12.5	35.9	42.7	—	—	—	—
1891–5	9.9	20.5	2.0	1.1	26.7	11.8	43.5	38.9	—	—	—	—
1896–1900	9.5	19.5	2.8	1.8	30.3	10.6	37.9	37.9	—	—	—	—
1905–10	10.1	17.7	5.8	6.5	18.9	9.3	26.3	27.6	—	—	—	—
1991	9.9	18.0	6.0	9.2	19.9	9.2	24.3	19.9	2.8	3.9	—	—

Rows do not add to 100

X: share in exports *M*: share in imports * less than 0.0001

Source: *Commerciul* (1893–1915); *Statistika* (1889–99); *Statisticheski Godishnik* (1910, 1914, 1924); Sundhaussen (1989); Nestorović (1913); Mitchell (1981); Nebioglu (1941); McCartey (1982); Novichev (1937).

Notes:
[a] 1887–90 [b] 1888–90 [c] 1891–3 [d] 1899–1900 [e] 1901–04.

protectionist reasons. After protracted negotiations and mutual concessions, the two states concluded a definitive treaty in 1896. Bulgaria insisted neither on a veterinary convention nor on the official and separate abolition of the capitulations inherited from Turkey, which had been negotiated over a long time with Austria–Hungary. Austria–Hungary accepted the increase of several import duties by Bulgaria. According to the customs revenue data for 1897, the tariff rates averaged 17.5 per cent *ad valorem* (*Istoria* 1983: 182), but the rate on most items was closer to 14 per cent. The Austro–Hungarian treaty served as an appropriate basis for Bulgaria to settle its commercial relations with other European partners.

The dispute between Greece and the Dual Monarchy over a tariff convention remained unresolved and they granted each other only most-favored-nation treatment. The argument referring to the Austro–Hungarian imports duties on raisins lasted for decades without being resolved (*HHStA*).

The 1890s brought a decade of closer trade relations among the Central European countries in the context of the Caprivi treaty system, which moderated import duties in line with the new political course of Germany. The Balkan countries enjoyed reduced import duties with respect to Austria–Hungary, too, on the basis of the most-favored-nation clause (Suter 1930). When these treaties expired, a new upsurge in protectionism followed in Europe and in Germany, especially after 1902. The Dual Monarchy joined this trend relatively late because of conflict between Austria and Hungary with respect to the renewal of the Compromise of 1867. Meanwhile a movement emerged in the Dual Monarchy that tried to insulate the domestic market against agrarian imports, instead of balancing concessions from Germany against those given to exporters of agrarian products to Austria–Hungary (Gross 1962: 103–4). These circumstances and the need to prepare the way for new negotiations were the motives for the tariffs adopted in Romania, Bulgaria, and Serbia in 1904. The tariffs were reactions to the growing limits on access to Central European markets and new attempts to protect domestic industries. Romania raised tariff rates by 10–25 per cent; Bulgaria nearly doubled them from 14 to 28–30 per cent *ad valorem*, and Serbia quadrupled import duties for a number of articles (Jinga 1975: 79–80, 178; *Istoria* 1983: 183–4; Svrakov 1935–6, 28–9; Djordjević 1962: 156; Nestorović 1913: 34). All insisted again on assurances from the Dual Monarchy with respect to their livestock exports and transit.

The Balkan countries pursued rather different strategies, based more on political than economic grounds. In the case of Serbia, the key was the state of relations between Vienna and Belgrade. After the turn of the century, Serbia tried to emancipate itself from the close ties with the Dual Monarchy that had lasted for two decades and had benefitted the Serbian exports and trade balance. The rising conflict revealed itself in especially acute form during the so-called "gun crisis." The crisis, which concerned a loan to the Serbian government related to orders for armaments and railroad construction, burst forth in 1904 (Aleksić-Peiković 1965: 90–3, 169; Djordjević 1962: 54–61, 63, 74, 93–4, 135, 225) and deepened during commercial treaty negotiations in 1905. Serbia insisted on retaining the veterinary convention and clarifying the boundary exchange clauses, i.e. those dealing with trade between districts adjacent to the common boundary, and demanded protectionist duties on industrial imports. The Dual Monarchy sought limitations on imports of livestock, which were to be butchered, and asked Serbia to lift all restrictions on industrial imports (Djordjević 1962: 138–9). Not surprisingly, the diplomatic crisis between Vienna and Belgrade turned into a tariff war for which the treaty creating the Serbo-Bulgarian customs union was merely a pretext.

The tariff war lasted five years (1906–11) and was but one of the spheres in which the conflict between Serbia and the Dual Monarchy unfolded in wave-like fashion. The conflict passed through several crises, reached its peak during the more general Bosnian crisis in 1908–9, and ended ultimately in World War I. The tariff war caused each state to turn temporarily toward Germany, but trade between them did not collapse. Austria-Hungary remained the most important market for Serbia, although the importance of Germany in Serbia's trade increased in both absolute and relative terms (Table 13.1).

Up to this time Serbia had enjoyed unprecedented preferences in comparison with the other Balkan states. These included veterinary conventions that allowed the imports of Serbian livestock into and transit through the Dual Monarchy (Marchet 1901: 291) and zero or considerably reduced tariffs on Serbian imports without similar concessions in return. Perhaps this alone justifies calling the commercial treaty between Austria-Hungary and Serbia from 1892 an "indirect subsidy treaty" (Grünberg 1902: 272), although the previous treaty of 1881 had been no less favorable to Serbia. Under the changed conditions the new concessions on the most controversial issue – livestock imports into the Dual Monarchy – were continuously renegotiated between Austria and Hungary in the context of political controversies with Serbia. Of course, according to the pattern of the German concessions to Austria-Hungary, only fixed quotas of butchered livestock could be imported. The equilibrium benefited Romania in the 1909 treaty and less so Bulgaria in the 1912 treaty, although the latter did not make use of it before the outbreak of the Balkan Wars and World War I. The Serbian treaty of 1910, when implemented in 1911, ended the tariff war and benefited only Serbia. The average duties on Austro-Hungarian imports into Serbia were raised in the preliminary treaty of 1908 by 30 per cent over the level of 1892 and in the treaty of 1910 by 10–20 per cent over the level of 1908 (Djordjević 1962: 615–8; Nestorović 1913: 41–3).

Small Montenegro succeeded in concluding its first and only official commercial treaty with the Dual Monarchy in 1911. The treaty represented a political flirting with Austria-Hungary after a temporary break with Russia.

The most important clauses for Montenegro involved considerable concessions for the boundary exchange and duty free quotas on livestock and meat imports (Preshlenova 1989: 282). The clauses had more political than economic importance because they were regionally limited and merely ratified officially the existing smuggling trade (Hitrova 1963: 151).

One final example of the many commercial conflicts with the Balkan states should be mentioned; the boycott movement that emerged in Turkey and spread into Serbia and Montenegro. The annexation of Bosnia and Herzegovina by the Dual Monarchy in 1908 provoked a strong boycott of Austro–Hungarian goods and ships that lasted for almost five months. It was used by the Turkish government to achieve the maximum possible political and economic concessions from the Dual Monarchy. The boycott had almost the same effects as a tariff war. However, it did less harm to Austro–Hungarian imports than to Vienna's prestige by contributing to the image of the Dual Monarchy as an aggressive great power in the region (Hitrova 1963). Montenegro in its turn used the occasion to start a tariff war with Austria–Hungary (Mikić 1983: 102–14, 150–1, 182–3; Preshlenova 1989: 248–62). From an economic point of view, this could not have influenced the Austro–Hungarian markets on the Balkan peninsula; Montenegrinean trade was insignificant for the Dual Monarchy, amounting to an annual average of 1.6 million crowns, which was no more than 0.01 per cent of total Austro–Hungarian commodity trade and only 0.5 per cent of total Balkan trade with the Dual Monarchy. The conflict had only a propaganda effect. It strengthened the notion that the interests of some Southeastern European states were incompatible with those of the Habsburg Monarchy.

It can be argued that the protectionist trend in Central Europe and the corresponding reaction in some of the Balkan states hampered trade between the two regions. In this respect, the Austro–Hungarian measures had a greater effect than the Balkan ones, especially in the Romanian and Serbian cases when the clash ended in tariff wars. The decrease of their exports into the Dual Monarchy was a consequence of their shift partly to markets with more liberal regimes for agricultural goods – chiefly to Belgium, a state with a dynamically expanding foreign trade during the period under review (Bairoch 1973a: 14–18, 25–9; Lampe and Jackson 1982: 180) and partly to Turkey, especially after 1905 (Table 13.1). An undetermined amount of Romanian and Bulgarian grain funneled through the port of Antwerp for wider distribution, chiefly to the UK and Western Europe, with little to Germany and virtually none to Austria–Hungary. The shift did not affect livestock, which for a long time lost its importance as an export article for Romania. In Serbia it was replaced by exports of processed meat, which were less dependent on transportation factors. The Serbian government actively supported these shifts to other markets and the substitution of livestock exports by related processed goods. By the end of the conflict the

Serbian economy may have converted over three-quarters of its meat exports into sales of processed meat, which revealed more favorable price trends than did livestock. Success, however, was achieved only with great difficulty (Djordjević 1962; Lampe 1975: 64–5).

Austro-Hungarian restrictions on livestock imports affected the long-term trade patterns of Romania, Serbia, and Bulgaria, but the effects were not irreversible. These countries persistently tried to gain access to the Austro-Hungarian market for their livestock imports during the entire period under review, perhaps because of the relatively more favorable prices of livestock compared with grain.[14] The Romanian and Bulgarian response to the agrarian tariff protectionism in Austria-Hungary was a kind of "limited elasticity," i.e., a change in the direction rather than in the structure of exports, unlike Serbia, which faced less favorable transportation possibilities with respect to other markets.

The concessions that the Dual Monarchy gave Serbia and to some extent Romania prior to the tariff wars, plus several other factors – geographical proximity, traditional connections, etc. – oriented trade toward the neighboring Monarchy. The situation often gave rise to the characterization of Austro-Hungarian trade as hegemonic. The abolition of these concessions in the early stages of their economic transformation did not, however, reduce the potential attractiveness of the Austro-Hungarian market for Romania and Serbia. It did, however, force a redirection of the Romanian and to a lesser degree the Serbian exports in several directions, which reduced the one-sided orientation of their exports and made them more like the other Balkan states that did not have special privileges from Austria-Hungary. The opportunity was missed for establishing closer economic relations consistent with their favorable geographic proximity. This was due, on the one hand, to Hungary's jealous guarding of its internal market against agrarian producers, and on the other hand, to the "Empire's pathological relations with its neighbors on the southeastern frontier" (Macesich 1970: 27).

THE IMPACT OF TRADE ON GROWTH IN THE BALKAN COUNTRIES

The argument that Austria-Hungary exploited the Balkan countries through exports of industrial goods and capital and by its transport policy (Müller 1979: 88; Woodruff 1973: 656) is not justified except perhaps in the case of Serbia before 1906. The Balkan states to some extent encouraged Austro-Hungarian ties, e.g., by means of liberal regimes for imports of capital goods (Gross 1937: 153). Even Turkey, which until 1913 did not implement explicit policy promoting domestic industry, allowed duty free imports of steam engines for factory equipment after 1873 (Novichev 1937: 111). Instead the tariff barriers were directed against

Austro–Hungarian consumer goods that competed with already existing or nascent domestic industries.

Except for the era of the tariff wars, trade with Austria–Hungary more-or-less matched the overall growth of Balkan foreign trade. Before 1906 the trade of Turkey, Greece, and Serbia with Austria–Hungary paralleled their overall trade.[15] During the 1887–1911 period total Greek imports grew by 1.2 per cent annually, while Greek imports to Austria–Hungary grew by 1.4 per cent. For total exports and for exports to Austria–Hungary, the respective increases were 1.3 and 2.9 per cent. In the case of Serbia from 1886 to 1905 total imports grew 1.7 per cent, while imports to Austria–Hungary grew 3.2 per cent. Bulgarian and Romanian trade show a similar pattern. In the Bulgarian case the total imports increased by 4.6 per cent per year while imports to Austria–Hungary by 4.2 per cent; total exports grew by 5.3 per cent while exports to Austria–Hungary grew by 6.0 per cent. For Romania (1887–1911), the corresponding figures are 2.5 per cent for the growth of total imports and 4.0 per cent for imports to Austria–Hungary; 4.1 per cent for total exports and 4.6 for exports to Austria–Hungary.

These patterns of trade between Austria–Hungary and the Balkans coincide with the general trend in international trade in the nineteenth and early twentieth centuries. The growth of trade reflected the increasing interrelatedness of economic regions and not simply the political will of mercantilist-type states (Woodruff 1973, 658). Along with the lack of correlation between the rates of growth in trade and trends in commercial policies, Balkan trade confirms another general trend (Bairoch 1973a: 29). Even though the correspondence was not perfect, the phases of growth in individual countries coincided in the main with the phases of growth in European trade as a whole. Thus, the slow growth of Balkan trade from the 1870s to the mid-1890s mirrored a similar pattern for European foreign trade. The acceleration in the total trade and in the Austro–Hungarian trade of the Balkan countries (except for the Serbian trade with Austria–Hungary during the tariff war) after the turn of the century corresponds to a very strong increase in European trade (Bairoch 1973a: 9; Lampe and Jackson 1982: 161, 164, 168; Pamuk 1987: 33–5).

In contrast to the regional distribution of Balkan trade, the commodity composition of trade did not change significantly, except, perhaps, in the case of Serbia. Throughout the period under review the Balkan states retained the typical profile for the periphery – they exported chiefly primary goods, raw materials, and/or agricultural products; they imported overwhelmingly manufactured goods (Berend and Ránki 1982: 111, 120, 123–7).

The composition of the foreign trade of the Balkan countries and Austria–Hungary shaped the commodity trade between them, although not as a carbon copy.[16] It also reflected the framework created by the bilateral commercial agreements and on the character of transportation (see Table 13.2).

About one-third of the total value of the *Veredelungsverkehr* (the imports of raw materials and semifinished goods into the Dual Monarchy, which were then reexported as manufactures to the same countries after processing) between Austria–Hungary and the Southeastern European countries fell in the 1890s. In the early 1890s, Romania and Serbia accounted for 95.5–99.3 per cent of the total value of the *Veredelungsverkehr* with Southeastern Europe, while in the late 1890s the share of Turkey and Romania in the total was between 77.4 to 91.3 per cent.[17]

Being favored rather well by the protected customs union within the Dual Monarchy, Hungary accounted for between 16 and 18 per cent of the monarchy's exports and 12–17 per cent of its imports (Eddie 1977; Komlos 1983: 123, 212–3, 217). Hungary's role in the Balkan trade of the Dual Monarchy was even greater. In the 1890s about 25 per cent of total exports to the Balkans fell to Hungary with over 70 per cent going to neighboring Romania and Serbia and only 12 per cent to Bulgaria.[18] Hungary's share was largest in iron and ironware (47 per cent in 1897), sugar (19 per cent), leather and leatherware (16 per cent), wooden articles (16 per cent), glass and glassware (13 per cent), and chemicals (13 per cent).[19] The composition of Hungarian exports to the Balkan countries confirms that with respect to them, Hungary was the more developed trading partner, exporting industrial goods and importing agricultural products (Good 1984: 138–42; Komlos 1983: 212).

No major changes in the composition of Austria–Hungary's commodity trade with the Balkan states took place, although there were small changes in the shares of different items and a trend toward greater diversification of the trade list. The relatively stable composition of trade implies that modernization in the Southeast European economies was occurring, but that it had not experienced any decisive turn. In light of this, the impact of Austro–Hungarian trade on Balkan modernization could be sought in two directions. On the one hand, the imported industrial goods from the Dual Monarchy along with the domestic industries in the Balkans competed with the region's handicrafts sector. By eliminating some of the non-viable firms in this sector, the competition accelerated the transition from production forms belonging to the past to more modern ones. On the other hand, the imports of raw materials, semi-finished goods, and machinery brought the Balkan producers closer to the production methods of their Central European contemporaries. In this sense, Austro–Hungarian trade played a intermediating role.[20]

If we consider the trade balances, Austro-Hungary had no importance as a source of the capital that all the Balkan countries needed so badly for their modernization, except for Serbia (Table 13.3). The Monarchy was a net importer in the region and contributed much more to their trade deficits. Only during the tariff war between them did Serbia display a trade deficit. With regard to the trade balance, no other Balkan country gained as much

Table 13.2 The composition of Balkan trade with Austria–Hungary

A: Main articles as share of country's total export value to Austria–Hungary (%)

	1891–1904		*1911–12*
Romania			
Grain	52.8	Grain	62.2
Fish	12.7	Timber	7.6
Timber	6.0	Fish	3.5
Wool	4.0	Wool	1.6
Raw oil	3.0	Hides	1.0
Eggs	3.0	Raw oil	0.9
Hides	2.6		
Serbia			
Livestock	59.3	Livestock	30.3
Grain	13.3	Grain	11.8
		Poultry	11.7
		Meat	9.9
Bulgaria			
Hides	49.1	Grain	29.6
Grain	18.9	Eggs	17.7
		Tobacco	14.7
		Bran	13.6
		Hides	8.8
Turkey		*European Turkey only*	
Tobacco	43.4	Tobacco	46.7
Hides	15.1	Carets	17.4
Wool	3.9	Hides	5.9
		Eggs	3.6
Greece			
Figs	23.8	Hides	21.6
Hides	20.7	Figs	17.7
Raisins	13.3	Raisins	9.2
Tanning matter	11.0	Olive oil	6.0
		Hazelnuts	5.8
		Iron ore	5.4
		Tanning matter	3.2

Table 13.2 Continued

B: Main articles as share of country's total import from Austria–Hungary (%)			
	1891–1904		*1911–12*
Romania			
Timber	21.4	Timber	16.4
Woolen articles	6.9	Iron and ironware	9.9
Other ironware	5.5	Cottonware	9.2
Horses	5.3	Woolen articles	8.1
Sugar	4.8	Cotton yarn	4.9
Machines	4.2	Horses	4.2
Serbia			
Iron and ironware	9.3	Ironware	8.7
Sugar	7.7	Machines	6.5
Cottonware	5.2	Cotton yarn	6.0
Woolen articles	4.9	Hides	5.7
Machines	4.4	Ships	5.3
Hides	4.2	Cottonware	4.9
Leather	4.1	Coal and charcoal	4.0
Leather articles	2.7	Clothes	3.8
Bulgaria			
Textiles	12.6	Iron and ironware	16.2
Iron and ironware	10.4	Sugar	9.8
Sugar	9.8	Cottonware	6.0
Cottonware	4.7	Woolen articles	4.9
Paper	4.4	Cotton yarn	4.7
		Agricultural machines	4.2
Greece			
Sugar	24.6	Sugar	32.3
Timber	15.6	Timber	9.6
Woolen articles	7.4	Woolen articles	4.7
Paper	6.6	Paper	3.9
Turkey			
Sugar	29.4	Sugar	24.9
Woolen articles, inclusive clothes	19.7	Cottonware	16.4
Paper	5.6	Clothes	8.5
Fezzes	5.4	Woolen articles	8.2
		Paper	8.0
		Ironware	4.7

Source: Estimated from Lang (1906); *Österreichisches statistisches Handbuch 1914* (1916) and Bazant (1894: 157–63).

from the commodity trade with Austria–Hungary as did Serbia. Only in Romania and Bulgaria did Belgium contribute more to capital accumulation through the channel of foreign trade than did the Dual Monarchy in Serbia. Also, the Bulgarian trade balance with Turkey resembled the Serbian balance with Austria–Hungary (Table 13.3).

The idea that foreign markets (including Hungary) played a limited role in Austria's industrial sector (Komlos 1983: 216–7) may be justified. Nevertheless the drive for tariff protection of the Dual Monarchy's common market appeared first among Austrian industrial circles. On the other hand, the same circles regarded Southeastern Europe as a natural and even vital market for the Austrian industries throughout this whole period. Both the level of trade between the two regions and the trade balances reveal that the Balkans were more important as a market for exports than as a source of raw materials for Austria. Thus, the goal of penetrating Southeastern Europe united commercial elites, who sought diplomatic support for their trade ventures, and political elites, who regarded trade as an instrument of foreign policy in the Balkans. These elites recognized clearly the need to improve transport facilities in the Balkans as a way of promoting trade relations in the region. The issue was settled in international agreements in which Austria–Hungary played, overtly or covertly, a very active role, e.g., in the 1878 Berlin treaty, in the 1883 railroad convention signed by Austria–Hungary, Serbia, Bulgaria, and Turkey, in the international agreements on Danube navigation, and in the bilateral agreements with Balkan states.

To ensure prerequisites for increased commercial penetration into the Balkans, Austria–Hungary contributed greatly to railroad construction in the region. On its initiative, Bulgaria and Serbia assumed the obligation, taken by Turkey in 1875, to complete the railroad link Vienna–Constantinople–Thessaloniki that passed through their territories (by articles 10 and 38 of the Berlin treaty from 1878). The terms were later specified at the conference in Vienna that resulted in a formal convention in 1883 between Austria–Hungary, Serbia, Bulgaria, and Turkey. As is well known, the railroad was put into operation in 1888 although after its completion a considerable portion of the shares of the company that built it (*Betriebsgesellschaft der Orientalischen Eisenbahnen*) were bought by the Deutsche Bank so the Dual Monarchy could not really influence it. Despite the heavy-handed way Austria–Hungary dealt with the problem, this railroad connected the Balkan market and two of its most important harbors – Constantinople and Thessaloniki – with the European railroad network. In addition, it did not guarantee preferences for Austria–Hungary (Palotás 1980: 25–8; Palotás 1989: 596–607; *Österreichische Monatsschrift* 1880 (2): 25, 1880 (12): 195–6). Austro–Hungarian ambitions in railroad construction in the Balkans provoked numerous competing projects that might have impeded the Monarchy's expansion toward Thessaloniki, the most important among them being the Danube–Adriatic projects (May 1952).

These, however, were not realized because of the rivalry between the great powers.

The struggle over establishing Austro–Hungarian predominance in the Danube met with some success at the Berlin Congress (materialized in article 55 of the Berlin treaty) where the Dual Monarchy was allotted an active role in regulating and supervising navigation from the Iron gates to Galats. The promising plans ended in a total fiasco only five years later because of Romania's and Bulgaria's rejection (Palotás 1989: 607–9). The Ballhausplatz partly compensated for this failure through the regulations regarding navigation in nearly all commercial treaties with the Balkan states or through special conventions like those with Serbia (1882) or Bulgaria (1881).

Nevertheless the Dual Monarchy played an active role in navigation on the Danube. The k. k. privilegierte Donau–Dampfschiffahrts–Gesellschaft, established in 1829, maintained its supremacy in Danube navigation up to World War I due partly to the state subsidy it received (the payments were suspended only between 1871 and 1892). By 1878 it owned 193 steam ships and 699 barges. With its shipping fleet and capital stock fund in 1914, it ranked among the greatest river navigation companies in the world (Bachinger 1973: 308–10; *Österreichische Monatsschrift* 1880 (2): 3). Also influential on the Danube was the Hungarian River- and Sea-Navigation-Co. AG, which was founded in 1894 and enjoyed significant state financial aid. A similar example was the Austrian Lloyd Navigation Company, which operated on the Mediterranean, the Adriatic, and the Black Sea (*Österreichische Monatsschrift*, 1880 (6), 1882 (6, 7), 1904 (1), 1912 (12). The commercial traffic between the Balkans and the Dual Monarchy was served mainly by Austro–Hungarian companies such as Internationale Transport-Gesellschaft AG, Wien, AG Kohn & Mittler, Wien, and Internationale Transporte Schenker & Co.

In a similar way, Austria–Hungary contributed to the construction of infrastructure in the region. In the Ottoman empire the Habsburg Monarchy established its own postal administration to cater to its trade interests. By 1902 there were 38 Austro–Hungarian post offices in Turkey, which functioned well according to the annual report of the Austro–Hungarian Chamber of Commerce in Constantinople (*Österreichische Monatsschrift* 1904 (1). Upon gaining independence, Bulgaria took over the Austro–Hungarian post offices inherited from Turkey, after having joined the World Post Union in 1879 and the International Telegraph Convention in 1880 and presenting the Dual Monarchy with some assurances of regular and adequate services. Nevertheless the Bulgarian government concluded in 1881 a treaty with the Erste k.k. privilegierte Donau–Dampfschiffahrts–Gesellschaft AG in which both sides granted each other facilities for postal and navigation services (*Vanshnata politika* 1978: Nos. 41, 66, 89, 90). In this way the Dual Monarchy again assured preferential post services in Bulgaria for its subjects. Austria–Hungary also had special agreements on

Table 13.3 Trade balance of the Balkan countries with main trading partners, 1886–1911 (value in national currency, current prices)[a]

	Total	*Austria–Hungary*	*Germany*	*France*	*England*	*Belgium*	*Turkey*
Romania							
1883–5	−90,233	−59,623	−40,167	−8,815	+15,566	−725	−1,236
1886–90	−64,820	−40,940	−83,619	−8,460	+54,774	+11,606	−1,137
1891–5	−96,938	−58,970	−57,867	−24,582	+12,615	+38,366	−1,026
1896–1900	−74,666	−41,371	−77,429	−15,871	−17,590	+82,365	−1,306
1901–5	+61,728	−33,648	−59,624	−5,578	−19,328	+147,334	−885
1906–10	+92,335	−52,097	−107,634	+10,077	−13,281	+135,302	+8,826
1911	+121,975	−74,166	−150,789	+13,517	−29,615	+235,354	+7,447
Bulgaria							
1886–90	−8,162	−17,602	−2,968	+9,825	−10,540	−994[a]	+16,696
1891–5	−6,013	−27,045	+1,895	+12,193	−4,312	+563	+11,979
1896–1900	+548	−13,930	+424	+4,287	−442	+3,979	+10,169
1901–5	+25,015	−14,246	−3,540	+1,477	+3,032	+27,921	+9,880
1906–10	−21,613	−28,459	−9,653	−1,848	−8,991	+16,283	+13,308
1911	−14,711	−37,649	−16,925	−13,808	−5,797	+48,743	+13,224
Serbia							
1886–90	+884	+8,106	−1,286	+175	−3,908[b]	—	+1,150
1891–5	+10,627	+20,087	−1,906	−84	−4,420[c]	−344[c]	+296
1896–1900	+15,653	+27,566	−2,825	−921	—	−222[d]	−84
1901–5	+13,702	+26,207	−3,526	−1,030	−4,177[e]	+378	−136
1906–10	+14,697	−684	−2,346	+86	−7,576	+11,242	+9,419
1911	+1,491	+985	−2,414	+686	−9,437	—	+8,171

Table 13.3 Continued

	Total	*Austria–Hungary*	*Germany*	*France*	*England*	*Belgium*	*Turkey*
Greece							
1887–90	−23.0	−9.0	−1.5	+12.7	+16.4	—	−11.5
1891–5	−28.8	−8.4	−4.6	+1.4	−0.4	—	−9.2
1896–1900	−38.6	−6.4	−4.6	−2.6	−2.8	—	−7.0
1901–5	−51.8	−11.8	−5.6	−2.4	−6.2	—	−8.4
1906–10	−29.6	−6.8	−2.6	−0.4	−1.0	—	−6.8
1911	−33.0	−10.0	+3.0	+4.0	−7.0	—	−4.0
Turkey							
1886–90	−7,734	−2,904	+2	+1,640	−4,188	—	—
1891–5	−8,858	−3,359	+31	+1,161	−2,760	—	—
1896–1900	−9,132	−3,259	−14	+1,941	−3,458	—	—
1905–10	−12,024	−3,718	−924	+908	−3,608	—	—
1911	−20,476	−5,459	−2,590	+473	−3,110	−1,056	—

[a] Romania, thousands of leis; Bulgaria, thousands of levas; Serbia, thousands of dinars; Greece, millions of drachmas; Turkey, thousands of pounds.

Source: as Table 13.1.

Notes: [a] 1887–90 [b] 1888–90 [c] 1891–3 [d] 1889–1900 [e] 1901–4.

telegraph services with Romania and Serbia (*Österreichische Monatsschrift* 1912 (9); *Sapisnici* 1952: No. 864).

Yet Austria–Hungary's achievements in promoting trade with the Balkans through transport and postal facilities should not be overestimated. Despite the favorable geographic preconditions, the Dual Monarchy missed the chance to create an adequate and relatively cheap transport system that would have promoted trade inside its own territory, not to mention with Southeastern Europe (Bachinger 1973: 292–315; Macesich 1970: 27–8). On the other hand, improved transport facilities would have meant increasing foreign competition, especially from Germany, to the extent they made the Balkan market more accessible and reduced the transportation costs.

The exports of the Dual Monarchy remained relatively strong in Southeastern Europe even though the Monarchy was not a first-rate industrial power. To be sure, the Austro–Hungarian share in the total imports of the Balkan countries reveals a smooth downward trend (except for the tariff wars with Romania and Serbia when the decrease occurred abruptly), while the share of Germany rose. On the other hand, this trend should not be exaggerated. It is valid above all for Romania. But in the other Balkan countries, the Dual Monarchy remained ahead of Germany, especially in absolute terms. In any case, the relative strengthening of Germany's trade position in the Balkans still fell short of its greater level of economic development and its industrial growth compared with Austria–Hungary.

Along with some general theoretical explanations (Ohlin 1967, 170–1, 179–80, 196; Jones 1985: 130–224), there are also some other features of Austro–Hungarian trade in the Balkans that account for its strength. The most often emphasized explanations are the geographical proximity of the Dual Monarchy to the Balkans and the long tradition of commercial relations. But contemporaries stressed other factors as well. Austro–Hungarian importers observed the Balkan market rather carefully and reacted quickly to its changing demands. For this purpose they maintained regular contacts through a system of agents. For example, from the total of 183 licenses given by the Turkish government to foreign traveling sales agents in 1910, 89 were given to Austrians, 35 to Germans, and nine to Englishmen (Issawi 1980: 88). In addition, the Austro–Hungarian goods were usually cheaper than German, English, or French goods. Although sometimes they reflected lower quality, low prices were important because price was a decisive factor for the customers in this region. In this respect, Austro–Hungarian commodities, mainly consumer goods, were directed to a wider market, not only to the elite. This implies that the terms of trade with the Dual Monarchy were more favorable for the Balkan states than with other core countries.

Austro–Hungarian sales agents in Southeastern Europe had significant advantages over their English or French competitors with respect to supplying goods on trust by granting four, six, nine months, or even a year's grace in making payment. On the other hand, banks with Austro–Hungarian capital in the Balkan countries routinely offered short-term credit on foreign trade (Lampe and Jackson 1982: 228–9, 261–2). Some or all of these features of Austro–Hungarian trade in Southeastern Europe were emphasized by English and French contemporaries, especially diplomatic officials (Issawi 1980: 86–7; Damianov 1971).

CONCLUSION

The pattern of development before 1914 implies that foreign trade, although dynamic, did not cause any crucial upturn in the Balkan economies unlike in other peripheral countries such as Denmark or Hungary (Berend and Ránki 1980a: 566–70, 578–9). It was, however, one of the factors that brought them closer to the European path of development and integrated them more into the rest of the continent as World War I approached. Austro–Hungarian trade helped to activate competition, led to a decline of non-viable domestic handcrafts, and supplied raw materials and machinery for domestic industries whose output was insufficient to satisfy demand. Trade between Southeastern Europe and Austria–Hungary was accompanied by considerable tensions due to the strong agrarian protectionist policy of the Dual Monarchy, which harmed Balkan export interests, and to the close interrelation between trade and foreign policy (Matis 1971: 175; Preshlenova 1990, 1991). It appears that the deterioration of their commercial relations was mostly due to the non-economic factors that promoted the disintegration of the Habsburg Monarchy itself (Good 1984: 256). Nevertheless despite this generally unfavorable environment, commodity trade between them expanded except during the periods of tariff wars.

What are the implications of the Balkan experience before World War I for the current transformation in Central and Eastern Europe? The last four decades have divided the Southeastern European countries into countries with quite different economic systems and foreign orientation. Greece and Turkey retained their market economies and West European economic and political orientation. Romania, Bulgaria, Albania and to some extent former Yugoslavia adopted the Soviet central planning model and participated in the Council for Mutual Economic Assistance (CMEA), which to a high degree limited international economic relations outside the East bloc.

With the collapse of the Soviet empire the Balkan states face, at least in the short run, perhaps even greater economic difficulties than a century ago. Together with the other former East bloc countries (except for East Germany) they form a new periphery with little chance in the near future of participating in European economic integration. The prospects for them are much smaller than for Hungary, Poland, or the Czech Republic not only because of their poorer economic situation, but also because of the unstable political situation in former Yugoslavia, which recalls the image of the

Balkans as a powder-keg of Europe. Their foreign trade is faced with the legacy of the post-World War II decades – inconvertible currencies, stagnating production, growing inflation, remnants of the foreign trade patterns of centrally planned economies, and collapsed relations in the CMEA. They have to seek out new markets in a time of bad economic performance and protectionist trends in the European Community. A new version of the CMEA seems unlikely due to the negative sentiments against this form of forced cooperation. As an alternative they can strive to cooperate with more advanced partners who could be investors as well. The economic history of Southeastern Europe shows that foreign trade alone unaccompanied by adequate capital flows cannot promote a radical transformation in this region. Yet the same economic history also suggests a near-term strategy with two elements. One strategy is to specialize in non-competing production that could be allowed more easily into the protected European market. Of course it would require capital investment and the ability to respond to changing market demand. The other strategy is to cultivate, naturally on the basis of freely negotiated relations, the large, close-by, and less pretentious market of the former Soviet Union, which the Balkan states know better. They could play a role similar to that of Austro–Hungarian exporters in the Balkans a century ago.

NOTES

1 I do not use "core" and "periphery" in the sense of Immanuel Wallerstein or dependency theorists, but as convenient terms for describing regions at a high compared with a low level of economic development.

2 For a more detailed analysis see among others Lampe and Jackson (1982), Jackson and Lampe (1983), Lampe (1975), Berend and Ránki (1977, 1982), Ránki (1982), Damianov (1979), Gross (1937), *Istorie* (1979), Leonties (1971), *Ikonomika* (1989), Gerschenkron (1962), Aleku (1973), Voyatzis (1969), Pamuk (1987), Issawi (1980).

3 The state expenses for public debt and military purposes accounted in 1911 in Romania to 33 per cent of all expenses, 51 per cent in Serbia, 43 per cent in Bulgaria, 58 per cent in Greece. Estimated from data in Lampe and Jackson (1982: 234).

4 The average annual imports of agricultural machinery and tools increased as follows: 1886–90 – 199 tons; 1891–99 – 356 tons; 1900–05 – 551 tons; 1906–11 – 2,612 tons (*Ikonomika* 1989: 329). Even on the eve of the Balkan wars the ratio between imported and domestic machinery was more than 20:1 (*Ikonomika* 1989: 347).

5 Behind this figure stand impressive figures for some individual branches: electricity – 100 per cent; metals – 95 per cent; paper – 85.6 per cent; chemicals – 76 per cent; leather – 67 per cent; textiles – 62.2 per cent; mining – 42 per cent; ceramics – 41 per cent. Thus six of the eight industrial branches in the statistics relied on imports for over 50 per cent of raw materials. Estimated from data in *Statisticheski godishnik na Balgarskoto Tsarstvo 1911* (1914: 239).

6 The beginning of the "modern phase of industrialization" occurred between 1825 and 1830 first in Bohemia, the region around Vienna, and in Vorarlberg. These

regions did not lag behind the advanced Western European areas at that time – UK, Belgium, and the Rhineland – and kept pace with them (Komlos 1983: 90, 100, 109; Good 1984: 42–8, 238–41; Gross 1973: 28; Rudolph 1973: 243–4).

7 Growth impulses diffused gradually eastward into Hungary, and to some extent into eastern Austria (Galicia) as well, and affected both agriculture and industry. As a result, uneven development, at least in statistical terms, diminished. After 1870 agriculture grew faster (at an annual rate of 1.5 per cent) in Hungary than in Austria (1.3 per cent) as did industry (2.5 per cent in Austria against 3.0 per cent in Hungary) (Good, 1984: 240).

8 Good 1984: 240–1. The relative lagging of the Dual Monarchy behind the other great powers, with the exception of Russia and Italy in some respects, is evident from statistical data on GNP per capita, industrial output, and shares in European and world trade (Gross 1973: 18–27; Bairoch 1976: 77, 154–5).

9 Estimated from data in Láng (1906) and *Österreichisches statistisches Handbuch*.

10 Of a total 5,500 million crowns invested abroad by Austrians at the beginning of the twentieth century, 4,700 million was transferred to Hungary (Fink 1969: 125), i.e., over 85 per cent. In 1913 Austrian investments accounted for 44.3 per cent of the total capital invested in Hungary (estimated from data in Komlos 1983: 183). By contrast, the share of Austria–Hungary in foreign investment in the Balkans was low. Of the 1,250 million dollars invested in the Balkan countries, 100 million was British (mainly in Greece), 540 million was French, and 400 million was German. The remaining 210 million was split among Sweden, Belgium, Denmark, and Austria–Hungary (Berend and Ránki 1982: 82).

11 Eddie (1977: 354–5). The share of sales to Austria remained remarkably stable at around 73 per cent of the total Hungarian exports (Eddie 1977: 334), while imports from Austria fluctuated between 84 and 73 per cent of total Hungarian trade with a slight downward trend (Eddie 1977: 336). Overall Austria had a much greater share in the value of Hungarian trade – over 70 per cent – while the Hungarian share in Austrian trade constituted less than 40 per cent. The western parts of the Austrian half of the Dual Monarchy relied overwhelmingly on the outside world, although the share of over 80 per cent might be overstated (Eddie 1980: 232–1).

12 The average is, of course, only a crude measure because there were great discrepancies between the duties on the individual items.

13 Perhaps an exception here is Greece, whose tariffs of 1884 and revisions in 1892 were protectionist. They provided for import duties on some industrial articles on a basis of 22–30 per cent *ad valorem* (Aleku 1973: 45, 47).

14 With the great increase of world grain production from the 1870s to the end of the century, the price of wheat dropped by more than 50 per cent between 1871 and 1894. From the 1890s until 1914 prices tended to rise. Other grains entering Western European ports showed similar price trends. While meat prices also followed the general downward trend, they did not fall as sharply as grain prices (Woodruff 1973: 662).

15 Computed from the data underlying Table 13.1.

16 The main Austro-Hungarian export items in 1875–1910 were sugar, grain, coal and charcoal, iron, and ironware (Rudolph 1973: 232–4).

17 Estimated from data in Schwaighofer (1900: 232).

18 Estimated from data in Schwaighofer (1900: 224, Tables 1 and 2).

19 Estimated from data in Schwaighofer (1900: 229–31).

20 See also Pollard (1981: 226).

REFERENCES

Aleku, P. (1973) "Zur Entwicklung des Kapitalismus in Griechenland bis zum Zweiten Weltkrieg," *Jahrbuch für Wirtschaftsgeschichte*, 2.

Aleksić-Peiković. L. (1965) *Odnosi Srbie sa Frantsuskom i Engleskom 1903–1914* (Serbia's Relations with France and England 1903–1914), Belgrade.

Antonescu, C.G. (1915) *Die rumänische Handelspolitik von 1875–1910*, Leipzig.

Bachinger, K. (1973) "Das Verkehrswesen," in A. Brusatti. (ed.) *Die Habsburgermonarchie 1848–1918*. I: *Die wirtschaftliche Entwicklung*, Vienna.

Bairoch, P. (1973a) "European foreign trade in the XIX Century: The development of the value and volume of exports (preliminary results)," *The Journal of European Economic History*, 2.

Bairoch, P. (1973b) *Commerce exterieur et dévelopment économique de l'Europe au XIX siècle*, Paris: La Haye.

Bairoch, P. (1976) "Europe's gross national product: 1800–1975," *Journal of European Economic History*, 5: 273–340.

Battaglia, R. (1917) *Ein Zoll- und Wirtschaftsbündnis zwischen Österreich-Ungarn und Deutschland*, Vienna, Leipzig.

Bazant J.v. (1894) *Die Handelspolitik Österreich-Ungarns 1875 bis 1892 in ihrem Verhältnis zum Deutschen Reiche und zu dem westlichen Europa*, Leipzig.

Berend, I.T. and Ránki, G. (1977) *East Central Europe in the 19th and 20th Centuries*, Budapest.

Berend, I.T. and Ránki, G. (1980a) "Underdevelopment in Europe in perspective of East–West relations in XIX century," in *XV-eme Congres international des sciences historiques. Rapports* III, Bucharest.

Berend, I.T. and Ránki, G. (1980b) "Foreign trade and the industrialization of the European periphery in the XIXth century," *The Journal of European Economic History*, 9: 539–84.

Berend, I.T. and Ránki, G. (1982) *The European Periphery and Industrialization*, Budapest.

Berov, L. (1985) "The effect of the West European economy on the market conditions in the Balkan countries in the 19th and the early 20th C," *Etudes balkaniques*, 1.

Bindreiter, U. (1976) *Die diplomatischen und wirtschaftlichen Beziehungen zwischen Österreich-Ungarn und Rumänien in den Jahren 1875–1888*. Vienna, Graz, Cologne.

Black, C.E. (1966) *The Dynamics of Modernization. A Study in Comparative History*, New York, London.

Bridge, F.R. (1972) *From Sadowa to Sarajevo. The Foreign Policy of Austria–Hungary 1866–1914*, London, Boston.

Brusatti, A. (1967) "Die wirtschaftlichen Folgen des Ausgleichs von 1867," in *Der österreichisch-ungarische Ausgleich von 1867*, Vienna, Munich.

Carlgren, W.M. (1955) *Iswolsky und Aahrenthal vor der bosnischen Annexionskrise*, Upsala.

Comerciul exterior al Romaniei in 1812 . . . 1912 (1893–1915), Bucharest.

Crampton, R.J. (1989) "Modernization: Conscious, unconscious and irrational," in R. Schoenfeld (ed.) *Industrialisierung und gesellschaftlicher Wandel in Südosteuropa*, Munich.

Damianov, S. (1971) *Frenskoto ikonomichesko pronikvane v Balgaria. Ot osvoboshdenieto do Parvata svetovna voina (1878–1914)* [The French Economic Penetration in Bulgaria. From the Liberation to the First World War], Sofia.

Damianov, S. (1979) "Sur le dévelopment industriel du sud-est européen a la fin du XIX et du XXe siècles," *Etudes balkaniques*, 4.

Diószegi, I. (1970) "Die österreichisch–ungarische Monarchie in der internationalen Politik im letzten Drittel des 19. Jahrhunderts," in *Etudes historiques*, I, Budapest.

Djordjević, D. (1962) *Tsarinski rat Austro-Ugarske i Srbie 1906–1911* [The Tariff War of Austria–Hungary and Serbia 1906–1911], Belgrade.

Eddie, S.M. (1977) "The terms and patterns of Hungarian foreign trade, 1882–1913," *The Journal of Economic History*, 37: 2.

Eddie, S.M. (1980) "Austria in the Dual Monarchy: Her trade within and without the customs union," *East Central Europe*, 7, 2.

Fellner, F. (1960) *Der Dreibund. Europäische Diplomatie vor dem ersten Weltkrieg*, Munich.

Fink, K.M. (1968) *Die Österreichisch-ungarische Monarchie als Wirtschaftsgemeinschaft*, Munich.

Fink, K. (1969) "Spezielle Aspekte der Wirtschafts- und Sozialentwicklung seit der Jahrhundertwende in Ungarn," in *Wirtschaftliche und soziale Entwicklung Südosteuropas im 19. und 20. Jahrhundert*, Munich.

Galanter, M. (1966) "The modernization of law," in M. Weiner (ed.) *Modernization. The Dynamics of Growth*, New York.

Gerschenkron, A. (1962) *Economic Backwardness in Historical Perspective*, Cambridge.

Good, D.F. (1984) *The Economic Rise of the Habsburg Empire 1750–1914*, Berkeley, Los Angeles, London.

Gross, H. (1937) "Südosteuropa. Bau und Entwicklung der Wirtschaft," *Beihefte zur Leipziger Vierteljahrsschrift für Südosteuropa*, I.

Gross, H. (1962) "Mitteleuropäische Handelspolitik 1890–1938 und der Donauraum," *Der Donauraum*, 2–3.

Gross, N.T. (1973) "Die Stellung der Habsburgermonarchie in der Weltwirtschaft," in A. Brusatti (ed.) *Die Habsburgermonarchie 1848–1918*. I. *Die wirtschaftliche Entwicklung*, Vienna.

Grünberg, K. (1902) *Die handelspolitischen Beziehungen Österreich-Ungarns zu den Ländern an der Unteren Donau*, Leipzig.

Grunzel, J. (1892) *Die Handelsbeziehungen Österreich-Ungarns zu den Balkanländern*, Vienna

Grunzel, J. (1901) "Die handelspolitischen Beziehungen Deutschlands und Österreichs," in *Beiträge zur neuesten Handelspolitik Österreichs*, Leipzig.

Grunzel, J. (1906) *System der Handelspolitik*, Leipzig.

(HHStA) *Haus-, Hof- und Staatsarchiv*, Administrative Registratur, F.34, K.78, F.37, K.74.

Hitrova, N.I. (1963) "K voprosu ob ekonomicheskom rasvitii Chernogorii v kontse XIX i nachale XX veka" [To the Question of the Economic Development Montenegro's in the Late XIX and Early XX C], *Ucheonie zapiski instituta slavianovedenia*, XXVI.

Ikonomika na Balgaria do sotsialisticheskata revoliutsia [Economy of Bulgaria till the Socialist Revolution], (1989) L. Berov (ed.), Sofia

Issawi, C. (1980) *The Economic History of Turkey 1800–1914*, Chicago, London.

Istoria na finansovata i kreditnata sistema na Balgaria [History of the Financial and Credit System of Bulgaria], (1983) 2, Varna.

Istorie economica [Economic History]. (1979) Bucharest.

Jackson, M.R. and Lampe, J.R. (1983) "The evidence of industrial growth in Southeastern Europe before the Second World War," *East European Quarterly*, 16: 4.

Janos, A.C. (1989). "The politics of backwardness in continental Europe, 1780–1945," *World Politics*, 41: 3.

Jelavich, B. (1969) *The Habsburg Empire in European Affairs, 1814–1918*, Chicago.

Jinga, V. (1975) *Principii si orientari ale comertului exterior al Romaniei (1859–1916)* [Principles and orientation of the foreign trade of Roumania 1859–1916], Cluj-Napoca.

Jones, R.A. (1985) *International Trade Theories and the Evolving International Economy*, London.

Komlos, J. (1983). *Habsburg Monarchy as a Customs Union. Economic Development in Austria–Hungary in the Nineteenth Century*, Princeton, NJ.

Kuznets, S. (1966) *Modern Economic Growth. Rate, Structure and Spread*, New Haven, London.

Lampe, J.R. (1975) "Varieties of unsuccessful industrialization: The Balkan states before 1914," *The Journal of Economic History*, 35: 56–85.

Lampe, J.R. (1989) "Imperial borderlands or capitalist periphery? Redefining Balkan backwardness, 1520–1914," in D. Chirot (ed.) *The Origins of Backwardness in Eastern Europe*, Berkeley, Los Angeles, Oxford, 177–209.

Lampe, J.R. and Jackson, M.R. (1982) *Balkan Economic History, 1550–1950. From Imperial Borderlands to Developing Nations*, Bloomington.

Láng, L. (1906) *Hundert Jahre Zollpolitik, 1805–1905*, Vienna, Leipzig.

Leonties, D. (1971) "Die Industrialisierung Rumäniens bis zum Zweiten Weltkrieg," *Acta scientarium socialim* IV, Monachii.

Macesich, G. (1970) "Theory of economic integration and experience of the Balkan and Danubian countries before 1914," in *Actes du premier congress international des etudes balkaniques et sud-est europeennes*, V, Sofia.

Marchet, G. (1901) "Internationale Veterinärkonventionen," in *Beiträge zur neuesten Handelspolitik Österreichs*, Leipzig.

Matis, H. (1971) "Die Wirtschaft der Franzisko-Josephinischen Epoche," in *Die Wirtschaftsgeschichte Österreichs*, Vienna.

Matlekovits, A.v. (1891) *Die Zollpolitik der österreichisch-ungarischen Monarchie und des deutschen Reiches seit 1868 und deren nächste Zukunft*, Leipzig.

Matlekovits, A.v. (1901) "Die handelspolitischen Interessen Ungarns," in *Beiträge zur neuesten Handelspolitik Österreichs*, Leipzig.

May, A. (1952) "Trans-Balkan railway schemes," *Journal of Modern History*, 4.

McCartey, J. (1982) *The Arab World, Turkey and the Balkans (1878–1914): A Handbook of Historical Statistics*, Boston.

Mikić, D. (1983) *Austro–Ugarska i mladoturtsi 1908–1912* (Austria–Hungary and the Young-Turks 1908–1912), Banjaluka.

Mitchell, B. (1981) *European Historical Statistics: 1750–1975*, London.

Müller, I. (1979) Die Handelspolitik der österreichisch-ungarischen Monarchie am Balkan zwischen 1890 und 1914. Unpublished dissertation, Vienna.

Nebioglu, O. (1941) *Die Auswirkungen der Kapitulationen auf die türkische Wirtschaft*, Jena.

Nestorović, I. (1913) *Der Aussenhandel Serbiens*, Leipzig.

Novichev, A. (1937) *Ocherki ekonomiki Turtsii do mirovoi voinoi* [Outline of the Economy of Turkey till World War], Moskva, Leningrad.

Ohlin, B. (1967) *Interregional and International Trade*, Cambridge.

Österreichische Monatsschrift für den Orient (1880, 1882, 1904, 1912).

Österreichisches statistisches Handbuch für die im Reichstrat vertretenen Königreiche und Länder 1914 (1916), Vienna.

Palotás, E. (1980) "Ziele und geschichtliche Realität. Wirtschaftsbestrebungen Österreich-Ungarns zur Zeit des Berliner Kongresses im Jahre 1878," *Etudes historiques hongroises*, I.

Palotás, E. (1989) "Die aussenwirtschaftlichen Beziehungen zum Balkan und zu Russland," in *Die Habsburgermonarchie 1848–1918*, VI. *Die Habsburgermonarchie im System der internationalen Beziehungen*, 1. Teil, Vienna.

Palotás, E. (1991) "Die Rolle der Wirtschaftsbeziehungen zwischen Österreich-Ungarn und den Balkanländern in den letzten Jahren des 19. Jahrhunderts," in *Wirtschafts- und Kulturbeziehungen zwischen dem Donau- und dem Balkanraum seit dem Wiener Kongress*, Graz.

Pamuk, S. (1987) *The Ottoman Empire and European Capitalism, 1820–1913. Trade, Investment and Production*, Cambridge.

Paulinyi. A. (1973) "Die sogenannte gemeinsame Wirtschaftspolitik in Österreich-Ungarn," in A. Brusatti (ed.) *Die Habsburgermonarchie 1848–1918*. I. *Die wirtschaftliche Entwicklung*, Vienna.

Peez, A. (1892) "Die österreichische Handelspolitik der letzten fünfundzwanzig Jahre," in *Die Handelspolitik Nordamerikas, Italiens, Österreichs*, Leipzig.

Petrosian, J. (1976) "Die Ideen der 'Europäisierung' in dem sozial-politischen Leben des Osmanischen Reiches in der Neuzeit (Ende des 18. Anfang des 20. Jh.)," in *La revolution industrielle dans le sud-est européen*, XIX e, Sofia.

Pollard, S. (1981) *Peaceful Conquest. The Industrialization of Europe 1760–1970*, Oxford.

Preshlenova, R. (1989) *Targoviata na Avstro-Ungaria s Balkanskite strani v kraya na XIX i nachaloto na XX vek* [*Austro-Hungary's trade with the Balkan countries in the late 19th and early 20th C*], Unpublished dissertation, Sofia.

Preshlenova, R. (1990) "Protektionismus und die Handelsbeziehungen zwischen den Balkanstaaten und Österreich-Ungarn Ende des XIX. und Anfang des XX. Jahrhunderts," *Etudes balkaniques*, 2.

Preshlenova, R. 1991. "Probleme der Handelsbeziehungen Österreich-Ungarns zu den Balkanstaaten am Ende des 19. und Anfang des 20. Jahrhunderts," in *Wirtschafts- und Kulturbeziehungen zwischen dem Donau- und dem Balkanraum seit dem Wiener Kongress*, Graz.

Ránki, G. (1982) "Die ökonomische Entwicklung auf dem Balkan in den 1870er Jahren. Die ersten Wirkungen der westlichen industriellen Revolution," in R. Melville and H.-J. Schröder (eds.) *Der Berliner Kongress von 1878. Die Politik der Großmächte und die Probleme der Modernisierung in Südosteuropa in der zweiten Hälfte des 19. Jahrhunderts*, Wiesbaden.

Rudolph, R.L. (1973) "Quantitative Aspekte der Industrialisierung in Cisleithanien 1848–1914," in A. Brusatti (ed.) *Die Habsburgermonarchie 1848–1918*. I. *Die wirtschaftliche Entwicklung*, Vienna.

Sapisnici sednica Ministarskog saveta Srbije 1862–1898 [*Records of the Sessions of the Serbian Government 1862–1898*]. (1952) Belgrade.

Schwaighofer, W. (1900) "Österreich-Ungarn und der Orienthandel," *Statistische Monatsschrift*, April.

Sieveking, H. (1905) *Auswärtige Handelspolitik*, Leipzig.

Sosnosky, T.v. (1914) *Die Balkanpolitik Österreich-Ungarns seit 1866*, Stuttgart, Berlin.

Statisticheski Godishnik na Balgarskoto Tsartsvo (1909, 1911, 1913–22, 1910, 1914, 1924), Sofia.

Statistika za targoviata na Balgarskoto Kniashestvo za 1887–1898, (1889–1899), Sofia.

Stokes, G. (1980) "Dependency and the rise of nationalism in Southeast Europe," *International Journal of Turkish Studies*, I.

Stojanoff, A. (1914) *Die handelspolitische Situation der Balkanstaaten gegenüber Österreich-Ungarn*, Vienna.

Sugar, P.F. (1976) "Some thoughts on the pre-conditions of modernization and their applicability to the European provinces of the Ottoman empire," in *La revolution industrielle dans le sud-est européen XIXe*, Sofia.

Sundhaussen, H. (1989) *Historische Statistik Serbiens 1834–1914. Mit europäischen Vergleichsdaten*, Munich.

Suter, E. (1930) *Die handelspolitische Kooperation des Deutschen Reiches und der Donaumonarchie 1890–1894*, Marburg.

Svrakov, G.K. (1935–1936) "Balgarskata mitnishka tarifa za vnosnite stoki v neinoto razvitie" [The Bulgarian import tariff in development]. *Godishnik na vissheto targovsko uchilishte Varna*, IX.

Tamborra, A. (1986) *Studii storici sull' Europa orientale*, Rome.

Tipps, D.C. (1973) "Modernization theory and the comparative study of societies: A critical perspective," *Comparative Studies in the Society and History*, 15:2.

Vanshnata politika na Balgaria. [The Foreign Policy of Bulgaria]: (1978) I: 1879–1886, Sofia.

Voyatzis, B. (1969) "Spezielle Aspekte der Wirtschafts- und Sozialentwicklung in Griechenland seit der Jahrhundertwende," in *Wirtschaftliche und soziale Entwicklung Südosteuropas im 19. und 20. Jahrhundert*, Munich.

Woodruff, W. (1973) "The emergence of an international economy 1700–1914," in C.M. Cipolla (ed.) *The Fontana Economic History of Europe*, 4 (2). *The Emergence of Industrial Societies*, London, Glasgow.

14

BETWEEN POLITICAL DISINTEGRATION AND ECONOMIC REINTEGRATION

Austrian trade relations with the successor states after World War I

Jürgen Nautz

The defeat of the Central Powers in World War I and the following peace treaties drastically changed the political map of Central and Southeastern Europe, but the peace treaties of Versailles, Saint Germain, Sevres, and Trianon did not succeed in reorganizing the European system of states. It is symptomatic that the unsolved problems and the unstable areas were to be found primarily in those critical regions that needed a new order most urgently. Their "first steps to new sovereignty sometimes had desperately small chances of development and depended for their existence upon the insecurity, relics and atmosphere of the war being replaced by orderly new foundations and an internationally sanctioned consolidation" (Krüger 1985: 6ff.). The critical regions were situated where dangers to the peaceful order of Europe traditionally started and also where as a result of the collapse, the great powers who had previously been dominant, had become extremely unpredictable.

That the allies were unable to bring about peaceful affairs in Europe in the shortest time possible was initially due to the revisionist endeavors of the defeated states. In the immediate post-war years, the most important prerequisites for a stable European system of states were often lacking. Thus the situation remained unstable in spite of the many issues that were solved at the peace conferences. The prevailing nationalism and the failure to establish basic rules for economic relations delayed peace on the continent.

In Krüger's judgment, the example of Austria and the successor states shows that the allied policy of restoring order achieved at best only limited results when "it should have been a priority to direct all possible energy towards the political and economic order" (Krüger 1985: 8). Rumpler has argued that the basic foreign policy problem of the new Austrian Republic was its almost complete isolation and the fact that no – or only incomplete plans – had been developed to overcome this. European politics, as coordinated by Western Europe, Italy, and the successor states had created an independent state, according to Rumpler, that was then not given the consistent support it needed to preserve its independence (Rumpler 1983). If Krüger is right that the peace settlements of Paris remained problematical, Rumpler's view must be questioned in several respects. In reality, the Austrian government was able to enter negotiations with the allies and the successor states very early after the armistice in 1918 on economic and financial matters and on the role of these states in supporting Austria with foodstuffs, raw material, and energy (Fellner 1983: 90; Karner 1981; Šorn 1981). Until recently the bad effects of the economic disintegration of the Monarchy have been overestimated. Teichova (1989: 237) has rightly argued that historical research often underestimates the degree to which economic unity continued even in face of political fragmentation. What economic impact did the political reorganization of states in the area of the Danubian Monarchy have? Was Austria really so isolated after the war? Did the old economic ties really break? Did the political uncoupling of the states of the former Monarchy lead to a break in trade relations?

THE DEVELOPMENT OF THE AUSTRIAN BALANCE OF TRADE

After the war the Austrian economy was faced with a greatly reduced domestic market. The traditional economic structure meant that a large proportion of production had to be exported in order to guarantee survival. The same was true for Czechoslovakia, which was home to more than half of all the former Monarchy's industrial capacity. The increase in the importance of foreign trade was inopportune because foreign trade initiatives as a whole had reached a nadir. In 1922 the level of trade of the European states was still between 15 per cent and 20 per cent below that of the last pre-war year. Only the USA increased foreign trade, perhaps by one-third (Pinder 1986: 380).

On the other side of the trade balance, Austria had depended to a significant extent upon imports to supply food, raw material, and energy needs. Agriculture's high degree of foreign dependence was partly a result of the war and partly due to antiquated agricultural methods, which kept down yields. The dependency upon coal and other kinds of fuel imports also influenced foreign trade. In addition, almost all the demand for raw materials for textiles, metals, and rubber had to be met with imports (Bachinger and Hemertsberger-Koller 1987: 539ff.; Butschek 1985: 31; *Der Außenhandel Österreichs* 1946: 36–72). As a consequence, the Republic's balance of trade was in deficit from the start, which is shown by data from the Austrian Central Statistical Office in Table 14.1.

Table 14.1 The development of the Austrian balance of trade from 1920–37 (schillings)

Year	*Imports*	*Exports*	*Deficit*
1920	2,453.9	1,347.7	1,106.2
1921	2,448.4	1,302.0	1,146.4
1922	2,530.5	1,589.3	941.2
1923	2,768.0	1,615.6	1,152.4
1924	3,448.0	1,970.0	1,478.0
1925	2,891.4	1,922.8	968.6
1926	2,766.0	1,703.1	1,062.9
1927	3,088.5	2,036.8	1,051.7
1928	3,239.2	2,208.2	1,031.0
1929	3,262.6	2,188.5	1,074.1
1930	2,699.1	1,851.4	847.7
1931	2,161.4	1,291.1	870.3
1932	1,383.5	764.4	619.1
1933	1,149.2	772.6	376.6
1934	1,152.8	857.0	295.8
1935	1,206.2	895.0	311.2
1936	1,249.2	951.0	298.2
1937	1,453.7	1,216.9	236.8
1938	1,307.2	785.9	521.3

Außenhandel Österreichs (1946: 20); parity: 1 goldcrown = 1.44 schilling.

Figures for 1938 (excluding the old Reich): *Monatsberichte des Wiener Instituts für Wirtschafts- und Konjunkturforschung* (13 January 1939: 85). Exchange rate: 1 Reichsmark = 2.17 Austrian schillings.

THE REGIONAL DISTRIBUTION OF AUSTRIAN FOREIGN TRADE

Both contemporaries and later scholars hold that Austrian exports were badly hurt by the restrictive foreign trade policies of the successor states (Kluge 1988: 34ff.; Kerekes 1979: 62ff.; Stadtler 1968; Wessely 1970). The figures for the regional distribution of Austrian foreign trade argue against this view. In the years until 1922 the share of the successor states in Austrian foreign trade did not fall dramatically. For the first months after World War I the only available figures are those of the Austrian *Warenverkehrsbüro*[1] (Foreign Trade Office), which show the value of export permits for industrial articles issued by the trade office within the framework of existing compensation agreements. The records of the Warenverkehrsbüro, which are quoted in a study by the Viennese Chamber of Commerce import and export traffic between Austria and the successor states for the period between 1 December 1918 until 21 January 1921, reveal the pattern shown in Table 14.2.

Table 14.2 Values of imports and exports in the period 1 December 1918–21 January 1921 in millions of crowns which were transacted via the Warenverkehrsbüro

Land	*Imports*	*Exports*
Total	5,703	11,668
Yugoslavia	2,560	3,680
Czechoslovakia	1,567	1,301
Hungary	702	2,047
Poland	533	1,542
Italy	203	382
Romania	138	2,716

Source: *Exportberichte der Kammer für Handel, Gewerbe und Industrie in Wien*, Bericht No. 22, 27. Jänner (1921) Beilage 1, in *Archiv der Republic Wien*, HM 3015.

The first published trade statistics of the Republic of Austria show that in the second half of 1919 the percentage of Austrian imports from the successor states was 55 per cent, or 50.2 per cent excluding Italy. The share of Germany was 34.1 per cent. The percentage of imports from the successor states remained relatively constant until 1922, while at the same time the share of Germany fell by just under 12 percentage points. Among the successor states, the share of Czechozlovakia in imports fell by 16 percentage points between 1919 and 1922 after having risen by 41 per cent in 1921. In this period there was a clear increase in the shares of Romania (by 2.4 percentage points) and Hungary (by 8.9 percentage points). Yugoslavia's share increased by 1.3 percentage points and that of Poland by 2.4 percentage points. In the case of Hungary a clear increase in the import of foodstuffs lies behind the change. In 1919 just under 68 per cent of exports, or 37.5 per cent (without Italy) was accounted for by the successor states, 21.5 per cent by Germany. The percentage of Austrian exports going to Germany fell just under 7 percentage points by 1922. The changes within the successor states are illuminating. The share of the successor states in Austrian exports fell significantly due to the 20 percentage point fall in Italy's share and the 13 percentage point reduction in Czechoslovakia's share. On the other hand, the proportion of exports to the other successor states greatly increased: Poland by 4.4 percentage points, Romania by 4.5, Yugoslavia by 9.0, Hungary by 8.7. Thus excluding Italy, the share of the successor states in Austrian exports increased by 13.8 percentage points (Nautz 1994: 130).

One explanation for the increasing share is the legal regulation of trade relations, which helped Austria to export output that could not be fully utilized by Austrian industry as a result of shortages of raw materials and energy. But the shift in export shares may have other causes, e.g., the

Table 14.3 Destination of Austrian foreign trade 1919–41 (%)

A: Imports 1919–39					
Country	*1919*	*1924*	*1929*	*1933*	*1939*
Germany	34.10	14.90	21.00	18.70	—
Switzerland	1.18	5.60	4.40	3.30	3.40
France	0.05	2.30	2.70	2.40	1.70
Great Britain	0.32	2.80	2.80	2.90	3.40
USA	1.10	5.50	6.00	5.20	5.40
Italy	4.75	7.20	3.60	4.20	7.60
Poland	5.10	4.70	8.80	6.40	3.90
Romania	0.10	1.70	3.80	4.50	10.00
Yugoslavia	3.12	4.10	4.00	8.90	6.80
Czechoslovakia	39.67	22.60	18.10	18.60	8.00
Hungary	2.22	11.70	9.90	11.30	18.00
Successor states	54.96	52.00	48.20	53.90	54.30
Without Italy	50.21	44.80	44.60	49.70	46.70

B: Exports 1919–39					
Country	*1919*	*1924*	*1929*	*1933*	*1939*
Germany	21.50	13.10	15.70	15.20	—
Switzerland	6.86	6.60	5.70	8.10	5.00
France	0.13	2.50	3.40	4.00	2.50
Great Britain	0.03	4.30	4.50	4.30	7.20
USA	2.09	2.10	3.40	2.30	4.60
Italy	30.30	10.10	9.00	10.70	9.80
Poland	4.76	9.70	4.80	3,80	4.70
Romania	1.94	2.50	5.10	5.60	7.30
Yugoslavia	3.45	10.30	7.70	7.00	7.70
Czechoslovakia	23.13	11.00	13.50	7.80	7.00
Hungary	4.22	8.80	7.50	10.00	9.40
Successor states	67.80	52.40	47.60	44.90	45.40
Without Italy	37.50	42.30	38.60	34.20	35.60

Sources:
1919: Statistische Übersichten (1919).
1924–33: *Außenhandel Österreichs* (1946) 31ff.
1939: *Monatsberichte der Wiener Institutes für Konjunkturforschung* (1939) 191.
1919: only second half of year. As the figures given by official statistics which have been published for the second half of 1919 only slightly differ from those of the whole of 1920, one may presume that those for the whole of 1919 would not be significantly different.
1939: January–March.

currency devaluations that occurred in nearly all these states after the war (Nautz 1994: 162ff.).

The integration of Austria within the area of the former Danubian Monarchy continued to be very strong after the currency stabilization. Official statistics show that the share of the successor states in Austrian trade fell, but was still substantial in the 1930s.[2] According to Table 14.3, Austrian ties with the successor states remained considerably stronger than with Germany throughout the whole period from 1918 to 1938 (see Stiefel 1988: 313ff., and for 1928 Karner *et al.* 1987). The share of exports to Western Europe (Belgium, France, Great Britain, the Netherlands, and Switzerland) increased from 15.8 per cent to 18 per cent. The share of "others" rose from 12.1 per cent to 18.7 per cent. In 1923 12.7 per cent of Austrian goods were exported to Germany, in 1937 it rose slightly to 14.8 per cent. From these data, it can be inferred that the share of the successor states in Austrian exports did indeed fall, but that there was no serious shift in favor of Western Europe, let alone Germany. In 1923 Austria imported goods worth 431.3 million schilling (15.6 per cent) from the West European states of Belgium, France, Great Britain, the Netherlands, and Switzerland. In 1929 the figure was 393.7 million (12.1 per cent) and in 1937 it was 208.4 million or 14.3 per cent (*Außenhandel Österreichs*, 1946: 82ff.).

The annexation of Austria by Germany had to lead to a shift in regional patterns of foreign trade. First of all Austria's trade with Germany (14.8 per cent of exports and 16.1 per cent of imports in 1937) disappeared from the balance of payments and became domestic trade. Germany was greatly interested in increasing the flow of goods for its war economy that did not have to be paid for in foreign currency, so trade barriers between Austria and Germany were quickly abolished. For 1938 Felix Butschek (1985, 62) estimates a tripling of the real flow of goods from Austria to the Reich compared with 1937. By comparison, exports to third world countries fell after the third quarter of 1938. Statistics for 1939 show that the annual average was 24 per cent below that of the previous year. In 1938 the export share of those countries with which the Reich already had intensive trade relations, namely Southeastern Europe and overseas, increased while exports to Central and Western Europe decreased. Preliminary data for the period from January to March 1941 (Table 14.4) show that the successor states were still among the most important trading partners for the Austrian part of Greater Germany.

AUSTRIAN TRADE POLICY AFTER THE DISMEMBERMENT OF THE HABSBURG MONARCHY

After World War I, the new government had to confront grave problems resulting from the war and its consequences. The widespread crisis in supplies accompanied by the revolutionary events of the immediate post-war period made it appear to those responsible that the most important goal should be domestic stabilization (Haas 1989: 11ff.). A most important precondition for the consolidation of the new democratic order and of the state in general was mastering the food shortages. To get domestic production started again the energy crisis and the shortage of raw materials also had to be overcome (Stiefel 1978: 13ff.; Butschek 1985: 28ff.). In addition to these problems the state suffered from increasing financial difficulties. The economic difficulties not only provided fertile ground for revolutionary social and political movements, but also the dynamite that threatened to destroy the republic from within. Provincial particularism and the willingness of individual provinces to secede from Austria took on a threatening intensity (Goldinger 1954; Haas 1989; Teichova 1989: 125; Bachinger 1981: 139ff.; Kernbauer and Weber 1984; Jedlicka 1970).

These domestic problems presented Austrian foreign policy with clear, short-term tasks: to surmount shortages, above all in supplies of food and energy, and to procure the means, mainly through foreign loans, for financing the functions of state and necessary imports. In addition to these most urgent tasks the Republic's foreign policy had to be directed so that the state could obtain some elbow room in international affairs. To achieve this, three

Table 14.4 Destination of Austrian exports January–March 1941 in 1,000 Reichsmark

Countries	*Value*	*Shares (%)*
Italy	13.346	20.17
Hungary	8.189	12.37
Yugoslavia	7.975	12.05
Romania	6.762	10.22
Netherlands	4.622	6.98
Slovakia	3.427	5.18
USSR	2.410	3.64
Switzerland	2.260	3.41
France	1.931	2.92
Generalgouvernement	1.674	2.53
Great Britain	—	—
USA	—	—
Total		
Successor states	39.699	59.99
Total exports	66.179	100.00

Source: *Spezialausfuhr nach Herstellungsbezirken* (January 1941–June 1941). Ausgearbeitet vom Statistischen Reichsamt, Berlin, versendet von der Reichswirtschaftskammer, Außenhandelstelle Wien, Akt-Zahl 27.249/41, in Archiv der Handelskammer Wien, IV.6285.

tasks had to be carried out satisfactorily: to put Austria's relations with the victorious allied powers on a new basis and prepare for peace negotiations, to clarify Austria's relationship with its World War I ally Germany, and to re-order its position *vis-à-vis* the other successor states in the Danubian basin (Verosta 1983).[3]

For the first few months after the armistice, Austrian foreign policy was dominated by the issue of Anschluß, i.e., unification with Germany. This was backed above all by the Social Democrats and German nationalist forces (Low 1974; Schausberger 1978) while within Christian Social party (Goldinger 1954: 95; sächsische Gesandtschaft) and business circles[4] it had much cooler support. The Social Democrats – especially the wing represented by Otto Bauer – regarded the *Anschlußpolitik* as a suitable means for achieving domestic political aims. They believed that attachment to Germany would help reduce the economic and financial crises to a bearable level. More importantly, they believed that dependency on social democratically ruled Germany would help them achieve their social and economic–political goals in Austria (Low 1974; Haas 1989).

This hope soon proved to be misguided. The German leadership was not in a position to give effective economic aid and the allied and associated states were not prepared to accept the absorption of Austria into Germany. The increasing gravity of the food and energy crises alone made a turn towards the allies necessary, as only they could help secure the physical needs of the population and establish a democratic order (Haas 1989; Schausberger 1978).

Turning towards the allies and distancing itself from Germany allowed Austria to move relations with the other successor states more strongly into the political arena. In this context, trade policy became more important. Since the armistice, the government in Vienna had been making efforts to prevent economic relations with the new states from breaking off. With the help of compensation agreements, Austria managed, at great effort, to take the first steps towards building economic relations on the basis of the new political circumstances. Turning to the successor states enjoyed the special support of Austrian industry and commerce, which viewed their old markets as the best chance for making a successful new start after the war.[5] Representatives of trade and industry were not proponents of the idea that the new Austria lacked viability.[6] For trade and industry, easing foreign trade and creating larger economic areas, although not through annexation by Germany, were the decisive interests (Nautz 1994: 70ff).

Contemporaries and some later scholars repeatedly argued that the successor states hindered trade for nationalist, political reasons and had thus plunged Austria into grave difficulties (Berl 1923: 5; Gruntzel 1918; Riedl 1919; Rumpler 1983). According to one of the dominant theories, the nationalism of the governments in Eastern and Southeastern Europe was essentially economic in nature (Bachinger 1981, 173). Although the impact of economic nationalism should not be underrated, a large part of the difficulties in trade among the states was due to general economic difficulties that were a direct consequence of war exhaustion, which had been felt clearly before the breakup of the Monarchy.

During the discussions on Anschluß and while efforts to obtain aid deliveries were underway, Austria tried intensively to rebuild trade relations with the successor states. In the period before the peace negotiations started and the Anschluß negotiations broke off, Austria and the successor states agreed on a large number of compensation treaties. Fellner (1983: 90) has correctly argued that available source material does not support the oft-repeated theory that Austria was deliberately isolated in the period between the armistice and the signing of the peace treaty. The compensation deals received much attention in the negotiations on financial and economic questions. In the first few months, the deals served mainly to regulate the exchange of goods. With the passing of time they increasingly became instruments for establishing regular trade relations and for normalizing Austria's political relations with the other successor states. In some provinces the compensation deals actually contributed significantly to surmounting the supply and distribution crises (for Carinthia see Karner 1981). Thus the relevant Vienna ministries regarded both the nature and extent of trade that was transacted on a compensation basis as altogether satisfactory.

In general, the economic negotiations fulfilled a foreign policy purpose that should not be underestimated. They gave the Austrian government the opportunity to start discussions that formed the basis for normalizing relations with its neighbors.

With the peace negotiations in Paris, Austrian foreign policy clearly entered a new phase. While on the one hand distancing itself from a one-sided orientation towards Germany, Austria placed establishing good relations with the successor states and the Entente within the framework of the League of Nations at the center of its efforts. This change, of course, was the precondition for developing commercial relations and for solving the country's financial and currency problems (Nautz 1994: 72ff.).

To build an Austrian national economy, it was first of all necessary to rebuild the transport system and to reduce legal and bureaucratic obstacles to trade, above all through trade agreements. In his first governmental declaration, Karl Renner said that Austrian foreign policy was primarily economic policy.[7] Thus from 1919 onwards Austrian foreign policy aimed primarily at restoring the flow of goods and hard currency to the successor states on the basis of trade agreements. A further task was to consolidate foreign relations. In December 1919 the Council of Ministers decided to start negotiations with the governments of neighboring states with the purpose of overcoming the antagonisms caused by the war and achieving normal, regular relations.[8] The path to understanding was to be reached by means of economic cooperation among the states of Central and Southeastern Europe. Accordingly work was started on a new concept for regulating Austrian trade policy. This policy, which was started by Renner, was continued by the non-socialist cabinets (Hochenbichler 1971).[9]

Part of the concept was the policy of seeking rapprochement with the Little Entente without actually joining it. Reconciliation with Czechoslovakia and the Little Entente counted as an important precondition for building up better economic relations with the successor states. Only when this precondition was fulfilled could one reckon with the necessary credits from the Western powers.[10] In time, Vienna's accommodating policy, whose intent was peaceful compromise regarding the resolution of territorial disputes, led to a greater openness towards Austria in the other successor states (Burian 1970: 458ff.). At the same time, the Austrian government continued to work closely with Berlin because Austria reckoned very early on that Germany would achieve lasting hegemony in Southeastern Europe.[11]

A significant element in Austria's diplomatic offensive was the beginning of negotiations with its neighbors on matters relating to trade policy, which then led to the signing of most-favored nation agreements with Yugoslavia and Romania in 1920. The way to such agreements was opened by the secret agreement between Renner and Beneš of 12 January 1920. Austria consistently pursued rapprochement with its neighbors. A further important foreign policy step was the treaty with Czechoslovakia concluded by Chancellor Schober in December 1921 (Ladner 1963). A closer connection between the successor states was also the aim of the allies in the period after the Paris peace negotiations. The conferences of the successor states in Rome and Portorose, whose results are frequently underestimated, served this purpose. However, the far-reaching plan for establishing a Danubian Confederation that was pursued during those years above all by France, lacked almost any real foundation.

After the Anschluß was removed from the catalog of immediate political aims of both German and Austrian foreign policy, Austrian trade policy concentrated on regulating trade relations with Germany. The result was a wide-ranging trade agreement in 1920 (Nautz 1994: 342ff.).

Although Anschluß with Germany had faded into the background of Austrian foreign policy, another alternative became important during the summer of 1922. This was the option of a customs and currency union with Italy, which the Seipel government favored in the event efforts by the League of Nations to restore financial soundness were unsatisfactory. An agreement with Italy seemed ready for signing at the start of the League of Nations consultations in Geneva in autumn 1922. The Italian project was then given up as efforts in Geneva achieved success (Ladner 1963; Nautz 1994: 252.). A rapprochement with Czechoslovakia and Yugoslavia, but also with Hungary was weighed by the Ballhausplatz, but then pigeonholed in consideration of the likely effects upon domestic and foreign policy.[12]

By the spring of 1923 when the financial reform under the auspices of the League of Nations began, Austria had built up a basic network of trade agreements with the other successor states. These efforts correspond to the economic importance of these states; they accounted for about half of Austria's foreign trade. While still negotiating with Germany on procedures for Anschluß, the government in Vienna was at the same time working on reestablishing and maintaining economic relations with the other successor states. By using the path of economic negotiations, Austria sought political compromise with its neighboring states and more freedom of movement in foreign policy. This policy was accompanied by long and strenuous efforts to restore the country's financial and monetary soundness, which were successfully completed with the Geneva Protocols. The large problem of Austrian foreign trade, the persistent trade imbalance, could not be solved by means of trade policy. The primary causes of this imbalance lay in the structural problems of the domestic economy, which could not be resolved even in the long term, and in a lack of Western markets.

Austria's foreign trade remained bound to the Danubian area. The protectionist policy of the other successor states brought a reduction of the overall volume of trade, but not a change in its geographic patterns. Austrian trade and foreign policy in the first years after the war created the basis for a relatively high degree of trade integration with the successor states. The world economic crisis brought some changes (Stiefel 1988: 393ff.), yet the country's traditional trade relations with the other successor states continued to be important.

IMPLICATIONS

The geographic patterns of Austrian foreign trade changed only after 1945. Austria's entry into the Organization for European Economic Cooperation (OEEC) foreshadowed its Western orientation after World War II. The creation of distinct economic blocs from the mid-1950s brought a change in the regional structure of foreign trade. European Community (EC) and European Free Trade Association (EFTA) countries occupied a prominent position in Austrian foreign trade, with the main share accounted for by the Federal Republic of Germany (Bachinger and Hemetsberger-Koller 1987: 580ff.; Matzner 1970; Butschek 1985: 133ff; Nautz 1993). The latest figures for Austrian trade with the former East bloc show a strong expansion (*Die Presse* 1992). This trend toward reintegration cannot be understood without reference to the traditional trade channels that pre-dated the cold war.

Against the backdrop of the collapsed cold-war order in Europe, there will be a reordering of trade relations, especially in Central and Southeastern Europe. It is obvious that the former members of Council of Mutual

Economic Assistance (CMEA) must move towards integration into the EC. But it is quite questionable if a "rapid Westernization" (Good 1992) is the correct way. We have seen that Austria's traditional trade relations – and its financial relations, too (Matis 1983) – persisted over the entire interwar period and that Austria got a footing in Western markets only after World War II and the formation of the two cold war blocs.

The formation of Yugoslavia after World War I also shows the difficulties in joining regions of different economic and social standards and economic ties. The breakdown of the economy within the area of the German Democratic Republic (GDR) shows what happens when traditional economic ties are neglected. Not only these lessons from history, but also the current experience of the former Yugoslavia and the former GDR, make clear that the reorganization of the former CMEA economies involves more than a simple "Westernization." Rather, Europe must move toward a more complex continent-wide reorganization based on a specialization and division of labor that reflects the differences in resource endowment and technology of its countries and regions (Good 1992: 7). Last but not least, the former East bloc countries need protection for a time to bring up their economies and societies to a competitive standard before opening completely to European trade, much like the Saarland in the 1950s or Spain and Portugal in the 1980s.

NOTES

This chapter draws on my book and research project on Austrian foreign trade policy 1918–38, generously financed by the Fritz-Thyssen-Stiftung. For more detailed information on sources and literature, see Nautz (1994).

1 The duty of the Warenverkehrsbüro was to coordinate the whole compensation trade. All private contracts had to be agreed by the office (Rundschreiben des Deutschösterreichischen Staatsamtes für Kriegs- und Übergangswirtschaft and die Landesregierungen vom 13 Dezember 1918, in *Archiv der Republic, Wien* (*AdRW*), 14 HP 448). The official statistics start with the second half of 1919.

2 Haass and Peschel (1982) present a theoretical framework for foreign trade, which makes it possible to analyze international trade integration without regard for the differing dimensions of trade as a whole. This prevents large states with the corresponding foreign trade capacities from automatically appearing to be well integrated. The work of Haass and Peschel makes it possible to classify the economies being studied according to decreasing integration. Based on this method of calculation Karner *et al.* (1987) in their examination of the intensity of Austria's foreign trade with the Danubian region in 1928 – the time when world trade was at its most developed during the interwar years – reach the conclusion that Austria, Czechoslovakia, Hungary, and Yugoslavia had the second highest relative rate of integration of the most important trading nations worldwide. Trade between the successor states was still more strongly integrated in the area of the former Monarchy than in world trade (Karner *et al.* 1987). See also Stiefel (1988).

3 Mr. Lindley (Vienna) to Earl Curzon (Received 9 December), No. 28, Vienna, 1 December 1919, in DBFP (1947), First Series, **VI** (33): 452.

4 Staatsamt für Äußeres, Kanzleibogen, Z.2243 – 1919/10, Ggst.: Anschluß an Deutschland, Besprechung mit den Handelskammern, Verf.: Wildner, 19 February 1919, in *AdRW*, 14HP 454.

5 Ibid.; "Bericht des Deutschösterreichischen Wärenverkehrsbüros vom 21. mai 1920," in *AdRW*, HM M.B. 714; März (1981: 352ff).

6 "Anschluß an Deutschland oder Donaubund?," in *Die Industrie*, 10 January 1919: 1.

7 Protokoll der Sitzung des Ausschusses für Äußeres 22 November 1919, in *AdRW*, NPA Präs. 1.

8 Memorandum Staatsamt für Äußeres, December 1919, in *AdRW*, NPA 412.

9 Text der Redes des Bundeskanzlers im Ausschuß für Äußeres am 9. Juli anläßlich der Übernahme des Ressorts für Äußeres, in Wiener Zeitung, 10 July 1921.

10 Karl Renner, Leitsätze für ein politisches und ökonomisches Programm der Koalition, o.D., in *AdRW*, NL Renner 3, fol. 36–38; Pro domo. Unser Verhältnis zur Kleinen Entente [memorandum for Chancellor Schober from Egger and Eichhoff], 2 December 1921, in *AdRW*, NPA 822.

11 Pro memoria. Z. 1215/1A. Unser Verhältnis zu den Nachbarstaaten, in *AdRW*, NPA 694.

12 Übertragung des Stenogramms über Punkt 1 der Ministerratssitzung No. 220 op 28 August 1922, in *AdRW*, Ministerratsprotokolle; Goldinger (1954: 70) Unterhändler, 129ff.; Washburn to Secretary of State, dispatch 1120, 31 July 1926, in: National Archives, M 695, r. 41, fr. 292ff.

REFERENCES

Bachinger, K. (1981) *Umbruch und Desintegration nach dem Ersten Weltkrieg. Österreichs wirtschaftliche und soziale Ausgangssituation in ihren Folgewirkungen auf die Erste Republik*, Habilitationsschrift (Ms.) Vienna.

Bachinger, K. and Hemetsberger-Koller, H. (1987) "Österreich von 1918 bis zur Gegenwart," in W. Fischer (ed.) *Handbuch der europäischen Wirtschafts- und Sozialgeschichte*, Stuttgart, 6: 513–97.

Basch, A. (1942) *The Danubian Basin and the German Economic Sphere*, New York.

Berend, I. T. and Ránki, G. (1970) "Die wirtschaftlichen Probleme des Donaubeckens nach dem Zerfall der österreichisch-ungarischen Monarchie," in R. G. Plaschka and K.-H. Mack (eds.) *Die Auflösung des Habsburgerreiches. Zusammenbruch und Neuorientierung im Donauraum*, Vienna: 350–65.

Berger, P.-R. (1982) *Der Donauraum im wirtschaftlichen Umbruch nach dem Ersten Weltkrieg. Währung und Finanzen in den Nachfolgestaaten Österreich, Ungarn und Tschechoslowakei 1918–1929*, Dissertation der Wirtschaftsuniversität Wien No. 35, Vienna.

Berl, O. (1923) *Die Chinesische Mauer. Österreichische Betrachtungen zur Absperrungspolitik der Nachfolgestaaten*, Vienna.

Bloomfield, J. (1984) "Trade and inflation in the Czechoslovak and Austrian Republics," in: G. D. Feldman, C.-L. Holtfrerich, G. A. Ritter and P.-C. Witt (eds.) *Die Erfahrungen der Inflation im internationalen Zusammenhang und Vergleich*, Berlin, New York: S.228–69.

Burian, P. (1970) "Politische Probleme zwischen Österreich und den Nachfolgestaaten," in R. G. Plaschka and K.-H. Mack (eds.) *Die Auflösung des Habsburgerreiches. Zusammenbruch und Neuorientierung im Donauram*, Vienna: 456–61.

Butschek, F. (1978) *Die österreichische Wirtschaft 1938–1945*, Stuttgart.

Butschek, F. (1985) *Die österreichische Wirtschaft im 20. Jahrhundert*, Stuttgart.

Der Außenhandel Österreichs in der Zeit zwischen den beiden Weltkriegen. (1946) Bearbeitet vom Österreichischen Statistischen Zentralamt (Beiträge zur österreichischen Statistik. Herausgegeben vom Österreichischen Statistischen Zentralamt vol. I), Vienna.

Der Staatsvertrag von St. Germain samt Begleitnote vom 2. September 1919 und einem alphabetischen Nachschlageverzeichnisse (1919), Vienna.

"Die Handelspolitik und der Außenhandel Österreichs in den Jahren 1918 bis 1936," (1936) in *Monatsberichte des Österreichischen Instituts für Konjunkturforschung*, Vienna, 10: 246–51, 269–79.

DBFP. (1947) *Documents on British Foreign Policy 1919–1939* First Series, London.

Fellner, F. (1983) "Der Vertrag von St. Germain," in E. Weinzierl and K. Skalnik (eds.) *Österreich 1918–1938. Geschichte der Ersten Republik*, Graz, Vienna, Cologne: 85–106.

Goldinger, W. (1954) "Der geschichtliche Ablauf der Ereignisse in Österreich 1918–1945," in H. Benedikt (ed.) *Geschichte der Republik Österreich*, Vienna, Munich: 15–288.

Good, D. F. (1992) "Economic transformation in Central Europe: The view from history," *Working Papers in Austrian Studies*, 92–1.

Gruntzel, J. (1918) "Die wirtschaftliche Wirkung des Selbstbestimmungsrechtes," *Das Handelsmuseum*, 33: 329–30.

Gschließer, O. (1960) "Die Katastrophe von St. Germain," in *Der Donauraum*, 2: 2–90.

Haas, H. "Österreich un die Alliierten 1918–1919," in *Saint Germain 1919*, 11–40.

Haass, J. M. and Peschel K. (1982) *Räumliche Strukturen im internationalen Handel. Eine Analyse der Außenhandelsverflechtung westeuropäischer und nordamerikanischer Länder 1900–1977* (Schriften des Instituts für Regionalforschung der Universität Kiel, vol. 3), Munich.

Handbuch der europäischen Wirtschafts- und Sozialgeschichte, (1987) W. Fischer (ed.) Stuttgart, vol. 6..

Hochenbichler, E. (1971) *Republik im Schatten der Monarchie*, Vienna.

Jedlicka, L. (1970). "Aufteilungs- und Einmarschpläne um Österreich 1918–1934," *Festschrift Franz Loidl zum 65. Geburtstag*, Vienna, 1: 96–112.

Karner, S. (1981) "Die Abtrennung der Untersteiermark von Österreich 1918/19. Ökonomische Aspekte und Relevanz für Kärnten und die Steiermark," in H. Rumpler (ed.) *Kärntens Volksabstimmung 1920. Wissenschaftliche Kontroversen und historisch-politische Diskussionen anläßlich des internationalen Symposions in Klagenfurt 1980*, Klagenfurt: 254–96.

Karner, S., Kubin, I. and Steiner, M. (1987) "Wie real war Mitteleuropa? Zur wirtschaftlichen Verflochtenheit des Donauraumes nach dem Ersten Weltkrieg," *Vierteljahrshefte für Sozial- und Wirtschaftsgeschichte*, 74: 153–85.

Kerekes, L. (1977) "Österreichs Weg zur Sanierung (1922)," *Acta Academiae Hungaricae*, 23: 75–97.

Kerekes, L. (1979) *Von St. Germain bis Genf. Österreich und seine Nachbarn 1918–1922*, Vienna, Cologne, Graz.

Kernbauer, H. and Weber, F. (1984) "Die Wiener Großbanken in der Zeit der Kriegs- und Nachkriegsinflation," in G. D. Feldman, C.-L. Holtfrerich, G. A. Ritter and P.-C. Witt (eds.) *Die Erfahrungen der Inflation im internationalen Zusammenhang und Vergleich*, Berlin, New York: 142–87.

Kluge, U. (1988) "Bauern, Agrarkrise und Volksernährung in der europäischen

Zwischenkriegszeit. Studien zur Agrargesellschaft und -wirtschaft der Republik Österreich 1918 bis 1938," *Vierteljahrschrift für Sozial- und Wirtschaftsgeschichte*, Sonderheft 86.

Koren, S. (1961) "Die Industrialisierung Österreichs – vom Protektionismus zur Integration. Entwicklung und Stand von Industrie, Gewerbe, Handel und Verkehr," in W. Weber (ed.) *Österreichs Wirtschaftsstruktur gestern-heute-morgen. Strukturwandlungen der österreichischen Volkswirtschaft in der Vergangenheit und ihre Bedeutung für Strukturprobleme der Gegenwart und der Zukunft*, Berlin, vol. 1.

Krüger, P. (1983) *Die Außenpolitik der Republik von Weimar*, Darmstadt.

Ladner, G. (1963) Seipel als Überwinder der Staatskrise vom Sommer 1922. Zur Geschichte der Entstehung der Genfer Protokolle vom 4. Oktober 1922, Vienna, Graz, vol. 1.

Low, A. D. (1974) *The Anschluss Movement 1918–1919 and the Paris Peace Conference*, Philadelphia.

März, E. (1981) *Österreichische Bankpolitik in der Zeit der großen Wende 1913–1923. Am Beispiel der Creditanstalt für Handel und Gewerbe*, Vienna.

Matis, H. (1983) "Disintegration and multi-national enterprises in Central Europe during the post-war years (1918 1923)," in A. Teichova and P.L. Cottell (eds.) *International Business and Central Europe, 1918–1939*, Leicester, New York: 73–96.

Matzner, E. (1970) *Trade Between East and West: The Case of Austria*, Stockholm.

Monatsberichte des Wiener Instituts für Wirtschafts- und Konjunkturforschung, (12 January 1938–13 January 1939).

Nautz, J. (1994) *Die österreichische Handelspolitik der Nachkriegszeit 1918–1923. Die Handelsvertragsbeziehungen zu den Nachfolgestaaten*, Vienna, Cologne, Graz.

Österreichisches Jahrbuch 1920. (1921) Vienna.

Piétri, N. (1981) "La Reconstruction Économique et Financière de L'Autriche par la Société des Nations (1921–1926)," Thèse pour le Doctorat d'État dès Lettres et Sciences Humaines. Université de Paris, 6 vols. Ms., Paris.

Pinder, J. (1986) "Europa in der Weltwirtschaft 1920–1970," in C. M. Cipolla and K. Borchardt (eds.) *Europäische Wirtschaftsgeschichte*, Stuttgart, New York vol. 5: 377–412.

Presse (1992) "Vor Rekord Überschuß in Österreichs Osthandel. 'Billigkonkurrenz' ist keine Gefahr," in *Die Presse*, 31 August: 6.

Ránki, G. (1983) "Inflation in Post-World War I East Central Europe," in N. Schmukler and E. Marcus. (eds.) *Inflation through the Ages*, New York: 475–87.

Riedl, R. (1919) *Bemerkungen zu den deutschösterreichischen Friedensbedingungen*, Vienna.

Rumpler, H. (1983) "Die innen- und außenpolitischen Determinanten der Wirtschaftsentwicklung der Ersten Republik," in *Christliche Demokratie*, 37–41.

Schausberger, N. (1978) *Der Griff nach Österreich. Der Anschluss*, Vienna, Munich.

Schwarzer, O. and Schneider, J. (1987) "Europäische Wechselkurse seit 1913," in *Handbuch der europäischen Wirtschafts- und Sozialgeschichte*, vol. 6: 1049–93.

Šorn, J. (1981) "Die Handelsbeziehungen zwischen Slowenien und der Republik Österreich vom November 1918 bis November 1919," in Kärnten–Volksabstimmung 1920. Voraussetzungen, Verlauf, Folgen, Vienna: 117–33.

Stadler, K. R. (1968) *Hypothek auf die Zukunft. Die Entstehung der österreichischen Republik 1918–1921*, Vienna, Frankfurt, Zürich (Original: *The Birth of the Austrian Republic 1918–1921*, Leiden 1966).

Statistik des auswärtigen Handels Österreichs im Jahre 1923. (1924) Vienna.

Statistische Übersichten über den auswärtigen Handel Österreichs im zweiten Halbjahre 1919. (1920) Vienna.

Statistische Übersichten über den auswärtigen Handel Österreichs im Jahre 1920. (1921) Vienna.

Statistische Übersichten über den auswärtigen Handel Österreichs im Jahre 1921. (1922) Vienna.

Statistisches Handbuch der Republik Österreich. (1922) Vienna.

Stiefel, D. (1978) "Konjunkturelle Entwicklung und Struktureller Wandel der österreichischen Wirtschaft in der Zwischenkriegszeit," Forschungsbericht no. 135, Instituts für Höhere Studien, Vienna.

Stiefel, D. (1988) *Die große Krise in einem kleinen Land. Österreichische Finanz- und Wirtschaftspolitik 1929–1938*, Vienna, Cologne, Graz.

Stolper, G. (1920–21) "Der deutschösterreichische Handelsverkehr," in: *Der Österreichische Volkswirt,* Vienna: 115.

Teichova, A. (1983) "A comparative view of the inflation of the 1920s in Austria and Czechoslovakia," in N. Schmukler and E. Marcus, (eds.) *Inflation Through the Ages*, New York: 531–67.

Teichova, A. (1989) "Der Aufbau der Wirtschaftsbeziehungen Österreichs zu den Nachfolgestaaten 1918–1926. Vom geschützten Binnenmarkt zur Konkurrenz am Weltmarkt," in F. Glatz (ed.). *Gazdaság, Társadalom, Történetirás. Emlékköny Pach Zsigmond Pál 70. Születésnapjára* [*Economy, Society, Historical Science. Festschrift für Zsigmond Pál Pach zum 70. Geburtstag*], Budapest: 237–53.

Unterhändler des Vertrauens. (1990) "Aus den nachgelassenen Schriften von Sektionschef Dr. Richard Schüller," J. Nautz (ed.) *Studien und Quellen zur österreichischen Zeitgeschichte*, Vienna, Munich.

Verosta, S. (1983) "Die österreichische Außenpolitik 1918–1938 im europäischen Staatensystem 1914–1955," in E. Weinzierl and K. Skalnik (eds.) *Österreich 1918–1938. Geschichte der Ersten Republik*, Graz, Vienna, Cologne, 1: 107–45.

Wessely, K. (1970) "Die Pariser Vororte-Friedensverträge in ihren wirtschaftlichen Auswirkunger," in R.G. Plaschka and K. Mack (eds.) *Die Auflösung des Habsburgerreiches. Zusammenbruch und Neuorientierung im Donauraum*, Vienna: 436–55.

15

FOREIGN TRADE IN AUSTRIA AND EAST–CENTRAL EUROPE

Retrospective and perspective

Jan Stankovsky

INTRODUCTION

Fundamental changes in the political and economic setting of Europe are underway. The East bloc, with its economic, political, and military institutions and its social system no longer exists; its hegemonial power, the Soviet Union, has been dissolved. All Eastern countries aim at establishing parliamentary democracies and market economies. The European Community (EC) has taken new steps toward deepening integration. Germany has been united. A "new architecture" is emerging on this continent. The core of the future Europe will be the EC, which most probably will include also some countries of Central Europe.[1] Austria will join the EC in the next few years; for Hungary, the Czech and Slovak Republics, and Poland an EC-membership within a ten-year period is a realistic possibility.

The close economic relations of Central Europe – formed by a common history as well as geographical and "cultural" proximity – survived the end of the Habsburg empire. The most decisive turning point in the history of this region was the establishment of Communist rule after World War II. Austria and East–Central Europe were separated by different social systems and became parts of two isolated economic blocs. The foreign trade was completely reoriented. The Iron Curtain multiplied the economic distances between the West – including Austria – and East–Central Europe.

The reintegration of East–Central Europe into the West will be a difficult task. The growth, composition, and regional structure of foreign trade in this region will be determined in the first place by the speed and the success of the current transformation. However, some deep-rooted tendencies, based on history, will also emerge. Therefore, economic history may give some clues for future developments. In this chapter the foreign trade of East–Central Europe – both in the pre-1939 and in the Communist period – is analyzed and compared with the foreign trade development of Austria to see what legacies may have persisted.

THE PRE-1939 TRADE PATTERNS OF CENTRAL EUROPE

The Austro–Hungarian Monarchy was characterized by far reaching differences in levels of economic development (Butschek 1985: 20). "Due to its sheer size and geographic location the monarchy was in a sense a microcosm of Europe as a whole. In the western territories – the Czech lands, the Danube basin, and the Alpine regions of the hereditary lands – conditions resembled those of the relatively advanced areas of France and the German states. In contrast, in the eastern territories of the monarchy – Galicia and Transylvania – the elements of Modern Economic Growth were virtually absent" (Good 1980: 251).

The industrialization of the Austrian part of the monarchy started in the second decade of the last century. It was concentrated in the area of today's Austria and in Bohemia, Moravia, and Silesia. Industrialization began in Hungary after the Dual Settlement of 1867 (see Good 1984: 126ff., 141ff.), in other parts of the region as late as the beginning of this century. For this reason Butschek (1985) and others reject the hypothesis that industrialization in the Austrian part of the monarchy was delayed; the picture of delay results from aggregating rapid growth and slow growing regions together. Only three countries, Austria, Hungary, and Czechoslovakia, are "true" successor states of the Habsburg empire in the sense that they were established almost entirely from areas of the old Monarchy. Poland, Romania, and Yugoslavia were formed mainly from territories outside the Monarchy that were generally less developed than those within (Schacher 1932: 3). In this connection it is interesting to note that the true successor states Czechoslovakia and Hungary (and also Slovenia, whose present-day territory was wholly within the Monarchy) have been more successful in the transition than other post-Communist economies. This experience should not be exaggerated, but it does suggest the importance of economic history in understanding the region.

When they were part of the Habsburg empire the Central European countries developed close economic ties. This high degree of economic integration survived the dissolution of the Austrian–Hungarian Monarchy. In 1928 between one-fourth and one-half of total exports from the four Central European countries stayed within these former Habsburg territories (Tables 15.1, 15.2).

There were, however, some important differences in the foreign trade orientation of the region, especially regarding the ties with Germany. Trade within Central Europe had the greatest importance for Hungary with a share in exports of 54.9 per cent and in imports of 42.8 per cent. Hungary's most important export market was neighboring Austria (34 per cent) and Czechoslovakia (17.6 per cent), followed by Germany (11.9 per cent). On the import side Czechoslovakia (22.4 per cent) and Austria stood in first and third place, while Germany was in second.

Table 15.1 Foreign trade orientation of Central Europe 1928

	Shares in total exports/imports (%)						
	A,CSR, H,P	*Y,R,B*	*G*	*I,S*	*GB,F, USA*	*Other*	*Total*
Exports from							
Austria	26.5	14.1	18.4	13.9	9.3	17.8	100.0
CSR	25.9	9.5	26.8	6.7	13.9	17.2	100.0
Hungary	54.9	12.7	11.9	10.3	4.5	5.8	100.0
Poland	25.9	3.2	34.7	2.5	11.3	22.4	100.0
Imports to							
Austria	35.8	9.4	19.9	8.2	12.5	14.2	100.0
CSR	18.5	5.6	38.7	5.8	14.6	16.8	100.0
Hungary	42.8	13.6	19.6	7.8	8.9	7.3	100.0
Poland	14.2	1.6	27.0	5.2	30.9	21.2	100.0

A: Austria; B: Bulgaria; CSR: Czech and Slovak Republic; F: France G: Germany; GB: Great Britain; H: Hungary; I: Italy; P: Poland; R: Romania; S: Switzerland; Y: Yugoslavia.

For Austria, Czechoslovakia, and Poland, Central Europe accounted for approximately 26 per cent of total exports; the leading single export partner was Germany with shares of 18.4 per cent, 26.8 per cent, and 34.7 per cent, respectively. With respect to imports, Central Europe was most important for Austria (35.8 per cent share) and less so for Czechoslovakia (18.5 per cent) and Poland. Germany accounted for 38.7 per cent of imports into Czechoslovakia, 27 per cent of Poland's imports and only 19.9 per cent in the case of Austria.

The data reveal that significant elements of the former integration of Central Europe under Habsburg rule survived the creation of independent states and the erection of tariff barriers. By the end of the 1920s the closest links were maintained between Hungary and Austria. Trade relations between Austria and Czechoslovakia, and Hungary and Czechoslovakia, were still important, but less intense. In contrast, trade between Austria and Poland and between Hungary and Poland was relatively small.

For all countries of Central Europe, especially for Poland and Czechoslovakia, Germany was an important trading partner. In addition, some special trade relations, which can partly be explained by the commodity structure of the trade, can be detected in the foreign trade orientation of Central Europe in the 1920s. For Austria and Hungary, trade with Yugoslavia, Romania, Italy, and Switzerland was important. Czechoslovakia had close links with Western Europe (Great Britain and France) and the USA. For Poland trade with Great Britain, with the USA (only for imports) and with Sweden played a role.

The independent states of Central Europe started after World War I from different levels of development and pursued different economic policies. Trade integration within this region did diminish over time, especially in the 1930s as all countries applied protective measures to combat the worldwide recession. Yet the economic ties within Central Europe remained important. In Austria, for instance, the share of this region in total trade was still 21 per cent for exports and 25 per cent for imports as late as 1937 (Tables 15.3, 15.4).

After World War II, the states of Central Europe quickly resumed their pre-war trade relations. In 1947 the share of East–Central Europe in Austria's trade was still 16 per cent for exports and 21 per cent for imports,

Table 15.2 Foreign trade structure of Austria, CSR, Hungary and Poland 1928

	Shares in total exports/imports (%)							
	A	*CSR*	*H*	*P*	*Y*	*R*	*B*	*G*
Exports from								
Austria	—	12.5	8.5	5.5	7.3	5.8	1.0	18.4
CSR	4.7	—	7.0	4.2	4.4	4.2	0.9	26.8
Hungary	34.0	17.6	—	3.3	6.6	5.3	0.8	11.9
Poland	12.4	11.8	1.7	—	1.1	2.1	0.0	34.7
Imports to								
Austria	—	8.3	8.4	9.1	4.0	4.5	0.9	19.9
CSR	7.4	—	4.5	6.6	2.4	2.8	0.4	38.7
Hungary	16.2	22.4	—	4.2	5.0	7.8	0.8	19.6
Poland	6.6	6.3	1.3	—	0.3	1.1	0.2	27.0
	I	*Swi*	*GB*	*F*	*USA*	*Swe*	*Total*	
Exports from								
Austria	7.9	6.0	3.6	2.3	3.4	1.0	100.0	
CSR	3.8	2.9	7.0	1.3	5.6	1.4	100.0	
Hungary	6.6	3.7	2.9	0.8	0.8	0.4	100.0	
Poland	1.9	0.6	8.8	1.7	0.8	4.4	100.0	
Imports to								
Austria	3.3	4.9	3.2	2.7	6.6	0.3	100.0	
CSR	3.3	2.5	4.4	4.3	5.9	1.4	100.0	
Hungary	3.9	3.9	2.8	2.5	3.6	0.3	100.0	
Poland	2.5	2.7	9.4	7.5	14.0	2.0	100.0	

A: Austria; B: Bulgaria; CSR: Czech and Slovak Republic; F: France; G: Germany; GB: Great Britain; H: Hungary; I: Italy; P: Poland; R: Romania; SWE: Sweden; SWI: Switzerland; Y: Yugoslavia.

Table 15.3 Foreign trade orientation of Central Europe 1928, 1948, 1989

		Shares in total exports/imports (%)			
		Central Europe[a]	*Germany*	*Other countries*	*Total*
Exports from					
Austria	1928	26.5	18.4	55.1	100.0
	1948	13.3	6.0	80.7	100.0
	1989	4.4	35.8	59.8	100.0
CSR/CSFR	1928	25.9	26.8	47.3	100.0
	1948	14.2	3.4	82.4	100.0
	1989	17.1	15.1	67.8	100.0
Hungary	1928	54.9	11.9	33.2	100.0
	1948	21.4	3.8	74.8	100.0
	1989	14.6	17.3	68.1	100.0
Poland	1928	25.9	34.7	39.4	100.0
	1948	12.5	7.8	79.7	100.0
	1989	10.6	18.3	71.1	100.0
Imports to					
Austria	1928	35.8	19.9	44.3	100.0
	1948	10.4	4.7	84.9	100.0
	1989	3.6	44.1	52.3	100.0
CSR/CSFR	1928	18.5	38.7	42.8	100.0
	1948	10.6	2.3	87.1	100.0
	1989	18.9	17.2	63.9	100.0
Hungary	1928	42.8	19.6	37.6	100.0
	1948	19.8	1.1	79.1	100.0
	1989	16.9	22.0	61.1	100.0
Poland	1928	14.2	27.0	58.8	100.0
	1948	11.8	6.1	82.1	100.0
	1989	13.3	20.2	66.5	100.0

[a] Austria, CSR, Hungary, Poland

CSR/CSFR: Czech and Slovak Republic; Czech and Slovak Federal Republic (1989–1992)

figures very similar to those for 1937.[2] The persistence of the trade flows within Central Europe in face of shocks from the two world wars gives some clues about the future trade patterns within the region. Close relations seem possible especially within the "triangle" Austria–Hungary and Austria–Czechoslovakia. Trade flows between 1990 and 1992 strongly support this view.

Table 15.4a Foreign trade ties in Central Europe 1928, 1948, 1989 (exports)

		Shares in total exports (%)			
		Austria	*CSR/CSFR*	*Hungary*	*Poland*
Exports from					
Austria	1928	—	12.5	8.5	5.5
	1948	—	7.9	3.9	1.5
	1989	—	1.2	2.0	1.2
CSR/CSFR	1928	25.9	—	7.0	4.2
	1948	14.2	—	3.0	7.1
	1989	17.1	—	4.0	8.5
Hungary	1928	54.9	17.6	—	3.3
	1948	21.4	12.6	—	2.3
	1989	14.6	5.0	—	3.1
Poland	1928	25.9	11.8	1.7	—
	1948	12.5	8.2	0.8	—
	1989	10.6	5.5	1.6	—

		Shares in total exports (%)		
		Central Europe[a]	*Other countries*	*Total*
Exports from				
Austria	1928	26.5	73.5	100.0
	1948	13.3	86.7	100.0
	1989	4.4	95.6	100.0
CSR/CSFR	1928	25.9	74.1	100.0
	1948	14.2	85.8	100.0
	1989	17.1	82.9	100.0
Hungary	1928	54.9	45.1	100.0
	1948	21.4	78.6	100.0
	1989	14.6	85.4	100.0
Poland	1928	25.9	74.1	100.0
	1948	12.5	87.5	100.0
	1989	10.6	89.4	100.0

[a] Central Europe: Austria, CSR, Hungary, Poland
CSR/CSFR: Czech and Slovak Republic; Czech and Slovak Federal Republic (1989–1992)

TRADE PATTERNS IN CENTRAL EUROPE DURING THE COMMUNIST ERA

With the introduction of Communist rule in Czechoslovakia, Hungary, and Poland, trade barriers – in different forms – were erected on both sides of the Iron Curtain. As a consequence, trade within the region declined sharply. The share of East–Central Europe in Austria's exports fell from 16.2 per cent

Table 15.4b Foreign trade ties in Central Europe 1928, 1948, 1989 (imports)

		Shares in total imports (%)			
		Austria	*CSR/CSFR*	*Hungary*	*Poland*
Imports from					
Austria	1928	–	18.3	8.4	9.1
	1948	–	5.6	2.4	2.4
	1989	–	1.2	1.5	0.8
CSR/CSFR	1928	7.4	–	4.5	6.6
	1948	2.4	–	2.8	5.4
	1989	5.5	–	4.8	8.6
Hungary	1928	16.2	22.4	–	4.2
	1948	4.3	12.7	–	2.8
	1989	8.5	5.1	–	3.3
Poland	1928	6.6	6.3	1.3	–
	1948	0.6	10.4	0.8	–
	1989	6.0	5.7	1.6	–

		Shares in total imports (%)		
		Central Europe[a]	*Other countries*	*Total*
Imports from				
Austria	1928	35.8	64.2	100.0
	1948	10.4	89.6	100.0
	1989	3.6	96.4	100.0
CSR/CSFR	1928	18.5	81.5	100.0
	1948	10.6	89.4	100.0
	1989	18.9	81.1	100.0
Hungary	1928	42.8	57.2	100.0
	1948	19.8	80.2	100.0
	1989	16.9	83.1	100.0
Poland	1928	14.2	85.8	100.0
	1948	11.8	88.2	100.0
	1989	13.3	86.7	100.0

[a] Central Europe: Austria, CSR, Hungary, Poland

CSR/CSFR: Czech and Slovak Republic; Czech and Slovak Federal Republic (1989–1992)

in 1947 to 6.8 per cent in 1960 and to 4.4 per cent in 1989. For imports, the relevant shares were 24.7 per cent; 5.7 per cent; 3.7 per cent (Table 15.5). Trade composition changed fundamentally, too. This can be illustrated by Austria's imports of machinery, which in 1988 were approximately the same from Malaysia as from Czechoslovakia or Hungary.

Some remnants of the common history survived, however, and benefited the Austrian export sector. In the 1980s Austria's market share in total Organization for Economic Cooperation and Development (OECD) exports was approximately 1.6 per cent. Its share of OECD exports to neighboring Switzerland was only 4 per cent, while its share of OECD exports to Hungary reached 10 per cent, to Czechoslovakia 15 per cent, and to Poland 6 per cent (Stankovsky 1990).

Foreign trade of Austria

Austria's foreign trade after World War II was determined by policies of trade liberalization at the international level, e.g., via General Agreement on Tariffs and Trade (GATT) negotiations and Western European integration.[3] Austria's openness as measured by the share of exports in gross domestic product (GDP) doubled from less than 20 per cent in 1955 to more than 40 per cent in 1990.[4]

Austria's economy became highly integrated into Western Europe. The share of this region in total Austrian exports increased from 66 per cent in 1955 to 75 per cent in 1992. The figures for imports are almost the same. The European Community (EC) accounts for 66 per cent of Austrian exports and 68 per cent of imports (1992). Austria's leading trade partner is Germany with a share in exports of 40 per cent and a share in imports of 43 per cent. The importance of Austria's economic ties to Germany is also reflected in the policy of tying the Austrian schilling closely to the German mark.

Table 15.5 Foreign trade orientation of Central Europe 1989

	Shares in total exports/imports (%)						
	CE	*USSR*	*OE*	*G*	*WG*	*OC*	*Total*
Exports from							
Austria	4.4	2.7	2.8	35.8	34.5	54.3	100.0
CSFR	17.1	30.5	7.4	15.1	8.6	29.9	100.0
Hungary	14.6	25.0	6.3	17.3	11.9	36.8	100.0
Poland	10.6	20.8	5.7	18.3	14.2	44.6	100.0
Imports to							
Austria	3.6	1.7	1.5	44.1	43.6	49.1	100.0
CSFR	18.9	29.7	7.2	17.2	9.4	27.0	100.0
Hungary	16.9	22.0	6.0	22.0	15.9	33.1	100.0
Poland	13.3	18.1	6.4	20.2	15.7	42.0	100.0

CE: Central Europe; G: Germany; OC: Other countries; OE: Other East: Bulgaria, Romania, Yugoslavia; WG: Western Germany.

Austria's market share in international trade increased from 1.2 per cent in 1955 to 1.7 per cent in 1992; it fell only in the 1960s due to protective measures within the EC market. In the context of favorable international conditions, successful economic policies, and increased international competitiveness, the commodity structure of Austria's exports altered significantly. The share of machinery in total exports rose from 13 per cent in 1955 to 39 per cent in 1992, the share of raw materials fell from 28 per cent to 4 per cent in the same period. The share of machinery in exports – a rough indicator of export "sophistication" – is higher in Austria's exports to Germany than in its total exports.

Foreign trade of East–Central Europe

Foreign trade in the Communist systems of East–Central Europe was determined by the nature of the system itself. Central planning and state ownership of the means of production served primarily as instruments of political power for the ruling elites. A description of how the planned economy worked in the past may illuminate the current situation and the prospect for foreign trade.

The most important feature of the system was the scarcity of almost all goods. Kornai (1980, 1986) characterized the planned economy as an "economy of shortage." The overhang of demand relative to supply was caused – among other reasons – by the "soft budget constraint" of the enterprises, which provided no incentives for increasing the efficiency of inputs. The high demand for resources in turn required high investment, especially in the area of raw materials, fuels and semi-finished products, which were themselves extremely resource-intensive. As a result a vicious circle of "investment for investment" and an economic structure with an extremely high share of heavy and extractive industries emerged in all Eastern countries. As an indicator of this, Czechoslovakia had the highest per capita production of steel in the world. Also, the planned economy had an anti-innovation bias at the enterprise level, as the penalties for failure were high and the rewards for success were low.

With the exception of the first Stalinist period, neither the countries of Eastern Europe nor the Soviet Union pursued an explicit policy of autarchy. On the contrary, since the 1960s a "socialist division of labor" and later a kind of "economic integration" within the Council of Mutual Economic Assistance (CMEA) was promoted. Various comparisons reveal that in the 1980s the Eastern economies were quite open by Western standards (Williamson 1991).[5]

But the foreign trade of the East was highly concentrated in intraregional trade, i.e., within the region. A major part of this trade was with the Soviet Union; although trade relations among the smaller Eastern European countries were also important.[6] On the other hand, the trade share of the

West – including Western Europe, the traditional and "natural" partner for Eastern Europe – was low.

The regional structure of foreign trade in Eastern Europe, with the possible exception of the Stalin era, was not imposed on Eastern Europe by Soviet political pressure, but was primarily a consequence of the economic system ruling Eastern Europe. One factor was that the planning authorities preferred stable trade relations with the other planned economies. In addition, the enterprises preferred exporting to other Eastern countries, especially to the Soviet Union. Due to the high demand, CMEA markets were easy to exploit, even easier than selling at home. The easily satisfied CMEA markets and the lack of competition reinforced the built-in anti-innovation bias of the economic system.

Up to the early 1970s and the beginning of detente, the low level of East–West trade was not determined by trade restrictions, but by the systemic features described above. From this point, both the planning authorities and the enterprises in the East were highly interested in imports from the West. Western products provided better technology and better services, and they were available when an unplanned demand emerged or when the delivery obligations from the CMEA countries were not fulfilled. The limiting factor was the low level of exports from the East to the West and the resulting lack of foreign exchange. Eastern European products, easily sold on other CMEA markets, were not competitive in the West. The Eastern countries continuously lost market shares for manufactures in the West. Most dramatic were the losses of the more advanced countries, e.g., the German Democratic Republic and Czechoslovakia (for details see Levcik and Stankovsky 1988). Foreign exchange was generated mostly by shipments of raw materials, coal, oil products (refined from Soviet oil) and some semi-finished products. The resources for these commodities were limited, however, and the production costs in most cases were high.

An attempt in the 1970s – eagerly supported by Western governments – to overcome this problem by granting Western credits led at the beginning of the 1980s to an unavoidable disaster – a debt explosion in all East bloc countries with the exception of the Soviet Union. In this situation the only possible remedy – although not ultimately a solution – was a severe austerity program. The import and investment restrictions aggravated the tensions and scarcities in all Eastern countries and provided some of the most important factors in the ultimate collapse.

TRADE PROSPECTS FOR EAST–CENTRAL EUROPE

The transition from planned to market economy

The events of 1989 buried the old regime in all of Eastern Europe. The changes in the political system and the shift to a parliamentary democracy have been implemented – at least in the three countries of East–Central Europe – surprisingly fast and propitiously. Establishing an efficient market economy is proving to be much more difficult.

The system transformation contains the following elements (see Gelb and Gray 1991): macroeconomic stabilization, price and market liberalization, institutional and legal reforms, privatization, and restructuring of the economy. Whereas a broad consensus about the ultimate aims of the transformation exists, the speed, the instruments, and the sequencing of the elements are being heatedly discussed. The international funding institutions and much of the Western world favor a rapid transition (sometimes labeled "shock therapy'). For the three countries in question (not necessarily for the former Soviet Union) a rapid transition provides a far greater chance for success than a more gradual approach. The rapid transformation, however, contains political risks and by no means guarantees prosperous economic development. Along with inherited legacies, e.g., heavy debt burdens, mistakes in economic policy could lead to failure.

The three countries of East–Central Europe started to transform from different positions. Hungary had a reform tradition, which had begun as early as 1968, while Czechoslovakia's orthodox regime impeded almost all changes until the end of 1989. Hungary and Poland inherited high external indebtedness from the previous governments, and Poland alone inherited economic anarchy. Hungary preferred the gradualistic approach to transformation, while Poland and Czechoslovakia preferred more radical therapy. The Polish "bang," however, was even greater than that of Czechoslovakia.

All three countries liberalized their domestic economies and foreign trade and introduced current account convertibility. Privatization is under way. The greatest problem is the deep decline in production, which has been aggravated by the collapse of intra-CMEA trade, especially exports to the former Soviet Union and the former German Democratic Republic. The contraction bottomed out in 1992; significant improvement seems possible perhaps for 1993, but at least for 1994.

The Czech Republic, Poland and Hungary have the best chances for successful reforms; the situation in Slovakia is more complicated. This assessment is the basis for the following discussion of the role and the prospects for foreign trade.

The role of foreign trade in the transition period

After the end of Communist rule, all countries of East–Central Europe have to pass the painful transition from a planned to a more efficient market economy. Foreign trade plays a decisive role during this period. Above all, it serves as a factor of economic growth. The technical qualifications of the labor force in East–Central Europe are similar to those in developed industrial countries, but the productivity is far below that of the West.

Exports serve directly as an engine of growth and at the same time help to finance the imports of investment goods that raise productivity further. Of course, this also works in reverse: flourishing foreign trade presupposes a functioning domestic economy. In addition to its role as an engine of growth, foreign trade also serves another important purpose during the transition period in Eastern Europe: it stimulates competition in the domestic economy and breaks the dominant position of monopolistic suppliers.

Several development strategies for the foreign sector are possible. The strategy of running a deficit in the current account, which involves borrowing from abroad, is effective if productivity growth in the domestic economy is higher than in other economies. However, this development strategy mostly shelters the new industries, which in turn weakens the international competitiveness. The history of developing countries shows very few positive examples of this strategy.

The most impressive results have been attained when countries pursue a strategy of export surplus. The main instrument used by these countries was an effective devaluation based on low wages. But the cost has been a long period of low living standards, so this strategy cannot easily be pursued in East–Central Europe.

Austria has been quite successful with its strategy of balancing its current account. In the first years after World War II, however, foreign aid, mostly in the form of Marshall Plan support, was necessary for this (for details see Butschek 1985: 96ff.). This approach may be suitable for East–Central Europe as well, particularly if it were possible to finance moderate deficits through direct foreign investment. For Poland and Hungary, however, this may be feasible only if the debt burden were reduced substantially. In the Czech Republic and Slovakia, too, the room for additional debts is small. In principle, therefore, the Eastern European countries must try for a balanced current account, or, in view of the debt service for old debts, a trade surplus. It means, too, that Western industrial countries must either be prepared to accept deficits in trade with the East or agree to substantial debt relief.

Comparative advantage in East–Central Europe

The future position of East–Central Europe in world markets depends on finding sectors that have a comparative advantage in international trade. In the pre-Communist era, Czechoslovakia had a comparative advantage in manufactured products (for details see Begg 1991). It had the fourth largest industrial production in 1938 in Europe and played a pioneering role in the automobile industry. However, a comparative advantage in the past is by no means a guarantee for a similar advantage in the future, as can be seen in the case of Argentina (Siebert 1991).

Based on normal measures, the East–Central European countries had a comparative advantage in machinery, especially in investment goods. The share of output of these products was higher than the world average (for details see Collins and Rodrik 1991). However, these products were almost exclusively sold in other Eastern countries, or in developing countries; on the Western market they were barely competitive.

The results of the available studies differ regarding the future competitiveness of Eastern products. A Center for Economic Policy Research (CEPR 1990) study analyzed the available data on human capital. The figures for Eastern Europe are similar to those for Western Europe. The report argues that Eastern Europe should use its skilled labor force to focus in on products with a high technological content: "These factor abundances suggest that among manufactures it is high-tech goods rather than labour-intensive goods that represent Eastern Europe's area of comparative advantage" (CEPR 1990: 12).

For Collins and Rodrik, the CEPR scenario is a plausible one. Its realization depends on a number of factors including "the level of capital flows into the region, how foreign investors evaluate the labor skills potential of the region, and the exchange rates at which these countries integrate themselves into the world economy" (Collins and Rodrik 1991: 59). According to these authors "large capital inflows attracted in part by the skill potential of the region would validate and unlock domestic human capital and set the stage for exports of relatively sophisticated, skill-intensive manufactures – especially if those flows came hand in hand with transfer of technology. Within ten years, Eastern Europe could look like Central or Western Europe rather than Southern Europe" (Collins and Rodrik 1991: 59). Without sufficient amounts of capital and the associated transfer of technology, however, it is doubtful that human capital can be transformed into a source of comparative advantage for exports. Without sufficient amounts of capital, Eastern Europe would have to compete on the labor cost advantage "mainly as a low-cost producer of relatively standardized commodities rather than as a producer of human capital-intensive products" (Collins and Rodrik 1991: 61).

Similar conclusions are obtained by Siebert (1991). In his opinion Eastern Europe will export labor-intensive products, especially human capital-intensive commodities in the medium range that require technical skills and for which production and research can be separated.[7]

The importance of foreign capital

The inflow of Western capital coupled with technology is crucial in determining the pattern of future economic development, and therefore the position of East–Central Europe in the international division of labor. The amount of capital required for the modernization of Eastern economies is high; the estimates (without the former Soviet Union) vary between 75 and 420 billion dollars per year. Of this amount, the greatest part will have to come from abroad.[8]

Policy-makers have given little thought to which part of the existing capital stock would have to be scrapped and which part, e.g., the largely modern capital stock of the armaments industry, could be restructured or cheaply revitalized. The experience of the former German Democratic Republic, which had to scrap the biggest part of its old capital stock, does not necessarily hold true for all of Eastern Europe. On the other hand, prolonged use of the old capital stock would weaken the building of high-tech sectors and reinforce the tendency toward specializing in cheap, labor-intensive products.

Two factors will determine how much and how fast foreign capital will come into Eastern Europe: future profits and future risks as assessed by investors. The availability of a skilled labor force, combined with an undervalued currency, could make investors assess the profitability of investments in East Central Europe favorably. The labor force in the East has, however, some important deficiencies, which lower the productivity and thus reduce the attractiveness of capital investment in the region. These deficiencies are a heritage of the previous system. In a narrow, technical sense, it is the lack of several professions that were not required in a planned economy, e.g. those like banking that are related to finance. In a more fundamental sense, it is the absence of a genuine understanding and acceptance of how a market economy functions. Historical experience suggests that these deficiencies cannot be eliminated quickly. How foreign investors evaluate future risks depends on the likelihood of political stability and the character of the legal system protecting their interests. The countries of East–Central Europe, of course, try to create optimal conditions for foreign investors. The still existing shortcomings are mostly a consequence of slow legislative procedures, mistakes, and lack of experience.[9] Western technical assistance in this area constitutes probably the most valuable support for the transition.

The amount of Western capital invested in East–Central European countries up to now has not been overwhelming. This is mainly due to the unfavorable environment that Western investors must face. There are some indications, however, that foreign investors are gaining confidence in this region, especially in Hungary and the Czech Republic. By the end of 1992 the amount of Western investment in Hungary was 4.9 billion dollars, in all of Czechoslovakia 1.8 billion dollars. According to statistics of the German Ministry of Economics, Czechoslovakia ranked sixth in terms of German direct investment abroad in the first six months of 1991, which placed it second among non EC-countries.

Regional structure of foreign trade

Collins and Rodrik also estimated the likely regional structure of Eastern European trade as a consequence of trade liberalization. They based their calculations on the trade patterns of the pre-war period (1928) and on the changes in the foreign trade orientation of comparable Western countries. According to this calculation the predicted share of the EC for almost all Eastern countries is above 50 per cent. The highest gains will be achieved by Germany. Trade relations with the Soviet Union will diminish dramatically, while the share of other Eastern countries will be reduced, but still high. The biggest shift will naturally occur in countries that have the highest trade orientation toward the East; the change for Hungary and former Yugoslavia will be smaller.[10]

The foreign trade changes in the East will certainly be mirrored in the trade patterns of the West. Up to now the East has been a relatively unimportant foreign partner of the West. This has been true even for countries like Austria with a relatively strong trade with East Europe.

SOME CONCLUSIONS

The dynamics and the regional structure of foreign trade in East–Central Europe will be heavily influenced by the product mix of exports. In the transition, the East–Central European countries will have to export their traditional, less technologically sophisticated products, e.g., steel, textiles, and agricultural products. In a medium term perspective, an upgrading of the exports will occur. Specialization in high-tech exports would aid these countries in catching up and give them the chance to integrate fully into the Western European economy. In this case the Czech Republic would regain the relatively favorable position Czechoslovakia enjoyed before 1939 while Hungary and Poland would improve their relative pre-war standing even more. The gains would be facilitated by opening Western markets for Eastern products because it would reduce the need to keep Eastern currencies undervalued.[11] Of course, if they export only cheap, labor-intensive products, the East–Central European countries might become only a "periphery" of Western Europe. The Eastern products would compete mostly with products from the less developed countries of Southern Europe and from overseas. In this case their import capacity and therefore their importance as an export market for the West would be more limited due to low purchasing power.

The chances that the countries of East–Central Europe will be successful in producing and exporting more sophisticated, skill intensive and human-capital intensive products in the near future seem limited. These chances could be significantly improved by early admission into the EC; the association agreements between the Community and the East–Central European countries are only the first step in this direction. The precondition for full EC-membership should be only a functioning market economy, not full-scale competitiveness. The EC has instruments for integrating less developed countries, as has been shown in the case of its Southern European members.

Rapid and complete integration of East–Central Europe into the European Community will probably be opposed by Southern European countries, which fear – for good reasons – an increased competition both for markets and subsidies. The "Southern enlargement" of the EC shifted the core of Europe more to the West. In the long run this could cause new tensions within the continent.

For Austria, as a close neighbor and natural trade partner of the Eastern European countries, all these developments are of utmost importance. Austria would profit more than other Western countries from strong economic growth in Eastern Europe. On the other hand, stagnation and failure of the transition process would cause more difficulties for Austria[12] than for other Western European countries. As a member of the EC, Austria would be well-positioned to help promote success rather than failure in the East.

NOTES

1 Czechoslovakia (Czech and Slovak Republic), Hungary, and Poland constitute East–Central Europe, and these three countries together with Austria, Central Europe. The broader term Eastern countries (East) is used for the European members of the former Council of Mutual Economic Assistance (CMEA) and former Yugoslavia, Eastern Europe for those countries excluding the former Soviet Union.

2 For details see Breuss (1983), Richter and Stankovsky (1992).

3 European Free Trade Association (EFTA) integration/EC discrimination 1960–1972; free trade agreements (for non-agricultural products) with the EC since 1972/73 (see Breuss and Stankovsky 1988).

4 It should be noted that in Austria the export ratio (exports as share of gross national product (GNP)) is relatively low for goods (25 per cent), but is very high for services (15 per cent), mainly due to the great importance of tourism.

5 The export ratio (exports as share of GNP) of Eastern European countries is not significantly lower than for Western countries of comparable size and level of development. These results are obtained, however, only when the gross domestic product (GDP) estimates in local currencies are translated into dollars by applying the market exchange rate, which is currently very low. Based on purchasing power parity calculations, a higher GDP and therefore lower export ratios emerge. These comparisons are further complicated by the conversion problems for intra-CMEA trade: the transferable ruble (the common currency in CMEA trade) was highly overvalued against the dollar. CMEA trade was based on lagged world market prices; the CMEA trade price level was therefore in general lower than the actual level of world market prices (with the exception of periods with falling oil prices). For details see ECE *Economic Bulletin* 1990 no. 42, box 2.1: 30ff.; 1991 no.43, box 2.1.1: 52ff.

6 The share of the USSR in the trade of Eastern Europe fluctuated in the 1970s and 1980s depending on oil prices. For details see Levcik and Stankovsky (1988). The

conversion problems (mentioned in note 5) also influence the calculation of the trade shares. In the 1980s, Hungary as well as some other Eastern countries, tried to reduce the dependence on Soviet trade. For details see Richter (1989).

7 These commodities are classified as "mobile Schumpeter industries" in contrast to the "immobile Schumpeter industries," in which research and development have to be connected with production. To the first category belong computers and household appliances, to the second aircraft products. See Klodt (1991).

8 For details see Handler *et al.* (1991).

9 In this connection the issue of the "restitution" (indemnification of the owners expropriated by the Communist regime) has to be mentioned; it may serve desires for fairness, but makes the privatization (including foreign participation) more difficult.

10 Abandoning the CMEA trade mechanism (using actual world market prices, switching from clearing accounts to the use of convertible currency) and liberalizing foreign trade was expected to change profoundly the regional pattern of exports and imports of all Eastern countries. The above mentioned collapse of the intra-CMEA trade accelerated the expected development.

11 The results of liberalization up to now are not very encouraging. "Yet the Community's generosity seems to vanish when talks turn to the industries in which the East Europeans could be most competitive, such as textiles and farming . . . Instead of opening itself wide to the brave new capitalists from the East, the EC is busy protecting Spanish clothes makers, Irish beef farmers and Scottish raspberry growers. This is crazy. Opening up to the East is not charity; it is in the West's interest" (*The Economist* 3 August 1991).

12 For details see Butschek (1990).

REFERENCES

Begg, D. (1991) "Economic reforms in Czechoslovakia. Should we believe in Santa Klaus," *Economic Policy* (October): 244–86.

Breuss, F. (1983) *Österreichs Außenwirtschaft 1945 bis 1982*, Vienna.

Breuss, F. and Stankovsky, J. (1988) *Österreich und der EG-Binnenmarkt*, Vienna.

Butschek, F. (1985) *Die österreichische Wirtschaft im 20.Jahrhundert*, Vienna.

Butschek, F. (1990) "Geopolitische Situation und Wirtschaftsentwicklung," *WIFO-Monatsberichte*, 63(3).

Butschek, F. (1991) "Erste Auswirkungen des wirtschaftlichen Umbruchs im Osten auf Österreich," *WIFO-Monatsberichte*, 64(4).

CEPR (1990) *Monitoring European Integration: The Impact of Eastern Europe*, Annual Report, Center for Economic Policy Research, London.

CIA (1991) *Handbook of Economic Statistics 1991*, Washington.

Collins, S.M. and Rodrik, D. (1991) *Eastern Europe and the Soviet Union in the World Economy*, Washington.

Debs, R.A., Shapiro, H. and Taylor, Ch. (1991) *Financing Eastern Europe*, Washington.

Dornbusch, R. (1991) "Priorities of economic reform in Eastern Europe and the Soviet Union," Center for Economic Policy Research (CEPR) Occasional Paper no. 5, London.

ECE (1990) *Economic Bulletin for Europe*, Geneva 42 (November).

ECE (1991). *Economic Bulletin for Europe*, Geneva 43 (November).

Gelb, A.H. and Gray, Ch.W. (1991) "The Transformation of Economies in Central and Eastern Europe," *World Bank Policy and Research Series*, no.17, Washington.

Good, D.F. (1980) "Modern economic growth in the Habsburg Monarchy," *East Central Europe*, 7: 248–68.

Good, D.F. (1984) *The economic rise of the Habsburg Empire 1750–1914*, Berkeley.
Hamilton, G. *et al.* (1990) "Trade patterns and trade policies," in *Monitoring European Integration: The Imports of Eastern Europe*, Annual Report, Center for Economic Policy Research, London.
Handler, H., Kramer, H. and Stankovsky, J. (1991) "Capital, financial requirements and debts of Eastern countries," *WIFO-Gutachten*, Vienna.
Hughes, G. and Hare, P. (1991) "Competitivness and industrial restructuring in Czechoslovakia, Hungary and Poland," *European Economy* no.2.
IMF (1991) "Macroeconomic developments and systemic reforms in Eastern Europe and in the USSR," *World Economic Outlook*, 26–37.
Klodt, H. (1991) "Comparative advantage and prospective structural adjustment in Eastern Europe," Working Paper no. 479, Kiel.
Kornai, J. (1979) "Resource-constrained versus demand-constrained systems," *Econometrica*, 4.
Kornai, J. (1980) *Economics of Shortage*, Amsterdam.
Kornai, J. (1986) "The soft budget constraint," *Kyklos*, 39: 1.
Kosta, J. (1975) "Die sozioökonomische Entwicklung der CSR. Wirtschaftliche und soziale Probleme," in K. Bosl (ed.) *Die demokratisch–parlamentarische Struktur der Ersten Tschechoslowakischen Republik*, Munich, Vienna.
Levcik, F. and Stankovsky, J. (1985) "East–West economic relations in the 1970s and 1980s," in Ch. Saunders (ed.) *East–West Trade and Finance in the World Economy*, London.
Levcik, F. and Stankovsky, J. (1988) "Eastern Europe's trade problems between the USSR and the West," in J.-P. Hardt and C.H. McMillan (eds.) *Planned Economies: Confronting the Challenges of the 1980s*, Cambridge, MA.
Lipton, D. and Sachs, J. (1991) "Creating a market economy in Eastern Europe: The case of Poland," *Brookings Papers on Economic Activity*, no.1.
Richter, S. (1989) "The economic relations of Austria, Finland, Yugoslavia and Hungary with the Soviet Union," *WIIW-Forschungsberichte*, no. 161.
Richter, S. and Stankovsky, J. (1992) "Die neue Rolle Österreichs im Ost–West-Handel," *Studie des WIFO und des WIIW*, Vienna.
Schacher, G. (1932) *Die Nachfolgestaaten Österreich, Ungarn, Tschechoslowakei und ihre wirtschaftlichen Kräfte*, Stuttgart.
Siebert, H. (1991) "Die Integration Osteuropas in die Weltwirtschaft," Institut für Weltwirtschaft, Arbeitspapier no.491, Kiel.
Stankovsky, J. (1990) "Economic policy and foreign trade in Austria: Relations with West and East," in M. Marrese and S. Richter (eds.) *The Challenge of Simultaneous Relations with East and West*, Basingstoke.
Williamson, J. (1991) "The economic opening of Eastern Europe," Institute for International Economics, Washington.

INDEX

(Page numbers which are italicised refer to figures or tables where these are separated from their textual references. n = note, thus n11 = Note no. 11.)

ƒ 50,-